PATRONS, CLIENTS, BROKERS

S.J.R. NOEL

Patrons, Clients, Brokers

Ontario Society and Politics, 1791–1896

UNIVERSITY OF TORONTO PRESS
Toronto Buffalo London

© University of Toronto Press 1990
Toronto Buffalo London
Printed in Canada

ISBN 0-8020-5858-2 (cloth)
ISBN 0-8020-6774-3 (paper)

∞

Printed on acid-free paper

Canadian Cataloguing in Publication Data

Noel, S.J.R. (Sidney John Roderick), 1938–
Patrons, clients, brokers

ISBN 0-8020-5858-2 (bound) ISBN 0-8020-6774-3 (pbk.)

1. Ontario – Politics and government – 1791–1841.*
2. Ontario – Politics and government – 1841–1867.*
3. Ontario – Politics and government – 1867–1905.*
4. Patron and client – Ontario – History.
5. Political culture – Ontario – History. I. Title.

FC3072.2.N63 1990   971.3'02   C90-093478-6
F1058.N63 1990

The illustrations in this book are courtesy of the Regional Collection of the
D.B. Weldon Library, University of Western Ontario.
SOURCES   p 119: *Atlas of Huron County* (1879); p 173: *Punch in Canada*
(1849); pp 247, 261, 265, 284, 289, 290, 301: the cartoons of
J.W. Bengough in *Grip* (1876–94)

This book has been published with the help of a grant from the Social Science
Federation of Canada, using funds provided by the Social Sciences and
Humanities Research Council of Canada.

For Carol

Contents

Preface

This is not at all the book I intended to write when I first embarked upon this enterprise. My initial and perhaps more practical aim was to write a descriptive-analytical account of modern Ontario politics in which I would draw upon the past only when necessary – for example, to explain the character of the province's political culture or the development of its party system. But the further I went, the more I came to realize that the really interesting trails all led back to the eighteenth and nineteenth centuries, that my attempted explanations were unsatisfactory, and that a large and complex subject – the formation and early evolution of Ontario as a political society – could not be avoided. It would have to be tackled first, head-on. In other words, I was forced to go back to the beginning, which is always a salutary lesson for a political scientist. What follows is my attempt to make sense of what I found.

The field of Ontario studies is nearly as old as the province itself and encompasses a remarkably rich and varied body of literature. Moreover, in recent years it has been greatly augmented by an outpouring of scholarly monographs exploring diverse aspects of the province's economy, institutions, cultural life, and socio-economic structure, often from fresh perspectives and employing modern quantitative methods. My debt to other scholars, old and new, is consequently large and is in part acknowledged in the footnotes, which I hope will also serve as a guide to further reading. There is one important group of scholars who are not named, however, but to whom I am especially indebted: the many authors of the Upper Canada–Ontario entries in the *Dictionary of Canadian Biography* and the editors of that magnificently executed project. Nearly always I found in their entries – particularly those for the lesser-known figures, obscure local notables and officials – exactly the kind of information I was seeking: for example, details of their subjects' land dealings, their milling and other business enterprises, their family and commercial connections, and their appointive as well as elective offices. The appearance of volume VII (1836–50) was particularly timely and saved me an immeasurable amount of effort. Taken together, the entries in volumes V (1801–20) through XI (1881–90) constitute a major portion of the data-base on which the book rests.

In the writing of the manuscript and its preparation for publication I have received much generous help that it is my pleasure to acknowledge. I am grateful to my colleagues at the University of Western Ontario, especially those 'down the hall' in the History Department, for giving so unstintingly of their time and expertise. To have one's manuscript read in instalments by James J. Talman, whose vast contribution to the study of Ontario history spans more than six decades, is an experience not to be missed. It is to catch the glint of a sharp mind at work, and to come away not only with the inevitable list of errors but also with new insights and enthusiasm, and often with a stack of material thoughtfully culled from his personal library. Fred Armstrong's careful reading and constructive comments, particularly on the Upper Canadian section of the manuscript, were similarly helpful and greatly appreciated. George Emery, too, went far beyond what one could normally expect of a colleague by writing a wide-ranging, penetrating, and immensely helpful methodological and historiographical critique. Brian Beaven, now of the National Archives of Canada, gave me the benefit of his extensive knowledge of the press and politics in late nineteenth-century Ontario. Ed Phelps, head of the Regional Collection of the D.B. Weldon Library, helped me to locate the material used in the illustrations, and photographer Alan Noon rendered expert assistance in readying it for publication.

I have also been well served by the process of peer review. Both of the anonymous referees' reports, one in French and one in English, offered valuable suggestions that were eventually incorporated into the manuscript. The author of the English report, in addition, called my attention to a number of relevant sources of which I had previously been unaware. Perhaps because I am neither a social anthropologist nor a historian, I genuinely have no idea who the referees might be, but I wish them to know that their efforts were very much welcomed.

Financial assistance for this work, which I gratefully acknowledge, has been provided by the Social Sciences and Humanities Research Council of Canada and the J.B. Smallman Publications Fund of the

University of Western Ontario. At University of Toronto Press I thank Gerry Hallowell for his keen interest and able guidance along the road to publication, Laura Macleod for her assistance at various times, and Susan Kent Davidson for her meticulous copy-editing. My debt to Rik Davidson requires acknowledgment beyond the conventional thanks of author to editor. He was enthusiastic and positive from the beginning, served as a creative sounding-board, and again and again revived my sense of excitement in the project when it seemed in danger of slipping away. I greatly value his contribution.

Above all, my thanks go to my wife Carol for help with practically everything, from research assistance, especially with the microfilm files of nineteenth-century newspapers, to editing, to indexing; and lastly to my trusty assistant and adviser, Ginger P. Cat, who literally logged as much time on this book as I did. All the above-named helped me to make improvements and eliminate errors. None, of course, bears any responsibility for the 'wild blunders, and risible absurdities' – from which, as Dr Johnson reminds us, no book of multiplicity is ever completely free – except the last named, who has kindly agreed to share with me the responsibility for those that remain.

PATRONS, CLIENTS, BROKERS

Introduction:
The Culture of Clientelism

This book is about the nature of political relationships, the influences that shape them, and their consequences. More specifically, it is a study of a particular type of relationship, based upon the roles of patron and client, that grew indigenously out of the social and economic environment of Upper Canada, became an elemental feature of its political life, and long persisted. As the province evolved through various stages of agricultural, resource-based, and industrial development, so too did the patron-client bond. Transformed but not supplanted, it became the cement that held together the decentralized, brokerage-based political formations of the mid-nineteenth century. And later, to meet the new exigencies of post-Confederation politics, it was brilliantly crafted into the structure of Ontario's first large-scale, cohesive, recognizably modern political party – the Liberal party of Oliver Mowat.

What follows, therefore, is not a comprehensive political history of the period from 1791 to 1896. It focuses primarily upon political processes rather than institutions; upon political economy rather than the administrative organization of government; upon leaders, parties, and factions rather than legislatures or cabinets; and above all, after 1867, upon Ontario politics rather than federal politics *in* Ontario.

The actual practice of politics, however, can rarely be categorized quite so tidily. Confederation, for example, did not lead immediately to a sharp distinction between federal and provincial electoral competition; indeed, before 1872, when dual representation was banned, it was not uncommon for the same individual to sit in both the Ontario legislature and the Parliament in Ottawa, and it was much later before any meaningful organizational separation occurred at the local level. Moreover, throughout the period we are dealing with, the roles of individual political actors tended to be much less functionally differentiated and specialized than they are today. Hence, to make sense of the ways in which individuals in a given era combined in pursuit of political power it is frequently necessary to explore the larger context of their activities, including not only the 'rules of the game' as determined by the law and the constitution, but also how they customarily combined in pursuit of other goals, particularly economic or commercial ones, and the general set of community outlooks, assumptions, and expectations that they shared.

Inevitably, to embark upon a study of this kind is to run straight into that most elusive and problematical of subjects – the Upper Canadian / Ontario political culture.[1] Since my approach is in some respects at variance with the approaches of other writers who have ventured to offer their interpretations, it is as well to make clear where the variance lies. In order to do so, however, two distinctions must briefly be made. The first and most obvious is between the *contemporary* and the *historical* uses of the term 'political culture' – that is to say, between its application to present societies and its application to past ones; and the second is between what may be labelled the *ideational* and the *operative* dimensions of political culture – that is to say, between the ideas, principles, ideologies, or theories about politics that are present in a society, often most visibly in the rhetoric of political debate, and the usually unarticulated assumptions, expectations, and understandings of the people of that society about the way their political system actually works. These dimensions are related, of course, and in certain circumstances their relationship may be crucial, but they are rarely, if ever, identical. And often there is a world of difference between them.

The concept of 'political culture' itself is too solidly entrenched in the language of political analysis to require extensive explanation here. As generally understood, it consists of both ideational and operative elements as previously defined (though they might not be identified as such), a time component, and an explanatory logic; in short, it commonly refers to a certain identifiable mixture of attitudes, beliefs, and sentiments that a people hold over some extended period of time

---

1 See John Wilson, 'The Red Tory Province: Reflections on the Character of the Ontario Political Culture,' in Donald C. MacDonald, ed., *The Government and Politics of Ontario* (2nd ed., Toronto 1980), 208–26; S.F. Wise, 'Ontario's Political Culture' (ibid., 3rd ed., Toronto 1985), 159–73; and David J. Elkins and Richard Simeon, *Small Worlds: Provinces and Parties in Canadian Political Life* (Toronto 1980), 31–76.

and that broadly governs their political behaviour.[2] In contrast to public opinion, which is short-term, oriented to issues or personalities, and liable to be volatile, political culture is long-term, oriented to values and habits of mind, and liable to persist even through radical changes of regime. Though not without weakness as a mode of explanation – since the link between culture and behaviour is typically complex and interactive rather than demonstrably causal – it is nevertheless a concept of proven utility.[3]

In the study of contemporary politics the concept of political culture directs our attention towards the ingrained patterns of community and national identity that are so often the well-springs of political action; it provides a basis for the comparison of both national and subnational political systems; and it locates key socio-psychological variables that can be empirically measured. Through standard methods of survey research it is then possible to determine, for example, the degree to which members of a community are attached to (or alienated from) the symbols and offices of government, their level of confidence in the honesty and efficacy of their institutions, their expectations of fair (or unfair) treatment in their dealings with figures of authority such as police or civil servants, the relative importance they assign to such values as freedom, equality, and order, where they stand on a left-right scale, and other similar orientations towards political objects and ideals. Today, no study of a political system is complete if it does not deal with the political culture; in many texts political culture is considered so basic that it occupies the very first chapter.

But the concept is also widely applied to *past* political systems – though not without some major differences, if not in sense then certainly in method. The dead, unfortunately, do not respond well to questionnaires. Nor, with rare exceptions, do they leave behind a written testimony of their political beliefs. In dealing with historical political cultures, therefore, we are obliged to seek alternative methods and sources, and these will naturally vary depending upon the society

2 For an excellent brief introduction to the concept, see the entry (by Lucien W. Pye) in *International Encyclopedia of the Social Sciences* (New York 1968), vol. 12, 218–25. The landmark modern study, to which most subsequent research is indebted, is Gabriel Almond and Sidney Verba, *The Civic Culture* (Boston 1963).

3 For the history of the concept and a critical discussion of methodological and other questions see Gabriel Almond and Sidney Verba, eds., *The Civic Culture Revisited* (Boston 1980).

and the period in question. In some cases there exist profound contemporaneous accounts of the popular ideas, practices, and 'character' of a country (such as, to take a classic early nineteenth-century example, Tocqueville's *Democracy in America*); and in others, such as England, a substantial educated class and numerous astute foreign observers from Montesquieu to Ostrogorski have contributed to a rich if unrepresentative archive.[4] From these relatively solid starting points it is then possible to fill in the detailed contours of a political culture by various means, but above all through inferential generalization from known political behaviour. In other words, if enough is already known about the history of a people, and if it can be established that under certain conditions they responded collectively in certain ways, reasonable inferences may be drawn about their likely political beliefs, sentiments, and assumptions at that time. This is admittedly a tenuous procedure, however, and prone to gross anachronism. In the absence of more direct evidence it is unlikely to yield very satisfactory results.

Yet in the case of Upper Canada it is practically the only procedure that we have at our disposal. The problem dates from the very beginning, and may be simply illustrated: very little is known of the political beliefs of the loyalist founders of Upper Canada (whose influence upon the political culture is generally acknowledged to have been seminal), in spite of all that has been written about them – and in spite of all the ideologies, ancient and modern, that have been variously attributed to them. Scarcely more is known about their political behaviour. And to add to the confusion, what is known can be used, and is used, with about equal plausibility, to support totally contrary inferences.

The Upper Canadian loyalists were very largely an illiterate people, and since they never attracted the scholarly attentions of a Tocqueville, it is not surprising that their political culture remains essentially a mystery; nor, perhaps, that around it swirls not only serious historical debate but also an entertaining farrago of speculation, assertion and popular mythology, both laudatory and debunking.[5] The temptation is to accept the judgment of Wallace Brown and Hereward Senior that at the time of its creation Upper Canada 'was the least political and least

4 Montesquieu, *De l'esprit des lois* (Paris 1748), and M. Ostrogorski, *Democracy and the Organization of Political Parties*, 1: *England* (London 1902)

5 The total number of works is vast. For a useful guide see Robert S. Allen, *Loyalist Literature: An Annotated Bibliographic Guide to the Writings on the Loyalists of the American Revolution* (Toronto and Charlottetown 1982).

intellectual of the British provinces in America,'[6] treat the search for its political culture as equivalent to the hunt for the Snark, and discount the importance of the loyalists accordingly. After all, they were few in number (like so much else about them, their population is a matter of conjecture, since there is no agreement on who is entitled to be counted: they were possibly as few as six thousand, probably not more than ten thousand);[7] they were soon outnumbered by later arrivals from the United States, the so-called late loyalists; and, in the 1820s and 1830s, they and their descendants, along with the American latecomers, were inundated beneath a rising tide of immigrants from the British Isles.[8]

Would it not make more sense, then, it must be asked, to trace the true origins of the Upper Canadian political culture to this latter British group? Though such an approach cannot be dismissed out of hand, and in certain respects might prove enlightening, on balance I believe the answer must be no. In Upper Canada, no less than in other societies founded through colonization, ultimately neither the smallness of the founding colony nor the obscurity of its beginnings can detract from the primacy, legitimacy, and perpetuation of its influence. The Upper Canadian loyalists, like the Puritans of New England and the original *habitants* of Quebec, must therefore be accorded a significance that extends beyond their number, not only because they were the first to arrive but also because of the drama and symbolism of their journey.

For theirs was no ordinary migration, no casual drift westward in search of new land and opportunities, but an exodus forced upon them by a great political upheaval, a direct result of the cataclysm of war and revolution that shattered the British Empire in North America between 1776 and 1783. Out of that cataclysm they had emerged as United

6 *Victorious in Defeat: The Loyalists in Canada* (Toronto 1984), 163

7 'Simply put, no one really knows how many original loyalists there were in Upper Canada, how many "late" loyalists followed, or how many nonloyalist Americans crossed the border from the south. This is a strange black hole in our knowledge.' D.H. Akenson, *The Irish in Ontario* (Kingston and Montreal 1984), 108–10. Official records set the number at 5,969, and by 1791, according to J.J. Talman, it had risen to only 10,000. 'The United Empire Loyalists,' in Ontario Historical Society, *Profiles of a Province: Studies in the History of Ontario* (Toronto 1967) 4

8 The population approximately doubled in each of these decades to reach 487,000 in 1842. Of that number only 6.7 per cent had been born in the United States and 1.4 per cent in continental Europe. The overwhelming majority of new immigrants came from the British Isles. The 1842 census is reprinted in *Census of Canada, 1870–71*, vol. IV, Censuses of Canada, 1665 to 1871, 134–40. See also Helen I. Cowan, *British Emigration to British North America: The First Hundred Years* (Toronto 1961).

Empire Loyalists: the variously celebrated, denigrated, mythologized American opponents of republicanism who had chosen, or had been driven, to seek the rebuilding of their lives and fortunes under the British flag. But unlike so many of their number, they had not retreated to Britain or to any of the more secure British colonies: instead they had trekked into the wilderness of the North American interior, there to suffer the agony of exile, the resurrection of hope, and finally, triumphant renewal – a secular procession in unmistakable parallel to the deepest themes of the Christian religion.[9] Their lives thus became the very stuff of which enduring myths are made. When later, in the aftermath of the War of 1812, loyalism would be formalized and cast into a semi-official ideology, that ideology would not be wholly spun out of thin air. Any attempt to account for the development of Upper Canada's political culture (or even that of modern Ontario, it may be argued) must therefore, sooner or later, come to grips with the meaning of the original loyalist experience.

But how is that experience to be approached? At this point it is necessary to recall the distinction made earlier between the ideational and the operative dimensions of political culture, for the loyalists would seem to present the clearest possible case for the adoption of a point of view that stresses the former. Their very identity, indeed, would seem to dictate such an approach, since they were defined – as singularly as any people in history has ever been defined – in terms of a political idea, and not in terms of religion or language or any other of the more commonly found bases of community. The war that imposed that identity upon them, moreover, while no doubt in large measure a naked struggle for power, had also been seen at the time (and was even more sharply defined in retrospect) as a struggle between rival ideologies and principles of government – republicanism versus monarchism, independence versus the unity of empire, the right to rebel versus the duty to obey, popular sovereignty versus traditional authority – and the loyalists, having defended the Crown, were naturally presumed to represent the entire canon of one side; to be, in other words, the living embodiment of a more or less coherent set of political doctrines. For understandable reasons, therefore, given the undeniable interest and importance of these matters, virtually every attempt to interpret their

9 For an exploration of biblical and other mythic themes in Ontario's literary culture, see Dennis Duffy, *Gardens, Covenants, Exiles: Loyalism in the Literature of Upper Canada / Ontario* (Toronto 1982).

political culture has concentrated primarily, or even exclusively, on the ideational aspect of their experience. And of modern interpretations, the best-known and most influential places the emphasis specifically on the role of political ideology, following in this regard the approach of the American historian Louis Hartz, whose theory of cultural 'fragmentation' is the starting point of much that has been written on the subject.[10]

Initially, in 1964, Hartz put forward his theory (in rather grandiose terms) as a new model for American historiography; but it fell on stony intellectual ground in its country of origin, made no great impression, and soon vanished into a dusty obscurity. In Canada, by contrast, in startling parody of Hartz's own central thesis, it took root and flourished. It is now impossible to deal with the loyalists without encountering it.

According to Hartz, the reason why societies that were founded through colonization (for example, the United States, English Canada, Quebec, Australia) have evolved political cultures that differ markedly from those of the societies from which they broke away is that, in each case, the founding 'fragment' was ideologically incomplete. Thus, because the New England colonists were predominantly a bourgeois group of religious dissenters – rather than a cross-section of seventeenth-century English society, with its still-powerful aristocratic and feudal elements – the range of American ideology was narrowed and given a singular thrust in the direction of liberal individualism, which triumphed so completely that it became popularly accepted simply as 'Americanism.' Lacking feudal elements, the founding American fragment had no potential to foster the growth of either conservatism or socialism, both of which, Hartz theorizes, have their roots in a feudal past. In Europe, however, both conservatism and socialism evolved as parts of a broader and more complex ideological spectrum. In a widely influential essay adapting the Hartzian thesis to Canada, Gad Horowitz accordingly ascribed the relatively greater strength of conservatism and socialism (the latter in the form of the CCF/NDP) in modern English Canada, as compared with the United States, to the presence of a stronger 'tory touch' in the original founding fragment of loyalist

10 *The Founding of New Societies* (New York 1964). Chapter seven of this volume, 'The Structure of Canadian History,' is contributed by Kenneth D. McRae. In an illuminating analogy, David Bell and Lorne Tepperman liken Hartz's fragment model of political culture to 'a kind of *genetic code* that does not determine but sets limits to later cultural developments.' *The Roots of Disunity: A Look at Canadian Political Culture* (Toronto 1979), 23

settlers.[11] The latter were in effect a fragment of a fragment, and their migration removed the last remaining vestige of toryism from the United States (thereby ensuring that the American political culture would be even more homogeneous than it might otherwise have been). But when transplanted, as it was in Canada, toryism became proportionately a much stronger part of the political culture than it had ever been in the original American colonies. And, as a result, so too did socialism.

This is an ingenious thesis whose appeal to Canadians is not hard to fathom. It offers a logical cultural explanation of the political differences that distinguish contemporary Canada from the United States, and it usefully directs attention to such underlying (but measurable) variables as attitudes towards authority and expectations of government to account for those differences.[12] With a little imagination, it can even suggest a reason for believing in the existence of that curious, uniquely Canadian (but possibly chimerical) ideological hybrid, the 'Red Tory.'[13]

When applied historically to the loyalist era of Upper Canada, however, the Hartz-Horowitz approach leads only to a cul-de-sac: its propositions are untestable, given the dearth of evidence on the ideational aspects of loyalist culture, and its assumptions are potentially misleading on a number of grounds.

First, it is not clear whether the loyalists were simply those Americans who, for whatever reasons, gave their allegiance to the king but whose political views and inclinations were otherwise scattered across a broad spectrum, or whether they were in some prior sense the bearers of a specific ideology of 'toryism' – or a 'tory touch' – which determined their allegiance in the first place and which they then brought with them to Upper Canada. Second, it is not clear whether those who settled in

11 'Conservatism, Liberalism, and Socialism in Canada: An Interpretation,' *Canadian Journal of Economics and Political Science* 32 (1966): 143–71
12 See, e.g., Tom Truman, 'A Scale for Measuring a Tory Streak in Canada and the United States,' *Canadian Journal of Political Science* 10 (1977): 597–614; and S.M. Lipset, 'Historical Traditions and National Characteristics: A Comparative Analysis of Canada and the United States,' *Canadian Journal of Sociology* 11 (1986): 113–55. The debate over the Hartzian thesis is extensive. See S.F. Wise, 'Liberal Consensus or Ideological Battleground: Some Reflections on the Hartz Thesis,' Canadian Historical Association *Papers*, 1974, 1–14; and H.D. Forbes, 'Hartz-Horowitz at Twenty: Nationalism, Socialism and Toryism in Canada and the United States,' *Canadian Journal of Political Science* 20 (1987): 287–315.
13 See Rod Preece, 'The Myth of the Red Tory,' *Canadian Journal of Political and Social Theory* 1 (1977): 3–28; and Gad Horowitz, 'The 'Myth' of the Red Tory?' ibid., 87–8.

Upper Canada (who constituted but one small stream in the great exodus of loyalists)[14] held to basically the same outlooks and values as the majority (who settled mainly in Britain or New Brunswick or elsewhere in the British Empire) or whether they held to significantly different outlooks and values. In other words, was it only their adventitious destination that distinguished them from the rest? Or were they a self-selected minority in the sense of being disproportionately composed of those who were by culture and experience more 'American' than other loyalists – and for that reason, perhaps, less daunted by the prospect of starting over in a remote inland territory far removed from the protection of British sea power? And if so, is there any additional evidence that might allow us to infer that they were also more 'liberal' in their political outlook and hence *less* touched by toryism? While it is known, for example, that there were more farmers, frontiersmen, and artisans and fewer drawn from the professional classes than among loyalists as a whole, and more from the inland areas of New York state and Vermont than from the Atlantic seaboard,[15] it can only be speculated whether these demographic variations had any significant effect upon their outlook at the time, to say nothing of their later political orientations. And finally, it is not clear whether *their immediate pre-settlement experience* (of revolutionary war, of loss and dispossession) in fact exerted a greater influence upon their cultural and political development than either *their earlier experience* (of generally successful colonization on the North American frontier) or *their immediate post-settlement experience* (of an all-absorbing primal encounter with the new land on which they had staked their future and on which all their hopes had come to rest).

These latter questions point us in a different direction, specifically towards an approach to historical political culture that primarily stresses the operative rather than the ideational dimension. This is the approach that will be followed here. To proceed thus, however, is not to deny the significance of the ideational in general or of ideology in particular; on the contrary, considerable significance is attached to both in subsequent chapters. In the 1812–41 era, especially – as the studies of S.F. Wise, Jane

14 The Upper Canadian loyalists probably constituted between 6 to 10 per cent of the total number of American emigrants, generally estimated to have been around 100,000. Brown and Senior, however, estimate that the true total (not counting the 'late loyalists') was not more than 70,000. *Victorious in Defeat*, 31–2

15 Ibid., 31; see also A.L. Burt, *The Old Province of Quebec* (Toronto 1968), 76–115.

Errington, and others have shown[16] – the governing oligarchy of Upper Canada cobbled together an ideology that influenced at least their own behaviour and which for that reason must be treated as politically consequential (even if it was so transparently self-serving that it may be questioned whether the population at large ever swallowed very much of it). But it should also be made clear that a shift of focus is required, as well as a wider casting of the analytical net, with the objective being to capture certain salient features of the political culture that elude analysis in term of conventional ideological categories. To illustrate, in the case of the loyalists this means setting aside the attempt to weigh and label the contents of whatever ideological baggage they might (or might not) have carried with them in favour of concentrating upon such factors as their adaptation to their new environment, and specifically their relationship to the land, the nature of their economic and political transactions, and generally the *non*-loyalist aspects of their culture, which are easily overlooked but which (it will be argued) are vitally important to an understanding of the society they founded.

Thus, while it may well be true that ideology in a fragment culture, in Hartz's phrase, 'becomes a universal, sinking beneath the surface of thought to the level of an assumption,'[17] and while it may further be granted that a shared assumption may as surely govern the political behaviour of a people as any explicit doctrine, ultimately, if the evolution of a political culture is to be properly understood, the realm of ideology must be tested against the realm of action – *theoria* must eventually confront *praxis*. And if this is done Upper Canadian politics appears in a sharply different light.

As something that might reasonably be called a political life began to unfold for the inhabitants of Upper Canada in the late eighteenth century, it was from the start overwhelmingly dominated by one thing: land. It could hardly have been otherwise. Land was what in almost all cases had attracted settlers to Upper Canada, whether they had come as loyalists or as later immigrants; or if they had first come as soldiers, it was land that induced them to stay. For a great many settlers, moreover,

16 S.F. Wise, 'Upper Canada and the Conservative Tradition,' in Ontario Historical Society, *Profiles of a Province: Studies in the History of Ontario* (Toronto 1967), 20–33; Jane Errington, *The Lion, the Eagle, and Upper Canada* (Kingston and Montreal 1987); and Terry Cook, 'John Beverley Robinson and the Conservative Blueprint for the Upper Canadian Community,' in J.K. Johnson, ed., *Historical Essays on Upper Canada* (Toronto 1975), 338–60
17 *New Societies*, 5

land had a symbolic value above and beyond its value as real estate; it could stir passions; it was not merely a commodity. This was especially true for those who, as loyalists, had earlier been deprived of land they believed to be rightfully theirs: for them each new grant of land from the Crown was a recognition by the highest authority that their service and sacrifice had been worthy, their allegiance legitimate, their claims valid. Little wonder, therefore, that loyalists and their heirs acquired land with an avidity and on a scale out of all proportion to its real or even speculative worth: in their eyes land was the measure of their righteousness, confirmation that they were indeed 'a people highly favoured of God.'

Later settlers were often not basically different from the loyalists in this respect. Many of them too had suffered the loss of land that had once been theirs, losses legally forced upon them in the nasty and brutal little worlds of Ireland or the Scottish highlands, or, if they were Moravians, Mennonites, Dunkards, or members of other German-speaking sects who had migrated from the United States, losses made prudent by their indifference to the growing nationalism of the new American republic. Even for the most affluent who had arrived with sizable accumulations of capital, the acquisition of land represented a vindication of what they had done, of the risks they had taken. For nearly all, land was the main and for many years virtually the only source of wealth; whoever came to Upper Canada of necessity lived in close and elemental contact with it, its symbolic significance bonded indissolubly to its real and immediate primacy in their lives.

The result was to make politics, from the very beginning, an activity that arose out of and overwhelmingly revolved around questions relating to the ownership and use of land. Such a situation is not unusual, and may even be inevitable in societies based on agriculture, but in Upper Canada it assumed a rare degree of dominance and some distinctive peculiarities. For whatever may have been the connection *in theory* between loyalism and liberalism or toryism or any other set of beliefs or principles, *in practice* the most basic and conspicuous connection of all was between loyalism and entitlement to land. In other words, for the typical flesh-and-blood Upper Canadian loyalist, loyalism had a focus that could hardly have been less abstract or more specific, concrete, and material. It meant land – and lots of it. The documentary evidence of this is voluminous. Indeed, land claims and registration records constitute the only comprehensive and systematic body of data on the behaviour of the loyalists that exists, since initially the only legal means of acquiring land was through government grants of surveyed lots (private purchase from Indians being prohibited).[18] This compelled the loyalists to press their claims upon government in writing, which they did with great enthusiasm and no little success. According to J. Howard Richards, 'The group which benefited most from the system of free grants was the loyalists, who with their children received 3,200,000 acres of the 5,786,946 acres of non-fee grants disbursed previous to the year 1838. Another 1,276,526 acres were given to militiamen and to discharged soldiers and sailors.'[19] That is to say, during the time when the choicest lands of what is now southern Ontario were being transferred to private ownership, the loyalists and their heirs managed to get no less than 55 per cent of the total allocation, and the military group (with whom they had a close affinity) a further 22 per cent.

The reciprocal basis of the original and archetypal Upper Canadian political transaction is thus clear: in effect, it was land for loyalty. But reciprocity as such is not logically or historically part of any particular ideology. Hence, while there is no reason to doubt that the loyalists, as a people of their own time and place, naturally brought with them a fair measure of whatever abstract political notions happened to be current in the American colonies in the late eighteenth century, which quite possibly included elements of both liberalism and toryism, what they actually most assiduously practised from the moment they arrived in Upper Canada is better described as 'clientelism.'[20]

What I wish to suggest by the use of that term is emphatically more than that the loyalists were, for the brief moment required to register a deed, the clients of the Crown or the government. For land acquisition in the loyalist era, and for decades thereafter, was anything but a short, simple, impersonal, one-shot official transaction: instead it was typically a complex, long-drawn-out affair, a process rather than a discrete event, often lasting the best part of a lifetime, and involving much face-to-face interaction with those who, in some legitimate capacity, controlled

18 Gerald M. Craig, *Upper Canada: The Formative Years, 1784–1841* (Toronto 1963), 5
19 'Lands and Policies: Attitudes and Controls in the Alienation of Lands in Ontario during the First Century of Settlement,' *Ontario History* 50 (1958): 195
20 This term has gained a wide currency in political analysis, both contemporary and historical. See, e.g., Steffen W. Schmidt et al., eds., *Friends, Followers and Factions: A Reader in Political Clientelism* (Berkeley 1977), and Christopher Clapham, ed., *Private Patronage and Public Power: Political Clientelism in the Modern State* (New York 1982). For an excellent brief discussion of the concept and its historical application, see M.I. Finley, *Politics in the Ancient World* (Cambridge, 1983), 24–49.

access to the land. In other words, settlers tended to acquire land incrementally rather than all at once, a practice sensibly related to their needs and opportunities but also immensely encouraged in the case of the loyalists by the fact that on the birth of each child, and on the coming of age of a son, or on the marriage of a daughter, a loyalist family automatically became entitled to claim an additional two hundred acres.[21]

To complicate matters further, the possession of land was not a straightforward all-or-nothing proposition. Rather, it consisted of various types of possession and gradations of security of tenure, ranging all the way from occupancy without title (or squatting) at one extreme through to fully patented, unmortgaged ownership at the other, with the possibility of moving up or down the scale as one's circumstances changed. Also, of course, it was possible, and not unusual, for a single individual to possess different pieces of land in different ways. Inevitably, the relationships arising out of such arrangements were correspondingly subtle and multifaceted. The whole business of land acquisition, indeed, was so closely related to the development of agriculture and so inextricably intertwined with other aspects of Upper Canada's social, economic, and political life that it makes very little sense to consider it in isolation. To describe what the loyalists practised as 'clientelism,' then, is to suggest that the roles of patron and client were inherent in the process by which they were settled in Upper Canada (stemming initially from the system of land allocation and sustained thereafter by other factors), and that consequently their political behaviour can best be understood if viewed within the framework of a clientele model of transactional exchange.

It should be obvious that I am here using the term 'clientelism' in its generally recognized anthropological sense to denote a network of relationships based upon 'vertical dyadic alliances,' – that is, upon patron-client bonds.[22] The core interaction is thus a type of reciprocity, an exchange of mutually valued goods or services between individuals who are of unequal status and in control of unequal resources. Less abstractly, a patron is typically in a position to bestow upon a client some

---

21 The evolution of loyalist land entitlements is complex. These particular entitlements were created by order-in-council in 1789. See Lillian F. Gates, *Land Policies of Upper Canada* (Toronto 1968), 20.

22 See Carl H. Lande, 'The Dyadic Basis of Clientelism,' in Schmidt, *Friends, Followers and Factions*, xiii–xxxvii.

tangible benefit, such as access to land, credit, employment, or other material reward, or (less tangibly) security, information or the opportunity to profit. In return a client is typically able to offer loyalty, service, personal acclaim, and support – including support for the patron's commercial enterprises, the carrying of arms under his leadership should the need arise, and political support in circumstances where numbers count, as in voting or campaigning (either for the patron himself or for his nominee). Such relationships are conditioned by the customs of the community and the character of the economy in which they are located, but they are invariably personal, face to face, and reinforced by other ties, such as those of a common religion or ethnicity or (as in Upper Canada) of common service in the local militia regiment. The patron-client bond also tends to be durable and capable of withstanding both pressure from without and friction from within, since, in the final analysis, it is firmly rooted in material self-interest. Politically, few types of association are more dependable. While overlaid in modern political systems by layers of more formal and organizationally complex relationships, it nevertheless stubbornly survives and often flourishes in the interstices of such systems; indeed, once established as a customary form of political linkage, it rarely disappears completely.[23]

Most of those who have written on Upper Canadian politics have of course noted the importance in it of 'patronage,' meaning the practice of awarding land grants, jobs, contracts, and other public benefits to the friends and supporters of the government.[24] This usage is perfectly compatible with the term 'clientelism' but not an adequate synonym for it, since it is generally used to identify (and often to condemn) an exclusively political phenomenon – treating it, in fact, in isolation from its context. The advantage of the term 'clientelism' is that it is more broadly analytical: it identifies a *pattern* of patron-client relationships that is woven into the total fabric of the community, and whose political effectiveness and durability are all the greater precisely because it is *not* exclusively political. To say, therefore, that clientelism was the operative principle of Upper Canadian politics, or that the political culture of

23 For the persistence of clientelism in Canada, see Reginald Whitaker, *The Government Party: Organizing and Financing the Liberal Party of Canada* (Toronto 1977), and S.J.R. Noel, 'Dividing the Spoils: The Old and New Rules of Patronage in Canadian Politics,' *Journal of Canadian Studies* 22 (1987): 72–95.

24 E.g., Craig, *Upper Canada*, 189–90, and Wise, 'Upper Canada and the Conservative Tradition,' 26–8

Upper Canada was basically clientelist, is to say more than that the government dispensed patronage. It is to focus attention upon a *type* of relationship that was prominent in the life of the province from the very beginning and was long assumed to be a normal part of the political process *because it was a normal part of practically everything else.* In other words, there was a general 'culture of clientelism' in Upper Canada, and strictly political patronage is better understood if viewed from this broader perspective.

After the loyalists, there were few newcomers to the province who would have found such a culture altogether foreign. Pre-1832 settlers from Britain, for example, came from a society that was still largely agricultural, where over vast stretches of the countryside access to the land was monopolized by the aristocracy, where every post of church or state was part of a pervasive patronage system, and where even seats in the House of Commons were routinely in the gift of great landed patrons or 'magnates.'[25] Upper Canada, then, can in no sense be considered the 'cradle' of clientelism. Nevertheless, it did evolve its own version of it along lines that had no exact parallels elsewhere. In other words, in Upper Canada clientele relationships were freely modified to meet local circumstances – becoming, in effect, an indigenous variant of a universal type, conditioned to some extent by ideational factors but above all by the dictates of the physical environment and sheer economic necessity.

One of the central themes of this book is to trace the evolution of Upper Canadian clientelism from its earliest beginnings through several stages of development, each progressively more elaborate and organizationally sophisticated than the last, each giving rise to an archetypal figure – the grand patron, the broker, the party boss – and each corresponding chronologically to a well-demarcated era in the province's economic and constitutional life. Thus, Part One examines the ideational elements of the loyalist heritage and the environmental and economic realities that combined to produce a deeply ingrained pattern of dyadic patron-client alliances during the formative era of Upper Canada (1791–1841). Part Two examines the rise of more extensive, complex, essentially triadic clientele networks, both financial and political, and the key role played in both by a new class of professional brokers and

---

25 Michael Brock, *The Great Reform Act* (London 1973), 15–41. See also Lewis Namier's classic study of eighteenth-century clientage, *The Structure of Politics at the Accession of George III* (2nd ed., London 1957).

intermediaries, the products of a curious conjunction – of burgeoning capitalist development and a totally unworkable constitution – during the era when Upper Canada (now constitutionally redesignated 'Canada West' but in popular usage and for all practical purposes retaining its old name) was twinned with Quebec in the Union of the Canadas (1841–67). Lastly, Part Three examines the emergence of the party machine as an efficient, functionally specific instrument of patron-client exchange – a prototypically modern adaptation of clientelism to mass democracy – that in the years between Confederation and the end of the long dominance of Oliver Mowat in 1896 decisively tipped the balance in Ontario's favour in its struggle against the federal government for 'provincial rights' and control of a vast northern resource frontier.

In adopting the developmental model of clientelism outlined above, however, I do not mean to suggest that the operative political culture of Ontario in the nineteenth century was marked by sharp discontinuities. On the contrary, each of the stages identified in the model should be understood to refer to a type of behaviour that was politically dominant in its time but not necessarily the only type present in the society. For it is characteristic of clientele systems that at a given time more than one type of patron-client bond (and often several types) will be simultaneously functional, the variations depending upon such factors as regional economic differences, level of urbanization and a number of less tangible influences such as religion and ethnicity. It is not uncommon, for example, for simple dyadic alliances or incipient stages of brokerage to persist in some areas or among some groups (usually the least economically advanced) long after machine-based clientelism (or, in contemporary systems, the newer phenomenon I have elsewhere identified as 'bureaucratic clientelism')[26] has become generally dominant. This naturally tends to produce a certain dissonance, at least until the latter manages to incorporate the former into its structure. This was the process at work in Ontario and which the model is designed to amplify in the chapters that follow.

There are two further preliminary points that should be made. First, in the course of this study I attempt to show that clientele relationships persisted in Ontario politics not because they arose out of some residually feudal or 'organic' conception of society – of which I find no evidence, and in any case no such explanation is necessary – but because

26 'Leadership and Clientelism,' in David J. Bellemy et al., eds., *The Provincial Political Systems* (Toronto 1976), 197–213

they were useful, practical arrangements that were capable of being intelligently adapted to changing conditions; in short, they filled a great gap in nineteenth-century social organization, and the reciprocal benefits on which they were based were real. It must be added, however, that no simple classification can do justice to the many subtleties they entailed or the rich varieties of exchange they encompassed, especially in earlier eras before they came to be formally regulated through the mediation of a party machine.

Second, although implicit in the approach taken here is an image of Ontario as a political society that is substantially at variance with the image traditionally projected, it is important to note also that it is substantially compatible (even though it does not conform in every respect) to the image that is beginning to emerge from quantitatively oriented studies of Ontario's nineteenth-century social demography and ethnicity. While those studies are local in focus and tend to treat politics as tangential to their main concerns, they nevertheless shed much light on the conditions of family, agricultural, and commercial life that form the background to the political behaviour explored in this book. For example, Ontario is here characterized as a society in which pronounced inequalities of wealth and status – the myth of the 'egalitarian frontier' notwithstanding – are combined with social and political structures of formidable solidity and durability. This view is in keeping with the findings of Michael B. Katz's study of *The People of Hamilton, Canada West*[27] and of David Gagan's *Hopeful Travellers: Families, Land and Social Change in Mid-Victorian Peel County, Canada West.*[28] Neither of these studies deals explicitly with political clientelism, but that phenomenon (it will be argued) can usefully be seen as offering at least a partial answer to the paradox of Ontario's stability in the face of what would seem to have been overpoweringly high levels of economic insecurity, immigration, and transiency. Similarly, D.H. Akenson's *The Irish in Ontario* (which ranges widely beyond its ostensible subject of ethnicity in eighteenth- and nineteenth-century Leeds and Landsdowne townships) paints a vivid portrait of a society in which 'acquisitiveness, aggressiveness and outright greed acted as centrifugal forces, while the need to form alliances, strike economic pacts, and collectively control violence was centripetal.'[29] Although Akenson does

27 Cambridge, Mass., and London 1975
28 Toronto 1981
29 115

not employ the concept, his account of the rise of the loyalist Joel Stone to a position of eminence as a leading merchant-miller, militia officer, pillar of the local elite, and 'the largest landowner in Leeds and Landsdowne' may be read as a classic case study of a standard figure in Ontario clientelism, the 'mid-level' patron.[30] Similarly, his account of the conversion of the Irish Protestant demagogue Ogle Gowan into a more or less orthodox political broker aptly illustrates the process of assimilation to clientelist norms that the Ontario political system imposed as a necessary pre-condition of long-term electoral success. 'To a degree unusual among political leaders Gowan came to personify his followers, to encapsulate their experiences and aspirations, and to symbolize their social migration and interaction with their New World society.'[31] And that society was one in which the sense of local identity was strong, in which alliances were formed in response to local needs, in which political and economic roles were fused, and in which political morality centred upon the keeping of promises rather than the separation of public from private interests.

Finally, a brief caveat. While this study focuses specifically upon clientele relationships, it is not intended to deny the efficacy, still less the existence, of other forms of political association. Indeed, as a complex society, Ontario has always manifested a considerable range of associative behaviour. As will be shown in subsequent chapters, there were periods when the political dynamic of the province arose out of the interaction between clientelist structures and organizations based on agrarian ideals, such as the Patrons of Industry, or religion, such as the Protestant Protective Association. Clientelism, then, should be understood as a central tendency rather than as an exclusive or uniformly dominant pattern – as the glue that held the political process together rather than as the whole of that process.

30 Ibid., 66–78
31 Ibid., 192

Part One

Upper Canada

1

The Upper Canadian Outlook

*Possessing, as this District does, a vast tract of unoccupied territory, of transcendent
excellency of soil ... we want only a population proportionate to our extent of soil, to
render our situation enviable beyond that of any people on earth.*

– Edward Talbot, *London Sun*, 1830

I

At some time in the geological past, nature dealt generously with that
region of North America that is today the province of Ontario. In the
notoriously unequal distribution of the world's resources, few places
were endowed with more fertile land than its southern portion, fewer
still with greater forest and mineral wealth than its northern. A society
planted in such an environment in the late eighteenth and early
nineteenth centuries was bound to have its subsequent development
profoundly affected by it, not only economically but also, in so far as
such matters are interrelated, socially, culturally, and politically; and to
the extent that there existed regional variations in that environment,
between east and west, but far more strikingly between south and
north, the specific type of development also would vary. Most obviously, the experience of those southern communities that arose along the
upper St Lawrence and across the broad, fertile peninsula between the
Great Lakes, and were based on an economic foundation of agriculture,
would differ in many respects from the experience of those northern
ones that, a century later, arose upon the glacier-thinned soil of the
Canadian Shield and whose *raison d'être* was the extraction of the
Shield's abundant forest and mineral wealth.

Moreover, since the two developed at such widely separated times, the historical sequence of their development was bound to influence both the type of relationship that would be established between them and, ultimately, the impact of the one upon the other. Of particularly crucial importance is the fact that, before the north (or, as it came to be habitually and revealingly referred to in the south, 'new' Ontario) was legally incorporated into the province in 1889, there was already a well-established 'old' Ontario, or Upper Canada, which had existed for nearly a century – and which owed its substantial population, its wealth, and its position of pre-eminence in British North America primarily to the success of its people in unlocking the land's agricultural potential. Little wonder, therefore, that when 'old' Ontario at last acquired possession of the vast northern domain that it had long coveted and aggressively claimed, its people tended to view that domain through the prism of their own quintessentially southern and agrarian past, and to evaluate its utility accordingly. But the social and political ramifications of this will be explored more fully in a later chapter. Here we must begin at the beginning, with the formative era of agricultural settlement in the old province of Upper Canada, where so many of Ontario's outlooks and attitudes had their genesis.

II

That era may be said to have begun in the 1780s and to have lasted into the middle of the nineteenth century, covering in all a period of roughly seventy years, during which the province's population grew from a few thousand to approximately one million and virtually all of its arable southern land had been occupied by settlers. The margins of agriculture had been extended west to Lake Huron and north into Grey and Bruce counties, where the last important concessions of good agricultural land were opened to settlement in 1849.[1] Effectively, by mid-century Upper Canada had run out of frontier (thus becoming, arguably, the first major North American community to do so: by contrast, in the United States at this time the western frontier was in its heyday). Bounded by the Great Lakes, and with the north blocked by a forbidding barrier of pre-Cambrian rock and coniferous forest, the area that contained the bulk of

1 J. Howard Richards, 'Lands and Policies: Attitudes and Controls in the Alienation of Lands in Ontario during the First Century of Settlement,' *Ontario History* 50 (1958): 200–1

its people was in reality more like an island. And amazing though it must have seemed to those who in their own lifetime had experienced it as a pristine wilderness of seemingly limitless horizon, it had been transformed into a measured, organized, richly productive, agricultural landscape in which the dominating presence of man was everywhere in evidence.

For most of the hundreds of thousands of new immigrants who had poured into the province in the quarter-century before 1850 and who had played a vital role in its development, the process of agricultural settlement was significantly different from what it had been for the loyalists and their immediate successors. Above all, their settlement was much more likely to take the form of 'in-filling' through the occupancy of vacant lots in already established townships – a process of social development that D.H. Akenson terms 'sub-infeudation' and compares to the creation of feudal subtenancies: 'As with the many subtenants in a fully articulated feudal society, the ever increasing number of local inhabitants came to hold the means of livelihood on similar terms one with another, and, as in feudal social order, there was only a small number of individuals of high economic and social status.'[2]

Acquiring land, and bringing it into production, consequently meant entering into private arrangements with those who had accumulated large amounts of it, such as the Canada Company or the many local merchant-speculators who were at one and the same time suppliers of land and credit and purchasers of surplus grain. A meeting (in 1826) between a merchant and a prospective client is described thus by Gordon Sellar, a Scottish immigrant: 'They entered into a large store, opposite the market-place, of which the gentleman was owner ... When he had learned all, Mr. Dunlop, for that was his name, said: 'You may give up your notion of getting land for the fees. All the good land, so far surveyed, either is in the hands of our gentry (who live by selling it), or of speculators. The lots the surveyor-general would give you would be dear for nothing, they are so far away. You want to be as near the lake, or a town or village as you can manage ... I am busy now; come back at four o'clock and I will find out what can be done.'[3] As it transpired, of course, the merchant happened to have exactly such a block of land available, which Sellar agreed to inspect and on which he eventually settled.

2 *The Irish in Ontario* (Kingston and Montreal 1984), 202
3 Robert Sellar, *A Scotsman in Upper Canada: The Narrative of Gordon Sellar* (Toronto 1969), 47

Much, however, remained the same as it had been for the loyalists. The pressure to acquire land was still intense, for it was still the only commonly accepted measure of worth. Little wonder, therefore, that even two decades later, as David Gagan points out, 'land, lots of land, apparently was still the prescription for economic success and social improvement in the community.'[4] To have too little of it was to be disadvantaged, and to have none at all was virtually to be invisible – it was to be without social standing or political rights, to be condemned to a limbo of transiency and insecurity.

The result was a society singularly rooted in the soil, whose accommodation with the land took the form of a cellular pattern of agricultural townships, one much like another, spread widely across the province and sustaining a large number of small towns and villages. The geographer Jacob Spelt writes: 'The urban village pattern of 1851 consisted of a large number of small service centres or central places whose growth was determined largely by transportation facilities, population density and waterpower resources. These centres were focal points for trade and transportation, for workshop manufacturing, and a variety of other services ... A large number of these centres were never incorporated, and there is no information about them in the censuses.'[5]

In 1851 only 7.5 per cent of the population lived in cities, of which Toronto, with 30,775 inhabitants, was the largest, followed by Hamilton with 14,112 and Kingston with 11,585. Overall, only 16.2 per cent lived in incorporated places.[6] Consequently, as Lord Durham had somewhat dismissively observed in his report of 1839: 'The province has no great centre with which all the separate parts are connected, and which they are accustomed to follow in sentiment and action; nor is there that habitual intercourse between the inhabitants of different parts of the country, which ... makes a people one and united, in spite of extent of territory and dispersion of population. Instead of this there are many petty local centres, the sentiments and interests ... of which are distinct, and perhaps opposed.'[7] Durham aside, however, there were sound economic reasons for decentralization, and those 'petty local centres' existed in close symbiosis with the type of agriculture for which the province was at the time best suited and which had brought it a burgeoning prosperity.

4 *Hopeful Travellers* (Toronto 1981), 44
5 *Urban Development in South-Central Ontario* (Toronto 1972), 95
6 Ibid., 89
7 Gerald M. Craig, ed., *Lord Durham's Report* (Toronto 1963), 78

For in the mid-nineteenth century the growing industrial cities of Britain possessed a prodigious appetite for cheap grain, especially wheat – and Upper Canada possessed a prodigious capacity to produce it.[8] It therefore rarely made sense for Upper Canadian farmers to engage in the intensive cultivation of small plots to grow a variety of crops, even where the land itself was superbly appropriate for such use, for domestic markets were generally too small to absorb the output. Fortunately, a more profitable alternative was readily at hand: through extensive cultivation the land could be made to yield substantial surpluses of a single marketable commodity for export. Hence, as settlers spread back from the lakeshores into the southwestern interior, there were few among them who had in mind the pursuit of small-scale peasant agriculture on the European model: the vast majority saw clearly that their surest route to prosperity lay in commercial agriculture, and specifically in producing grain. But to accomplish that goal they required access to relatively large quantities of land and linkage to a lengthy chain of credit and trade. Concomitantly, therefore, a pattern of dispersed, low-level urban development had become established that was finely attuned to the provision of both, with corresponding patterns of socio-economic and political interaction. Businesses, for example, were rarely branches of larger firms; instead, in township after township there would be found merchants and millers in crossroads villages and on river sites who operated essentially independent enterprises, though with credit links to the larger St Lawrence trading system.[9] And political alliances likewise tended to be independent and township-based, articulated to the wider system only at the top.

8 John McCallum, *Unequal Beginnings: Agriculture and Economic Development in Quebec and Ontario until 1870* (Toronto 1980), 9–24

9 This was the overall pattern, though there were some exceptions. Douglas McCalla, in a study of one of the more complex mercantile enterprises of the period, observes that 'those who tried in these years to operate branch systems generally withdrew from them. Retailing seemed to function best where the retailer owned his business and had the greatest incentive to manage it well ... Although the Buchanans always involved themselves in the affairs of their customers, they did not have to exercise as continuous a scrutiny as would have been required if they were themselves partners in the retail business ... In a climate of expansion, they had no incentive to challenge the developing Upper Canadian pattern of distinct wholesale and retail trades.' *The Upper Canada Trade, 1834–1872: A Study of the Buchanans' Business* (Toronto 1979), 28. See also T.W. Acheson, 'The Nature and Structure of York Commerce in the 1820s,' in J.K. Johnson, ed., *Historical Essays on Upper Canada* (Toronto 1975), 171–93.

What did it all amount to? On the surface at least, Upper Canada at mid-century must have seemed – as it had no doubt seemed to Lord Durham a decade earlier – a most peculiarly diffuse and unfocused creation. It displayed innumerable fissures, some inherited, some imported, but most of its own making: ancestral grievances dating back to the eighteenth century, religious quarrels, incipient class antagonisms, and, perhaps most pervasive of all, sheer stubborn localism (the route of a royal tour could inspire paroxysms of civic jealousy, the promotion of grandiose public works – including everything from ornate town halls to civicly financed railway lines – could be ruinously competitive).[10] And seemingly with a dynamic of its own, a provincial politics was carried on, with no little enthusiasm, that was as personal as it was chaotic and byzantine, an endless haggling over power, place, and preferment among rival leaders and their factions. Further complicating matters, the whole process was improbably tied to the politics of Quebec through a legislative union that Britain, in its wisdom, had seen fit to impose in 1841. Yet underneath all this lay some formidable strengths. The wheat-based economy was a dynamic generator of capital, the commercial and industrial benefits of which were largely retained within the province.[11] Extensive clientele networks existed that were both economically and politically integrating. Localism could also be a stabilizing influence and, at its best, a potent motivator of community effort. And not least, paradoxically mixed with localism and occasionally even transcending it, there had developed among the people a certain socially cementing pride in what they had collectively achieved as a British province, against all the odds of history, in the very heartland of North America.[12] In short, a provincial identity had been cast, which, if not altogether unique, nevertheless could hardly be mistaken for any other.

It was not a new 'nationality' (at least not in any modern sense of that term), nor do there appear to have been any significant aspirations to make it one. On the contrary, whatever its constitutional or political designation, whether Upper Canada or Canada West (or, later, Ontario),

10 See, e.g., Peter Ennals, 'Cobourg and Port Hope: The Struggle for Control of the "Back Country,"' in J. David Wood, ed., *Perspectives on Landscape and Settlement in Nineteenth Century Ontario* (Toronto 1975), 183–95.
11 McCallum, *Unequal Beginnings*, 6–8
12 See Frederick H. Armstrong and Neil C. Hultin, 'The Anglo-American Magazine Looks at Urban Upper Canada on the Eve of the Railway Era,' in Ontario Historical Society, *Profiles of a Province: Studies in the History of Ontario* (Toronto 1967), 43–58.

one of the most basic assumptions seems always to have been of its rightful and important place in some larger, grander national entity. This was first and foremost the British Empire (just as later it became the British Empire *and* Canada, and later still Canada alone). Indeed, to speak of a provincial identity is to imply the existence of some such larger context within which the provincial society exists as a recognizable variation, differing from the whole and from other parts of the whole in certain respects, resembling them in others. Culturally and intellectually, moreover, the larger context to which Upper Canada belonged was not exclusively the British Empire but rather 'the English-speaking world' – which encompassed not only Britain and her overseas colonies but also the United States.[13] Since the full spectrum of human civilization was of course much wider, it is as well to state an obvious fact that can too easily be forgotten: namely, that the cultural particularisms that distinguished the various members of that far-flung linguistic constellation from one another, while important, were rarely extreme. In the case of Upper Canada, therefore, what we are dealing with is largely a matter of varying emphasis rather than sharp contrast.

It should not be surprising, then, if what had come to distinguish Upper Canadian politics was not the presence of original or uniquely distinctive formal institutions (of which in fact there were few, and none of any great consequence). It was much more a matter of informal differences in outlook and attitude and behaviour – in other words, of political culture – which amounted to a persistent difference in perspective. To understand this perspective, however, it is necessary to look beyond the narrowly political to the broad thread of common experience that runs through Upper Canadian life, an experience that for the overwhelming majority of the people, in an overwhelmingly agrarian society, had to be dominated by one ever-present reality: namely, their encounter with the land itself, and their struggle to bring it to productivity. What must primarily concern us here, because it lay at the root of their political life and exerted a lasting influence upon it, is the effect of that experience upon their understanding of two fundamental relationships: the first is their relationship to the natural environment; the second (which is treated at greater length in the next chapter) is their relationship to government. The latter has traditionally been a central concern of political science, and while the former has not, it is no less

13 For the interplay of British and American influences see Jane Errington, *The Lion, the Eagle, and Upper Canada* (Kingston and Montreal 1987).

important to our present inquiry. Where we must begin – albeit inferentially and, to a degree, speculatively – is with the loyalists and their approach to the new environment into which they had so precipitously been thrust.

III

Some notion of what constitutes man's place in the natural order of things may presumably be found in every society's pattern of culture, and whether erected into an elaborate scientific or philosophical principle or held simply as a traditional belief, it will normally provide a framework for understanding the material environment and a rationale for actions taken in relation to it. In societies that are long settled, however, the effect of such notions is inevitably blurred and attenuated by the cumulative imprint left upon the environment by preceding generations; hence, whatever the currently prevailing notion might be, the realistic possibilities of present action are always constrained by what has been done in the past. But in the case of colonists in a new land – of which there is no more perfect archetype than the loyalists in Upper Canada – such constraints are absent and the effect sharply discernible. For they are confronted with what they perceive to be a 'wilderness' – a land whose history is unknown to them.[14] Yet in it they must urgently establish a means of livelihood and reconstitute their existence as a community.

How they set about these tasks and what they achieve, individually and collectively, will therefore depend not only upon what they find, in terms of the land's inherent economic potential, nor upon the capital, skills, and experience they bring with them, vital though each of these may be, but also, and perhaps above all, upon how they view themselves in relation to the land that lies before them. For it is that view that will determine what they believe to be achievable in their new circumstance; and it in turn will inevitably reflect the prevailing notion of man's

14 The idea of a 'wilderness' does not, of course, imply the absence of native inhabitants but only their exclusion from history, which is presumed to begin with colonization. Louis Hartz argues that in a fragment culture such exclusion is crucial both to the maintenance of the internal logic of the fragment and its political cohesion: 'Had the Indian population, or a mestizo variant, constituted a class within the American fragment, at the very least racial tensions would have distorted the usual alignments. Jackson, instead of rationalizing the extinction of the Indian from the White House, might well not have been there: or he might not have been a "democrat."' *The Founding of New Societies* (New York 1964), 95

place in nature of the age in which they live and of the culture in which they share.

It must be admitted, however, that to generalize about such matters is to risk over-simplifying something that is rarely if ever simple. For example, it is easy in retrospect to exaggerate the degree of diffusion of a particular new idea or mode of thought that only later became dominant, forgetting that at a given moment in any society a large residue of old and sometimes contradictory beliefs may be found coexisting with those of more recent origin, or that important new scientific theories or new trends in philosophy, art, or literature may for many years excite only a tiny minority without spreading very far into the community at large. Yet in spite of such necessary caveats it is possible to discern certain broad historical patterns of thought and action that, though far from being universally shared, may nevertheless fairly be treated as characteristic of an age.

Among the most important of such notions in the eighteenth century was the tendency to look upon nature as a realm from which man could stand apart and over which he was capable of exercising mastery by virtue of his reason and his free will.[15] These unique capacities, it was believed, were divinely bestowed; hence it could be reasoned that the subordination of nature was divinely ordained, and even, carried to its philosophical extreme, that the *purpose* of nature was to serve man. Thus, at its most absurd, the density of water could be held to be precisely calculated by God to facilitate man's navigation upon the seas; and mineral resources could likewise be held to be purposefully distributed: as one scientist sagely theorized in 1782, 'all the metals are placed at convenient distances ... the most useful are those nearest to the surface of the earth.'[16] Such Panglossian faith in a benevolent and perfectly arranged universe, while inviting satire, nevertheless reflected a new predisposition to look upon nature as something to be used, as something understandable and, if properly understood, capable of

15 See Keith Thomas, *Man and the Natural World* (London 1983). For an earlier but still valuable study of the idea of 'nature' in eighteenth-century thought, see Basil Willey, *The Eighteenth-Century Background* (London 1940; reissued 1972). For a general survey see Norman Hampson, *The Enlightenment* (London 1968). Of more immediate relevance to Upper Canada, since they deal extensively with the American cultural milieu of the period, are Daniel Boorstin, *The Lost World of Thomas Jefferson* (New York 1948); Russel Blaine Nye, *The Cultural Life of the New Nation* (New York 1960); Michael Kammen, *People of Paradox* (New York 1973); and Leo Marx, *The Machine in the Garden* (New York 1964).
16 Clément de Boissy, as quoted in Hampson, *The Enlightenment*, 82

responding to man's interventions in predictable and rewarding ways. The emergence of those assumptions marked an intellectual liberation from the perception of nature as a realm corrupted by the Fall and disfigured by the Flood, terrifying in its hostility and subject to malevolent supernatural forces, a perception that had been common to the Christian world for many centuries. As might be expected, the effect was to set in motion corresponding developments across a wide range of human endeavour. Aesthetically, for example, the qualities that came to be most highly prized, in everything from art and poetry to architecture and furniture-making, were those of order, balance, and harmony; while what came to be considered most beautiful in nature was that which showed to best effect the moderating and civilizing influence of man – as in a well-ordered agricultural landscape.

In the popular imagination and in everyday life the distillation of this way of thinking probably amounted to little more than a predisposition to view nature in terms of its potential, and especially its *economic* potential; in other words, to view the undeniable chaos of so much of the natural world as a mere surface attribute concealing an ordered reality that man could discover and profitably exploit. Originally this may have been a fragile European conceit – but, it must be stressed, it was not one that was shattered by experience when translated into a North American context. On the contrary, there it seemed to be unambiguously confirmed by the success of the American colonists in domesticating their new land. For, indeed, by the latter part of the eighteenth century there were few places anywhere that showed the transforming power of man's intervention quite so dramatically. And although the experience of colonization must also have taught that in practice nature could be unpredictable and at times deadly, the overriding fact remained that the North American environment did respond productively, even bountifully, to man's touch. The result was to give the American colonists a uniquely strong faith in their capacity to dominate it, while also promoting among them the belief that order, while perhaps theoretically inherent, in practice was something they could successfully impose.[17]

17 The most influential and illustrious popularizer of this outlook (on both sides of the Atlantic) was, of course, Benjamin Franklin, who exemplifies the strong practical streak in American rationalism. See Adrienne Koch, 'Pragmatic Wisdom and the American Enlightenment,' *William and Mary Quarterly* 18 (1961). The easy material success of the American colonies was a matter of concern to Puritan moralists: the Reverend Charles Turner, preaching in 1773, worried because he could not 'point out a country, founded in oeconomy, industry, frugality and temperance, that has arrived to such a degree of luxury, in so short a time as ours.' Quoted in Kammen, *People of Paradox*, 155

IV

Hence, in the case of those colonists who left the United States after the War of Independence and moved north into British-held territory in what was then the western region of Quebec, and who thus became the founders of Upper Canada, the fact that they were United Empire Loyalists should not be allowed to obscure a prior fact: namely, that they were also a people who were culturally and intellectually the product of their own time and place. That is to say, they had come to maturity in the second half of the eighteenth century; and although they were known as 'British Americans' their immediate experience was of America rather than Britain. It would have been strange indeed if they had not carried with them the quintessential outlooks and habits of mind of those American communities from which they had come and in which, in some cases, their families had lived for several generations. This is not to suggest that their loyalty to the Crown was in any way unreal or unimportant; but to focus too exclusively upon it is to lose sight of other equally salient aspects of their past. For all that can be said with certainty about their politics is that what had divided them from their neighbours had been their loyalty to the Crown: in a bitter civil conflict, the side they had supported, or had become identified with amid the chaos of war, had eventually lost, thereby rendering their situation intolerable and forcing them to undertake their historic exodus.[18]

Yet in their new situation, ironically, their politics were of less immediate consequence than the non-political qualities of their culture, which would have to sustain them through the toil and hardship of resettlement – and in this respect they were fortunate. For they seem to have carried with them, in addition to a considerable reservoir of practical skills, something that was no less important to their future, a basically optimistic colonial-American view of the natural environment

18 In the historiographies of loyalism and the American revolution there are many hypotheses about the possible ideological, social, economic, and regional correlates of loyalism and republicanism, but no consensus. See Robert S. Allen, *Loyalist Literature: An Annotated Bibliographic Guide to the Writings on the Loyalists of the American Revolution* (Toronto and Charlottetown 1982), 13–18. In Kenneth McRae's succinct summation, 'American society split vertically almost from top to bottom. Factors of geography, military campaigning, local politics, and private vendettas all added their weight to political and economic considerations. Many, as the Loyalist claims amply prove, changed allegiance during the war, and families were often split within themselves. All of which demonstrates that we are not dealing here with a simple social revolution of class against class.' 'The Structure of Canadian History,' in Louis Hartz, *New Societies*, 237

and their rightful place in it – a view that in their case was no mere abstraction but firmly based upon first-hand knowledge. That is to say, they possessed the inestimable advantage of knowing that what they were setting out to do could in fact be done. For even if they themselves had never been pioneer homesteaders, their parents or grandparents had; and in any case, no American colony was so long settled that the frontier was far away or the colony's origins lost in time.

To say this, however, is in no way to minimize the difficulties the loyalists faced, or their courage and resourcefulness in facing them. While most had been farmers, others had been uprooted from comfortable professional lives, and neither they nor their families were accustomed to the back-breaking work of land-clearing. Many were veterans of the king's loyal regiments who after long years of war were not accustomed to any civilian pursuits. Many were no longer young and had to face the prospect of starting over, knowing they would not live to see any but the most meagre return on their labour. The wonder therefore is not that some failed and some were broken by the effort, or that some eventually gave up and returned to their former homes in the republic, but that the majority took to pioneering with such determination and energy, and, on the whole, with such success. That they did so cannot be explained simply in terms of their 'survival instinct' (those who gave up were presumably no less concerned with survival – they merely chose a different means to achieve it); nor by the generous support and encouragement they received from the British government; nor by their past experience of farming, though all of these were important, as no doubt were other more private and personal motivations such as pride, stubbornness, and ambition. But in addition, subtly colouring everything they did, there may be detected a common approach to their environment which suggests that they were truly the children of their age, imbued in full measure with its unblunted optimism and its faith in man's ability to unlock the potential of his natural surroundings. Justus Sherwood, for example, after surveying the virgin forest of the upper St Lawrence in 1783, before the first acre had been cleared, could hopefully pronounce: 'I think the Loyalists may be the happiest people in America by settling this country.'[19] Joel Stone, though a later arrival, was no less pleased: 'Verily,' he wrote in 1787, 'I find it as good land in general as ever I set my foot on.'[20]

19 E.A. Cruickshank, *The Settlement of the United Empire Loyalists on the Upper St. Lawrence and Bay of Quinte in 1784* (Toronto 1934), 13
20 Akenson, *The Irish in Ontario*, 69. For the Reverend John Stuart of Kingston, writing in 1798, the quality of the land was proof of divine favour: 'How mysterious are the

Equally, it may be inferred from the way in which they proceeded to establish themselves upon the land that they were a people who believed implicitly that order and discipline were high virtues, and that in their circumstances success, and probably happiness too, would be measured by the degree to which they could impose these virtues upon their unordered new landscape.[21] Theirs was thus no unruly or haphazard assault upon the wilderness. In the great westward flow of population into the fertile central regions of the continent (of which demographically they formed but one small tributary) their migration was the most orderly and disciplined of all. Indeed, in all important respects it was carried out as a military operation, with even the vital phase of settling families upon the land being administered by the army. It was also a peaceful migration. In contrast to the hostile conditions prevailing in American territory on the other side of the Lakes, relations between the loyalists and the native Indians, while not altogether untainted by chicanery, were generally cordial and even friendly. This was partly because they had fought as allies during the war, but it is unlikely that such an alliance could have been sustained had it not been for the fact that the private purchase of Indian land had been strictly prohibited by the British government, which itself took sole responsibility for the acquisition of land through negotiation and public purchase. This prevented freebooting individuals from making profitable incursions into Indian territory and so removed a potent source of friction which on the American side led to endemic hostilities.[22]

It also meant that the organizing presence of government, particularly as represented by the military, was strongly felt from the very beginning. The effects of this upon the subsequent development of political institutions will be explored later, but first we must note the significant and highly symbolic presence of a most characteristic figure: the government (usually army) land surveyor.[23] With his scientific

---

ways of Providence! How shortsighted are we! Some years ago I thought it a great hardship to be banished into the wilderness ... Now the best wish we can form for our friends is to have them removed to us.' Catherine S. Crary, ed., *The Price of Loyalty: Tory Writings from the Revolutionary Era* (New York 1973), 452

21 These values still occasionally surface: 'Without order and regulations you have a rabble.' Staff Superintendent John Webster of the Metro Toronto Police, justifying disciplinary action against Constable Edward Murphy, who had refused to trim his moustache when ordered to do so. *Globe and Mail*, 4 Dec. 1980

22 'Unlike the nearby American states,' Gerald M. Craig observes, 'Upper Canada never had an angry Indian frontier.' *Upper Canada: The Formative Years* (Toronto 1963) 5

23 See R. Louis Gentilcore, 'Lines on the Land: Crown Surveys and Settlement in Upper Canada,' *Ontario History* 61 (1969): 57–73.

instruments and his knowledge of mathematics it was his task to apply to the natural world the ordering concept of accurately measured rectilinear space. He preceded settlement and typically had already imposed a form of geometrical order upon the landscape even before the first settler could legally take up residence. His precise rectangular shapes were mere lines on a map, empty abstractions, (and, of course, like all abstractions, sometimes in error), but important nevertheless because they also represented a way of thinking and perceiving, of reducing the wilderness to intellectually manageable proportions. At the same time they offered an image of the future, a kind of land-use plan that amounted to a self-fulfilling prophecy. For in due course, as the land yielded to cultivation, its physical reality came more and more to resemble the surveyor's original abstract design in its regularly chequered pattern of straight roads and rectangular farms. To this day, when viewed from the air, the agricultural landscape of southern Ontario still reveals a functional and aesthetic symmetry of classical eighteenth-century proportions.

V

For the loyalists, therefore, the frontier was not in fact an uncharted wilderness, a realm of nature where they were free to appropriate as much as they saw fit. Under the direction of General Frederick Haldimand,[24] a Swiss professional soldier long in the service of the British Crown, specific tracts of land were first surveyed and authorized for settlement before families were allowed to move on to them from the camps in lower Quebec in which they had been temporarily sheltered. The whole process was firmly under government control and, on the whole, efficiently administered. Moreover, a familiar and well-understood system of inequality was built into it from the very beginning, for land was granted only in surveyed blocks and according to a fixed formula based upon military rank. Thus a private was entitled to 100 acres, a corporal or sergeant 200, plus in each case a further 50 acres for each member of his family. A staff sergeant, warrant officer or subaltern was entitled to a straight grant of 500 acres, a captain 700, and a major or higher rank 1,000. A non-veteran was entitled to 50 acres if single, or to the same entitlement – 100 acres – as a private if the head of a family. This scale of grants was subsequently raised to between 200 and 5,000 acres,

24 *Dictionary of Canadian Biography*, v, 887–904

and there were numerous exceptions, but the principle of allocation by rank remained.[25] Moreover, it was part of Haldimand's plan to resettle loyalist veterans and their families as far as possible in groups corresponding to their regiment of service. This meant that they could be quickly remobilized if necessary, but also incidentally tended to encourage the carrying over into the civilian life of the community of at least some of the social cohesion and organizational discipline of the army.[26] And, initially, like an army in the field, they were supplied by the government with the basic necessities of life – including food rations, firearms, clothing, tools, hardware, agricultural instruments, seed, and livestock. In the entire history of colonization, there are few people who have ever been given a better start.

Or had better luck. It was an ironic consequence of their forced migration that it gave them first choice, and secure possession, of some of the continent's richest remaining agricultural land, land that they or their children might well have had to seek in any case as the population expanded and the thin soils of the eastern United States became exhausted. For most of southern Ontario turned out to be immensely fertile. In some areas small crops of grain could be grown even before the forest was cleared, in the open spaces between the enormous trees that covered much of the land. And for at least the first two years many settlers had no need even to plough, cultivation with a light harrow being sufficient to produce good results from the deep humus-rich soil.[27] Such obvious potential could not help but spur them on and sustain them: they could see that their effort would not be in vain; that their new environment would indeed respond predictably and profitably to their intervention.

By contrast, new settlers elsewhere in British North America had not fared nearly as well. Those loyalists who had made their way by sea from New York to Nova Scotia found no urban centre large enough to support them in their professions (they were on the whole of a higher social class than those who settled in Upper Canada) and the few areas of good agricultural land already occupied; in New Brunswick the dense coniferous forest proved a more daunting barrier to cultivation (and the

25 Lillian F. Gates, *Land Policies of Upper Canada* (Toronto 1968), 15–16
26 The settlers were also divided, at their own request, according to ethnicity and religion. The first five townships were allocated to 'Catholic Highlanders, Scottish Presbyterians, German Calvinists, German Lutherans, and Anglicans.' Craig, *Upper Canada*, 6
27 D'Arcy Boulton, *Sketch of His Majesty's Province of Upper Canada* (London 1805), 51

timber trade a more attractive alternative) than anything encountered in Upper Canada's more tractable landscape; while in Newfoundland English and Irish fishermen who tried to settle on its barren shores were opposed equally by an unyielding nature and harsh imperial laws that made permanent residence illegal, hence allowing them neither title to their land nor even the minimal protection of government.[28] In each case, the experience of colonization differed profoundly from that of the early settlers in Upper Canada. On the whole, the latter found their hopeful expectations of nature confirmed; in less hospitable regions a harsher reality imposed itself, nature proved more obstinate, hope turned more easily into despair – or into that dogged determination to survive that is sometimes (mistakenly) held to be the definitive Canadian cultural trait.[29]

Upper Canada also differed from the rest economically in that its sole resource was considered to be the land itself, the sole object of settlement being to bring it as quickly as possible to a state of agricultural productivity. There were supplementary sources of income but no realistic alternatives. The fur trade was centred elsewhere, no large-scale commercial fishery was possible, and because of the lack of economical means of transportation, except along rivers, throughout much of the province there was not even a market for the abundant supplies of timber, fine growths of pine and hardwood being burned to produce potash or simply to be rid of them. The single-minded pursuit of agriculture was therefore an economic necessity, but it was also totally in conformity with the dominant economic and social ethos of the eighteenth century. In that last pre-industrial age the ideal society was almost invariably pictured as having an agricultural base; it was hard to

28 Wallace Brown and Hereward Senior, *Victorious in Defeat: The Loyalists in Canada* (Toronto 1984), 31, 39; Graeme Wynn, *Timber Colony: A Historical Geography of Early Nineteenth Century New Brunswick* (Toronto 1981), 3–25; and S.J.R. Noel, *Politics in Newfoundland* (Toronto 1971), 4–6

29 One prominent source of this confusion is Margaret Atwood's *Survival: A Thematic Guide to Canadian Literature* (Toronto 1972), which daringly extrapolates from a reading of selected works of poetry and fiction to the characteristics of the national culture. Dennis Duffy, on the other hand, in an *envoi* to his study of loyalism, writes: 'I began it with the expectation that I was after a particular aspect of the English Canadian mind ... I planned, in short, another CanLit theme book. Eventually I realized that my limits lay between Lake Huron and the Ottawa River. Even the Loyalist Maritime provinces proved off limits, because the military component had given Upper Canadian Loyalism a combative and triumphal flavour I detected nowhere else.' *Gardens, Covenants, Exiles: Loyalism in the Literature of Upper Canada/ Ontario* (Toronto 1982), 131

imagine any other. And not only was agriculture thought economically essential; it was also thought (perhaps especially by city-dwellers) to be in some way morally virtuous. Success in agriculture was therefore the most orthodox of goals, easily understood, and regarded by all as worthy of pursuit.[30]

VI

To leap ahead once again to the mid-nineteenth century, there can be no doubt that the people of Upper Canada had to a remarkable degree achieved their aim. For in spite of the disappointments and setbacks to which agriculture is always inherently prone, their overall record, by any measure, had been one of phenomenal accomplishment: in acreage cleared and planted, in the volume and value of production, in the creation of wealth. And while the benefits were by no means equally distributed, either geographically or socially, they were everywhere conspicuously in evidence: in the many commodious new houses of brick or stone construction that were springing up, in new churches and public buildings, in rising property values, in investment in new farm technology (and in the small-scale local industries that increasingly supplied the technology), in improved livestock, in land drainage, in the growing consumption of luxury goods, and in the beginnings of a railroad boom that would last for decades.[31]

John McCallum calculates that Upper Canada's net exports of wheat 'rose by about 500 per cent during the 1840s and doubled again to reach their peak in 1861,'[32] while the value of those exports tripled in the years between 1850 and 1856 alone. His comparisons are striking: Upper Canadian farmers, he estimates, were on average between five and ten times more productive than their Quebec counterparts; and their wheat output, per capita and per farm, exceeded that of American farmers in

30 For an insightful examination of these themes, and their social and ideological implications, see Robert Lochiel Fraser, 'Like Eden in Her Summer Dress: Gentry,
Economy, and Society: Upper Canada, 1812–1840,' PHD thesis, University of Toronto
1979. There were also strong literary evocations: according to Sandra Djwa, 'the
transformation of a rude landscape into a cultivated garden was a central preoccupation of English Canadian verse from 1628 to approximately 1860.' 'Litterae ex
Machina,' *Humanities Association Report* 1973, 23

31 See G.P. deT. Glazebrook, *Life in Ontario* (Toronto 1971), 107–25; J.M.S. Careless, *The
Union of the Canadas* (Toronto 1967), 132–49; Armstrong and Hultin, 'The Anglo-
American Magazine,' 43–58.

32 *Unequal Beginnings*, 4, 18

all but the most westerly, least populated states.[33] The beneficial results are graphically illustrated in the case of Oakville, a typical small urban centre: 'The townspeople financed and built the road that tapped the agricultural hinterland, and the transportation of wheat to the port was handled locally. The town's foundry made the machinery that milled the wheat, and most of the ships used in the export trade were built in the town and commanded by Oakville captains. Consequently, almost all aspects of the process starting with the planting of the wheat and ending with its delivery as grain or flour in Montreal were performed by the local economy.'[34]

In effect, Upper Canada had reached a stage of self-sustaining economic growth, financed largely by its own high rate of capital accumulation; and there can be no doubt that the engine of that growth had been agriculture.[35] It was an achievement that few agrarian societies, either before or since, have ever been able to equal. From a national perspective, Upper Canadian agriculture was probably the single most prolific creator of wealth in Canadian history; and in terms of the development it engendered, Upper Canadian agricultural land was probably the nation's single most valuable natural resource.[36]

It is in light of this extraordinary economic performance – more important in many respects than anything that happened politically or constitutionally – that the province's evolution must be viewed. For the essential fact is that the loyalists and those who followed after them encountered a land that held out great promise of future betterment, and in little more than the span of a single lifetime fulfilled that promise. The environment, in other words, turned out to be both manageable and beneficent. If certain things were done – sufficient land acquired, the land properly cleared, the right crops planted; in short, if orthodox

33 Ibid., 22–4, 47
34 Ibid., 8
35 As Douglas McCalla points out, however, Upper Canada's exports-led growth would not have been possible had it not been for the long chain of credit that had earlier fuelled the province's development: 'In effect, imports preceded exports ... British credit, nominally short-term, was relayed through the commercial system to the frontier and through store credits financed a great deal of the capital investment required to being new areas of staple production into being.' *The Upper Canada Trade*, 5
36 McCallum states that 'Ontario wheat was perhaps the most successful staple product in Canadian history,' but, writing in 1980, adds in a footnote that 'the honour should perhaps be shared with Alberta oil.' *Unequal Beginnings*, 8n. That, however, was before the steep decline in world oil prices.

methods were followed – nature did indeed respond in a satisfyingly orthodox way and produce the hoped-for rewards. There were hazards: crops could fail or markets collapse, but these were common to agriculture everywhere and in Upper Canada were but isolated occurrences punctuating a sustained economic advance. The formative Upper Canadian experience, therefore, was not of struggle and failure, or even of struggle and survival, but rather of struggle and success.

2

Political Ideals and Economic Realities

At present the Farmer has no other means of obtaining such necessaries as he may want, but by bartering the produce of his Land for them with the petty Merchant, who by this means sets his own price on both commodities ...

– John Graves Simcoe, 28 April 1792

I

Some three months before writing the above, while in Quebec City preparing to assume his post as lieutenant-governor of the newly created Province of Upper Canada, Simcoe had received a long letter from one Robert Hamilton, a merchant at Niagara, which was unusual in that it contained neither a flowery address of welcome nor a request for patronage. Instead, it contained Hamilton's well-informed reflections on issues of trade and his rather presumptuous advice on the policies that he believed Simcoe's government ought to pursue in order to safeguard and promote British trading interests (which were, of course, in his view, identical with his own). But there was nothing parochial or 'petty' about his concerns. On the contrary, his perspective embraced the whole of the interior of North American and his vision of the future was grandly imperial: 'Possessed of the two Posts of Quebec and New Orleans, without further effect than regulating to the best advantage the internal policy of the extensive country,' he argued, Great Britain 'would, in time, enjoy a market for her manufactures, extensive almost beyond calculation. In return, she would exclusively receive the furs of the North and all the most desirable products of perhaps the finest soil in the world in all the different latitudes from Michillimackinac to New

Orleans.'[1] Naturally, the type of government he envisioned for Upper Canada was one that would be strongly interventionist in economic affairs, but only for the purpose of assisting commercial expansion (which would, of course, be left profitably in the hand of merchants like himself).

There is no record of Simcoe's reaction, but if he had any it was probably to dismiss Hamilton's letter as merely the opinion of an up-country trader with pretensions above his station. Had he troubled to take it seriously, however, he could have learned much from it that would later be useful to him. Above all, had he been able to read betwen the lines he would have gained a startling insight into the social and political structure that had already been established in the nascent province – a province that he believed it was his mission to build from the ground up, according to his own detailed ideological blueprint. He had assigned no place in that blueprint to a self-made merchant oligarchy. Yet here was Hamilton pronouncing on matters of state with all of the assurance of one accustomed to exerting influence in high places, of one who seemed to *assume* that his views on such matters would be treated with respect, even, and perhaps especially, by the new lieutenant-governor.

However, from Simcoe's perspective – which was the conventional perspective of the English landed gentry of his day – those who engaged in trade were inherently of low status and not to be entrusted with such influence because, as he put it, 'it is unreasonable to expect Disinterestedness among the Mercantile Part of the Community, nor do their habits or Education in the least entitle them to a shadow of preeminence.'[2] Merchants such as Robert Hamilton, on the other hand, were naturally just as inclined to believe the opposite: that status should be earned, and that 'pre-eminence' was precisely what they were entitled to by virtue of their wealth. Thus was the stage set, even before the political curtain had been officially raised, for two years of intermittent skirmishing between the leading mercantile interests of Upper Canada and the Simcoe administration.

Hamilton, in fact, was so rich and well connected that he had no need

1 E.A. Cruikshank, ed., *The Correspondence of Lieut. Governor John Graves Simcoe*, 5 vols. (Toronto 1923–31; hereafter *Simcoe Correspondence*), I, 97–100, Robert Hamilton to Simcoe, 4 Jan. 1792; see also Bruce G. Wilson, *The Enterprises of Robert Hamilton: A Study of Wealth and Influence in Early Upper Canada, 1776–1812* (Toronto 1983), 107–8, and *Dictionary of Canadian Biography*, v, 402–6.
2 Quoted in Wilson, *Enterprises of Robert Hamilton*, 110

of Simcoe's patronage (though, with good reason, he probably expected to receive his share of it in any case). Within the small but expanding empire of Laurentian commerce his rise had been spectacularly swift. In 1780, at the age of twenty- seven, he had set up shop as a trader in furs and general goods at Niagara, initially in partnership with Richard Cartwright (a shrewd and profitable association, since Cartwright was a loyalist with a record of military service and valuable official connections: his family had long been part of the clientele of Sir John Johnson, head of the patronage-soaked Indian Department). By this means their fledgling business was able to gain a foothold in the always lucrative business of supplying the army and the Indian Department with goods at wartime prices.[3] But in the long run it was Hamilton's commercial connections that were to prove even more valuable. For in the course of an apprenticeship served in the fur trade at Montreal he had acquired a wealthy and influential patron in the person of the merchant Isaac Todd, of the old and prominent trading firm of Todd and McGill, through whom he received the credit necessary to exploit Cartwright's contacts (and, equally critically, the long-term credit necessary to survive the post-war slump when military expenditure slowed to a trickle). He also received useful contacts with other of Todd's clients in the up-country, and above all, a share of the steadily profitable shipping, receiving, and portaging business on the Great Lakes route, which he and Cartwright soon parlayed into a near-monopoly.[4] At the same time, as the population of loyalist settlers increased, he began to speculate in land – by purchasing, or accepting in payment of debt or as collateral for mortgages, portions of land originally granted to loyalists but surplus to their immediate needs – and to expand his retail and wholesale trade. In classic clientelist fashion, his links to the small merchants he supplied with credit were invariably reinforced by bonds of kinship, ethnicity (many were his fellow Scots), and personal friendship, as well as being selectively reinforced by small plums of political patronage that had come under his control. For, as his commercial success had grown, he had become both the major recipient of government patronage in the Niagara region (again, through the influence of his Montreal connections), and hence also – being at one and the same time judge of the local Court of Common Pleas, justice of the peace, and a member of the District Land Board – the major dispenser of it.[5]

3 Ibid., 17–22; see also the entry for Cartwright in DCB, v, 167–72, and for Johnson in DCB, VI, 352–4.
4 See Wilson, *Enterprises of Robert Hamilton*, 28, 68–87.
5 Ibid., 42, 53

In short, Hamilton was a political figure to be reckoned with, and not only at the local level. Ever calculating, before Simcoe had even arrived he had pulled strings in Quebec City to have himself, as it were, 'pre-appointed' to the Legislative Council (the upper chamber of the as-yet unformed legislature of the new province), where he would be joined by his old friend and partner Richard Cartwright, now a resident of Kingston, who had made similar provision for himself.[6] Mercantile interests would thus be well represented under the new regime, whatever the lieutenant-governor's wishes in the matter. Indeed, nothing could have been more obvious in the autumn of 1792, as Simcoe began to set the machinery of government in motion, than the strength and vitality of those interests, in whose hands the economy of Upper Canada very largely rested. And if he needed reminding, he had only to leave his vice-regal residence at Newark – according to his own description, 'an old hovel that will look exactly like a carrier's ale house in England when properly decorated and ornamented'[7] – and visit nearby Queenston. For there, on a lush estate overlooking the Niagara River, sat a magnificent stone house built in the English country style, with side wings and covered galleries, fittingly vice-regal in every aspect but one: it was the home of Robert Hamilton.[8]

II

'Mr. Hamilton is an avowed republican in his sentiments,' Simcoe was soon darkly suggesting, 'and altho' the merchants are justly obnoxious to the settlers of this Province, and he is particularly so, yet the ascendancy [of] He and his friend Mr. Cartwright ... is of that nature, that there is nothing to prevent them from exercising it to the detriment of the Government, if they have any particular Object to promote, that may gratify their avarice, ambition or Vanity.'[9] His words are revealing, not only because of his vitriolic (and unwarranted) raising of the spectre of republicanism but also, and more importantly, because the 'settlers' to whom he refers are the loyalists, and his placing of them in

---

6 Ibid., 42. Their appointments were secured through the influence of Sir John Johnson. See *Simcoe Correspondence*, I, 10, Lord Dorchester to W.W. Grenville, 15 Mar. 1790.

7 *Simcoe Correspondence*, I, 205, Simcoe to James Bland Burges, 21 Aug. 1792

8 Wilson, *Enterprises of Robert Hamilton*, 1; H.C. Boultbee, 'Willowbank: The Old Hamilton Homestead at Queenston,' Welland County Historical Society, *Papers and Records* 5 (1938): 11–12

9 *Simcoe Correspondence*, II, 55, Simcoe to Henry Dundas, 16 Sept. 1793

juxtaposition to the merchants is both ideologically and politically significant. For just as he believed merchants to be uniquely unqualified to govern, by virtue of their lack of 'disinterestedness,' so too he believed loyalists – and specifically ex-military loyalists – to be uniquely well qualified. (The few who were also merchants, such as Richard Cartwright, were presumably exceptions to the rule.) Accordingly, in his view, positions of official power and influence in Upper Canada should ideally be filled by 'upright & disinterested Military Men'[10] – and he was determined to use the substantial patronage prerogatives of his office to ensure that in fact they would be.

Simcoe, of course, was no stranger to the loyalist ex-military, nor they to him. Indeed, a large part of his adult life had been spent among them in service in America. Over the course of a long war he had earned a reputation as a brilliant leader of loyalist troops, rising in rank to lieutenant-colonel and command of his own regiment of New York and Connecticut volunteers, many of whom would later become settlers in Upper Canada.[11] With them he had suffered the pain and exhaustion of defeat, and again with them he had found in Upper Canada a new focus for his ambitions and energies. Little wonder, therefore, that they regarded his elevation to the highest office and triumphant return to their midst as events of talismanic significance: 'Now I am content – content, I say – and can go home to reflect on this proud day,' declaimed one loyal veteran in his speech of welcome. 'Our Governor, the man of all others, has come at last.'[12] It was as though they had been waiting for him to appear, and he did not disappoint. They were the people towards whom he felt an 'ardent and undeviating attachment.'[13] They were his natural clientele. Upon them he would shower gifts of office, militia commissions, emoluments, honours, and above all, land. And they would reciprocate with their political and military support, their trust, and their public acclaim.

While mistrustful of the elected Legislative Assembly, and never satisfied that the supply of official patronage at his disposal was

---

10 Quoted in Wilson, *Enterprises of Robert Hamilton*, 110
11 For accounts of Simcoe's early career (and various aspects of his administration, such as Indian and defence policy, which are beyond the scope of this book), see W.R. Riddell, *The Life of John Graves Simcoe* (Toronto 1926); DCB, V, 754–9; and Gerald M. Craig, *Upper Canada: The Formative Years* (Toronto 1963), 20–41.
12 D.B. Read, *The Lieutenant-Governors of Upper Canada and Ontario, 1792–1899* (Toronto 1900), 21
13 *Simcoe Correspondence*, I, 153, Simcoe to Phineas Bond, 7 May 1792

sufficient to keep it properly under control – since in his view it was axiomatic that 'persons who shall compose the Assemblies must ... be dealt with as our Parliaments are *& be purchased to their duty*'[14] – Simcoe in fact possessed more than adequate inducements to ensure that he would encounter no opposition from that quarter. The loyalist ex-military were strongly represented, and with their support he was able to override the opposition of the merchant coterie in the Legislative Council and push through a series of acts that were designed to effect a major restructuring of judicial and local government offices. The merchant-dominated Courts of Common Pleas established in 1788 (which numbered among their many functions the right to order the seizure of land in payment of debt) were abolished and replaced by a Court of King's Bench and district courts, from which merchants would be excluded and whose judges would be lawyers appointed by the Crown. New county lieutenancies were created whose Crown appointees would have 'the recommendatory Power for the Militia and the Magistracy as is usual in England'[15] and who would thus act as a check upon mercantile influence. And, most important of all from a patronage point of view, the District Land Boards – 'the only effective local authority for the granting of land, the selection of townsites, the laying out of new roads and the improvement of primitive ones'[16] – were abolished: henceforth such functions would be concentrated in the hands of the lieutenant-governor. Thus, seemingly with a single masterful strategy, Simcoe had stripped away the institutional bases of mercantile power and substituted his own, at the same time vastly increasing his supply of patronage. To understand his use of that patronage, however, it is essential to understand that his goals extended far beyond the immediate welfare of his clientele. Patronage was politically vital, but as a means, not as an end: with it he intended to construct an ideal British society.

III

Thus, when Simcoe told the members of the first Assembly in 1792 that they were 'singularly blessed ... with a Constitution which has stood the test of experience, *and is the very image and transcript of that of Great*

14 Simcoe to Peter Russell, 17 July 1791, as quoted in Lillian F. Gates, *Land Policies of Upper Canada* (Toronto 1968), 36 (italics added)
15 *Simcoe Correspondence*, I, 251, Simcoe to Henry Dundas, 7 Nov. 1792
16 Wilson, *Enterprises of Robert Hamilton*, 53

Britain,' he was not propounding some novel (and patently erroneous) constitutional doctrine that the government of Upper Canada was intended to be as completely independent as that of the mother country. Nor was he speaking in the precise legalisms of a constitutional scholar. Instead, it is clear from the context that he was using the word 'constitution' in its broad eighteenth-century sense to mean the general political and social arrangements of a people, and that his purpose was to reassure the members of his audience that Upper Canada was and would remain a British province. Yet he was also telling them something more. For, he continued, unlike the rebellious colonists in the United States, they would be subject to no unbalanced or 'mutilated' constitution, but as a British people would continue to enjoy 'as much freedom and happiness as is possible to be enjoyed *under the subordination necessary to civilized society.'*[17] Clearly implied in such a message was a model of the society he would strive to create, a society whose Britishness would be reflected not only in its relationship to the empire but in every detail of its internal structure, and eventually in the habits and character of its people.

He left no doubt that the value of freedom would be paramount, but British freedom was seen as a two-sided coin and on the other side was order, not equality. Indeed, in Simcoe's view, claims to equality were either mischievous or misguided, for men were manifestly not equal. They naturally possessed different capacities and occupied different roles and stations in life. Yet each in his proper place could contribute to the strength and well-being of society as a whole, each could securely enjoy certain liberties and certain privileges – as long as they accepted and deferred to the authority of those placed above them. It was essentially a static conception of society: hierarchical distinctions were presumed to be immutable, and to deny their validity was to invite disorder. This, of course, was not a new notion. Shakespeare, for instance, had expressed the same thought in *Troilus and Cressida*, in Ulysses' speech before the tent of Agamemnon: 'Take but degree away, untune that string, / And hark, what discord follows!'

But the rebellion of the American colonies had seemingly driven home its point with new force. Had his listeners, if they were loyalists, not themselves witnessed the consequences of insubordination? Was it not obvious that without the constraining influence of respect for established authority society fell with appalling ease into disorder and violent civil strife? Upper Canada had therefore to be immunized

17 Public Archives of Ontario, *Report*, 1909, 18 (italics added)

against such ills. In Simcoe's grand design it was to be a haven of order and civility, justice and moderation, a shining example of British ways and institutions. The question was, by what means could such a future be best assured?

Inevitably, any answer given at this time would reflect some explanation of the causes of the American débâcle. In Simcoe's analysis, which was commonplace in official circles in England, it was not the granting of *too few* constitutional liberties to the American colonies that had caused their revolt but the granting of *too many*. Indeed, it was argued, by revolting they had demonstrated their inability to use wisely those substantial rights and liberties they had already possessed. For, it could now be perceived with hindsight, colonial society had been allowed to develop in a way that was fundamentally defective. In particular, its lack of an aristocracy had created a drastic imbalance in favour of the popular element in the constitution – in contrast to England where the separate interests of Crown, peers, and people were all (at least in theory) finely in balance. The latter situation was happily conducive to stability and moderation in government and provided the securest defence against tyranny. In the thirteen colonies, however, because the Crown was weakly represented and there was no balancing aristocratic element, there was no adequate check upon what Simcoe called 'the spirit of democratic subversion.'[18] It was this perception of events, amounting to an interpretation of the history of his own time, that gave a sharp ideological impetus to his plan of action in Upper Canada.

That plan was remarkably comprehensive, but also very simple: what he proposed was nothing less than the direct and uncompromising transplantation of the British way of life. Nothing could be left out. It was essential, he believed, if British rule was to be successfully maintained, that the British people 'transfuse their manners, principles and attachments thro' the entire colony.'[19] To do less would be to repeat the identical error that had had such disastrous consequences for the empire elsewhere in America.

What the Constitutional Act of 1791 had actually called for, however, was merely a somewhat modified and strengthened form of colonial rule.[20] It gave the lieutenant-governor, as representative of the Crown,

18 *Simcoe Correspondence*, III, 265, Simcoe to the Duke of Portland, 22 Jan. 1795
19 Ibid., I, 27, Simcoe to Henry Dundas, 30 June 1791
20 Adam Shortt and Arthur G. Doughty, eds., *Documents Relating to the Constitutional History of Canada, 1759–1791* (Ottawa 1918), 1031–51

wide executive powers as well as a legislative role, which included an absolute power of veto. The legislature was to be bicameral, consisting of an appointed Legislative Council and an elected Assembly. Provision was also made for an appointed Executive Council to advise the lieutenant-governor, but this body was to be solely responsible to him rather than to the legislature. The act, however, was by no means a comprehensive blueprint for development. Even in terms of prescribing institutional arrangements it was in certain respects little more than a piece of enabling legislation, allowing many vitally important decisions (including the establishment of judicial and local government systems) to be taken at the provincial level, which gave Simcoe ample opportunity to exert his influence vigorously on the side of anglicization and in accordance with his own plan for a complete and balanced society.

First of all, since the Constitutional Act had not revoked the application to Upper Canada of the French civil law of Quebec, it was necessary for the provincial legislature to revoke it and put in its place a new enactment requiring that 'in all matters of controversy relative to property and Civil Rights, resort shall be had to the Laws of England as the rule for the decision of the same.' Further legislation introduced the English system of legally determining matters of fact 'by the unanimous verdict of twelve jurors, which jurors shall be summoned and taken conformably to the law and custom of England.' The 'Winchester measures' of England were adopted as the standard of weights and measures, the use of all others being prohibited. The names of the districts of the province were anglicized to Eastern, Midland, Home, and Western (from Luneburg, Mecklenburg, Nassau, and Hesse – names originally assigned in 1788, supposedly to honour the Hanoverian connections of George III). By proclamation, Simcoe had already subdivided the province into nineteen English-type counties: these he had named Kent, Essex, Suffolk, Norfolk, Lincoln, York, Durham, Northumberland, Hastings, Prince Edward, Lennox, Addington, Ontario, Frontenac, Leeds, Grenville, Dundas, Stormont, and Glengarry – the first eight being named after the counties of England that border on the Strait of Dover and the North Sea.[21] The new office of county lieutenant was modelled on that of the lord lieutenant of an English county, and its social purpose was explicit: 'In order to promote an Aristocracy, most necessary in this country,' Simcoe reported, 'I have

21 Arthur G. Doughty and Duncan A. McArthur, eds., *Documents Relating to the Constitutional History of Canada, 1791–1818* (Ottawa 1914), 72–85; Riddell, *Life of Simcoe*, 100; Craig, *Upper Canada*, 26–8

appointed Lieutenants to the most populous Counties.'[22] Similarly, justices of the peace were not simply local judicial officers but also agents of the central government who exercised an important administrative and supervisory role in the community, which was precisely the situation then prevailing in English local government.

Thus, the machinery of justice and of government, and even the nomenclature of the province, were cast in a mould that Simcoe deemed fitting for a model British society. These were later to undergo innumerable changes in detail as the society grew and developed in different directions, but their original features remained prominently discernible for many decades, and indeed have never been completely erased.

The British constitution, however, is as much a matter of tradition and symbol as of machinery, as Simcoe well understood, and his close attention to institutional forms did not cause him to neglect the less tangible or symbolic aspects of political power. In spite of the embryonic state of the province's public life, and the extremely modest scale of its public buildings, he took care to celebrate such occasions as the opening of the legislature and the king's birthday with as much pomp and ceremony as could be mustered. His own official residence may have resembled 'a carrier's ale house' but it did not deter him from entertaining in vice-regal style. On 4 June, 1793, after attending a levee, a military display, and a 'splendid ball' in honour of the king's birthday, an observant American diplomat confided to his diary: 'Governor Simcoe is exceedingly attentive to these public assemblies and makes it his study to reconcile the inhabitants, who have tasted the pleasures of society, to their present situation, in an infant province. He intends the next winter to have concerts and assemblies very frequently. Hereby he at once evinces a regard to the happiness of the people, and his knowledge of the world; for while people are allured to become settlers in this country, from the richness of the soil and the clemency of the seasons, it is important to make their situation as flattering as possible.'[23]

In the art of politics, Machiavelli tells us, a ruler guided by *fantasia* – by which he means a talent for the imaginative manipulation of illusion – will be more successful than one bound by the limitations of mundane reality; for, he explains, 'the great majority of mankind are satisfied with

22 *Simcoe Correspondence*, I, 251, Simcoe to Henry Dundas, 6 Nov. 1792
23 General Benjamin Franklin, *Journal*, as quoted in Mary Quayle Innis, *Mrs. Simcoe's Diary* (Toronto 1965), 10

appearances, as though they were realities, and are often even more influenced by the things that seem than by those that are.'[24] Thus, while the reality of Upper Canada was of a strategically precarious, straggling, scarcely formed colony existing in the remote vastness of North America, the illusion Simcoe strove to create was always of something greater; not of what was, but of what might be.

Yet for all the audacity of his vision, his basic political beliefs and assumptions were unexceptional. His concern to instil the qualities of balance and completeness in the institutions and social fabric of Upper Canada, for example, was clearly in keeping with the prevailing eighteenth-century idea of the good, alike in politics as in art. That such qualities were inherent in the English constitution was something he seems never to have doubted. 'Should all Nations be permitted to combine in one view of universal peace and goodwill,' he theorized, they would turn to the model of Great Britain, 'whose subjects, in morality and industry, and in the form of Government which naturally flows from them, and is best adapted to their security, claim as their birthright the priority of the world.'[25] Like his great contemporary Edmund Burke, he believed the perfections of that constitution were 'the happy effects of *following nature*' and that consequently 'our political system is placed *in a just correspondence and symmetry with the order of the world*.'[26] It might be thought that such a view was curiously out of touch with reality; but as a man of affairs and former member of Parliament, Simcoe must have known that in practice and application the constitution also exhibited some manifest defects. What mattered, as far as Upper Canada was concerned, was his absolute belief in its rightness as a *theory*, indeed as a *doctrine*. As Basil Willey so insightfully writes of Burke, in words that apply equally to Simcoe: 'probably what [he] really reverenced was less the English Constitution as it actually was in the reign of George III, than an ideal English Constitution, stripped of its ugly incrustations and working freely according to its inner intention; an ideal almost but not quite as remote as Plato's city which is in heaven.'[27]

Unlike Burke, however, Simcoe, through a twist of fortune, had been placed in a position of power where he could devote his talent to the task of infusing that ideal with life and reality. Upper Canada was to be his canvas; on it he would strive to reproduce a masterpiece, but without the cracks and flaws of the original.

24 *Discourses*, I, 25
25 *Simcoe Correspondence*, I, 154, Simcoe to Phineas Bond, 7 May 1792
26 Quoted in Basil Willey, *The Eighteenth-Century Background* (London 1972), 233–4
27 Ibid., 233

IV

Such a vision was bound to appeal to the loyalists, and more especially to the ex-officers among them who were assigned the most flattering (and lucrative) roles within it. All the new lieutenants of counties, for example, were drawn from this element, and they in turn tended to recommend others of their number for the lesser plums of vice-regal patronage, from justices of the peace to inspectors of shops, stills, and taverns. 'Nothing presents itself more naturally,' Simcoe declared, than placing local offices 'in the hands of Persons whom the Colonists, principally disbanded Soldiers, have long been accustomed to consider as their Leaders; by having exercised the Administration of Justice, or having commanded them in the Field.' Moreover, to bring Upper Canada into conformity with the British model, and to counteract 'the awful example of the late American Rebellion,' he wished to see the chief among them rewarded with 'an hereditary Seat derived from a Title of Honor being vested in their Families.'[28]

But that was not to be; the obstacles were simply too formidable. In the first place, Simcoe's vision was only to a small degree shared by the British government. Even his establishment of the county lieutenancies was acquiesced in only with reluctance and prompted the Duke of Portland, the minister responsible for colonial administration, to warn generally against such measures on the grounds that 'your adoption of them arises from the idea, that by assimilating the modes of the Government of the Province, to the modes of the Government of England, you will obtain all the beneficial effects which we receive from them – whereas to assimilate a Colony in all respects to the Mother Country, is not possible, and if possible, would not be prudent.'[29] In other words, the basic underlying premise of his approach was misconceived, and, it was plainly implied, the measures he deemed necessary for its implementation would not be automatically supported in London.

In addition, he had constantly to contend with the obstructive tactics of his immediate superior, Lord Dorchester, governor general of the Canadas, who made his headquarters in Quebec City. There, ensconced in the Citadel, 'old and irritable and emptied of ideas,'[30] Dorchester commanded a garrison that was utterly dependent upon British sea

28 *Simcoe Correspondence*, IV, 116–7, Simcoe to the Duke of Portland, 30 Oct. 1795
29 Ibid., 12, the Duke of Portland to Simcoe, 20 May 1795
30 Donald Creighton, *The Empire of the St. Lawrence* (Toronto 1970), 116

power, an alien presence in the midst of a conquered and resentful people. Simcoe, meanwhile, was acquainting himself with his new charge by travelling on foot around the Niagara region, staying en route in the homes of settlers, and making long excursions by canoe and on horseback to the furthest reaches of the province, being everywhere greeted with the utmost warmth and acclaim. The contrast between his situation and Dorchester's could hardly have been more extreme, and not surprisingly, their points of view diverged irreconcilably. For Simcoe, the loyalist settlers, with their energy and optimism and faith in the land's agricultural potential, were the best guarantee of the future. Nothing could better serve the interests of the British Empire, he believed, than a populous, prosperous, well-governed Upper Canada; and if adequately garrisoned, with the support of local militia and Indian allies, it could be successfully defended against an American attack. For Dorchester, however, Upper Canada was little more than an insecure hinterland of Montreal, so far beyond the range of the Royal Navy as to be militarily indefensible. Consequently, Simcoe's ambitious and costly scheme to promote its development he saw as an extravagant waste of British money, and Simcoe's single-minded concern for the security and well-being of its inhabitants as wilful disregard of imperial interests (and, no doubt, of his own superior judgment). Lord Dorchester, Simcoe was soon complaining with reason, 'in all his dispatches almost discovers a spirit of counteraction and opposition to whatsoever does not originate from himself.'[31]

Finally, perhaps the greatest obstacle of all to his grand design was the likelihood that, if too rigorously pursued, it would arouse domestic opposition. For although the loyalists genuinely welcomed his presence and had good reason to support the initial anglicizing thrust of his policies, they were by no means enamoured of the English class and religious structures that he additionally hoped to foist upon them. Many believed their prospects to be on the rise; many were of Scottish, Irish, or German descent, Presbyterians, Roman Catholics, or dissenters. What advantage could there be for them in attempting to reproduce in Upper Canada the static and discriminatory social order of rural England? As usual, the merchants were quick to spot the weakness. Simcoe, Richard Cartwright wrote to Isaac Todd, 'thinks every existing regulation in England would be proper here. Not attending sufficiently, perhaps, to the spirit of the constitution, he seems bent on copying all the

---

31 *Simcoe Correspondence*, III, 163, Simcoe to Lord Grenville, 30 Oct. 1794

subordinate establishments without considering the great disparity of the two countries in every respect. And it really would not surprise me to see attempts made to establish among us Ecclesiastical Courts, tithes, and religious tests, though nine-tenths at least of our people are of persuasions different from the Church of England, though the whole have been bred in a country where there was the most perfect freedom in religious matters, and though this would certainly occasion almost a general emigration.' While he and Robert Hamilton, he added, were 'by no means disposed to form cabals, and certainly have not, nor do, intend wantonly to oppose or thwart the Governor,' nevertheless, 'I do not think it necessary to bow with reverence to every sub-delegate of the Executive Government.'[32]

But Cartwright, like so many of Simcoe's critics – from that day to this – had underestimated both his grasp of Upper Canadian realities and his political adroitness; for in spite of his rhetoric, and however much he might have believed in such measures in theory, in practice Simcoe was not unaware of the dangers of pushing his program of anglicization too far. Nor, facing an almost total lack of support from Dorchester, was he about to compound his problems by stirring up a hornet's nest of opposition to his rear. Instead, by the end of 1794 his appreciation of the situation, ironically, was not very different from Cartwright's; and from that point he began to shift pragmatically towards policies designed to broaden his base of support – and that meant reaching an accommodation with the mercantile community.[33]

V

What Simcoe had attempted to accomplish by expanding and centralizing the machinery of government and by channelling patronage towards the loyalist military was to create a coherent, hierarchical system of official clientelism to counterbalance the commercial clientel-

---

32 C.E. Cartwright, ed., *Life and Letters of the Late Hon. Richard Cartwright* (Toronto 1876), 56–64

33 Political adroitness and pragmatism are not terms that are usually associated with Simcoe, since modern historians have tended to stress his other qualities. See in particular the condescending appraisal of S.R. Mealing, 'The Enthusiasms of John Graves Simcoe,' in J.K. Johnson, ed., *Historical Essays on Upper Canada* (Toronto 1975), 302–16. But in his handling of provincial issues (as opposed to his dealings with Downing Street), it is remarkable how seldom he allowed his 'enthusiasms' to override his political judgment.

ism of the merchants, and to a degree he had succeeded. But his creation was still a relatively puny thing (and was likely to remain so, since neither Lord Dorchester nor the Duke of Portland could see any need to nourish it with further infusions of imperial money), while the commercial system, which generated its own supply of patronage out of the rich and ever-increasing spoils of Laurentian trade, was thriving as never before. In practical terms, the consequences were important. In the case of a village trader and storekeeper, for instance, to be a client of a leading merchant such as Robert Hamilton was to be rewarded with credit, advance information on market conditions, a guaranteed supply of goods for resale, and a guaranteed outlet for the produce purchased from his own clients; it meant a lessening of the risks of speculation; and more broadly, it meant a chance to accumulate a measure of wealth, to rise in the community, to become a person of standing. And the fact that Hamilton could no longer deliver in addition an appointment to a local office or some other minor piece of political patronage that had previously been in his gift but was now in the gift of the county lieutenant, while no doubt disappointing, did not seriously detract from the strength or value of the commercial patron-client bond.[34] The commercial clientele system, in other words, was deeper in resources than the official system and more than capable of surviving and even growing in spite of the loss of its political prerogatives.

Moreover, Simcoe's one potentially equalizing source of domestic patronage – namely, his right to dispose of the Crown lands – had turned out to have no direct effect upon the economic dominance of the merchants and indeed indirectly worked to their advantage. For the unintended consequence of endowing the ex-military and other favoured individuals with large grants that were surplus to their needs (and that they therefore sensibly preferred to convert into cash or credit) was to fuel a speculative market in 'wild lands' for which the merchants were practically the only buyers. By this means the more affluent among them were able to accumulate huge holdings of prime agricultural land for future sale or development without the need to be themselves the recipients of vice-regal bounty[35] (though, after approximately a two-

---

34 'The success and influence of the merchants did not, as Simcoe thought, depend upon specific political privileges they enjoyed and the government had not touched the social and economic roots of the merchants' power.' Wilson, *Enterprises of Robert Hamilton*, 118

35 Gates, *Land Policies*, 43

year hiatus, by 1795 that bounty was beginning to flow once more in their direction in any case).

The factor that more than any other made possible an accommodation between Simcoe and the mercantile community was the growing convergence of their thinking on questions of economic policy. Simcoe had from the start believed that the only satisfactory economic foundation for the province had to be agriculture, which of course put him at one with the bulk of the loyalist population. It was also an entirely orthodox view, in keeping with English economic thought of the period and very typical of the class of landed gentry to which he belonged, for which agriculture was next to religion as the *sine qua non* of civilized society. But he had not thought the matter through in any detail. Hence he had not anticipated the significance of the grain trade (possibly because he had assumed that there would develop more or less self-sufficient estates on the British model, which would produce a varied output but no large marketable surplus of any one commodity). Yet even by the time of his arrival Upper Canadian farmers, having passed the point of self-sufficiency, were already provisioning the garrisons and shipping increasing quantities of grain down the St Lawrence to supply the Quebec market and for export.[36] He had also initially associated the merchants almost exclusively with their interests in the fur trade and military provisioning contracts (and had scant regard for their activities in either, suspecting them of debauching the Indians with the one and cheating the government with the other). 'I consider the Fur Trade on its present foundation to be of no use whatever, to the Colony of Upper Canada,'[37] he had confidently asserted in 1792, and at least part of his opposition to the merchants stemmed from his suspicion that the fur trade, rather than his cherished new province, would always claim their first allegiance. What he seems not to have realized was that merchants such as Hamilton and Cartwright engaged in that particular branch of trade because it was profitable, and that out of their profits they had financed the extensive shipping, portaging, and warehousing facilities that were so vital to the development of agriculture. But as that development progressed, and as the population grew, they had naturally shifted the focus of their enterprises accordingly, for it was now in supplying the agricultural

36 R.L. Jones, *History of Agriculture in Ontario, 1613–1880* (Toronto 1946), 23–5
37 *Simcoe Correspondence*, I, 141, Simcoe to Henry Dundas, 28 Apr. 1792

sector with imported goods, in land speculation, and in the grain trade that they increasingly saw their opportunities.

By the end of 1794 Simcoe's views of agriculture and trade – and of merchants – had undergone a dramatic transformation. In his travels about the province he had observed at first hand the land's extravagant productivity and had become more convinced than ever that it was destined to support 'a numerous and Agricultural people.' It had also become clear to him, as he observed in his well-informed and carefully thought-out report to the Committee of the Privy Council for Trade and Plantations in September of that year, that 'the produce of the Earth, which forms the staple of Upper Canada must be Wheat.' That report, indeed, marked the turning point in his thinking. In it Simcoe proceeded to outline in detail a scheme to hasten and assist the development of Upper Canada into the granary of the British Empire by means of massive government investment and intervention – a scheme that resembled nothing so much as the one proposed to him in more general terms by Robert Hamilton nearly three years previously. It called for a combination of ameliorative and regulatory measures, including the establishment of an Upper Canadian paper currency, the improvement of navigation and port facilities, the establishment of 'a principal Flour Inspector' to head a corps of 'inferior Inspectors' with power to ensure 'a strict and just attention to the quality of the commodity being sent for export,' and the creation of a Crown corporation to facilitate and oversee every facet of the trade.[38] These were remarkably progressive ideas for their time. And while it might be thought that the merchants would not welcome increased intervention of government in their business, they were essentially pragmatic mercantilists for whom the doctrine of 'free enterprise' was not an inhibiting concern: they had always benefited from government intervention in the past and no doubt fully expected to go on doing so. They also had the reassurance of seeing the lieutenant-governor converted from an opponent of their interests into an active lobbyist on their behalf.

This is not to say that Simcoe abandoned either his grand design or his loyalist clientele, but neither could he ignore the economic realities that stared him in the face. Ultimately, all his hopes and ambitions for Upper Canada hinged upon its economic development, and that meant

38 Ibid., III, 52–68, Simcoe to the Committee of the Privy Council for Trade and Plantations, 1 Sept. 1794

above all the development of agriculture, for only agriculture could support the rapid increase in settlement that he envisaged and that he was doing everything in his power to promote. Yet it was also plainly evident that without the merchants no such development was likely to take place, or if it did, its progress would be impossibly slow – too slow to prevent Upper Canada's absorption into the United States. 'Perhaps no maxim will bear less examination,' Simcoe had written in his report, 'than that "Trade should be left to itself." It is not true in theory nor in practice, unless on a limited scale, and in petty operations.'[39] He had come to realize that the commercial system of the St Lawrence was anything but a petty operation, that the mercantile elite were too solidly entrenched to be dislodged by political means, and that in any case both were indispensable to his purposes. Moreover he had found, no doubt to his pleasant surprise, that merchants such as Hamilton and Cartwright were men of ability whose advice in matters of economic policy was not to be lightly disregarded. Ironically, in their eye for the larger picture, in their capacity to plan, and in their understanding of the need for 'systematic Arrangement' they were also generally much closer to his outlook than were the loyalist officers with whom he had initially filled his administration. For the latter were the product of an unconventional frontier war, and the qualities that had made them admirable leaders then – such as courage, resourcefulness, and a readiness to depart from strict rules and conventional tactics – had not equipped them particularly well for the routine duties of civil office, which many tended to treat in desultory fashion or exploit scandalously, even by the lax standards of the time. A case in point is that of Lieutenant-Colonel John Butler, the first county lieutenant of Niagara, who, after an outstanding military career, had spent the peace scheming to cheat the Indian Department and importuning his former superiors, though with only indifferent success. It is indicative of the new realism of Simcoe's administration that when Butler died in office in 1796 he was replaced by none other than Robert Hamilton.[40]

The rapprochement between Simcoe and the merchants had important ramifications, not only at the top of the political system but throughout it, for each merchant appointed to a post, at whatever level, tended to produce a ripple effect upon other appointments. Hamilton,

---

39 Ibid., 65
40 Wilson, *Enterprises of Robert Hamilton*, 127. Richard Cartwright had already been made a county lieutenant. *DCB*, v, 170

for example, used his office to increase both the level of merchant participation in government and his own sphere of influence. For he was now once again able to combine political patronage with commercial patronage, and so widespread was his network of the latter that his effective political influence spread even beyond his own district, particularly to the rapidly developing agricultural settlements to the west and north. In all these areas his favoured candidates for local office were his relatives or friends and the small merchants who formed his clientele. On his first patronage list, which contained his recommendations for appointment to the magistracy, nine of the ten named were merchants and one a surgeon. Significantly, none were loyalist officers. 'Messrs. Crooks, McKay, Edwards and others,' he added, 'may be equally entitled with those recommended. They are all merchants and I feared that such an addition might, to his Excellency, have the appearance of professional preference.' He need not have been concerned, however: Simcoe approved his entire list and threw in the names of Crooks and Edwards for good measure.[41]

In a society as small and intimate as Upper Canada there were bound to be social ramifications as well, for such recognition could not help but enhance the status of the mercantile element. This may be seen also in their increased presence as officers in the local militia regiments, whereas previously the commissioned ranks of those regiments had been the jealously guarded preserve of the loyalist military. In the Niagara district, indeed, to the latter's chagrin, Simcoe went so far as to allow Hamilton to form a special corps of artillery officered predominantly by merchants.[42] Likewise, in the making of land grants, merchants became increasingly the beneficiaries of vice-regal patronage, at the top by virtue of the important civil or military posts they had been given and at the bottom by virtue of the influence of their patrons. The result was to tie them more closely to their communities, a process further strengthened by the growth of agriculture and the consequent shift in their business enterprises away from the fur trade; for although a diminishing band of old-style fur traders remained, the bulk of the mercantile community had become steadily more committed to the land and to the future of agriculture. And not surprisingly, their commitment to Upper Canada had deepened accordingly. At every level, from

41 *Simcoe Correspondence*, IV, 299, 328, Hamilton to E.B. Littlehales, 15 June 1796; Littlehales to Hamilton, 10 July 1796
42 Wilson, *Enterprise of Robert Hamilton*, 127

magnate to shopkeeper, most would probably have shared Richard Cartwright's sentiments, as expressed in a letter to Isaac Todd in 1794: 'All my prospects, as well for myself as my family,' he wrote, 'are confined to this Province; I am bound to it by the strongest ties, and with its welfare my interest is most essentially connected.'[43]

VI

Simcoe had deftly co-opted the merchants and made them partners in his grand design. Or, to put it slightly differently, as Bruce G. Wilson does, 'as he had come to understand the role of the merchants in the economy, so he came to recognize their power within the society ... Through commercial operations merchants had the only effective network of local contact and local influence. In the end, Simcoe decided to attempt to harness it to governmental purposes.'[44] But equally importantly, in so doing he had also substantially altered his grand design to make it conform more realistically to the economic structures of an emerging agrarian society – a society in which nothing could have been less likely to take root than a hereditary landed aristocracy composed of officials and loyalist officers, who for the most part would have possessed neither the capital nor the expertise to develop their estates. The merchants, on the other hand, had behind them a wealth-creating system of proven effectiveness in the North American environment. And as Simcoe soon learned, they were far from being a levelling influence: many, indeed, were a match for even the most grasping of half-pay officers in their avidity for appointments, honours, awards, and other signs of social status and official preferment. The differences between him and them, while initially nettlesome and aggravated by misconceptions on both sides, were in fact neither ideologically nor politically profound. At root, both believed implicitly in inequality as the basis of social order; both believed in the value of strong, interventionist government; and in politics both operated totally within a framework of clientelist assumptions.

So much of Simcoe's time and effort as lieutenant-governor was taken up with other momentous issues – including defence, which was his constant preoccupation, his intractable difficulties with Lord Dorchester, and his controversial policy of increasing the population by inviting

43 Cartwright, *Life and Letters*, 57
44 Wilson, *Enterprises of Robert Hamilton*, 127

an influx of American settlers (the 'late loyalists') – that his impact upon the emerging political process of Upper Canada has generally been overlooked. But both immediately and in the long run that impact was of the utmost consequence. Above all, his efforts during the last two years of his governorship to integrate the merchants into the official clientele system significantly strengthened and stabilized the provincial political system as a whole, while helping to entrench a pattern of elite behaviour that would in time become customary. Thereafter, though the official and mercantile elites would never overlap completely in personnel, and though their interests would at times diverge, no unbridgeable gulf was ever allowed to develop between them: in effect, Simcoe's accommodation of mercantile interests and ambitions would become an enduring feature of the political landscape.

The importance of this to the very survival of the province would soon be demonstrated. Much has been made of the role played by the War of 1812 in the forging of the Upper Canadian identity. As Jane Errington writes, the war 'came to symbolize the unity and loyalty of all residents of the new land and prompted the development of a new colonial consciousness, one which was distinctly Upper Canadian.'[45] But it is doubtful whether such a development could have taken place if the merchants – who formed a vital tier of local leadership in the province's thinly spread communities – had been a disaffected and potentially disloyal element, or even if they had maintained a disinterested neutrality. Instead, by 1812 their links to the political system had grown strong and permanent. Laden with magistracies, shrivalties, militia commissions, land grants, and other entitlements, they had become, as Simcoe had hoped they would, ardent defenders of the Crown and of Upper Canada.[46] The war, moreover, served to enhance the legitimacy of their leadership and of the clientele system through which they had risen. When peace returned, that system reverted once more to its familiar pattern of localism, with its casual and often chaotic mix of commercial and political patronage, its strong dyadic patron-client alliances, and its endemic fractiousness. But, although loosely articulated, its toughness and resilience had been demonstrated; when threatened, its leaders had shown that they could set aside their differences; and its structure had withstood the tests of time and of war. In short, it had become finely attuned to the realities of Upper Canadian society.

45 *The Lion, the Eagle, and Upper Canada* (Toronto 1987), 89
46 See H.V. Nelles, 'Loyalism and Local Power – Niagara District, 1792–1837,' *Ontario History* 58 (1966): 104

3

Patrons and Clients

What is capital but property unequally distributed?

– John Elmsley, Chief Justice of Upper Canada, 1796–1802

It is in the nature of men to be as much bound by the benefits that they confer as by those they receive.

– Machiavelli, *The Prince*

I

The line between using land grants to reward loyalty to the Crown or to promote social stability and using them as unvarnished political patronage is at best an exceedingly fine one – and in Upper Canada it soon became so fine as to be indistinguishable. Both of Simcoe's immediate successors, Peter Russell (1796–99)[1] and Peter Hunter (1799–1805),[2] were men of practical bent who had made their careers in organizations that knew no other principle but patronage, Russell's in the army and colonial administration, Hunter's exclusively in the army; they had thrived on official plums, and it is not surprising that, when finally given a whole tree, they assumed the right to shake it vigorously and often. Thus, seizing upon the familiar patronage prerogatives of their office, they proceeded to distribute land in stunning volume, often on the flimsiest of claims, and always with an eye to their own personal

1 *Dictionary of Canadian Biography*, v, 729–32. Russell was not appointed lieutenant governor but rather 'administrator' in Simcoe's absence – that is, acting lieutenant-governor.
2 Ibid., 439–43

financial advantage. Their hope, of course was that such a distribution would at the same time give rise, if not to Simcoe's cherished ideal of a landed aristocracy, then at least to a sizable 'propertied interest' whose leaders would become the pillars of the established order – but even if it did not, the resulting payment of land registration fees (a percentage of which went straight into the lieutenant-governor's pocket) would have the happy incidental effect of supplementing their already substantial salaries. 'Russell is avaricious to the last degree,' Peter Hunter wrote of the man he was to replace, 'and would certainly as far as depended upon him have granted land to the Devil and all his Family (as good Loyalists) provided they could have paid the fees.'[3] His words were doubly ironic since they would later apply equally to himself.

The crux of the matter was land. There were few jobs carrying large salaries that were purely in the gift of the Upper Canadian administration, for the choice plums of official patronage were still jealously guarded by the imperial government. But in matters of land the administration's patronage powers were immense, indeed beyond the wildest imaginings of English domestic politics – and all because of a fortuitous moment in history that allowed it, in the span of a few brief decades, to dispose of truly enormous quantities of fertile land. To find a comparable moment in English history it is necessary to go back to the period of the Norman conquest. Hence those officials in Upper Canada whose posts were in the administration's gift – from legislative councillors and county lieutenants to magistrates, sheriffs, and customs collectors – profited far more from the land entitlements that their posts carried with them than from their stipends. Moreover, those engaged in certain favoured occupations, as well as their wives and children, were also eligible for grants. The staggering extent of the bounty showered upon them is indicated by Lillian F. Gates, who writes of Russell: 'With the ready help of the Executive Council, he proceeded to exercise the discretion vested him him of making land grants up to 1,200 acres ... To magistrates and barristers the maximum grant was allowed. Grants of 1,200 acres were made to "old" merchants, 600 to young ones, and 400 to merchants' clerks. The wives of barristers and Members of Parliament received 600 acres of wild land to help sustain their dignity, and the children of loyalist officers, not content with the common portion of 200 acres, petitioned for, and received, several times that amount, according to their father's rank.'[4]

3 As quoted in Lillian F. Gates, *Land Policies of Upper Canada* (Toronto 1968), 65
4 Ibid., 66

The seven sons of legislative councillor Robert Hamilton, for example, received among them 8,400 acres. 'A short time after this grant was made, an eighth son was born ... and hardly had the child drawn breath before the father petitioned for an additional 1,200 acres of land on its account.'[5] Eventually, Hamilton wound up with over 14,000 acres in direct grants and was allowed to purchase a further 24,000 acres from the Crown at the bargain price of nine pence per acre.[6] According to Bruce G. Wilson, 'the total known amount of land in which he held an interest by purchase, grant or mortgage was 130,170 acres.'[7]

Figures of this magnitude, however, while impressive on paper, in reality meant very little. In some countries the possession of even twenty thousand acres would have made a man a princely magnate with scores of tenant farmers labouring on his estate. But not in Upper Canada, where the one flaw in the whole great edifice of patronage, in so far as it was intended to gentrify the province, was that land had more potential than present value – and its potential could only be realized if new settlers wanted to locate on it. It could not be worked as a large estate because there was neither capital nor labour available to devote to the arduous task of clearing it. What twenty thousand acres made a man in Upper Canada, therefore, was a settlement promoter or land speculator, or more likely a bit of both.

At one extreme the system produced a small class of those who may be termed the 'grand patrons' of the province. These were individuals who, through a variety of means, all of which rested ultimately on their connections to the highest levels of government, managed to acquire the right to control access to truly huge tracts of land (ranging upwards of one hundred thousand acres, in addition to their often very substantial personal holdings), took up residence, and promptly set about the business of inducing settlers to join them by investing in facilities such as mills and roads, usually in conjunction with the promotion of group emigration schemes in the British Isles. While they were not the typical promoters of settlement (most of whom were small merchants who dealt in land on a relatively modest scale), their presence was widely felt. Indeed, over vast areas of the province they were the dominant agents of development. Our concern here, however, is not with the economic or demographic impact of their activities (of which, unfortu-

5 Ibid., 67
6 Ibid., 50–1
7 DCB, V, 403

nately, no comprehensive or comparative study yet exists) but with the social, political, and symbolic implications of their role. For – much like the role played by the Canadian Senate today – their very existence served as a reminder of the power of clientelism in the society and their example served to legitimize its practice at all levels. In their lives and careers, moreover, they usefully illustrate the cultural norms and conventions that regulated patron-client relationships. And finally, the fact that they were generally men of outstanding ability and colourful personality contributed in no small measure to the growth of a tradition of local political leadership and the entrenchment of local elites, which would become such striking features of the Upper Canadian political system.

Perhaps the best known and most successful of these grand patrons was Colonel Thomas Talbot,[8] who had first come to Upper Canada as secretary and aide to Lieutenant-Governor Simcoe. Captivated by the quality of the land, he had returned in 1803 to take up his entitlement as a ranking field officer of 5,000 acres, which he eventually expanded by 1821 to more than 65,000 acres through various additional government grants. He chose to settle in the then-remote southwestern region on the shore of Lake Erie, just south of the present city of London, where he began his enterprise in the traditional way by establishing saw and grist mills in order to make the numerous lots he had available more attractive to prospective farmers. He was sufficiently high-handed (and far enough away) to ignore the government at York when it suited him, yet sufficiently influential to enjoy its patronage. By having himself appointed road commissioner, for example, he was able to push ahead with the construction of roads designed to make his lands more accessible and hence more valuable, a blatant conflict of interest by modern standards but unquestionably effective: one result was the best road in Upper Canada, a three-hundred-mile artery that ended the isolation of the southwestern region by linking it to the settlements on Lake Ontario and hence to the St Lawrence waterway. Altogether, no less than half a million acres, extending over 130 miles from Long Point to the Detroit River, were settled through Talbot's agency. In this vast 'palatinate,' a contemporary observer noted, in matters of land the colonel's word was law.[9]

8 DCB, VIII, 857–62. For book-length biographies of Talbot, see Fred C. Hamil, *Lake Erie Baron: The Story of Colonel Thomas Talbot* (Toronto 1955); C.O. Ermatinger, *The Talbot Regime* (St Thomas, Ont. 1904); and Edward Ermatinger, *Life of Colonel Talbot* (St Thomas, Ont. 1859).
9 William Dummer Powell, as quoted in Gates, *Land Policies*, 128

The relationship that existed between Colonel Talbot and his settlers was basically one of simple, dyadic clientelism: it was personal, face to face, multifunctional, unequal, and reciprocal. As patron, Talbot's status was solidly based on his control over productive land; as client, what the settler received from him was access to that land, but that was only the beginning. Had the settler arrived with cash in hand to purchase his lot it would have been a straightforward transaction necessitating no further relationship between them, but few were in a position to do so, and fewer still had any wish to become tenant farmers or sharecroppers. Instead, the settler took up occupancy on a piece of land on the understanding that if he performed certain duties he would eventually receive freehold title to it. In the meantime, however, it was the colonel who personally superintended the performance of his 'settlement duties' and generally provided leadership, planning, advice, and credit in various forms to help him and his fellow client-settlers get started. If they wanted logs sawn into lumber, if they had grain to be ground into flour, there was no need of cash: the colonel's mills were at their disposal – for a share of the product. As they prospered they thereby made the region as a whole more attractive to new settlers, and as their small personal estates rose in value, so did the colonel's large one. In due course there were more applicants for lots than he could satisfy.

The key to the entire process was Talbot's rigid and at times ruthless insistence that his clients perform their settlement duties or face eviction. Those duties were supposedly standard throughout the province and were not in fact very onerous. They required only the erection of a 'habitable dwelling,' the clearing of at least ten acres, and some additional clearing and maintenance work on the road fronting the settler's lot, of which he would in any case be the prime beneficiary – but only if his neighbours did likewise. The latter condition was crucial: otherwise the labour of road work was pointless and the roads consequently impassable. But in the absence of a bureaucracy to police such matters, in some parts of the province settlement duties were commonly neglected and thus a great source of irritation to conscientious settlers. One considerable advantage of the patron-client system was that a strong patron such as Colonel Talbot could offer them the security of knowing that their own labours would not be thwarted by the inaction of lazy neighbours or absentee landholders.

It is essential to realize, however, that even in the case of Talbot's domain, the Upper Canadian patron-client relationship was complex and subtle, and far from being a matter of mere coercion. Ultimately it rested upon the perception of mutual interest by parties who were unequal in wealth and status, and mutual respect grounded in many years of close personal dealings, of promises on both sides that had been kept. According to one biographer, the colonel was a 'Lake Erie Baron,'[10] but the ascription of a feudal title to him is misleading. His was not a feudal domain, for there was not really a great deal that he could compel, ultimately, if his clients chose to challenge his authority.[11] Even the threat of dispossession ceased to be effective once a settler had completed his settlement duties and transformed himself into a freeholder. It would be a mistake, therefore, to portray his clients as hapless serfs with no choice but to do his bidding. Upper Canadian clientelism in practice owed little to European feudal models; it was less a relic of a distant and foreign past than a realistic and practical arrangement that was freely adapted to local circumstances. It was never based exclusively or even primarily upon tenantry, for example, and indeed its effectiveness in helping settlers without capital achieve the cherished status of freeholders was a unique feature that tended to strengthen rather than weaken the personal bonds that held it together.

In politics it was clearly facilitated by an electoral system that required open voting at designated polling places, thereby allowing patrons who were so inclined to monitor the votes of their clients.[12] At the same time, it must be borne in mind that elections were sporadic events and often more an excuse for drunken revelry or rowdy mischief than a sober exercise in political choice. For many electors, it would appear, a vote was no more than a minor asset to be sold to the highest bidder or traded for a jug of whisky; for others it was a part of their reciprocal relationship with the local patron, and to vote as he directed was simply to show a

10 Hamil, *Lake Erie Baron*. Anna Jameson refers to him as 'sovereign *de facto*, if not *de jure*' and as 'this grand bashaw of the wilderness' in her charming and sympathetic sketch of the old colonel in *Winter Studies and Summer Rambles in Canada* (London 1838; reissued Toronto 1965), 88–102.

11 See Paul Baldwin, 'The Political Power of Colonel Thomas Talbot,' *Ontario History* 61 (1969): 9–18.

12 They were capable of stronger measures, if required. To ensure the election of Mahlon Burwell for Oxford and Middlesex in 1812, for example, Talbot had located the poll in 'an *entire wilderness*. So that Mallory [the opposing candidate] and his friends were obliged to travel nearly 60 miles through the woods to the poll, – there they found the *"Father of the Settlement"* [Talbot] providing votes for his favourite ... by furnishing all who were willing to support the claims of the Young Aspirant to office, and who were not already qualified – with LOCATION TICKETS.' The observer of this scene was Asahel Lewis, quoted in the entry for Benajah Mallory, *DCB*, VIII, 608.

small courtesy to a man who had earned their trust in political as in commercial matters. Though there were many variations from place to place, these did not fundamentally affect the system. One patron might be highly active politically, another much less so; one might automatically command compliance at the poll, another might traditionally have to accompany his voting advice with bribes, his hold on a client's vote being in effect nothing more than a first option to buy. And everywhere it was a foolish patron indeed who wanted to quarrel over politics with a client who was a good farmer or a useful member of the local militia regiment. Nevertheless, elections could still at times be fiercely contested. The patrons' dominance was never absolute; outside their own immediate counties of residence their influence tended to diminish over distance; and some, through their actions and personalities, seemed positively to invite opposition. Colonel Talbot, for example, whose domain extended over twenty-nine townships, did not in fact entirely control the allocation of land in any one of those townships. He made no effort to make himself popular (indeed, as he grew older, he became increasingly high-handed and reclusive), while the rise of the town of London as the district's commercial and administrative centre inevitably weakened his political hold.

In this respect, it should be noted, the district was moving towards the structure of political power that was commonly found in the more populous and developed parts of the province, such as the Home District, which had Toronto as its focus. What Talbot had to contend with was the rise of an oligarchy of mid-level patrons in London who had their own direct lines of commercial and political patronage, who were building up their own clienteles, and who were thus not as amenable to his control as the official clique (the so-called Courtier Compact) with which he had surrounded himself – the surveyors, customs collectors, and others who owed their positions directly to him.[13]

Among the grand patrons, land and loyalism were invariably present as twin pillars of their status, but in other respects their backgrounds reveal no common pattern. Even with regard to land it was only necessary that they be able to secure it for their clients, which a few were able to do without owning vast amounts of it themselves. In the Eastern District,

13 Colin Read, 'The London District Oligarchy in the Rebellion Era,' *Ontario History* 72 (1980): 195–209; Graeme H. Patterson, 'Studies in Elections and Public Opinion in Upper Canada,' PHD thesis, University of Toronto 1969, 36–7; and DCB, VIII, 860

for example, the grand patron was Bishop Alexander Macdonell,[14] the ranking Catholic cleric in the province, who, like Colonel Talbot, had begun in the traditional way as a promoter of settlement schemes. Under his auspices whole townships in the Glengarry area were settled with Scottish highlanders, many of whom were ex-soldiers from disbanded highland regiments and their families.

It is everywhere essential to the maintenance of a patron's role, however, that he be able to deliver on his promises and obligations to his clients – and to be a grand patron in Upper Canada he had to be able to deliver land. This Colonel Talbot was able to do because he personally owned so much of it, and Bishop Macdonell was able to do it because of his consummate skill in manipulating the government patronage system. He personally occupied a position on the Land Board for the Eastern District and eventually reached the very pinnacle of patronage, the Legislative Council itself. There were few of his relatives or friends who did not benefit from his uncanny knack of loosening official purse strings, while to his wider clientele there flowed a steady stream of land grants, jobs, militia promotions, pensions, and emoluments of every kind. It helped that he was a fierce loyalist, a tory, and a militia leader. With a reservoir of highland veterans to draw upon, he had raised the formidable Glengarry Regiment for service against the Americans in 1812, serving with them in the field: 'Half bishop, half baron, he fought and prayed, with equal zeal, by the side of the men he had come to regard as his hereditary followers.'[15]

In electoral politics his influence was spread throughout the Eastern District, while in Glengarry itself (which normally elected one Presbyterian and one Catholic to the assembly) the filling of the Catholic seat was one of his personal prerogatives as patron. It was generally acknowledged to be part of his clients' duty to vote for his nominee – and should any feel inclined to stray from their duty, the bishop was not slow to remind them of who had secured them their land. But in general he had no need to intimidate, since even among those who were not his clients his authority was widely respected. His ultimate accolade, perhaps, was earned in in 1836, when, after the local rout of the reformers, he became very likely the only Catholic bishop ever for whom a grateful Orange

14 J.E. Rea, *Bishop Alexander Macdonnell and the Politics of Upper Canada* (Toronto 1974)
15 William F. Coffin, *1812: The War and Its Moral* (Montreal 1864), as quoted in Rea, ibid., 34

Lodge cancelled their July Twelfth parade and instead drank toasts in his honour.[16]

Another route to the status of grand patron was that taken by William 'Tiger' Dunlop,[17] the eccentric wit and *bon vivant* whose sway extended over a vast area in the west of the province stretching inland from the shores of Lake Huron. This area was part of a gigantic property of over a million prime acres known as the Huron Tract. 'It is impossible to find two hundred acres in the whole territory which will make a bad farm,'[18] wrote Dunlop, and he was not far wrong. Yet in 1826 the whole of it had been conveyed to a rather unlikely group of settlement promoters, made up of an English joint-stock company spearheaded by a Scottish novelist, John Galt (who shortly thereafter wrote *The Member* – one of the very few novels ever written on the theme of political patronage). Originally, Galt had intended to supervise the settlement scheme himself and had engaged Dunlop, a London reviewer and literary critic, to be his aide in Upper Canada, with the romantic-sounding (but empty) title of 'Warden of the Woods and Forests of the Canada Company.' As it turned out, however, it was not the novelist but the critic who possessed the experience and personal qualities that were essential to the success of the project. For in spite of his unlikely occupation, Dunlop was in fact intimately acquainted with the Upper Canadian wilderness, his involvement in the literary life being but a brief interlude in an adventurous career as a surgeon and army officer, in which capacities he had served in Upper Canada during the War of 1812. He was a huge and jovial figure, in the words of his eminent contemporary, Thomas Carlyle, 'one of the strangest men of his age, with an inexhaustible sense of fun.'[19]

Galt soon quarrelled with his partners in the company and returned to England, but Dunlop's attachment to Upper Canada proved strong and lasting. As the Canada Company's general superintendent in the Huron Tract during the socially formative early period of settlement, he was responsible for the day-to-day administration of the settlement program.[20] In effect, it was he who controlled access to the land and

16 Rea, ibid., 173. See also W.B. Kerr, 'When Orange and Green United, 1832–39: The Alliance of Macdonnell and Gowan,' *Ontario History* 34 (1943): 34–42.
17 W.H. Graham, *The Tiger of Canada West* (Toronto 1962); DCB, VII, 260–3; for a sample of Dunlop's writings, see Carl Klinck, ed., *Tiger Dunlop's Upper Canada* (Toronto 1967).
18 Graham, *The Tiger*, 43
19 Ibid., 28
20 Clarence Karr, *The Canada Land Company: The Early Years* (Toronto 1974), 56

generally represented the company in face-to-face dealings with the new settlers. But the company itself was an impersonal organization whose chief officers and shareholders were elsewhere. As their agent, Dunlop controlled the one resource necessary for him to assume the role of grand patron – and the fact that the land had not been granted to him personally did not seriously detract from his status. Thus, between him and those he assisted in settling on the Huron Tract there grew the classic Upper Canadian patron-client bond, a bond made distinctive by local circumstance, rooted in the soil, reciprocal in nature, and supported by strong personal ties of loyalty, trust, and affection. All of his clients knew very well who had obtained their land for them, legal niceties aside, and who had helped them in a thousand ways, with food and encouragement and personal credit during the lean early years of land clearing. It was he, too, who organized the building of roads, demanded the performance of settlement duties, insisted on militia service, and in other ways both serious and trivial imposed his authority as patron.

Dunlop's career illustrates in a particularly vivid way some of the key attributes of Upper Canadian clientelism. First, it required a relationship between patron and client that was more or less permanent. One could be a fly-by-night land speculator, or (like John Galt) a short-term promoter, or an absentee landholder – but no one could be a fly-by-night or short-term or absentee patron. To be a patron required one's *personal* presence upon the land and unremitting attention to the details of settlement, not just for a few months or a few years, and not intermittently, but continuously; in effect, for a lifetime. Likewise, frontiersmen who were merely 'passing through' would not become clients; the clientele relationship was effectively confined to those who had come to stay. In time it became largely a matter of habit – and like any habit, once established it was not easily broken. Thus in politics clientelism tended to live on, even long after the objective conditions that had initially nurtured it were overtaken by new trends towards rising prosperity and constitutional change.

Secondly, clientelism in Upper Canada was not something whose origins were lost in the mists of time or whose only justification had to be found in religion or ancient tradition. On the contrary, it was peculiarly modern in that the critical dyadic bond between patron and client, to a much larger extent than was usual in older societies, depended upon *performance*; in other words, the Upper Canadian patron had to earn his status by contributing to the success of his clients, and his clients had to reciprocate by being productive, which in turn further enhanced the patron's reputation and so brought new settlers into his clientele.

Viewed in this context, the powerful and at times almost obsessive emphasis placed upon the keeping of promises in Upper Canadian patron-client relations becomes more understandable. Dunlop once again provides an extraordinary example. Against the wishes of the Canada Company's Toronto directors, he had called out his clients for militia duty in the First Huron Regiment (known to themselves as the 'Huron Invincibles,' to others as the 'Bloody Useless'), of which he was of course the commanding officer, and kept them on duty for three harsh winter months in 1837–38, far from home, guarding against American attack across the St Clair River. In return he had promised them payment for their service in time to buy seed and instruments for the spring planting. But when week after week went by and in spite of his pleas still no money was forthcoming from army headquarters, he launched his most furious attack of the entire campaign – against his own superior officers to compel them to pay his men. His tactics were characteristically unorthodox: he rode his horse (a beast as huge and notoriously unkempt as its rider) on to the parade square at London to confront the chief staff officer with his demands; he dispatched a libellous diatribe against the commissary-general to the newspapers of the province; and he threatened to appeal to the British Parliament. By the end of March the army had surrendered. A money-box containing ten thousand dollars in coin was delivered to Amherstburg and from there the indefatigable Dunlop and a small party of his men lugged it over muddy roads and thawing rivers 256 misadventure-filled miles to Goderich.[21] But his farmer-clients were paid, as promised.

Thirdly, Dunlop's career demonstrates the basically non-institutional character of Upper Canadian clientelism: it was so thoroughly rooted in shared experience that it did not need to operate through or even require the support of formal institutions, whether of church or of state. In actual practice it generally did have institutional associations, partly because those wider institutions were themselves symbolically valued, and moreover their writ, however feeble most of the time, could if pressed extend to the furthest reaches of the province. But there were also ample opportunities for friction. Centralized institutions in Upper Canada were seriously hampered in the early nineteenth century, both by the slowness of communication and by their own lack of administrative manpower. The provincial government had therefore to rely a great deal upon local elites – and particularly upon the grand patrons – to provide on-the-scene political leadership. As they were to discover,

21 Graham, *The Tiger*, 163–78

however, the trouble with this arrangement was that the latter were an exceedingly difficult bunch to control. There were those of them such as Talbot who were socially superior and better connected in Britain than their would-be controllers, while others such as Macdonnell were politically shrewd and generally able to exact a high price for their support, which made dealing with them always a potentially touchy and awkward business. Even worse, from an administrative point of view, the grand patrons also had an infuriating habit of taking their obligations to their clients more seriously than they did the rules and regulations of the institution under whose orders they were supposedly operating. Nevertheless, though it was rarely appreciated by officials in Toronto, the conventions of clientelism frequently served provincial institutions well, if idiosyncratically – as in the case of Dunlop's regiment and the army. In such circumstances, indeed, it was *only* the patron-client bond that could keep the working levels of those institutions functioning at all, and even more remarkably, could do so on the strength of a promise and in the face of almost complete administrative breakdown.

The army in this respect was more pragmatic and accommodating than the Canada Company, whose absentee officials understood neither the nature of the society that had taken root in the Huron Tract nor Dunlop's role in it. As far as they were concerned he was their agent, and indeed it was that agency that had originally provided the basis of his economic power and the foundation of his status as patron; but in time the demands of the patron's role tied him ever more closely to the interests of his clients. Whenever possible, he personally made good on the company's failure to keep its promises in such matters as bridge construction or the location of mills; when disputes arose he found himself fighting his clients' battles with the company rather than enforcing company policy upon them. Increasingly, the authority he wielded became his own, something he had earned, and not something the company had bestowed upon him. Nor, as it turned out, could the company take it away. When eventually Dunlop was forced to choose between his position in the company (and the substantial salary that went with it) and his role as grand patron, his unhesitating choice of the latter served only to further enhance his status in the eyes of his clients.[22] Likewise, the hurried relocation of some high officials of the company to Goderich in an effort to countermand his authority proved ineffectual.[23]

22 Ibid., 179–80
23 It did, however, set the stage for a prolonged feud between the company's commis-

Too many of the settlers had acquired title to their lands and were prospering as farmers to be easily intimidated, and were too loyal to the Tiger to be impressed by ostentatious displays of wealth in the tiny district capital. The company, on the whole, had not been a wickedly exploitative organization; most settlers had reason to be satisfied that they had accepted its offer of land, but in the last analysis they felt they owed it nothing: there was no reciprocal bond between them and it as there was between them and the man who for so many years had been their patron.

Eventually, the old clientele pattern of Upper Canada would change as the times changed: parts of it would atrophy and others evolve in response to new technologies and new social and political developments, but in its own time it was impressively solid. As Dunlop's career shows, it could not be cracked by pressure from outside.

By the 1830s it had assumed a definitive overall shape and, as well, considerable uniformity in its detailed internal configurations. For example, with the growth of population and the spread of settlement further and further back from the lakeshores, a basically cellular structure had emerged, made up of repeated units of farmers on plots of land that were for the most part only partially cleared but growing increasingly productive, and whose most important economic, political, and social relationships took place within the context of a locally functional and locally sanctioned clientele system. From one district to another, and often within districts, there were differences of national origin, religion, and even language, but strikingly, at its lower levels the clientele structure of one district of Upper Canada was pretty much like the next. The most important variation occurred at the top. In districts where a grand patron presided there was invariably a certain hiatus in the system between the grand patron (and the political-*cum*-military clique that generally surrounded him) and the mid-level and local patrons (who were generally merchants and thus part of a separate, integrated system of commercial clientelism). In effect, the old cleavage between loyalist military and mercantile elites, which Simcoe had tried to bridge, persisted to a degree in some districts but was not at all a factor in others. In the London District, for example, because of Talbot's eminent presence, the struggle between the two groups for control of

sioner, Thomas Mercer Jones, who, with an entourage of officials, had been relocated to Goderich, and the already established social and political elite, the 'Colborne Clique,' who were loyal supporters of Dunlop. Ibid., 112–14, 133–43; Karr, *Canada Land Company*, 95–8; DCB, IX, 415–17

local patronage and local elective office became a constant source of discord;[24] but, as Frederick H. Armstrong has shown, in the Western District (the Windsor-Essex-Kent-Lambton area) – where there was no grand patron – a tightly knit oligarchy of mid-level patrons, composed predominantly of merchants, 'comfortably dominated.'[25]

II

Eventually it was this pattern of political and economic power that prevailed everywhere across the province, even in those districts where the grand patrons had once held sway. For the latter, while important figures in their own time, by the 1840s had become curious anachronisms, out of sympathy with the new generation of politicians and out of touch with the thrusting, ambitious men of business – the mid-level patrons – to whom the future largely belonged. When they passed from the scene, they left no successors.

In the Huron Tract, for instance, the career of J.C.W. Daly[26] is as illustrative as that of Tiger Dunlop, if on a smaller (though eventually very substantial) scale, and is unquestionably more typical. Daly too had begun as a Canada Company agent in the eastern portion of the tract centred on Stratford, and like Dunlop, although by a very different route, had gone on to become a patron of independent status. Though not a particularly colourful personality, and perhaps for that reason not much studied, he was a most effective occupant of the patron's role – and in his own way an archetypal figure in the general structure of Upper Canadian clientelism, in that it was he and numerous others like him across the province who filled the solid, reliable middle ranks of commercial and political leadership. The basis of Daly's rise to prominence was his well-earned reputation for sound judgment in matters of land, his sharp eye for speculative opportunities, and his ability to operate such essential facilities as mills, stores, and even an iron foundry both profitably and efficiently. His clients benefited from his business-like provision of credit, services, and advice, and he benefited from the success of their own small business endeavours or, in the case of farmers, from their rising agricultural productivity. Though he possessed neither the social status nor political connections of a Dunlop,

24 Read, 'The London District Oligarchy'
25 'The Oligarchy of the Western District of Upper Canada, 1788–1841,' Canadian Historical Association, *Historical Papers* (1977), 101
26 *DCB*, x, 212–13; Karr, *Canada Land Company*, 58

he was a loyal tory and, at his own level, a quietly skilful player of the official patronage game. As magistrate and militia officer (and also, at one time or another, everything from postmaster to coroner) he typically combined appointive (and later, as district councillor, elective) office with managerial expertise and political leadership. And in his case, as in similar situations elsewhere in the province,[27] his links with his clients grew out of local isolation and from roots planted in economic necessity – but they were also reciprocal, personal, and long lasting.

At a still lower level, in the innumerable villages that had sprung up wherever settlers had penetrated the bush, there could be found grass-roots clientelism in its most elementary dyadic form, consisting for the most part of farmers who as yet had only small quantities of surplus produce to sell or exchange, and storekeepers who as yet had few goods to offer them in return. Many of the latter also operated saw or grist mills[28] and farmed themselves – as well as speculating in land. For one of the inevitable consequences of the great land give-away of earlier decades was to place much good land in the hands of absentee owners or resident owners who could see no prospect of ever clearing all of their holdings for themselves, or who simply needed to raise cash. The resulting speculative market in uncleared and semi-cleared land was widespread and active, rising and falling in response to grain prices, changes in tax policies, the pace of local development, and the overall level of immigration into the province.[29] And among those who were best placed to take advantage of it were local storekeepers and millers who were linked, however tenuously, to distant markets and sources of credit, and whose occupations gave them the means of expertly appraising the potential value of local lots. It was a risky business, for their operations were generally too financially marginal to withstand

27 For the careers of mid-level patrons in other localities, see, e.g., the entries for the following in *DCB*, VIII: George Brouse (Matilda Township / Iroquois), 104–5; Zacheus Burnham (Newcastle District / Cobourg), 116–18; James Crooks (Gore District / West Flamborough), 185–90; James Bell Ewart (Dundas), 279–80; and William Morris (Perth), 638–42.

28 As Douglas McCalla observes, 'much of the local merchant's wealth, as he accumulated it, was geographically immobile. Given the lack of liquidity of the economy, he tended to find it easier to extend his local investments, for example into grist- and sawmills, than attempt a wider spatial diversification of his capital.' 'Rural Credit and Rural Development in Upper Canada, 1790–1850,' in Roger Hall et al., eds., *Patterns of the Past: Interpreting Ontario's History* (Toronto and Oxford 1988), 37

29 See Gates, *Land Policies*, 132–3.

serious errors of judgment. Bankruptcies were not uncommon. But if a shopkeeper-miller's expertise was sufficient, if his creditors were patient, if his evaluation of land was sound, if his farmer-clients were honest and industrious, he could in time do very well – especially in comparison with other occupations. Of all the possible careers that a man might pursue in Upper Canada, John Langton wrote in 1844, 'store-keeping is decidedly the most money-making and is carried on with very little capital; but it appears to me that those who have made it pay are invariably those who have started with next to nothing and have gradually crept up in the world, increasing their business as their capital, custom and experience increased.'[30] The evidence of mercantile success was everywhere to be seen. As Anna Jameson observed, in a new Canadian village 'the grocery store, or general shop ... is always the best house in the place.'[31]

At this local level Upper Canadian clientelism was essentially of a type that is still common in many of the less developed countries of the world and is perhaps typical of societies at an early stage of capital accumulation.[32] In such societies no sharp distinction is drawn between economic and political functions, with the process of exchange between patrons and clients tending to be broad and multifunctional rather than narrowly contractual; thus, in Upper Canada, 'land, animals, grain, apples, fish, furs, building materials, political influence and man-hours of labour, might all be employed in the intricacies of a single transaction.'[33] And the relationship between patrons and clients accordingly tended to be diffuse, whole person, and face to face rather than impersonal or explicitly professional in nature. The basis of the patron's role lay in his possession of certain valuable resources and his consequent ability to attract a clientele that lacked them. These resources could include his own land, Crown land (or land belonging to a large grantee) whose allocation he could influence, credit in the form of goods or mortgages, information, intervention with officials, and other discretionary favours and services that were within his power to bestow or withhold. It is important to note, however, that although himself a

30 W.A. Langton, ed., *Early Days in Upper Canada: Letters of John Langton from the Backwoods of Upper Canada and the Audit Office of the Province of Canada* (Toronto 1926), 220
31 *Winter Studies*, 35
32 See, e.g., René Lemarchand and Keith Legg, 'Political Clientelism and Development: A Preliminary Analysis,' *Comparative Politics* 4 (1972): 149–78.
33 Marion MacRae, *MacNab of Dundurn* (Toronto 1971), 71

client of others higher placed in the clientele network – such as a mid-level patron who might act as a regional supplier of credit and also hold one or more important government offices – the local patron was not primarily a 'middleman' or agent, nor was he generally perceived to be one. In other words, though he might on occasion function in such a capacity, for the most part he himself acted as the direct supplier of credit, service, and favours, and took the attendant risks. In return, his clients were required to deal exclusively through him in the disposal of their surplus produce and, in a variety of contexts, generally support his commercial enterprises and accept his social leadership. (In the district militia units, for example, it was commonly the local patrons and their sons who filled the ranks of junior officers and non-commissioned officers.) Their relationship was thus one of reciprocity and mutual dependence, but not of equality; for, as Peter M. Blau points out, while 'the patron may, of course, be dependent himself on having a large number of clients ... his dependence upon any *one* client is much less than the dependence of any one client upon him.'[34]

Clearly, in such a relationship some element of coercion is always potentially present, but its actual presence in a given patron-client dyad will vary depending upon a number of factors, the most critical being the degree to which the patron is able to monopolize the supply of needed resources.[35] In Upper Canada that degree was generally not very high. Typically, 'each side had choices and constraints.'[36] Local patrons, in particular, more closely resembled oligopolists than monopolists in that, to some extent at least, they were in competition with one another for new clients, and sometimes even for old ones, since in the fluid state of a young community – and with the growing importance of electoral politics – it was the *size* of a patron's clientele that largely determined his standing, both commercially and politically. This naturally tended to produce patron-client relationships that were not inherently coercive, and reciprocities that, while cemented by personal and social bonds, were also understood to be based on calculations of material self-interest. Both parties, in other words, had to be willing and able to deliver the goods.

Politically, the strength of the local patrons stemmed from their

34 *Exchange and Power in Social Life* (New York 1964), 137
35 See James C. Scott, 'Patron-Client Politics and Political Change in Southeast Asia,' in Steffen W. Schmidt et al., eds., *Friends, Followers and Factions: A Reader in Political Clientelism* (Berkeley 1977), 131
36 McCalla, 'Rural Credit,' 48

ability to mobilize their clients in circumstances where such mobilization had measurable (or at least demonstrable) value: as in elections, or in the mounting of shows of public support for political leaders, or even, in extreme emergencies, for military service. While no horizontal organization existed to link them politically to one another, the vertical linkages that connected them to the next highest level of the clientele system – that is, in most cases, to a mid-level patron – were typically strong. They were also essentially of the same type as those that connected the local patrons to their own clients, in that they freely blended commercial with political considerations, operated on a personal basis, and were commonly reinforced by kinship, ethnicity, religion, or some combination of these or other social ties. In return for their support the local patrons could normally count on obtaining whatever minor local offices or other pieces of political patronage the mid-level patrons (in some districts in conjunction with a grand patron) effectively controlled. As one critic of the system in the London District observed of Colonel Talbot and Mahlon Burwell (Talbot's chief surveyor and a considerable mid-level patron in his own right): 'Magistrates, officers of the excise, surveyors, and militia officers, commissioners to carry the appropriation of public money into effect, are all appointed through the recommendations of these sages of the District – thus forming a host of worthies who are ever at the back of their Patrons.'[37]

The local patrons' connections with the leaders of the executive government of the province, by contrast, tended to be remote and impersonal. While they had reason to be pleased with certain government policies, such as those that allowed them to flood or otherwise use portions of the Crown reserves in order to obtain water-power for their mills, on the whole they were not inclined to think of themselves as either highly privileged or richly rewarded. Rather, they were often the articulators of local discontent, especially over what they saw as the government's inadequate efforts to promote agricultural settlement (which they held responsible for retarding the progress of their district and, coincidentally, their own prosperity). Their position in the political system was thus an ambivalent one: it gave them a sufficient stake in the status quo to make them resistant to change in their own bailiwicks, but not enough to render them immune to the idea of change at the top. Consequently, if a political reform movement were to arise that threatened to disturb the established order, their role, as the leaders and mobilizers of local opinion, would be pivotal.

37 *Liberal* (St Thomas), 25 July 1833

4

Clientelism and Reform

In retrospect I shall remember the lessons the people of Upper Canada have taught me: and I feel it is my duty to declare that I leave the continent of America with my judgment perfectly convinced that the inhabitants of Europe, Asia, and Africa are right in their opinion that all men are not by nature equal.

   – Sir Francis Bond Head, lieutenant-governor of Upper Canada, 1836–38

... that man would make a rebellion anywhere.
    – Sir John Beverley Robinson, chief justice of Upper Canada, 1829–62

I

By the mid-1830s a political disturbance was definitely brewing in Upper Canada. Its origins were complex and lay in large measure in the processes of economic and social development that in less than half a century had transformed a thin and precarious chain of loyalist settlements into an increasingly populous, varied, and substantial agrarian society. Yet politically no significant adjustment had taken place since the inauguration of the constitution of 1791 – with the result that a governmental system that had once served well had become manifestly deficient and inadequate. It was also stubbornly resistant to change. As a British colony, Upper Canada could not legally alter its machinery of government on its own; and politically, those who controlled that machinery or who were influential in its operation were not disposed to pressure the imperial Parliament to enact changes that might undermine their own powers and privileges. Indeed, for reasons as historically understandable as they were self-serving, those in power obdurately identified any challenge to their own authority as disloyalty to the Crown, and any proposal for reform, however modest, as the thin edge of a revolutionary and republican wedge.[1]

The Upper Canadian governing elite looked anxiously across the American border, but a similar apprehension was not uncommon elsewhere; in Britain, for example, it was epitomized by the Duke of Wellington, who saw the spectre of the French Revolution behind every attempt to modernize the British constitution. But by 1832 the obstinate tory duke had been replaced as prime minister by the whig Lord Melbourne, and the Great Reform Act, that watershed in British constitutional development, had been passed. Some of the worst abuses of the old British electoral system, such as the 'rotten boroughs,' had been thereby eliminated or reduced and the popular element in the constitution increased and placed at last on a more regular and legitimate basis. The lesson that Melbourne had learned was that it was sometimes necessary to change political institutions in order to preserve them – that judicious reform was an antidote to, rather than a catalyst of, revolution.[2]

As part of the empire, and open to the free flow of ideas within it, Upper Canada could not remain immune to such important currents of political thought and action, nor did it. Internal pressure for change had been gradually building up for years, but after 1832 reform was more positively in the air, the old constitution of the province was more obviously than ever in need of change – and perhaps as important, those who had the temerity to say so could no longer be quite so easily dismissed as 'Yankee' or 'disloyal.'

But who were the leaders and spokesmen of reform in Upper Canada and what were their ideas of reform? Who supported them? And where did they and their supporters fit economically and in relation to the clientele system? Before turning to these questions, however, it is essential to recall once again the part played by land in the shaping of Upper Canadian society. Provincial politics in the 1820s and early 1830s had contained a surprising array of issues, controversies, and *cause célèbres* – ranging from routine wrangling over financial appropriations

1 S.F. Wise, 'Colonial Attitudes from the Era of the War of 1812 to the Rebellions of 1837,' in S.F. Wise and Robert Craig Brown, eds., *Canada Views the United States: Nineteenth Century Political Attitudes* (Toronto 1967), 16–43; Patrick Brode, *Sir John Beverley Robinson: Bone and Sinew of the Compact* (Toronto 1984), 161–2; and Aileen Dunham, *Political Unrest in Upper Canada, 1815–1836* (London 1927; reissued Toronto 1963), 136–49
2 Michael Brock, *The Great Reform Act* (London 1973), 314–36

between the elected Assembly and the appointed Executive Council to the tangled and thorny question (for a province founded by Anglo-American loyalists) of what should be the political and property rights of later American immigrants, to uproar over the lieutenant-governor's removal of an obstructionist judge from the Court of King's Bench.[3] Each of these and many similar issues could rouse affected individuals or groups to noisy fury, but essentially they were part of the normal passing parade of politics and not in themselves the stuff of which revolutions are made. Indeed, such issues could burn with bright intensity for those caught up in the affairs of Toronto when to a farmer in the Huron Tract, surveying the still-uncleared stumps in his pasture, they were scarcely visible and mattered not at all. Yet there was also one persistent, nagging source of irritation that, because it involved land, lay very close to the hearts of Upper Canadians. And such was the nature of it that as the population grew it was bound to become worse.

It was inevitable that at some point the wholesale give-away of land would have to cease – there was, after all, a physical limit to the amount of good agricultural land available – but the actual cessation, when it did come, was not imposed by nature but by government. More specifically, it was imposed by the government's adherence to land-use policies that dated from an earlier and very different era. Thus, by the 1820s new settlers were frustrated to find that they could not obtain land except by private purchase (and often at prices they regarded as exorbitant) or could not obtain enough land or could obtain grants only in the remotest or least fertile areas. What made this situation all the more galling was that in most of the already settled districts perfectly good land was still unoccupied, having been set aside as Crown or clergy reserves, or even worse, kept out of production by speculators or absentee owners. Eventually even such grand patrons as Colonel Talbot simply ran out of land and were forced to turn away skilled and otherwise well-qualified applicants for lots – the very type of people they had earlier endeavoured to attract as their settler-clients and of whom the province was still, in their opinion, very much in need. One consequence was a departure from the orderly process of settlement by a growing number who settled illegally on reserved or unoccupied land as 'squatters.'[4]

3 For these and other controversies see Dunham, *Political Unrest*, 73–116; and Gerald M. Craig, *Upper Canada: The Formative Years* (Toronto 1963), 188–209.
4 Lillian F. Gates, *Land Policies of Upper Canada* (Toronto 1968), 289–90; and Alan Wilson, *The Clergy Reserves of Upper Canada* (Toronto 1968), 109–10

Another was the emergence of a class of landless poor who gravitated towards the towns to form an embryonic urban working class.

Land, however, remained the *sine qua non* of Upper Canadian life: to be without it was to be drastically disadvantaged in wealth and status. It was also the foundation of the clientele system, and for an increasingly numerous minority, to be excluded from that system was to be consigned to an economic limbo. Their unfortunate position cast in sharp relief the advantages of security, land, credit, mutual assistance, and political influence that the clientele system provided to the majority who were part of it or in some way economically connected to it.

Upper Canada in the 1830s was thus not exactly a political powder-keg ready to explode into revolution at the first spark, but it did contain some dangerous pressures. If these were unrelieved, an eruption of some kind was a very possible outcome; already there were sufficient disaffected, alienated, and disappointed elements in the population to make it happen, if only they could be moulded into an effective political force.

In some respects the situation was similar to that which existed in Britain during the period immediately prior to the passage of the 1832 Reform Act – except that in Upper Canada there was no government of whig aristocrats to put themselves at the head of the reform movement and, by insisting on 'the bill, the whole bill and nothing but the bill,' safely enact a measure that satisfied all but the most extreme critics of the *status quo*. In Britain, moreover, the pressure for reform had come very largely as a result of industrial development and urban expansion, which had created absurd anomalies in the system of popular representation: such cities as Birmingham, for example, were practically without voice in the unreformed House of Commons, while abandoned hamlets such as the notorious Old Sarum continued to 'elect' members, though in reality such seats were in the gift of the local magnate or patron.[5] The reform consensus that eventually developed in Britain was therefore primarily a consensus to make the electoral system more equitable and less of an affront to common sense. Indirectly, it meant a considerable strengthening of the democratic principle in the British constitution, but it was by no means a frontal assault on the established order.

In Upper Canada, by contrast, reform had no such clear focus. The province's electoral system, by the standards of the age, was a good deal fairer than Britain's and not in itself a major source of agitation; the land

5 Brock, *The Great Reform Act*, 28, 80–1

problem was pervasive, but there was no consensus on a remedy to it (even a widespread feeling that the clergy reserves ought to be disposed of broke down when it came to a consideration of ways and means, since the different religious denominations squabbled fiercely over who should share in the proceeds);[6] while on questions of government there was likewise no agreement on specifics. To some, reform meant restricting the lieutenant-governor's powers of patronage; to others it meant increasing the protective tariff. To some it meant a cautious extension of the Assembly's rights and powers to bring them more closely into line with those enjoyed by the British House of Commons; to others it meant republicanism and outright annexation to the United States (thereby lending credence to the tory jibe that *all* reformers were really republicans in disguise). Still others saw reform as primarily a means of restricting the enormous Upper Canadian thirst for alcohol (thereby lending credence to Colonel Talbot's famous sally that reformers were really rebels who 'commenced their work of darkness under cover of organizing Damned Cold Water Drinking Societies.'[7]

What all this meant was that in Upper Canada reform sentiment was a stew of diverse and unblendable ingredients; it bubbled erratically and could seemingly flow in any direction – depending on whose hand tipped the pot. It is little wonder, therefore, that even such an experienced lieutenant-governor as Sir Peregrine Maitland, by the end of his tenure, was reduced to marvelling equally at the province's great economic progress and at its people's incorrigible political quarrelsomeness.[8] Nevertheless, there were two components of reform that were ultimately to prove of greater importance than the rest: the first was the idea of 'responsible government' and the second was the attack upon the Family Compact.[9]

6 Wilson, *Clergy Reserves*, 111–24

7 C.O. Ermatinger, *The Talbot Regime, 1791–1840* (St Thomas, Ont. 1904), 167

8 Craig, *Upper Canada*, 188

9 The term 'Family Compact' is variously defined but practically unavoidable in any discussion of Upper Canadian politics. It is used here to identify the close-knit, Toronto-centred tory oligarchy who dominated the Executive and Legislative councils in the period 1820–37 and who are generally acknowledged to have constituted the social, political, and financial elite of the province. For a discussion of historical usages of the term and the membership of the group to whom it is applied, see Robert E. Saunders, 'What Was the Family Compact?' in J.K. Johnson, ed., *Historical Essays on Upper Canada* (Toronto 1975), 122–39; and for a more rigorous methodological critique, D.H. Akenson, *The Irish in Ontario* (Kingston and Montreal 1984), 191ff. The term 'Compact' is also sometimes applied to local oligarchies in places other than Toronto, and while it can be used clearly in this sense, without further

The idea that government should be conducted by an executive of ministers (a cabinet) whose formal legal responsibility is to the Crown (whose advisers they are) but whose real political responsibility is to a popularly elected legislative body (from whose membership they must be largely or entirely drawn and whose confidence they must retain) is today the commonly understood principle of the British system of government wherever it is practised, including the province of Ontario.[10] But it is by no means a principle of ancient origin. In the early nineteenth century it was neither clearly formulated as a theory nor consistently followed in practice, even in Britain itself.[11] Indeed, not so many years earlier the effective genius of the British constitution was thought to lie precisely in an *opposite* principle: namely, that the executive and legislative branches ought to be substantially separate. This was the belief of the framers of the American constitution, but it was no less firmly held by loyalists; John Graves Simcoe, for example, saw the separation and not the fusion of powers as the best guarantee of the rights and liberties of the individual. Yet by the 1830s the idea of responsible government was clearly taking hold, and nowhere was it

explanation it tends to imply that they were simply the creatures of the Family Compact. (Saunders, indeed, goes so far as to assert that 'the local compacts generally owed their positions to the friendship of the York clique and ties between the two levels were very close.') As Frederick H. Armstrong and others have demonstrated, however, the relationship between them was more complex and reciprocal than that, and the independence of the local oligarchs correspondingly greater. In the Western district, Armstrong writes, in matters of patronage 'the Toronto Family Compact generally took the recommendations of the local oligarchy and of course they recommended their own ... Therefore, to a large extent, the main question was often how the spoils should be distributed internally, not whether or not the local elite would have the right to distribute them.' 'The Oligarchy of the Western District of Upper Canada, 1788–1814,' Canadian Historical Association, *Historical Papers*, 1977, 97. Local oligarchies thus tended to be internally fractious, and a too-narrow focus on the immediate period of the rebellion (when they generally managed, however briefly, to put aside their differences) is likely to produce an exaggerated impression of both their cohesion and the degree to which they could be politically mobilized and directed by the Family Compact. For other case studies of Compact-oligarchy relations, see Elva M. Richards, 'The Joneses of Brockville and the Family Compact,' *Ontario History* 60 (1968): 169–84; Colin Read, 'The London District Oligarchy in the Rebellion Era,' *Ontario History* 72 (1980): 195–209; and Graeme H. Patterson, 'Studies in Elections and Public Opinion in Upper Canada,' PHD thesis, University of Toronto 1969.

10 F.F. Schindeler, *Responsible Government in Ontario* (Toronto 1969)
11 See A.D. Harvey, *Britain in the Early Nineteenth Century* (London 1978), 199–204.

taking hold more strongly or finding a fuller or more sophisticated theoretical formulation than in Upper Canada.

That this was so was due in large measure to the work of W.W. Baldwin and his son, Robert Baldwin,[12] moderate reformers who were also political thinkers of unusual clarity. Like many others, they were convinced that the old political system of Upper Canada had reached an impasse, but, with rare insight, they also saw a hidden potential in the British constitution that offered a way out: through a responsible ministry, which would not necessarily solve every problem but would at least make solutions possible by removing the prospect of an endlessly immobilizing deadlock between the Executive and the Assembly. Their critique of the old system was penetrating, and their concept of responsible government flowed logically from it. They expressed it, moreover, with an intellectual elegance that is not often found in any age and is all the more remarkable when one remembers that they were also active politicians, fully engaged in the heat and battle of the day. They did not, of course, 'invent' responsible government; but better than anyone else of their era they grasped the possibility that it could be validly applied in the context of colonial government.

The objections were manifold. Since sovereignty was indivisible, it was argued, the Crown could not accept advice from one set of advisers in Britain and another set in Upper Canada, for the two might be in conflict; it would turn the lieutenant-governor into a mere cipher; it would lead to rule by political parties; it would make Upper Canada virtually an independent state; or it would lead to annexation to the United States. But in spite of its detractors, by the 1830s it was an idea whose time was not far off: in the next decade Robert Baldwin would hold high office under the very conditions of constitutional responsibility he had long advocated.

II

It was not by accident that responsible government emerged as an important idea of reform in Upper Canada, for it was in all essential respects an evolutionary product of the political culture. The Baldwins, moreover, did not flourish in isolation but were very much a part of Upper Canada's educated and politically conscious elite. As such, the

12 *Dictionary of Canadian Biography*, VII, 35–44 (W.W. Baldwin); ibid., VIII, 45–59 (Robert Baldwin); and J.M.S. Careless, 'Robert Baldwin,' in J.M.S. Careless, ed., *The Pre-Confederation Premiers: Ontario Government Leaders, 1841–1867* (Toronto 1980), 89–147

question they addressed was of general concern: what was original was their answer. As ardently as any tory the advocates of responsible government wanted to preserve their province's allegiance to the monarchy and its connection with the British Empire; where they differed was on the means that could best ensure that end. For them, unyielding resistance to change would make inevitable the very outcome that was most feared, but through reform – understood as responsible government – the monarchical and British connection could be strengthened and renewed and a drastic disruption of the established order avoided. Responsible government, as they conceived it, was thus a narrowly *political* device, and hence not directed towards economic or social goals. It posed no real threat to the operation of the clientele system. Indeed, as events were to prove, they meshed together very nicely – for the clientele system, too, was a most flexible and adaptable set of arrangements.

For some, however, a drastic disruption of the established order was exactly what Upper Canada needed. Their discontents were by no means confined to the constitutional sphere but spilled over into a wildly varied assortment of grievances; moreover, they were rarely restrained by any feelings of attachment to the loyalist tradition. A lack of land, or failure to secure adequate land, was in many cases the underlying source of their unhappiness, but radical ideas also played a part, and some were greatly influenced by them: they heard the voices of British radicalism echoing across the Atlantic, and even more strongly, the voices of American democracy echoing across the border.[13]

They also had constantly held up before them, especially in Toronto, a provocation they could scarcely endure in the shape of the Family Compact. That notorious tory oligarchy had sat atop Toronto society for years, presumptuously dishing out to themselves and their friends the choicest plums of office and privilege, or so it appeared to their critics – and by the 1830s their critics were legion. Though at least some of the members of the Compact were individuals of talent and distinction who would likely have risen to high positions in any society of the time, that was understandably never a popular perception. Still, for many years their authority, if not exactly unquestioned, had been generally accepted as legitimate. Now, increasingly, it was not. Memories of their military and moral leadership in the War of 1812 had faded for a new generation of Upper Canadians, while more recent immigrants knew nothing of it.

13 Craig, *Upper Canada*, 197–8; and Wise, 'Colonial Attitudes,' 32–7

They were becoming in fact a symbol of oppression, an *ancien régime*. They had no doubt done their share to earn that symbolic status, even if they could not possibly have been responsible for all of the social and economic ills for which they were now blamed. But it was a role thrust upon them, for along with the enlargement of the urban population there had come a rapid proliferation of newspapers – and some of them were aggressively and vociferously radical. The most important of these was the *Colonial Advocate*, whose founder and editor was William Lyon Mackenzie.[14]

Much has been written about Mackenzie's turbulent life and political career, including some admirably balanced and insightful accounts, yet he remains a figure of mythic significance. To those who are politically of the right he has always been unambiguously a villain, and to those of the left just as unambiguously a hero. In the 1920s a Conservative government in Ontario sponsored the publication of *Great Men of Canada*, two volumes of biographical sketches intended for use in the province's schools – from which Mackenzie was conspicuously omitted.[15] A decade later Canadians who fought on the republican (but also the *loyalist*) side in the Spanish Civil War proudly called themselves the Mackenzie-Papineau Battalion. Liberals, being caught in the middle, have uneasily stressed his democratic instincts while downplaying his revolutionary (or, as conservatives would have it, treasonable) ones.[16] Nevertheless, for present purposes, an attempt must be made to view Mackenzie within the context of the politics of his own day and in relation to the political culture and clientele structures of the society he so ardently wished to change.

It is sometimes said that Mackenzie owed his political rise to an incident in 1826 that suddenly lifted him into prominence. Up to that time, for all his verbal assaults upon members of the Compact, he had

---

14 *DCB*, IX, 496–510; William Kilbourne, *The Firebrand: William Lyon Mackenzie and the Rebellion in Upper Canada* (Toronto 1956); David Flint, *William Lyon Mackenzie: Rebel against Authority* (Toronto 1971); and Margaret Fairley, ed., *The Selected Writings of William Lyon Mackenzie, 1824–1837* (Toronto 1960)

15 John Henderson, *Great Men of Canada* (Toronto 1928; 2nd ser. 1929)

16 Also downplayed are certain of his other instincts. Mackenzie was evidently not a progressive employer (see Frederick H. Armstrong, 'The Reformer as Capitalist: William Lyon Mackenzie and the Printers' Strike of 1836,' *Ontario History* 59 [1967]: 187–96), while his political principles did not extend to 'one man, one vote': on the contrary, he thought it absurd to equate 'the ricketty and scrofulous little wretch that first sees the light in a workhouse or in a brothel' with 'the ruddy offspring of the honest yeoman.' *Colonial Advocate*, 26 Apr. 1827

made no real dent in their power or prestige, and the *Colonial Advocate* was slowly sinking in a sea of debt. Ironically, at that point his future was suddenly brightened by a misguided band of young tories who took it upon themselves to put him out of business by wrecking his printing press. This act of folly was for Mackenzie a piece of providential good fortune: the substantial damages he was awarded in court rescued him financially, and the resulting notoriety secured his election to the Assembly as member for York.[17] In a deeper sense, however, Mackenzie and the Family Compact were made for each other, and it is difficult not to believe that he would sooner or later have emerged as the leader of Upper Canada's radical reformers. He was well placed to do so, for newspapers were vital instruments in the popular politics of the era, not only through their columns but also through their offices and news-rooms, which were centres of political discussion, agitation, and organization. As Anna Jameson observed, they were 'absolutely the only place of assembly or amusement, except the taverns and low drinking houses.'[18] Out of them came individuals who were well equipped to join old grievances to new but potent notions of democracy and popular sovereignty. It was a role Mackenzie relished and to which he brought exceptional gifts. The essence of radical journalism is to probe for the feet of clay beneath the togas of the high and mighty, and no one probed more fearlessly or relentlessly than he. The Compact, by its very existence, goaded him on, and he pursued its members with obsessive zeal, a ferocious self-appointed watchdog of private morality and the public interest. As an orator he could stir a crowd; he had learned how to articulate the resentments of the powerless; he believed absolutely in his own righteousness; and neither success nor failure were able to tire or mellow him. He was, in short, a formidable enemy.[19]

17 *DCB*, IX, 497–8. Paul Romney argues that this incident and its aftermath provide a revealing insight into a streak of 'loyalist providentialism' in the political culture of Upper Canada's tory oligarchy that 'served, in the minds of its devotees, to legitimize abuses of the rule of law ... It also suggests that the connection between the types riot and the Rebellion of 1837 can be explained systematically, rather than in terms merely of Mackenzie's personal experience.' 'From the Types Riot to the Rebellion: Elite Ideology, Anti-legal Sentiment, Political Violence, and the Rule of Law in Upper Canada,' *Ontario History* 76 (1987): 113–44
18 *Winter Studies and Summer Rambles in Canada* (London 1838; reissued Toronto 1965), 73
19 According to R.A. MacKay, a strict Presbyterian upbringing had left Mackenzie with 'a puritan cast of mind,' which he transferred to politics. 'The Political Ideas of William Lyon Mackenzie,' *Canadian Journal of Economics and Political Science* 3 (1937): 3

All he needed was an opponent worthy of his talent, and in the Family Compact he had found one.

By the 1830s it was Mackenzie who churned the waters of Upper Canadian politics, and more moderate reform politicians had either to follow him or stand aside. Most chose to stand aside. For good or ill he had become the leader and symbol of the reform cause – even if it was by no means clear exactly where he would lead it. It was also unclear whether support for reform was on the rise or on the wane, for in spite of almost ceaseless uproar the unreformed system still stood very much as it always had, and so did the Family Compact. Their survival, moreover, was not simply the result of a rigid constitution (which in the last resort permitted the lieutenant-governor and his Executive Council to govern without the confidence of the Assembly, if they had to), for that constitution had not really been put to the test. No great legislative obstacle had been put in the government's way because the reformers, to their chagrin, had not been able to establish control of the popularly elected lower house. Each time they had managed to capture a majority of its seats, the tories had come back strongly in the very next election. Hence a reform majority in 1828 was followed by a tory majority in 1830, and a reform majority in 1834 by another tory majority in 1836.[20] Even the most optimistic of reformers could not see in these results much evidence of progress. Naturally, to Mackenzie the tory victories were so unpalatable they had to be the product of electoral corruption, engineered by fraud, deceit, intimidation, or conspiracy. But even granted that in the chaotic, week-long open polling of the day none of the above were entirely absent, neither were they confined entirely to one side. Elections, moreover, were still largely parochial affairs that were beyond the reach of anyone's centralized control. Much depended on how active the mid-level and local patrons were and whether in a given district they were united or squabbling among themselves. There is thus no accurate measure of province-wide opinion. All that can reasonably be concluded is that the reformers evidently had not established much of a hold over it; indeed, when it came to direct competition for public favour, the tories were at least as successful as they were.

It must be stressed, however, that to describe electoral outcomes in terms of 'reform' and 'tory' majorities is not to suggest that elections in this period were province-wide contests between organized, centrally

20 See S.F. Wise, 'Upper Canada and the Conservative Tradition,' in Ontario Historical Society, *Profiles of a Province: Essays in the History of Ontario* (Toronto 1967), 20–33.

financed and directed political parties, since no such parties as yet existed. Nevertheless, within the Assembly there had emerged a loose but fairly consistent pattern of alliances – following in this respect Duverger's classic model of the development of parties of parliamentary origin[21] – which consisted on the one hand of conservatives or 'tories' (though at the time none would have applied the latter derogatory label to themselves), who generally supported the government, and on the other hand of reformers, who generally opposed it. Neither grouping displayed much uniformity. The conservatives, while perhaps on the whole more moderate than the leaders of the government in the Executive and Legislative Councils, nevertheless represented a considerable range of views and behaviour: some were moderates, some were mavericks, and some were utterly reliable place-men. Likewise, on the reform side some were cautious gradualists who were deeply suspicious of Mackenzie, some were waverers, and some were radicals. To confuse matters further, there were some who were stubborn independents and some whose only consistent goal was the promotion of their own district's local interests. A perusal of entries in the *Dictionary of Canadian Biography* for members of the Assembly during this period reveals that political allegiances were often less than solid. To take but a few by no means untypical examples: Bartholomew Beardsley, a sometime reformer, is described as 'sufficiently independent to irk his colleagues as well as his opponents'; another reformer, George Brouse, 'does not appear to have had a strong political orientation prior to the 1828 election' and was listed by Mackenzie under 'political sentiments not known'; Francis Caldwell, 'elected as an independent ... proved himself to be in reality a moderate tory'; another 'moderate tory,' Colin Ferrie, 'lacked partisan zeal'; while Alexander Fraser supported the conservative cause 'and, especially, the interests of his friend Bishop Alexander McDonnell.'[22]

From one district to the next, moreover, there were wide variations in the level of popular interest, the degree of competitiveness, and the nature of the cleavages around which elections normally revolved. In one district popular interest might run high, while in another a candidate might be elected with the support of only a tiny coterie of electors; in one the outcome might be in doubt until the final vote had been cast (or, more likely, until the district court had ruled on the

---

21 Maurice Duverger, *Political Parties* (London 1959), xxxiv–vii
22 DCB, VIII, 69, 105, 120, 299, 303

charges of illegality that nearly always ensued), while in another the sitting member might have the seat 'in his pocket.'[23] Even clear province-wide issues, such as the 'alien question' in the 1820s,[24] could not prevent the muddying of the political waters at the constituency level by the usual dense blend of sectional and religious rivalries, candidates whose views were impossible to fathom, internecine feuding between those whose views were the same, and incessant bickering over the distribution of political patronage – which was, of course, almost entirely confined to the tories. But, since there was never enough patronage to go around, it also tended to make them more prone than reformers to engage in open faction fights.

Such a process obviously bears scant resemblance to the disciplined competition that takes place within modern party systems. A more illuminating analogy, in many respects, is with the struggle between 'court' and 'country' parties in eighteenth-century England and the American colonies in that the Upper Canadian tories resembled the 'court' party in their close identification with the apparatus of government, their self-interested defence of 'royal' (that is, executive) prerogatives, and their reliance on patronage rather than organization to secure electoral support.[25] S.F. Wise, indeed, *defines* the 'tory party' of this period as 'a quasi-official coalition of the central and local elites united for the purpose of distributing honours and rewards to the politically deserving.'[26] The reformers, by contrast, resembled the 'country' party in their belief in the virtue of rule by an 'independent yeomanry' (a stock phrase in the rhetoric of reform), their desire to make the executive

23 'Pocket' seats, however, could be very expensive to maintain, and even more expensive to acquire. After spending lavishly in an 1832 by-election to acquire the safe tory seat of Carleton (in a race against another tory), Hamnett Pinhey lamented: 'I might have a rotten borough seat in the Imperial Parliament for one half the sum this very enviable one has cost me.' DCB, VIII, 707

24 This question involved the application in Upper Canada of certain onerous British laws governing the naturalization of American immigrants. See Craig, *Upper Canada*, 114–23. For an exploration of its wider political and cultural ramifications, see Paul Romney, 'Re-inventing Upper Canada: American Immigrants, Upper Canadian History, English Law, and the Alien Question,' in Roger Hall et al., eds., *Patterns of the Past: Interpreting Ontario's History* (Toronto and Oxford 1988), 78–107.

25 For further discussion of the country-court distinction, see J.G.A. Pocock, *The Machiavellian Moment* (Princeton 1975). For an extended application to Canada, see Gordon T. Stewart, *The Origins of Canadian Politics: A Comparative Approach* (Vancouver 1986).

26 'Upper Canada and the Conservative Tradition,' 27

accountable to the legislature, and their preference for a small, economical form of government.

Beyond the tories' use of patronage, however, there are a number of other reasons why the reformers failed to establish a secure hold on the popularly elected Assembly. As a political leader Mackenzie was at his best when on the attack, publicly roasting the Compact or compiling his massive indictment of them in the famous *Seventh Report of the Committee on Grievances*. But such activities tended to intensify reform agitation without broadening its popular base. In spite of sporadic efforts to form a coalition of reform-minded groups, on the model of the political unions that radicals in Britain had successfully organized, who could work together in accordance with some agreed agenda, there was no common reform platform in Upper Canada and much confusion over specific goals.[27] The latter problem was made all the more acute by Mackenzie's erratic shifts of policy in response to nothing more than the dictates of his conscience and his enthusiasms of the moment, such as his sudden and in some respects bizarre infatuation with American republican institutions – including the spoils systems, which he saw as a means of getting rid of the Compact – oblivious to the embarrassment that this was bound to cause other reformers, such as the Baldwins, who had spent years trying to dissociate reform from republicanism.[28] There were still those who were his hard-core supporters and who would follow him anywhere, but there were many more who would cautiously wait and see.

Also the walls of the tory citadel had by no means crumbled before the trumpet blasts of reform, thus giving the tories inside time to prepare their counter-attack. And as is often the case in such circumstances, the prospect of imminent demise seems to have concentrated their minds wonderfully, for they emerged with some new weapons and some surprisingly modern tactics. Not for the last time, a threatened government realized that it could go a long way towards repairing its fortunes by adopting two basic policies: first, by borrowing to finance a vast program of public works, especially road construction, which quickly put cash into the pockets of large numbers of workers (while at the same time showing that something was at last being done about the state of the roads, a perennial source of complaint); and second, by

27 Eric Jackson, 'The Organization of Upper Canadian Reformers, 1818–1867,' in Johnson, ed., *Historical Essays*, 96–107
28 Careless, 'Robert Baldwin,' 104–5

courting the favour of new immigrants through measures designed to assist them in getting settled – which in the 1830s meant posting government agents along the routes west from Montreal to help them find suitable locations and using the Crown lands to provide the poor with fifty-acre lots with no payment required for three years.[29] New immigrants were pouring in, nearly all of them from Britain, and inclined in any case to support the Crown and the British connection. With a little encouragement they could be turned into solid supporters of the government.

Some tories, moreover, while abhorring the *principles* of democracy, were beginning to adopt its *techniques*. It was not that they had reached the level of sophistication that would be attained by the next generation of tory politicians, who, under John A. Macdonald, came to realize that parliamentary democracy was a game they could master; it was just that the game became slightly more attractive to them once they saw the possibility of winning. Moreover, as noted earlier, the performance principle was an important ingredient in the Upper Canadian clientele culture, and the tory record was far from being all bad. They could hardly claim credit for progress in political or constitutional matters, but in economic and financial ones they could point to the benefits that their policies had brought to the province, especially in the area of public investment in needed facilities, including the Welland Canal and the Bank of Upper Canada. In each case, Mackenzie retorted, members of the Family Compact had also profited personally, but at the same time he had little else to offer: in his own economic thinking, ironically, he was more conservative than the Compact, being a believer in pure metallic currency and minimal public expenditure.[30]

III

Left to their own devices, the tories might well have continued to evolve in the direction in which they were being pushed, gradually coming to terms with the inevitability of a greater role for the people in the constitution and perhaps even discovering that responsible government – when accompanied by fervent loyalty to the Crown – was really a tory idea after all. But in the event they were not left to their own devices. And their evolution was not without interruption.

29 Craig, *Upper Canada*, 227
30 DCB, IX, 498

First came a well-meant gesture on the part of the British Colonial Office which, as such gestures often do, had the opposite effect from that intended – the result of one of those catastrophic lapses of judgment that were endemic in the British system of aristocratic leadership: certainly no one who had witnessed the appointment and subsequent career of Sir Francis Bond Head as lieutenant-governor of Upper Canada could have been altogether surprised by the charge of the Light Brigade. Head was a former army engineer whose career in civilian life had been barely adequate to sustain him in his station, which was on the fringe of the upper class. He had been employed in a mining venture in South America, which failed, but wound up with a knighthood, allegedly for demonstrating the military usefulness of the lasso. Such talent as he possessed was mainly as a scribbler of opinionated travel books, the best known of which was entitled *Bubbles from the Brunnens of Nassau*. His connections with those in power were not exactly close: the only salaried patronage post he had managed to acquire was as one of the Poor Law commissioners for the county of Kent. Yet when in 1835 the whig colonial secretary Lord Glenelg decided it was time to appoint a more liberal chief official in Upper Canada, someone more sympathetic to reform and better able than his immediate predecessors to work with the Assembly (which then contained a large reform majority), his choice for that politically sensitive and demanding role was none other than Head.[31]

It was once thought that Glenelg had mistaken Head for his abler and more experienced cousin Edmund Walker Head, but it now appears that that was not the case. A more convincing explanation is that Glenelg was pressured into making the appointment by some reform members of the cabinet who had totally misinterpreted a typically muddled essay that Head had written on the Poor Law. Hence when the new lieutenant-governor arrived in Toronto in January 1836, he was puzzled to find himself welcomed as 'a tried Reformer,' which could hardly have been further from the truth. 'Head had so little political experience that he had never voted in an election; he had displayed no interest whatever in colonial policy; and even his essay on the poor law, though couched in the rhetoric of reform, was based upon the deepest social conservatism.'[32]

31 Head's improbable career is admirably summarized in DCB, X, 342–5. For a full-length biography, see Sydney W. Jackman, *Galloping Head* (London 1958). Head's own account is contained in *A Narrative* (London 1846; reissued Toronto 1969).

32 DCB, X, 343

Such handicaps, however, did not deter him from reaching a swift conclusion about the state of Upper Canadian politics: the struggle, he believed, was between the forces of good and evil, loyalty and disloyalty, monarchy and republicanism – and all reformers were therefore, by definition, evil disloyal republicans. Glenelg, to his credit, had issued Head with clear and sensible instructions: without conceding responsible government, he was to rectify specific grievances whenever possible and generally reassure Upper Canadians that the Colonial Office had no desire to meddle in their internal politics; in other words, he was supposed to co-opt or at least mollify the reformers without totally alienating the tories. Instead, within a matter of weeks he had managed to so embroil himself in conflicts with the Assembly that there was no possibility of his being able to carry out such a delicate assignment. On 28 May 1836 he dissolved the legislature and issued writs for a new election.

It was soon obvious that he did not intend to be a neutral observer. With the same instinct for self-promotion that had earned him the nickname 'Galloping Head' (for his habit of colourfully embellishing his exploits in the Argentine), he had evidently decided that what the forces of loyalty in Upper Canada needed most was a leader of heroic stature: namely, himself. As more knowledgeable men such as Robert Baldwin looked on aghast, he went plunging into the unfamiliar arena of electoral politics with all the enthusiasm of a novice discovering his true calling – and finding in the process that he did indeed possess a certain talent. His specialty was to stir up the patriotic but normally somnolent local militia regiments by appealing to their members' latent fear of an American attack. An invasion was imminent, he would proclaim: 'Let them come if they dare!' It seemed to work. Most of the reform candidates were defeated, including Mackenzie, and the tories once again assumed majority control of the Assembly.[33]

Ironically, the real effect of Head's vainglorious antics was to deny the tories a victory they might well have legitimately won on their own. As it was, their success was tainted by the atmosphere of hysteria and intimidation that surrounded it and to which Head had so mindlessly contributed. No reformer could accept the result as valid. Those who were already tempted by the idea of rebellion naturally saw it as final proof that the old political order of Upper Canada was unreformable. Their alienation would have serious consequences, as Robert Baldwin

33 Craig, *Upper Canada*, 237–9

foresaw. On 11 July he wrote to Lord Glenelg: 'I sincerely believe the crisis to have arrived which is to decide the ultimate destiny of Upper Canada as a dependency of the British Crown.'[34] But his appeal for the removal of Head went unheeded, and within a year the province was once again in turmoil. Mackenzie had organized a 'Committee of Vigilance' and was now urging his followers to overthrow the government and join the United States. By December he had convinced several hundred of his supporters that the time was ripe to emulate the rebellion of the thirteen American colonies in 1776.

Revolutionary fervour alone was not entirely trusted, however, and as usual in Upper Canada, land was not far in the background: Mackenzie promised each participant in the uprising three hundred acres in the new state that he intended to establish, while those who refused to join him 'might, like the tories of the American Revolution, have their land confiscated.'[35]

Head, meanwhile, was doing his bit to hasten events by sending the province's entire garrison of regular troops to Lower Canada to assist in putting down an uprising of the French Canadians, which was in progress under Papineau's leadership. He later claimed that he had done this deliberately in order to lure Mackenzie into open rebellion, and later still denied that he had done so, but whatever the truth of the matter Mackenzie cannot be faulted for his timing. He was surely correct when he told his followers: 'The whole physical power of the government, the mud garrison, redcoats and all, is not equal to that of the young men of one of our largest townships.'[36] Where he went disastrously wrong was in underestimating the strength of Upper Canadian conservatism, for when forced to choose, a great many of those same young men were tories.

IV

Few political acts can be more pathetic than a rebellion with too few rebels. Late in the afternoon of 5 December 1837 Mackenzie's confused and ill-equipped little army advanced down Yonge Street to a point just beyond Gallows Hill (near the present site of St Clair Avenue). There, in the gathering winter gloom, they encountered an even smaller party of

34 As quoted in Dunham, *Political Unrest*, 176
35 *DCB*, IX, 503
36 *Constitution*, 13 Sept. 1837

the Toronto militia, who had been hastily mobilized by Sheriff Jarvis for the defence of the city. Volleys of rifle shots were exchanged, doing little damage, but in the panic that followed both sides turned and ran: the rebellion was effectively finished. By this time militia units were pouring towards Toronto from outlying areas, and two days later a large force, armed with cannon and accompanied by two brass bands, marched up Yonge Street, put Mackenzie and his remaining supporters to flight, and burnt the tavern where they had made their headquarters.[37] Mackenzie, with a price on his head, managed to escape across the border and take refuge in the United States. The aftermath was singularly unpleasant: tory extremists felt they had been vindicated by events, while every old militiaman in Upper Canada seemed determined to squeeze back into his uniform for one last crack at the rebels – but since there were not enough genuine rebels to go around merely moderate reformers were in some cases persecuted and harassed for nothing more than an alleged lack of loyalist zeal.[38]

The most important political reality of Upper Canada, therefore, was not that a rebellion was attempted but that a system of government that was obsolete, largely unworkable, and even by the standards of its own time virtually indefensible was in fact stoutly defended.

Had it been simply a case of William Lyon Mackenzie leading the common people in revolt against the Family Compact, as he claimed and as it has often since been portrayed, clearly the old system would not have stood for a moment. But the old system was more deeply rooted in the society of the province than Mackenzie ever realized, and it was by no means synonymous with the Family Compact. Its real substance lay elsewhere, above all in the clientele economic and social structures that continued to function effectively in the villages and townships and backwoods concessions where the great majority of the people lived. There the most crucial of all political links, that of leader-follower, was

37 For an authoritatively documented account of these events, see Colin Read and Ronald J. Stagg, eds., *The Rebellion of 1837 in Upper Canada* (Toronto 1985). There was also a rather feeble attempt at insurgency in the western region of the province, provoked by false reports that Mackenzie had been successful at Toronto. See Colin Read, *The Rising in Western Upper Canada, 1837–8: The Duncombe Revolt and After* (Toronto 1982).

38 Lt Colonel Allan Napier MacNab, commander of the 1,500 eager volunteers sent to search out rebels in the London District, admitted that he had 'at least six times as many men as I require' (*DCB*, IX, 522); see also Fred Landon, *Western Ontario and the American Frontier* (Toronto 1941; reissued 1967), 161–5.

still largely based on that of patron-client, and the latter was a linkage that Mackenzie had never been able to break.

From the perspective of Toronto, moreover, it was easy to mistake the politics of the city for the politics of the province as a whole. Yet even in the 1830s Toronto stood somewhat apart from the rest. It was still small but it was recognizably a city, and politically it had acquired some distinctly urban attributes: an active press, a politically conscious public, the potential for mob action, and a generally more varied and intricate form of political life. Elsewhere politics for the most part retained a 'parish pump' quality and more often than not revolved around old loyalties, old feuds, and local personalities. It could rarely be understood in terms of the issues that excited Toronto – though this was often overlooked by those immersed in the furious conflicts of the capital. Curiously, Mackenzie and most members of the Family Compact were alike in this respect. They were also alike in their personal attachment to Toronto and in their exclusively urban careers and interests – which made them rather anomalous figures in a society that was overwhelmingly rural and agrarian. Perhaps in consequence neither was able to demonstrate much expertise when it came to politics 'out there' in the districts; and ironically, each tended to miscalculate by overestimating the extent of the other's influence. Thus Mackenzie seemed to assume that because the Compact loomed so large in Toronto its shadow had necessarily to extend across the province, whereas in reality it did not, or did so only weakly and intermittently, for outside Toronto the Compact's role was effectively circumscribed by two basic deficiencies.

First, since it was pre-eminently a governmental rather than a business elite, it did not control the broad commercial base of the clientele system, which, as we have seen, developed separately from the Compact and pre-dated it by many years. The mid-level and local patrons thus did not depend upon the Compact financially, nor were their lines of credit as yet concentrated in Toronto but still commonly extended to Montreal; indeed, to the extent that the Compact included a minority of able businessmen and bankers, such as William Allan,[39] whose inclinations were to centralize financial power in Toronto, their interests were liable to be in conflict. As a result, the Compact could never rely upon the commercial base for consistent or wholehearted support, much less direct it. Secondly, though the Compact dominated

39 DCB, VIII, 4–31; see also C.L. Vaughan, 'The Bank of Upper Canada in Politics, 1817–1840,' Ontario History 60 (1968): 185–204.

the machinery of government at the centre (and the very considerable patronage that went with it), this by no means guaranteed that its political dominance would necessarily extend to the local level in an unbroken 'line of command.' On the contrary, ironically, the very system of non-responsible government (the so-called balanced constitution) that ensured the Compact's position of privilege in the capital, and which its leaders were so adept at defending, also ensured a substantial measure of local autonomy. The reasons for this, however, are not obvious. To understand it we must look most closely at the relationship between the Compact and the local political elites, and in this regard the relationship between the Compact and the grand patrons of the province is especially instructive.

Within their own districts the grand patrons were unquestionably Upper Canada's symbolic patriarchs, its tribal elders, and (in so far as it could be led at all) its regional leaders. They were also without exception solidly loyalist and tory. It might be thought, therefore, that they would be, in effect, the Family Compact's subagents. Yet in fact no such sensible arrangement existed, for the grand patrons simply did not see themselves in a subordinate role. They did not defer to the Compact socially and saw no reason to do so politically – at times, indeed, they seemed to treat the Compact as *their* subagents in Toronto. Their loyalty to the Crown was beyond challenge, so they could not be brought into line by charges of disloyalty if they insisted on going their own way. They were in any case idiosyncratic and strong-willed individuals who were not much inclined to accept orders from anyone, except the lieutenant-governor himself (hence, perhaps, the ease with which they were mobilized by Sir Francis Bond Head in 1836). Their independence was partly a matter of wealth but even more a matter of status, for each of the grand patrons possessed status that in the last analysis the Family Compact could not affect one way or another.[40] First, it cannot be emphasized too strongly that each, within the conventions of the clientele culture, possessed a status that was earned and not ascribed. In their own districts, therefore, this made them dangerous political opponents, as Mackenzie and his followers discovered to their cost. Secondly, each possessed some means of going over the heads of, or

40 By the same token, as Paul Romney observes of Colonel Talbot, by 1823 the leaders of the Compact 'recognized that the York oligarchy was too securely entrenched to feel threatened any longer by his *imperium in imperio.*' 'The Spanish Freeholder Imbrolio of 1824: Inter-elite and Intra-elite Rivalry in Upper Canada,' *Ontario History* 76 (1984): 440

around, the Compact, either through financial connections elsewhere or through aristocratic birth and/or military background that linked them personally to the highest levels of British society, or even (as in the case of Alexander Macdonnell) through ecclesiastical eminence and skilfully cultivated British political contacts. This made them exasperating and unreliable political allies, very nearly as troublesome to the Compact as they were to the reformers.

It must be remembered, moreover, that the separation of powers in the old constitution of Upper Canada left the lieutenant-governor with extensive powers of patronage over both land and appointments. In spite of Mackenzie's jibe that they were all puppets of the Compact, most holders of the office jealously guarded those powers and did not hesitate to exercise them. The grand patrons thus had no need of the Compact to act as their intermediaries: they assumed, nearly always correctly, that they had automatic access to the very top of the province's political system – and if that failed to work they still had strings that could be pulled at a higher level, in the Colonial Office or beyond. Thomas Talbot, for example, was unlikely to be overawed by an official clique in Toronto when his old friend and companion of his youth, Arthur Wellesley, Duke of Wellington, was prime minister of Great Britain.[41]

Talbot's normal attitude towards members of the Compact was to treat them more or less as functionaries. When it suited him, he would turn up in Toronto to be entertained in their homes in suitably regal fashion, and though, like some of his hosts, he held a seat on the Legislative Council, he seems to have regarded his membership in that supposedly august body as no more than a trivial honour. There is no evidence that he ever bothered to attend a meeting. Other grand patrons had their own ways of dealing with the Compact. Alexander Macdonnell's approach was to court them assiduously with flattery and assurances of support, all the while manipulating them with the finesse of a chessmaster whenever he thought they could advance his own position or serve the interests of his clients in Glengarry. Most at least treated them with respect, except for Tiger Dunlop, who treated them as a joke. (He had, for example, provoked a characteristic mixture of mirth and outrage by publishing a spoof 'petition to the King' modestly proposing that all financial power be taken out of the lieutenant-governor's hands and given to the Compact, on the grounds of their

41 *DCB*, VIII, 857

unsurpassably wise use of the public funds they already administered!)[42] Their power, and their pretensions, made them a target no satirist could resist, though for Dunlop a potentially dangerous one in view of their close ties to his nominal employer, the Canada Company.[43] To their credit, however, the political leaders of the Compact in its heyday knew better than to challenge a grand patron on his own turf. But eventually Dunlop's antics proved more than the Toronto officials of the company could bear and, in 1841, as the old constitution of Upper Canada crumbled about them, they sent Bishop Strachan's son, James McGill Strachan, to run against him in the Huron District. The result was a humiliating failure for what remained of the Compact, and an expensive one for the company: Strachan was prepared to fight to the company's last penny but still could not muster a legitimate majority; after a week of riotous open polling and flagrant fraud and corruption the whole affair ended before a parliamentary commission, with the victory being awarded to Dunlop on a recount.[44]

Yet there was no more devoted loyalist than the Tiger, and no one more deeply tory in habit and outlook. Like Talbot and the other grand patrons, however, what he was loyal to was the Crown, not the Family Compact, and his toryism was a commitment to a way of life and a type of society that he himself had been instrumental in fostering, not a commitment to support a particular group of office-holders in Toronto. He could never have rallied his clients to defend the Compact; the very idea would have been absurd; but he could and did rally them to defend the Crown, the British connection, their own property, and their own community. And if in the process the Compact was propped up along with the rest of the established order, that was only an incidental outcome, and not the main object.

Toryism, then, for all its contradictions, lack of organization, and sheer eccentricity, had in the clientele system greater potential resources of leadership and support than were usually evident on the surface of events. That system was basically too anarchic to be led, but it nevertheless rested on a solid foundation of shared values and proven

---

42 W.H. Graham, *The Tiger of Canada West* (Toronto 1962), 62–3

43 William Allan had become one of two Upper Canadian commissioners of the company in 1829 (*DCB*, VIII, 9). The other commissioner, Thomas Mercer Jones, was the son-in-law of Bishop Strachan (*DCB*, IX, 416). Strachan's son, James McGill Strachan, was the company's lawyer (*DCB*, IX, 751).

44 Graham, *The Tiger*, 211–13. In the end Dunlop was credited with 149 votes to Strachan's 101.

patron-client relationships: when threatened, it could respond in concert and with surprising strength.

At the lower levels of the clientele system there was generally even less political coherence than at the top. Local patrons tended to be every bit as individualistic in their opinions as their grand counterparts – and much more quarrelsome in their relations with one another, for unlike the grand patrons, they were often in competition for such things as land grants, new clients, and local government offices. In the London District, for example, they feuded incessantly over such earth-shaking issues as the chairmanship of the quarter sessions and the location of the registry office, coming together only out of necessity to fight off a reform challenge – and then promptly picking up their squabbles exactly where they had left off.[45]

Some local patrons made no secret of their dissatisfaction with the provincial government. In their eyes it had become a barrier to progress, and they chafed under policies they regarded as old-fashioned and restrictive, such as the continued maintenance of the Crown and clergy reserves, the preference for centralized as opposed to local banking, and the prohibition against the private purchase of Indian lands, all of which they contrasted unfavourably with the more liberal, dynamic, and free-wheeling capitalism of the United States. They were thus at least potential supporters of a reform movement – but only one that was pro-business in outlook and politically liberal rather than radical.

V

Had anyone cared to notice, that potential had been demonstrated as early as 1822 with the publication of Robert Gourlay's *Statistical Account of Upper Canada*.[46] But Gourlay was such an exceedingly odd Scot ('when sane, he was a very reasonable man'[47] is probably the most charitable judgment of him) that the substance of his book was lost in the furore that invariably surrounded him. Originally, he had come to Upper Canada in the hope of himself becoming a grand patron and settlement promoter, but when thwarted in that unrealistic ambition

45 Read, *The Rising*, 199–200
46 All references here are to the Carleton Library edition, abridged and with an introduction by S.R. Mealing (Toronto 1974). For biographical studies of Gourlay see DCB, IX, 330–6, and Lois D. Milani, *Robert Gourlay, Gadfly* (Thornhill, Ontario 1971).
47 The description is Joseph Hume's, as quoted in Mealing's introduction, 3.

(for he was not a man of great wealth or impressive connections, and in any case the status he sought was not available merely for the asking) he turned to political agitation; his true mission, as he now saw it, was to issue 'a call for inquiry into corruption, mismanagement, and mis-rule.' His efforts predictably brought him a great deal of trouble, and it was while languishing in a Niagara jail on a charge of sedition that he conceived the idea of a statistical study. (He was thus, in more ways than one, a truly 'committed' scholar.) What is chiefly of interest to us here is his research method, for – inadvertently – it produced a unique and absolutely invaluable record of the views and values of local patrons, a vast compilation of their opinions, complaints, prejudices, dreams, and ambitions, a marvellous glimpse into the mentality of their subculture.

Gourlay deserves to be commemorated as a pioneer pollster, for his chosen method was to distribute a lengthy questionnaire to the public officers of each township, accompanied by an address urging them to call township meetings to prepare returns. As a sweetener, to encourage a good response rate, he promised to publish his findings in English and German, the latter to attract a people highly regarded in Upper Canada for their qualities as settlers. Most of the questions in his survey were of a disarmingly benign and factual nature: 'Number of stores?' 'Number of taverns?' 'Present price of a good work horse four years old; also a good cow, ox, sheep, of the same age?' The sting was placed in the tail, in the thirty-first and last question, which asked: *What, in your opinion, retards the improvement of your township in particular, or the province in general; and what would most contribute to the same?*[48] Obviously, what he was hoping to receive was a fresh supply of ammunition to use against the government. What he actually got was data that was ambiguous, or in many instances directly contrary to his preconceptions. His method, in fact, had practically guaranteed such a result, for it ensured that responses to his inquiries would come mainly from local patrons – they, after all, *were* the township officers in most cases – or would be prepared under their watchful gaze even if ostensibly the product of a meeting and returned over the signature of a clergyman or some other literate member of the community. No grand patron, of course, would dignify the efforts of a known troublemaker such as Gourlay by replying at all, and the majority of mid-level patrons seem to have felt the same way,

48 *Statistical Account*, 128

but others responded with enthusiasm. Altogether he obtained 57 reports covering 70 of the province's 158 townships.

These reports (which were fortunately published by Gourlay in their original, unedited form) constitute a remarkable treasury of information and attitudes – but the attitudes are not of the kind that could have brought even the slightest comfort to a radical reformer. The prevailing spirit was overwhelmingly one of optimism, of faith in the province's economic prospects and pride in its resources and achievements. The local patrons, evidently, were not nearly as interested as Gourlay in attacking the evils of the system; their aim rather was to improve the system's future. Many of their responses to his survey were for this reason comically at cross-purposes with the use he wished to make of them. Even their answers to his notorious thirty-first question were typically couched in a conditional form. Their most common complaint by far was the patron's standard litany: too much land was unproductively tied up in the reserves, or by absentee owners, or by the existence of Indian rights. (There was not one of them who did not feel that he could better develop such lands himself.) But, they would add, if this impediment were removed, their township would have a glowing future.

The reports vary widely in style and content, but the one factor that is present more often than any other is a favourable appraisal of the township's agricultural land, sometimes briefly stated ('The country is level with good soil')[49] and sometimes more rapturously described ('The soil of Beverly, rich loam, and intervals; West Flamboro' the same; both very healthy and pleasantly diversified with hill and dale; are well watered with spring streams').[50] Again and again they went on to praise the land's fertility, proudly listing the extraordinary yields of wheat that local farmers were obtaining, the rich diversity of produce that was being grown, and the superior dairy and other stock that were being raised. No prospective settler could fail to be impressed – which was no doubt precisely the intention.

In other respects some of the reports have a surprisingly modern ring to them. Indeed, they resemble nothing so much as the local boosterism of present-day Ontario municipalities and chambers of commerce, and would not be out of place today in the brochures that small-town development committees send out in their efforts to entice new firms to

49 Ibid., 132
50 Ibid., 187

locate in their hopefully named 'industrial parks.' For example, they shamelessly advertised their townships' assets and attractions, emphasizing such things as good roads ('The roads in this township are surpassed by none in the province'),[51] navigable waterways and port facilities, the availability of schools, mills, merchants, blacksmiths, local markets for produce, hotels and taverns, the quality of the natural scenery ('sublimity reigns in all her glories'),[52] potential tourist attractions, and any other features that were matters of local pride. Even a deficiency could with a little imagination be turned to advantage: 'We have no taverns,' admitted the township of Windham, 'but we profess to be a hospitable people, and do entertain strangers.'[53] And where the land tended to be undeniably rocky, as around Kingston, an abundance of good building stone could be truthfully stressed.[54]

In answer to the second part of the thirty-first question (which asked respondents to suggest improvements) a few chose to promote their favourite local development schemes, especially canal building, which was already coming into vogue; a few saw it as an opportunity to put in a plug for temperance or 'the improvement of morals'; while one Absolam Shade insisted that in his township 'the minds of the people want rousing up.'[55] On the whole, however, there was a consensus bordering on unanimity: what Upper Canada most needed was a fresh influx of 'men of capital.' Over and over, in virtually identical words, they suggested the same thing:
- nothing wanting but the filling up with industrious men, men of property;
- men of sufficient means to purchase land;
- persons of ability to purchase;
- capitalists;
- a monied capital directed in a general and liberal manner to agricultural pursuits.

If this need were met, ran their thinking, their township would 'no doubt, soon form a most delightful, populous, and wealthy settlement.'[56]

Though they did not use the term, it is clear that what the local patrons wanted, indeed avidly desired, was more rapid economic

51 Ibid., 252
52 Ibid., 269
53 Ibid., 149
54 Ibid., 245
55 Ibid., 195
56 Ibid., 145

growth. They were themselves heavily engaged in land speculation (of which, naturally, they made no mention in their identification of the factors retarding progress). They were beginning to see new opportunities for the capital they might raise from land sales, in such enterprises as brewing, tanning, and various other forms of local manufacturing. On the whole, they were the most economically restless and aggressive stratum of the clientele system. And they were itching to progress beyond the early stage of clientelism. Not for them the romantic attachment to a rural way of life that was so much a part of the toryism of the grand patrons.

By the 1830s, even though settlers were now pouring in, they were still complaining as vociferously as ever. Yet their complaints should not be misinterpreted: they did not contain the seeds of revolution. In the final analysis, what the local patrons were after was not so much the overthrow of the *status quo* as its expansion, even if in the long run the result would be much the same. A reform movement that promised economic growth *without social disruption* would therefore have appealed strongly to them, but no such movement existed. There was only Mackenzie. But his discontents were not theirs, and the wilder his pronouncements became, the more reason they had to fear that what he was more likely to bring about was the reverse of what they wanted: social disruption *without economic growth*. A few were drawn to him regardless, but when armed rebellion threatened, most turned upon him with a vengeance and mobilized their clients in support of the government.

VI

It is necessary at this point to stress once again the distinction between the political system and the clientele system. The Toronto tory oligarchy were rooted in the former and derived their power and influence mainly from a constitution whose structures and institutions had created substantial roles for them and whose process they had mastered through long experience. They had connections to the clientele system, but these were not the basic source of their eminence and indeed were normally attenuated and unreliable. The rural patrons, on the other hand, were rooted in the clientele system and derived their power and influence mainly from their symbiotic relationship with their clients in the social and economic development of an agrarian society. They had connections to the political system, but again these were problematical and not the source of their eminence. Mackenzie had unwittingly brought the two together more closely than anyone else had ever been able to do, but this abnormal and temporary unity should not be allowed to obscure their essential separateness. In the end it was the clientele system that proved the more dynamic, adaptable, and durable of the two.

The old political system, though it had proved too tough to be toppled by invasion from without or rebellion from within, faced another source of destruction against which it had no defences, and that was the British government. Sir Francis Bond Head and Mackenzie between them had, after all, inflicted irreparable damage, especially to what little remained of the system's tattered reputation in the corridors of the Colonial Office. Now thoroughly alarmed, and acting with unaccustomed swiftness, the British government extended its long shepherd's crook and yanked Head from the political stage. Unfortunately, by this time Melbourne's once-effective whig ministry had fallen into an advanced state of internal decay. To buy time on the Canadian issue, and to appease his disgruntled colonial secretary, Lord Howick, who was threatening to resign, Melbourne – with understandable trepidation – agreed to appoint Howick's notoriously erratic and altogether exceedingly strange brother-in-law, Lord Durham (the 'Radical Jack' of the 1832 reform movement) as governor general, with dictatorial powers and a sweeping commission to investigate affairs in both Upper and Lower Canada.[57]

Durham's brief mission turned out to be a worthy second act to Head's first. He arrived with a vast entourage, including a full orchestra (prompting one wag to explain that its purpose was to make 'overtures' to the Canadians), surrounded himself with a scandalous collection of rogues and racial bigots as his advisers, took to dressing himself up in outlandish costumes, and went sweeping around the country in whirlwind fashion, accomplishing precisely nothing. Later biographers would note that he was unwell at the time and 'under a strain.' Some five months after he arrived, shocked by Melbourne's disallowance of one of his ordinances, which happened to be illegal (it involved the summary exile of eight prisoners to Bermuda without trial), he resigned

---

57 See Ged Martin, *The Durham Report and British Policy* (Cambridge 1972), on which the following interpretation of Durham's mission to Canada is largely based. For a contrary interpretation, portraying Lord Durham as a liberal individualist, see Janet Ajzenstat, *The Political Thought of Lord Durham* (Kingston and Montreal 1988).

in a huff and returned to England – one step ahead of another outbreak of rebellion in the lower province.

In January 1839 he produced his report[58] – a document long venerated as a milestone in Canadian constitutional history. To read it, however, is to be mystified by its reputation: in spite of its assertive tone, it is plain that its author's grasp of the Canadian situation was at best very superficial, while as an example of political thought it is too muddled and jejune to be of any value. What it does reveal is a staggering conceit, a paucity of factual information, and a lurid racism on which its entire argument rests. Its only real importance lies in its two main practical recommendations, for both of these were eventually translated into reality (though a good case can be made that by linking the two together Durham made the achievement of each more difficult than it might otherwise have been). What he proposed as a solution to the Canadian problem was, first, the legislative union of the two Canadas, in the naïve hope that the French Canadians would thereby be compelled to abandon their 'vain hope of nationality'; and second, the granting of responsible government, in the equally naïve hope that political dissension would thereby give way to a new reign of 'harmony.' The first was the standard nostrum of the anti-French element in Lower Canada, and the second the standard nostrum of the Baldwinite reformers (though Durham's assertion that the United States possessed 'responsible government' must have given them pause to wonder how well he actually understood the concept).[59]

French Canadians were, of course, unanimously hostile to the report, but Upper Canadian opinion was, as usual, divided. The Family Compact were in high dudgeon: Durham had spent but a single day in Toronto (as against four gazing at Niagara Falls) and much of what he wrote about it was as unsubstantiated and insulting as anything he had written about the French Canadians. 'It absolutely made me ill to read it,'[60] fumed Chief Justice John Beverley Robinson. But protests were in vain; the game was over and the Compact had lost. In the end the British had to impose union because in reality there was very little else they could do: without it there was no way of breaking the English-French deadlock in Quebec. And though they did not have to impose responsible government, the Upper Canadian reformers (ironically, at

58 Gerald M. Craig, ed., *Lord Durham's Report* (Toronto 1963)
59 Ibid., 128
60 As quoted in Brode, *Sir John Beverley Robinson*, 210

the very moment when their fortunes had sunk to their lowest ebb) were suddenly given new life by the suggestion that they might. The reformers seized upon Durham's report as their personal and political vindication, a confirmation from highest authority that in demanding responsible government they were being no less loyal than those who opposed it. In effect, the stigma was removed from the concept, finally making it palatable and even attractive to many moderate tories.

Significantly, in their opposition to the substance of the report the Compact could not carry the local patrons of the province with them. The latter would not stand idly by and allow the Compact to be overthrown by force, as events had shown, but neither would they follow it without question. Once they had done their bit to save it, it appeared, few of them felt they owed it their undying allegiance, particularly once a now impeccably legitimate and attractive alternative had been put before them. They had no important economic interests that necessarily hinged upon the Compact's survival; indeed, they saw a great deal in the proposed new constitutional arrangements that would allow them to promote those interests more satisfactorily than under the old regime. Instinctively, moreover, they were attracted by Durham's proposal to cut the Gordian knot of provincial politics. They could see the force of Robert Baldwin's argument that greater popular control over the provincial government would strengthen rather than weaken the imperial connection. Moreover, secure in their own bailiwicks, and trusting the loyalty of their clients, they had less reason than the Compact to fear the growth of a more democratic form of politics.

Their instincts were sound. In economic as well as in political matters the future largely belonged to them. Already there were signs of development in the province that would as surely transform the lives of Upper Canadians as anything envisaged by Lord Durham. The Welland Canal, which opened in 1829, had broken the previously impassable barrier to navigation between the eastern and western sections of the province, greatly facilitating the flow of grain from the fertile western districts to overseas markets. By 1839 the first crude railway line was also in operation, its symbolism more powerful than its technology, but nevertheless a true harbinger of things to come. Everywhere there was a growing appetite for modernity, and none felt its pangs more sharply or were more eager to find the means of satisfying it than the local patrons. They were the province's chief source of entrepreneurial talent, and it was from within their ranks that men such as William Hamilton Merritt, the builder of the Welland Canal, emerged – men with the combinative skills necessary for success in the more complex commercial and financial era that was dawning.

VII

The new constitution came into effect on 10 February 1841, though not in the form proposed by Lord Durham. The upper and lower provinces were united, but the British continued to hedge on the question of responsible government. The effective unit of rule now comprised an enormous territory that stretched across half the continent from Gaspé to Lake Superior, and between its two twinned colonial semi-states there existed enormous divisions of language, culture, and economic interest. Its problems and prospects were in many respects more European than North American, though nowhere in Europe at the time would anyone have attempted to govern so strange a combination by other than autocratic means.

Yet it would in practice be far more democratic than either of the old provincial regimes it replaced, though also infinitely more complex and byzantine in its political processes. Opportunities were thus created for men of different political skills from those who had previously dominated, and in Upper Canada this meant men of pragmatic inclinations, negotiators who could bargain with their French-speaking colleagues, coalition-builders, accommodators, and political entrepreneurs. From the start, the men who would form the new political class in succession to the Compact were drawn predominantly from among the local and mid-level patrons, or were men of commercial or professional background (professional politicians in all but name) who relied upon local patrons for electoral support, courted their favour, and legislatively catered to their interests.

The clientele system, then, by no means vanished with the changing of the political guard. It is noteworthy, however, that the evolution that renewed it and secured its future occurred at its lower levels, not at its top. None of the old grand patrons had a role to play in the new era. They had been products of unique historical circumstances, their extraordinary lives built around land development on a scale that was not repeatable. In their day they were politically powerful, but their power died with them, even though their impact on the communities they founded long survived. In style and outlook they belonged to the eighteenth rather than the nineteenth century, their ideal society being Arcadian rather than industrial. They were patrons from choice, autocratic in temperament, paternalistic, unshakeably tory – paradigmatic figures of the old clientelism. The local patrons, by contrast, were patrons more from necessity, and from their less secure situations they struggled incessantly for the Victorian goals of advancement, improvement, progress – in business and in politics. From among them came men with new skills who in business could combine the surplus capital of the local patrons into larger enterprises than any of them could finance individually, and who in politics could put together the larger alliances necessary for success. In the new clientelism the paradigmatic figure would be a broker.

Part Two

Canada West

5

The Broker's Art

BROKER: 1. *A factor; one that does business for another; one that does bargains for another.* 'Brokers, who, having no stock of their own, set up and trade with that of other men; buying here, and selling there, and commonly abusing both sides, to make out a paultry gain.' *(Temple)* 2. *One who deals in old household goods.* 3. *A pimp; a match-maker.*

– Dr Samuel Johnson, *Dictionary of the English Language*

The years 1852 to 1857 will ever be remembered as those of financial plenty, and the saturnalia of nearly all classes connected with railways.

– T.C. Keefer, *Eighty Years' Progress of British North America* (1864)

I

Few human skills are so universally viewed with suspicion, or so denigrated by the denial that any skill is involved at all, as the ability to make a deal. Yet deal-making in some form is a common feature of human societies, a necessary basis for a wide variety of transactions between individuals, even if it is also a source of much conflict and mistrust. (For the actual outcome of a deal might not be as anticipated by all the parties to it, thus naturally leaving room for dispute over the line between high skill and low ethics.) Deal-making is perhaps most commonly exemplified in commerce, in the daily myriad of transactions to buy, sell, or exchange goods – or in politics, where a deal may be as specific as the exchange of a vote for a promised favour or as vague as a tacit bargain to 'live and let live' or to 'let sleeping dogs lie.' In general, however, the richer and more complex a society, the less it will rely on deals between individuals in face-to-face relationships and the more it will rely upon deals that are transacted through specialized third-party deal-makers, facilitators, or brokers, especially in financial and political affairs, and the more highly it will reward these intermediaries with money and power.

In the early stages of Upper Canada's economic and political development, for reasons already explained, the key functional relationship was basically dyadic, between patron and client. In that relationshp there was no room for specialist intermediaries and no perceived need of them. Even in circumstances where land granting was complicated by the existence of a corporate entity, as in the case of the Huron District and the Canada Company, the dominant role that evolved was that of patron and not of broker, for any mediation that was required between settlers and the company was subsumed under the patron's role: it was one more service that patrons such as Tiger Dunlop and J.C.W. Daly performed for their clients. But in time, population growth and agricultural development combined to create new needs – and new opportunities – that no patron could hope to meet on his own. The most a successful local patron could do, for example, was to invest his modest accumulation of surplus capital in improvements to his own milling and merchandising facilities, or in small-scale processing or manufacturing, which many of them did.[1] At that most dynamic and competitive level of the economic system, however, there were also those who saw that other more complex investment techniques could be profitably employed, such as the promotion of joint-stock companies and the floating of private (or better still, private but government-backed) bond issues, and used to finance large-scale investment. Financial brokerage, in other words, was their answer to the inherent limitation of simple dyadic clientelism: its weak or non-existent horizontal links between patrons. By pooling the surplus capital of local patrons, and by adding to it capital from any external sources that might be available, brokers would be able to put together the deals that would make possible development projects more ambitious than any previously undertaken, except by government. The traditional linkage between patron and client would remain undisturbed, at least for the time being, but in this

1 See, e.g., W.P.J. Millar, 'George P.M. Ball: A Rural Businessman in Upper Canada,' *Ontario History* 66 (1974): 65–78.

newly emerging stage of *triadic* clientelism the broker's role would obviously be a crucial and transforming addition.

The changes that were taking place in Ontario's society and politics during the Union era were extremely complex and far from uniform. Nevertheless, certain broad trends are evident and may be usefully viewed from the perspective of a developmental model of clientelism. Thus, while Part One of this book focused upon the local roots of the clientele system – and upon the political culture, elementary economy, and generally weak machinery of central government that were so conducive to its growth – Part Two will focus upon the political process that emerged at the provincial level in response to profound constitutional and economic developments. In that process the winning and holding of political power came to depend above all upon the ability of political leaders to put together supra-local coalitions in a legislature where loyalties were notoriously unstable but where control of all of the prizes of office had at last been concentrated. The result was a politics of brokerage and the emergence of a new class of political brokers whose essential skills paralleled those of financial middlemen in the economy. In many cases, indeed, these two roles were combined in the same person, for successful investment in such large-scale projects as canals and railways invariably required more capital than could be raised privately without the backing of government.

Sir Allan MacNab's famous remark, 'My politics now are railroads,'[2] even if apocryphal, was undoubtedly true. It was also true of a number of other political brokers. By the 1850s railway charters had become the richest of political prizes, and no railway promoter could hope to succeed if he did not at the same time either hold office in the government or have a close financial relationship with someone who did. Not surprisingly, factions in the legislature tended to crystallize around railway ventures and to be maintained by liberal distributions of railway stock. Indeed, the promoter of the Great Western Railway, Samuel Zimmerman, was known to boast that when the division bell rang in Parliament, more members 'were to be found in his apartments than in the library or any other single resort.'[3] He was also adept at putting together deals among local patrons in support of municipally

2 As quoted in Donald Creighton, *Sir John A. Macdonald: The Young Politician* (Toronto 1952), 176. Other sources give slightly different versions, such as 'all my politics are railroads.' *Dictionary of Canadian Biography*, IX, 524
3 T.C. Keefer, *Eighty Years' Progress of British North America* (Toronto 1864), 221–2. See also *DCB*, VIII, 963–7.

financed railway schemes. The patrons tended to monopolize local government offices and to exercise substantial electoral influence through their clienteles: with their votes the financial authorization of local councils could be obtained for borrowing from the Municipal Loan Fund (which the province had conveniently established in 1852 for precisely this purpose); and through their influence the ratepayers could be persuaded to endorse such schemes in local referenda. In consequence, 'lines could be built almost entirely at public expense.'[4] From enterprises of this kind Zimmerman profited from lucrative construction contracts, bonuses, fees, and the holding of negotiable mortgage bonds secured by the company's assets; while the local patrons profited in a variety of ways, from supplying the railway with goods and services to speculating in shares, but above all, as major landholders, from the speculative bonanza in land that railway construction typically brought in its wake. In London, for example, in 1851 Mayor Simeon Morrill cast the deciding vote to run the tracks of the Great Western across his own lands and adjacent to his tannery.[5]

Developments of this kind imparted a new dynamic to Upper Canadian economic life that spilled over into other areas of endeavour, producing a general quickening of pace and a broadening of horizons. As J.J. Talman so succinctly puts it, in writing of the United Canadas of the early 1850s, 'practically all observers during this brief period agree that there had been a change in thinking, particularly in Canada West; that it had come suddenly; and that it was associated with railways.'[6]

The impact of new economic forces, moreover, coincided almost exactly with a major shift in the constitutional underpinnings of the Upper Canadian political process. In particular, the final establishment of the principle and conventions of responsible government, combined with the quickly unfolding consequences of legislative union with Quebec, fundamentally changed both the 'rules of the game' and the practical requirements for political success. In order to govern it was now essential to find some means of holding together a majority in the Assembly – and that meant being willing and able, first, to deal for support among the diverse factions, interests, and independents who constituted the Upper Canadian section of the House, and second, to

4 DCB, VIII, 965
5 DCB, X, 533
6 'The Impact of the Railway on a Pioneer Community,' Canadian Historical Association, Annual Report, 1955, 6.

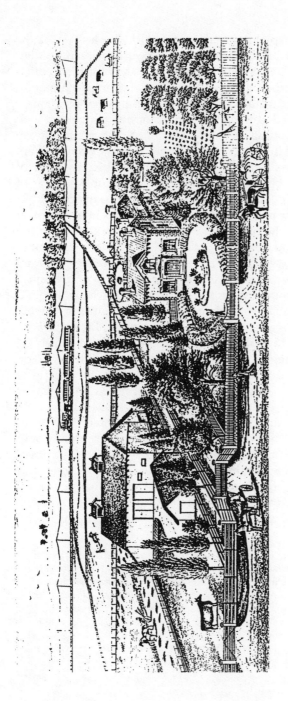

The new Upper Canadian ideal – a prosperous agriculture crowned by a railroad

come to a mutually acceptable arrangement with the leaders of the French Canadian bloc who dominated the Lower Canadian section, over such matters as the allocation of cabinet posts and the distribution of the spoils of office. Both of these enterprises placed a high premium on brokerage skills. And to both the railway boom was fortuitously related in that it produced new opportunities for bargaining and new incentives to combine politically if the right terms could be struck. In the process it became part of the broker's art to conjure into existence, from such brokered enterprises as railway construction, a dazzling array of new rewards that could be used to supplement traditional sources of political patronage and in whose allocation he would be instrumental.

Accordingly, one of the major themes to be elaborated in the chapters that follow is the rise of the broker to a role of vital importance in the burgeoning economy and complex politics of the Union era. Before proceeding further, however, it is necessary to explain more fully my usage of the terms 'broker' and brokerage' in the present context, since these terms are also commonly employed in everyday language in a variety of senses and shades of meaning. Here, following a well-established technical usage of anthropology and political science, I am using them specifically to denote a form of clientelism in which (1) patron-client dyads are aggregated at the top through an intermediary; and (2) the intermediary controls or has privileged access to 'the critical junctures and synapses ... which connect the local system to the larger whole.'[7] Originally, in the early stages of brokerage, these intermediaries may build their positions by promoting a common basis for co-operation among patrons (for example, in a chartered company or in concerted support for a particular political leader or party), but they soon come to exercise a dominant role in the organizations and networks thus created. The broker is therefore more than a neutral facilitator of exchange. Rather, he is an active participant, a 'gatekeeper' of the system who significantly affects the way the system operates.[8]

7 Eric Wolf, 'Aspects of Group Relations in a Complex Society: Mexico,' in Dwight Heath and Richard Adams, eds., *Contemporary Cultures and Societies of Latin America* (New York 1965), 97. For other illustrative usages within the framework of an analytical model of clientelism, see S.N. Eisenstadt and L. Roniger, *Patrons, Clients and Friends* (Cambridge 1984); Robert D. Paine, ed., *Patrons and Brokers in the East Arctic* (St John's 1971); and S.J.R. Noel, 'Leadership and Clientelism,' in David J. Bellamy et al., eds., *The Provincial Political Systems* (Toronto 1976).
8 Robert D. Paine draws the following useful distinction between a 'go-between' and a broker: where a transaction 'is made faithfully, without manipulation or alter-

Politically, the effectiveness of such brokerage depends 'on the broker's access to the organs of the state and to the channels of delivery of its resources, as well as on the ability to use them in a particularistic way to gather political support.'[9]

II

The true era of the broker dawned with the formation of the United Canadas, and throughout the whole period of the Union, from 1841 to 1867, there was no more characteristic or dominant figure. But this was not the period in which brokerage began: as in so many things, the earlier Upper Canadian experience had been formative, for already a prototypical broker of genius had come upon the scene in the person of William Hamilton Merritt,[10] the builder of the Welland Canal. Though his career stretched over several decades, it is particularly instructive at this point to consider the early part of it, for it classically illustrates the evolution of the broker's role. Also, Merritt was an original: in the years that followed his brokerage techniques were widely copied.

His background was a fairly standard one and contained nothing in particular to foreshadow the role he was later to play so successfully. His father was an American loyalist who had fought under Simcoe in the Queen's Rangers and subsequently settled at St Catharines, where William quickly rose from farming a portion of the family's land in Grantham township to become a substantial local and later mid-level patron. In the usual way he engaged in the St Lawrence grain trade using credit from Montreal, acted as a land agent, operated a general store and grist mill, and generally tied his fortunes to the productivity of his farmer clients in the surrounding area and the vagaries of a distant market. Such surplus capital as he was able to accumulate he invested in expanding his mercantile operations and developing local processing

---

ation, we may well speak of a *go-between*. The concept of a broker, on the other hand, essentially has to do with 'processing' of information (whether or not with the intent of mediation), and I reserve the use of *broker* to one who, while purveying values that are not his own, is also purposively making changes of emphasis and/or content.' 'A Theory of Patronage and Brokerage,' in *Patrons and Brokers*, 21

9 Eisenstadt and Roniger, *Patrons, Clients and Friends*, 231
10 *DCB*, IX, 544–8. See also Hugh G.H. Aitken, 'The Family Compact and the Welland Canal Company,' in J.K. Johnson, ed., *Historical Essays on Upper Canada* (Toronto 1975), 153–70; and J.P. Merritt, *Biography of the Hon. W.H. Merritt, M.P.* (St Catharines 1876).

facilities, including a potashery and a distillery. He was also a militia officer in the Niagara Dragoons with a record of active service in the War of 1812, a magistrate for the Niagara District, and a member of the Anglican Church. In politics (at this stage of his career) he was of course a tory.

Given his situation at St Catharines, it required no great feat of imagination on his part to realize that a canal bypassing Niagara Falls and linking Lake Ontario to Lake Erie would greatly improve trade; indeed, there could scarcely have been a merchant in the whole western region who did not realize it. Nor did he possess any great talent for engineering: his calculations were amateurish, and in any case the problem was not one of engineering. What distinguished Merritt was his grasp of the techniques of modern finance: he understood the means by which a project far beyond his own financial capacity (and even beyond his province's, as it turned out) could be successfully capitalized. More important still, he also brilliantly excelled in the application of those techniques, resourcefully stitching together deal after deal until the project was finally completed. With the Welland Canal Company (chartered in 1824) as his instrument, he set out to sell shares to local patrons wherever possible, ranging as far afield as Kingston and Cornwall, and when he came up short proceeded to tap investors in Lower Canada and the United States. From the start he recognized that no project of the kind he envisioned would get far in Upper Canada without the active support of the Family Compact, and one by one he somehow managed to lure the leading financial figures of the Compact into his enterprise as investors and members of the company's board of directors. Among those who, at one time or another, he managed to ease into directorial chairs were William Allan[11] (president of the Bank of Upper Canada), John Beverley Robinson[12] (attorney-general), and Henry John Boulton[13] (solicitor-general). The presidency of the company went to none other than John Henry Dunn,[14] the receiver-general (in effect, finance minister) of the province. By such means he assured the company of all the benefits of one of Upper Canada's most deep-seated political traditions: the conflict of interest. Moreover, both personally and as public officials, the Compact financiers were induced to go just a

11 DCB, VIII, 4–13
12 DCB, IX, 668–79
13 DCB, IX, 69–72
14 DCB, VIII, 251–7

little too far to turn back, a technique Merritt also used on his American backers; and when the canal badly overran its estimated construction costs, they had either to pour in more money or risk losing everything.

Clearly, the functions of the company's Compact directors were first to ease its path politically, including the passage of any necessary legislation and the granting of such favours as exemption from import duty on machinery and tools, and secondly to obtain direct public subsidies on its behalf. As Hugh G.J. Aitken writes: 'For evidence of how effectively the Company directors performed these functions we need only turn to the record of the various grants and subscriptions made to the Company by the Upper Canada Legislature. And an impressive record it is: £25,000 in 1826; £50,000 in 1827; £25,000 in 1830; £50,000 in 1831; £7,500 in 1833; £50,000 in 1834; and a magnificent promise of £245,000 in 1847, of which only £68,144 was actually realized ... Majorities were often slim – sometimes only the casting vote of the Speaker stood between success and failure – but the necessary votes were always mobilized somehow ... The power of the Compact, supreme in the Legislative and Executive Councils and usually dominant in the Assembly, opened the public purse on its behalf again and again, up to the limit of the province's financial resources and beyond.'[15] Even public support of this magnitude was not enough, however, and Merritt had to apply all his considerable ingenuity to the search for fresh capital, constantly juggling loans from banks and miraculously extracting a loan of £50,000 from the parsimonious British Treasury. Finally, at the scene of the canal, when things became desperate, he made deals with local shopkeepers, liverymen, suppliers and labourers to accept company scrip in lieu of cash.

On 30 November 1829, the first freight-laden schooner made its way through a rough channel from Lake Erie to Lake Ontario: the Welland Canal was open. Now, in an age when projects that dwarf it in size and cost are commonplace, it is easy to undervalue Merritt's achievement, or misunderstand its true nature and significance. But for its time it was a magnificent feat, not of engineering technology, which was ordinary, but above all of original and creative brokerage. Aitken concludes that what Merritt demonstrated was that in Upper Canada 'entrepreneurial success depended upon political rather than purely economic talents.'[16] From our perspective, however, it is necessary to put it in broader terms:

15 Aitken, 'The Family Compact,' 164
16 Ibid., 168

what Merritt demonstrated (though its full implications would not be understood until the 1850s) was that a new figure, the broker, had made his entrance upon the Upper Canadian stage, and his special talents were as relevant to politics as to economics.

The essence of successful brokerage is to put together a deal among parties who would otherwise not be in association with one another and whose interests may be at variance apart from a common denominator of which they may be unaware. By this standard, Merritt's performance as a broker was of astonishing virtuosity, especially when one considers that it was his first such venture and that he had gone, more or less in a single leap, from backwoods shopkeeping to the world of high finance. Anyone could have seen the desirability of the Welland Canal, any competent engineer could have built it: Merritt's great and creative contribution was to harness together the unlikely assortment of backers who made it financially possible – joining local patrons with a little surplus capital to invest to the sophisticated bankers and lawyers of the Family Compact, and the austere officials of the British Treasury to his principal American investor, a cash-rich New York lottery promoter. It must be remembered, moreover, that he did all this without surrendering effective day-to-day control of his company and, though often on the brink of ruin, without cheating or failing its shareholders.[17]

In the process he himself had advanced from a relatively low position in Upper Canadian society to a relatively high one, and significantly, he had done so on the strength of his brokerage skills alone. It is worth noting that when the Compact needed officials with specialized expertise, they had often to turn to Britain for them; but as Merritt showed, expert brokers were produced through the dynamics of the clientele system itself. The Compact, moreover, were no more able to master the broker than they had been able to master the patron: as deftly as a Bishop Macdonnell, Merritt had found a way to exploit their power without turning himself into their servant. On the contrary, as Aitken points out, 'within four years he not only was on intimate terms with half a dozen of Upper Canada's little oligarchy, but also, and more important, held their reputations in the palm of his hand.'[18] The lesson was not lost on aspiring brokers. When the Union of the Canadas

17 When the canal was finally brought under public ownership in 1843, long-term provisions were made to safeguard the shareholders' interests. DCB, IX, 546
18 'The Family Compact,' 157

opened fresh political vistas, and the coming of the railway age fresh economic ones, the lobbies of Parliament would be crowded with aspiring Merritts, all busily manoeuvring to involve office-holders or potential office-holders in their schemes. And the only means of governing would be through political combinations that were at times every bit as unlikely as the one Merritt had patched together to finance the Welland Canal.

6

The Reign of Harmony

Avoid useless discussions upon theoretical points of government.

– Charles Poulett Thomson (Lord Sydenham)

I

To understand the changes in the political process that followed in the wake of the new Union constitution it is necessary to look beyond that constitution to the goals and assumptions of its imperial framers. It was above all the response of a harried British government to the demand that they 'do something' about a long-standing problem, but in this case prospects of their doing something useful were slight. As Ged Martin states: 'The Canadian problem had long been virtually insoluble to the British because the solution which they desired, that the French Canadians should cease to be disaffected and preferably cease to be French, was beyond the reach of legislative fiat.'[1] In 1841 it was still beyond reach, but under pressure, the British decided to attempt it anyway by lumping together the two Canadas. In essence the purpose of the Union was to use the English population in Upper Canada as an instrument for the political domination, and hopefully the cultural annihilation, of the French population in Lower Canada. The result was a constitution whose first premise, unwritten but clearly understood, went a long way towards making it unworkable.

Since the French Canadians could hardly be expected to co-operate in their own demise, no serious attempt was made to persuade them to do

1 *The Durham Report and British Policy* (Cambridge 1972), 51

so. Instead, the British effort was concentrated on Upper Canada, for it was there that the fate of the new constitution would largely be decided. If the Upper Canadians could be persuaded to accept it there was at least a chance that it could be successfully imposed upon the French: obtaining their acceptance therefore became the first priority of British policy.

This delicate task was entrusted to an ambitious whig politician, Charles Poulett Thomson, MP for Manchester and a member of Melbourne's cabinet – but a politician who was losing his taste for politics. 'The interruption and noise which prevails so much in the House *cows* me,' he had confessed; 'I have certainly made no good speech for two years.'[2] He would no doubt enjoy life more in the House of Lords, but he had been passed over for a peerage once already and if he were now to go down with Melbourne's obviously sinking ship, his prospects for elevation would be slim indeed. The governor generalship of Canada, on the other hand, carried with it a virtual guarantee of at least a barony, and when (on the fourth round) the post was offered to him, he seized it with alacrity. His main chance had arrived.

He was to find, however, that Upper Canada too had its ambitious politicians; and just as he was intent upon using *them* for his purposes, so too were they intent upon using *him* for theirs. For the fact was that Upper Canada had interests of its own, which its politicians reflected, and these interests could not easily be squared with British interests. In all their calculations, what Durham, Glenelg, Poulett Thomson, and other British officials persistently failed to take into account was the extent to which a distinctive social and political community had taken root in Upper Canada, a community that was odd and difficult to understand in many respects, but also solidly established and well adapted to its North American environment – as ineradicable in its own way as the French in Quebec. In the context of the vast web of empire this perhaps did not count for very much. But in the small political arena of Upper Canada it counted for a great deal, and the result was a growing atmosphere of irritability and misunderstanding between the imperial centre and the colonial periphery.

The British naturally tended to take the long view in dealing with an empire that was always somewhere in flux: what did it matter if a small interest here had to be sacrificed to a larger interest there? In a decade, or

2 Adam Shortt, *Lord Sydenham* (Toronto 1908), 148. For an excellent modern account of his life and career, see the *Dictionary of Canadian Biography*, VII, 855–62.

a century, the balance would right itself. Thus Lord John Russell, the colonial secretary, in introducing the government's measures to implement the Union, could explain casually that the Constitutional Act of 1791 had, after all, been a mistake – implying that a separate province of Upper Canada should never have been founded, that in effect all the pieces on the chessboard should be returned to their original squares and the game restarted. His draft bill was revealingly titled 'A Bill for *Re*-uniting the Provinces of Upper Canada and Lower Canada.'[3] Upper Canadians, however, just as naturally saw the half-century since 1791 through the magnifying glass of their own experience. And in their eyes the creation of Upper Canada had been no mere move in some imperial chess game but an event of profound significance, a talismanic symbol of loyalist endurance and ultimate success; when they looked around them, many were inordinately proud of all that they had achieved, both as a people and individually. A politician in Westminster could remain ignorant of such sentiments, but no politician in Toronto could. Realistically, therefore, there was about as much likelihood that Upper Canada would passively allow itself to be turned into an instrument of some imperial grand design as there was that Quebec would passively allow itself to be anglicized. This did not mean that Upper Canada would necessarily reject the proposed new constitution out of hand – there were too many potential advantages in it for that – but it did mean that if it did participate it would do so for its own reasons and to serve its own purposes. And these did not include a profitless, assuredly quixotic campaign to assimilate the French Canadians.

On the contrary, Upper Canada's core interest was to ensure that it would not itself be politically submerged in a union with its more populous neighbour; but if that interest could somehow be safeguarded, the rest would amount to little more than haggling over the financial terms. It was not enough to use Lord Durham's simplistic arithmetic (which added the population of Upper Canada to the English minority of Lower Canada to come up with an overall English majority) because the gap between the two English segments was wider than Durham had realized – not only in terms of politicial experience and tradition but also in terms of hard economics. With the gradual improvement in transportation facilities, Upper Canada had found that its geographical location, so long a liability, was now becoming an asset: it allowed its merchants, for example, to play off Montreal against New York in the import-export

3 Shortt, *Sydenham*, 123 (italics added)

trade. But if Upper Canada's separate political identity were to be lost, what was to stop the English mercantilists of Lower Canada from combining with the French to turn it once again into a captive agrarian hinterland of Montreal?

II

Poulett Thomson, however, had come with authority to put before the Upper Canadian legislature some extremely attractive concessions, the first of which was the crucial one: Upper Canada would not be treated as part of 'the English' but would instead be accorded separate but equal representation in the proposed new parliament – in spite of the fact that its population stood at only 480,000 compared to Lower Canada's 670,000.[4] The remainder of the package contained financial inducements so lucrative as to be almost irresistible, above all the munificent promise (at Lower Canada's expense) that the huge public debt that Upper Canada had run up, mainly through its enthusiasm for canal building, which amounted to £1,226,000, would be pooled with the modest debt of Lower Canada, which amounted to only £95,000, and become a *joint* charge on the revenue of the Union.[5] It was a clever ploy: the English in the lower province were prepared to swallow anything to get the Union accepted, while the French were already so alienated that there was nothing to be lost by alienating them still further. Moreover, Poulett Thomson was a rarity, a governor general with a business background (as a merchant in the Baltic trade) who could talk persuasively about such things as economic growth, new public works, and the possibility of imperial loans, all tantalizing visions of sugarplums needing only acceptance of the Union to make them a reality.

4 In Upper Canada the French minority numbered less than 14,000; in Lower Canada the English minority numbered around 160,000. For a summary of the religious composition and geographical distribution of the population, see J.M.S. Careless, *The Union of the Canadas* (Toronto 1967), 24–8.
5 Shortt, *Sydenham*, 317–18. The British government would guarantee a consolidated debt of 1,500,000 pounds. From the Upper Canadians' standpoint this was a most satisfying turning of the tables on Lower Canada, whose low debt they attributed to the practice of cheating on the division of the customs revenue collected on goods imported through Montreal and Quebec: 'That revenue was chiefly paid by the Upper Province, where a majority of the consumers resided; yet Lower Canada had for years received the lion's share of it, and surrendered even the smallest proportion with reluctance.' J.C. Dent, *The Last Forty Years: The Union of 1841 to Confederation* (Toronto 1881; reissued 1972), 18

Opposition came mainly from the die-hard tories who could neither be cajoled nor bribed, but the tories as a whole were split: the remnants of the old regime, the Family Compact and a few of the grand patrons and their supporters, were on one side; the bulk of the mid-level and local patrons, especially those of the younger generation, were on the other. It is significant and typical that on this issue William Hamilton Merritt broke with the Compact to join a group of moderate conservatives who supported union on the terms offered.[6] The reformers, for their part, had no doubts whatsoever: they were wholeheartedly in favour of union, not least because they believed that responsible government would follow inevitably. (To ensure their support Poulett Thomson was not above hinting that this would be the case, but in fact he had neither the authority nor the desire to offer it as a concession.) Also, like the moderate conservatives, they were in general reassured by the political terms and attracted by the financial ones. In the end, union was carried in the Assembly on the strength of their combined votes – with the motion on the provision for unloading the public debt not even requiring a division of the House.[7]

It remained only for the Act of Union to be drafted and duly passed by the imperial Parliament. The two Canadas had their new constitution, for good or ill; and Poulett Thomson had his peerage, becoming Lord Sydenham ('of Sydenham in Kent and Toronto in Canada'). For the French Canadians, on top of all the rest, there was one final crowning humiliation thrown in for good measure: their representatives in the new united legislature would be allowed to speak French if they had to, but the sole language of record would be English. Ironically, the only Upper Canadian voice raised in their defence was that of John Beverley Robinson, arch-tory and spokesman of the Family Compact, who had wisely but vainly admonished the British not to legislate upon the assumption of 'the hopeless inferiority of the French Canadian Race,' tartly adding: 'it is not in that spirit that the domination over half a million of free subjects should be exercised.'[8]

---

6 George Metcalf, 'William Henry Draper,' in J.M.S. Careless, ed., *The Pre-Confederation Premiers: Ontario Government Leaders, 1841–1867* (Toronto 1980), 36
7 Gerald M. Craig, *Upper Canada: The Formative Years* (Toronto 1963), 265
8 While sympathetic to French Canadians, Robinson had draconian plans of his own for Quebec: he would have carved Montreal and the north bank of the Ottawa River out of its territory and attached them to Upper Canada. See Patrick Brode, *Sir John Beverley Robinson: Bone and Sinew of the Compact* (Toronto 1984), 214.

But for the members of the Compact too there was only humiliation at the end. Their power had been decisively broken, though by dismissal from office and not, as they had long feared, by the introduction of responsible government.

III

For the reformers, however, there were encouraging hints and intimations of progress towards the latter goal – but never an actual declaration of support for it. In fact, the Colonial Office and Sydenham himself were still wedded to the intellectually threadbare notion of governing through 'harmony' – but without being able to explain how anything so felicitous could be expected to arise out of the atmosphere of suspicion and hostility that they had done so much to promote. Though it was never openly declared at the time, what 'harmony' seems to have amounted to, at least in Sydenham's conception of it, was the continuation of the old system, in that the governor general would personally lead the Executive Council, whose members would hold office only at his pleasure.[9] The new Executive Council would therefore be no more responsible to the legislature than the Compact had been. But such would be the good intentions, wisdom, and efficacy of the governor general's administration, and so in accordance would it be with the true wishes of the people that the legislature would be happy to support it anyway. Such at any rate was the theory.

It could only be tested in practice after elections had been held to choose a new legislature. In terms of establishing basic legislative institutions, however, the Act of Union provided for nothing more than a replication of those it replaced, albeit on a grander scale. There would thus be the usual bicameral arrangement of a Legislative Council appointed for life and a House of Assembly elected on a broad property franchise. The only original provision was that in the Assembly, Upper Canada and Lower Canada (now designated Canada West and Canada East) would have equal representation, each with forty-two seats, a balance not alterable except by a two-thirds vote of both houses.[10] The danger, from Sydenham's point of view, was that elections would end

9 Shortt, *Sydenham*, 262–3. See also Stephen Leacock, *Baldwin, LaFontaine, Hincks* (Toronto 1907), 64–7.
10 For the text of the act see W.P.M. Kennedy, ed., *Statutes, Treaties and Documents of the Canadian Constitution, 1713–1929* (Toronto 1930), 433–45.

his reign of harmony before it could begin, for if they were honestly conducted it was reasonable to suppose that the die-hard tories of Upper Canada would win some seats, and given the way the French Canadians had been treated, it was certain that they would elect a solid bloc of anti-unionists. That the two combined might outnumber the expected pro-union combination of reformers, moderate conservatives, and Lower Canadian tories was an awkward but very real possibility. And nearly as awkward, though more remote, was the possibility that the reformers might sweep Upper Canada. Buoyed by such a result, they would then no doubt press for a clarification of the governor general's delphic utterances on the subject of responsible government. Sydenham, however, was not inclined to leave such matters to fate – or to the fickle whim of the electorate. Instead, his response was to manage the campaign of the pro-union forces – in effect, to act as their self-appointed party leader. In the process, his waning appetite for politics, which supposedly had brought him to Canada in the first place, underwent a miraculous revival: 'The worst of it is that I am afraid I shall never be good for quiet purposes hereafter,' he later wrote, 'for I actually breathe, eat, drink, and sleep on nothing but government and politics ... That, in fact, is the secret of my success.'[11]

The secret of his success in 1841 might more accurately be described as electoral corruption. Sydenham was not without a base of support, particularly, as noted earlier, among the politically influential local patrons who were attracted by his visions of commercial growth. Also, even among those who occupied important official positions, such as sheriffs or chairmen of the quarter sessions, who were normally the pillars of local toryism, there was evidently considerable sympathy for his aim of improving the machinery of administration, as long as it did not involve the granting of responsible government.[12] But – perhaps because he was too unfamiliar with the intricacies of Upper Canadian politics to appreciate the true extent of their influence – he was unwilling to trust the local patrons to deliver the votes of their clients. As a result, the elections for the first parliament of the United Canadas were probably the most blatantly crooked of any ever held in either province. And much of the crookedness was sanctioned by Sydenham or personally perpetrated by him.

11 Shortt, *Sydenham*, 339
12 See Carol Wilton-Siegel, 'Administrative Reform: A Conservative Alternative to Responsible Government,' *Ontario History*, 78 (1986): 105–25.

Correctly perceiving that the old provincial divisions were undimin-
ished in political importance, regardless of union, and that his only
chance of obtaining a more or less legitimate victory lay in Upper
Canada, it was there that Sydenham concentrated his effort to secure
support, devoting all the resources of the government to that end. There
was, of course, nothing particularly new in this; essentially, his tactics
were the same as those of Sir Francis Bond Head in 1836, only this time
they were directed *against* the tories. What distinguished Sydenham's
use of them were the unprecedented lengths to which he was willing to
go and his superior ability as an organizer. In his hands bribery, fraud,
intimidation, and every other abuse to which the electoral system
(which had not been significantly altered by the Act of Union) remained
susceptible were not resorted to haphazardly and locally amid the usual
chaos of an election; rather, they were adopted as government policy
and applied systematically and ruthlessly.

Sydenham himself campaigned across the province, parading his
hand-picked unionist candidates (the majority of whom were government officials) and promising a cornucopia of public works, but only for
districts where 'the right type of men are returned.'[13] This was one of his
more subtle approaches. More direct, and no doubt more effective, was
the simple expedient of rigging the electoral machinery. As governor
general he could do this with impunity, since for all practical purposes
he was also the chief electoral officer, with wide authority over the
organization and conduct of elections, and thus able to control such
vitally important matters as the drawing of constituency boundaries, the
appointment of returning officers, the location of polling places, and the
dates of polling. It must be remembered that in 1841 elections bore little
resemblance to their modern counterparts. Voting was still by open poll,
with each elector required to establish his right to vote and declare his
preference in public before a returning officer, who was a functionary
with much discretion over such things as voter eligibility, the opening
and closing of the poll, and the general orderliness or otherwise of the
voting. Polling, moreover, was restricted to one place in each constituency, which meant that the location of the poll could often go a long way
towards determining the outcome: for example, if located in a village
known to favour a particular candidate, it not only convenienced his
supporters but also made it possible for them to 'capture the poll' and

13 Irving Martin Abella, 'The 'Sydenham Election' of 1841,' *Canadian Historical Review* 47
(1966): 333

physically keep opposing electors at bay; or a whole area known to be unfavourable to a candidate could be effectively disenfranchised by making the distance to the poll too great to be readily travelled. A governor general was thus in an ideal position to subvert the electoral process if he were so inclined – and Sydenham was very much inclined. Indeed, it may be argued, he had virtually no choice but to do so, since, having stuck his neck out by claiming to be able to govern with popular support, the wrong result would have left him with the credibility of his regime in tatters, personally embarrassed, and perhaps open to charges of illegal and unconstitutional behaviour.[14]

His activities are well documented: ridings were gerrymandered; polling places chosen for the sole purpose of discrimination; returning officers appointed who were brazenly partisan, some actually being the election agents of unionist candidates; the franchise manipulated; appointments freely promised; government employees and pensioners compelled to vote as directed under threat of dismissal or loss of pension; troops selectively deployed to disperse supporters of opposing candidates who had captured polls, but not supporters of unionist candidates; opposing candidates bribed to withdraw; false results reported; and so on through an almost endless catalogue of electoral fraud and corruption. 'As a representative of Buckingham Palace, he acted more like an envoy from Tammany Hall.'[15]

Lower Canada presented a different problem. Practically all the English were securely in the unionist camp, but the attitude of the French towards Sydenham was one of such loathing that anything he might do to influence them, whether by threats or bribes, was liable to be counter-productive. With nothing to lose, he was thus free to adopt tactics that made even those he employed in Upper Canada seem restrained and scrupulous by comparison. First, through a gross gerrymander he ensured that in the largest towns the French would be almost totally disenfranchised and the seats handed over to English unionist candidates. Then, after polling was allowed to begin, the relentless application of force was relied upon to take care of the rest. His military secretary, Major Campbell, became his Quebec election agent. In some predominantly French areas polls were located in English hamlets and surrounded by troops to prevent French electors from voting; in others, gangs of thugs were recruited from among canal

14 See DCB, VII, 861
15 Abella, 'Sydenham Election,' 343

labourers and used to capture polls on behalf of English candidates. By such means Terrebonne, for example, which was 90 per cent French (and the riding of the leading French Canadian politician, Louis LaFontaine), was declared to have elected one Dr McCulloch.[16]

IV

What was the outcome of all this? In Lower Canada the English unionists emerged with nineteen or twenty seats, a plainly rigged result, but nevertheless an important victory for Sydenham. In Upper Canada the results were more problematical and the effects of Sydenham's tactics more difficult to gauge. Given the magnanimous terms upon which Upper Canada had entered the Union, and the widespread support for union on the part of the local patrons, many of whom no doubt shared Merritt's belief that the unionists were the 'commercial and industrial improvement party,'[17] it seems likely that a majority of the Upper Canadian seats would have gone to unionists even if the elections had been honestly conducted. Nevertheless, the tory die-hards still managed to capture no less than seven seats – a remarkably strong showing in the circumstances, and evidence that they might well have done even better in a fairer contest. Their leader was Sir Allan MacNab, the redoubtable magnate of the Hamilton area (whom Sydenham had unsuccessfully tried to bribe into withdrawing). Of the remaining thirty-five Upper Canadian seats nearly all were won by unionists of some description. The latter, however, were anything but a harmonious group, and still less a political party: even before the new Assembly could meet they had begun to disintegrate into factions, the chief of which may be identified as follows.[18]

The Moderate Reformers
These constituted the largest (and loosest) grouping, numbering around twenty-five. Their hard core consisted of Sydenham's place-men, all of

---

16 Ibid., 342. See also DCB, IX, 440–51.
17 Careless, The Union, 45
18 Not surprisingly, given the fluidity of political alignments in this period, the number of members in each camp can only be approximately determined. The most thorough study of parliamentary divisions is to be found in Paul G. Cornell, The Alignment of Political Groups in Canada, 1841–1867 (Toronto 1962), 3–9. But see also Careless, The Union, 45–7; Shortt, Sydenham, 291–2; and Leacock, Baldwin, LaFontaine, Hincks, 82–3.

whom were recipient of vice-regal largesse and who were 'reformers' only in the sense that they favoured change, as long as it was of a kind approved by Sydenham; also, and perhaps more to the point, they had not been members of the Family Compact. Their leader was S.B. Harrison,[19] an English barrister and recent immigrant to Upper Canada whom Sydenham had personally selected for preferment, appointing him to the Executive Council as provincial secretary and using him as a trusted election agent. (He was, however, temporarily without a seat – MacNab had defeated him in Hamilton).[20] Around this hard core there clustered the rest, who were attached to it by bonds of varying strength. Some were local patrons who were 'reformers' mainly in the sense that they looked to the Union to spur economic growth, and who could hardly wait to turn on the taps of public expenditure (which, they rightly believed, if Sydenham kept his promises, would flow bountifully into their coffers). Others were simply hopeful office-seekers who would soon grow disgruntled if their hopes were not fulfilled. Still others were supporters of responsible government who either believed that Sydenham would actually implement it or who were temporarily attracted by his vague talk of 'harmony'; for whatever reason, they were not prepared to make an immediate issue of it, though if no progress were made towards it they might quickly become disillusioned.

The Ultra-Reformers

These were the reformers whose commitment to responsible government was as strong, if not stronger, than their commitment to the Union itself. For them it was the *sine qua non* of constitutional change, the non-negotiable price of their co-operation with or participation in the government. Moreover, they wanted it at once, with no further procrastination or toying with ambiguous alternatives. They numbered only five, but their influence was much greater than this would suggest because their leader was Robert Baldwin.[21] He was the voice and conscience of reform, a moderate in everything except the one great

19 *DCB*, IX, 369–73
20 For an interesting account of this important election, see Donald R. Beer, *Sir Allan Napier MacNab* (Hamilton, Ont. 1984), 162–4. See also *DCB*, IX, 519–27.
21 *DCB*, VIII, 45–59; and J.M.S. Careless, 'Robert Baldwin,' in Careless, ed., *The Pre-Confederation Premiers*, 89–147. For earlier studies of Baldwin's life and career, see Leacock, *Baldwin, LaFontaine, Hincks*; George E. Wilson, *The Life of Robert Baldwin* (Toronto 1933); and R.M. and J. Baldwin, *The Baldwins and the Great Experiment* (Toronto 1969).

issue with which he had been for so long identified. There was no other reform leader of his reputation or symbolic stature. His moral authority extended to many of those who were nominally in the camp of the moderate reformers; given a slight shift of circumstance, they would regroup behind him without a qualm.

The Moderate Conservatives

These too numbered five but possessed influence beyond their number, in their case initially through Sydenham's powerful backing of them in order to split the tory ranks. But if they were thus essentially place-men, they also importantly represented the transformation of toryism into a more recognizable modern conservatism.[22] They would still claim guardianship of the loyalist tradition but were better able than the die-hard tories to appeal to the new business-minded, brokerage-inclined elements in the clientele system – elements which might otherwise have gone entirely over to the reformers by default. Unlike the die-hards, they saw the advantages rather than the dangers in union; and while they professed to want no part of responsible government in principle, when the occasion arose they were pragmatic enough to grasp it in practice. Their nominal leader was William Henry Draper,[23] a wily lawyer and former protégé of the Family Compact who had parted company with them over a number of issues, but particularly over what they regarded as his unconscionable and opportunistic support of Sydenham and the Union.

In the interval between the passing of the old constitutional order and the birth of the new the leaders of all three of these factions had uneasily shared office in the interim administration, but once union had been secured there was nothing to hold them together. Baldwin in particular had agreed to serve only because Sydenham had not yet revealed his opposition to responsible government. His presence in the administration, however, was regarded by Sydenham as 'the greatest possible *coup,*' for it meant that 'the man most esteemed and looked up to by the

---

22 For the intellectual and ideological aspects of the rise of moderate conservatism, see David Mills, *The Idea of Loyalty in Upper Canada, 1784–1850* (Kingston and Montreal 1988), 71–92, 117–24.

23 *DCB,* X, 253–9; Metcalf, 'Draper,' 32–88. For a critical reassessment of the careers of Draper and two die-hard or ultra tories, Henry Sherwood and Allan Napier MacNab, see Donald R. Beer, 'Toryism in Transition: Upper Canadian Conservative Leaders, 1836–1854,' *Ontario History* 80 (1988): 207–25.

whole of the Reformers of Upper Canada'[24] was not only fully behind union but also had apparently acquiesced in the notion of vice-regal government through 'harmony.' In fact the two were totally at cross-purposes. When it was clear that the reformers commanded a majority of the Upper Canadian seats, Baldwin confronted Sydenham with his demands: first, a reconstruction of the Executive Council along party lines (in other words, the introduction of responsible cabinet government); and second, the inclusion of French Canadians in the government. It is not recorded which of the two Sydenham regarded as the more outrageous. But Baldwin's move had forced him to show his cards at last, and he now made it clear that he intended to govern as his own prime minister, preferably with all-party advisers – and without the French.

Baldwin thereupon resigned from the Executive Council. When the first legislature of the United Canadas opened, he and his ultra-reformers sat in opposition, along with the tory die-hards and the sullen, leaderless supporters of Louis LaFontaine. 'I have got rid of Baldwin,' Sydenham boasted, 'and finished him as a public man forever.'[25] The reign of harmony had begun.

24 Careless, 'Robert Baldwin,' 115
25 Careless, The Union, 51

7

Francis Hincks and the Politics of Accommodation

I have got the large majority of the House ready to support me upon any question that can arise.

– Lord Sydenham to Lord Russell, 27 June 1841

Our dictator will be gone before another session and public opinion will bring the renegade Reformers back to their first faith.

– Francis Hincks to Louis LaFontaine, 29 June 1841

I

Few political systems have ever got off to a more unpromising or sordid start. On any reasonable assessment, the Union of the Canadas was a potentially sound idea that had gone horribly wrong, ending up so flawed in design, so deluded in purpose, and so infected with malice that its likeliest outcome would be civil war.

Yet ten years later the Union not only still stood but was in a state of almost unimaginable good health. The French Canadians were a fully participating and indeed indispensable part of government; Robert Baldwin and Louis LaFontaine were effectively co-premiers, working closely and harmoniously as the leaders of a great reform coalition; responsible government was an established fact; French was an official language of parliamentary record, and both of the Canadas were basking in a state of unprecedented peace and prosperity. The reasons for this stunning change of fortune are many and complex, but a contributing factor of no small importance was the early evolution of a politics of accommodation in which brokers and brokerage played an essential part. The Union, in other words, while meeting the material goals that had been so ambitiously set at its launching, operated politically in almost precisely the opposite manner from that which had originally been proposed, and with almost precisely the opposite result. To understand how this came about it is necessary to begin with one small but significant step that was taken quietly in the spring of 1839, in the midst of the great furore unleashed in the Canadas by the publication of Lord Durham's report.

II

On 12 April 1839, having thought long and hard about the possible political ramifications should Durham's major recommendations be implemented, as he hoped they would, a young Toronto reformer, Francis Hincks,[1] picked up his pen and wrote a letter to Louis LaFontaine. It was for Hincks a characteristic response to a perceived opportunity. 'Though I have not the honour of personal acquaintance with you,' he began, 'yet entertaining a high respect for your political and private character, I take the liberty of addressing you on the subject of the Durham Report, which you have no doubt perused long ere this.' His purpose in writing, he explained, was 'to learn how that document is received by you and your political friends,' but it is clear that he also had something more in mind: he wished to plant, however tentatively, the seed of an idea – that in a future united legislature the Upper Canadian reformers and French Canadian moderates might profitably work together. 'Lord Durham,' he continued, 'ascribes to you national objects. If he is right, union would be ruin to you; if he is wrong, and that you are really desirous of liberal institutions and economical government, the union would, in my opinion, give you all you could desire, *as a united Parliament would have an immense Reform majority.*'[2] He could not have known how such an opening gambit would be interpreted; but throughout his career, in business and politics, he had thrived on his

---

1 For biographical studies of Hincks, see *Dictionary of Canadian Biography*, XI, 406–16; William Ormsby, 'Sir Francis Hincks,' in J.M.S. Careless, ed., *The Pre-Confederation Premiers: Ontario Government Leaders, 1841–1867* (Toronto 1980), 148–96; R.S. Longley, *Sir Francis Hincks* (Toronto 1943); and Sir Francis Hincks, *Reminiscences of His Public Life* (Montreal 1884).
2 National Archives of Canada (NAC), LaFontaine Papers, Hincks to LaFontaine, 12 Apr. 1839

ability to make new contacts – and if all went well he could see the possibility of putting together a deal. 'A broker's *capital*,' as Jeremy Boissevain insightfully observes, 'consists of his personal network of relations with people, and his *credit* of what others think his capital to be.'[3] Viewed in this light, Hincks was attempting to increase his political capital and perhaps in the long run create new credit on which he might one day be able to trade, activities that came naturally to one of his instincts and experience.

The son of an Anglo-Irish clergyman, Hincks had early been drawn to the world of commerce. After an apprenticeship in a Belfast shipping firm, which provided him with many valuable overseas contacts, he had settled in Toronto in 1832. After briefly engaging in the import trade as a commission agent and wholesaler, he had found his métier in the field of finance, where he rose quickly through a series of intricately brokered banking and insurance ventures. He had also entered politics as a supporter of Robert Baldwin and responsible government. But in contrast to the patrician Baldwin, who was generally inept as a politician and who affected 'a certain arrogant disdain of many of the "ways and means" of politics,'[4] Hincks was a brilliant political practitioner, possessed of all of the zest for the game itself that Baldwin lacked – and who always took the trouble to master whatever 'ways and means' were necessary in order to win. He was more than Baldwin's follower; he was his ablest colleague, and with Hincks to advise him, Baldwin's influence and popular following had soared. Even the Baldwinite newspaper, the Toronto *Examiner*, was Hincks' personal creation which he had founded, financed, and edited to give the advocates of responsible government for the first time an articulate, politically acute, and frequently very witty public voice.

Now, through a shrewd and timely speculation, Hincks had made contact with the one man who could lift the reform movement from the depths of opposition to the heights of office and power. The beleaguered LaFontaine, in spite of his large following, knew that he was powerless to prevent the Union from being imposed regardless of the wishes of the French Canadians and indeed with the object of eventually obliterating them as a people; but what prospect did that leave him, as

---

3 'Patrons and Brokers,' ms, quoted in René Lemarchand, 'Political Clientelism and Ethnicity in Tropical Africa,' in Steffen W. Schmidt et al., *Friends, Followers and Factions* (Berkeley 1977), 109

4 George E. Wilson, *The Life of Robert Baldwin* (Toronto 1933), 86

the leading French Canadian politician, apart from becoming a *vendu* or trying to start a new rebellion?

He therefore had nothing to lose by replying with a cautious show of interest in the new possibility that Hincks had so intriguingly raised. And for Hincks that was encouragement enough. He wrote to LaFontaine again, elaborating on his proposal; over the following year a stream of correspondence flowed between them; at an appropriate point Baldwin was brought into the negotiations, as was LaFontaine's lieutenant, A.N. Morin; secret visits were exchanged; personal, face-to-face relationships were established; and in the process, slowly and with immense difficulty, a bridge of trust was built, spanning the very chasm that Lord Durham had imagined to be unbridgeable.

Throughout Hincks had played the part of the consummate broker, admitting no obstacle to be final, sifting tiny points of consensus out of mounds of disagreement, omnivorously digesting every new scrap of information, explaining away misunderstandings, smoothing ruffled feathers, soothing wounded pride, flattering, cajoling, urging upon both sides his own persuasive version of political reality. As his first letter reveals, he had started out in total ignorance of LaFontaine's nationalist sensitivities; but he had learned quickly and was soon cleverly appealing to them. He could also be disarmingly frank: the consolidated public debt, he admitted, 'is of course downright robbery,'[5] but, he insisted, it should not be treated as an insuperable barrier to union. Likewise, equal representation was unfair to the French, but '*can you at present hope for more?*'[6] And while the provision establishing a civil list was 'abominable,' the only sensible course was to 'work it if we can, and afterwards improve it. *What else can we do?*'[7] This was his constant refrain. Co-operation would close no doors: 'A representative Govt. & a united Legislature must give us all we want or *Separation*.'[8] But first, he urged, give union a fair trial; in other words, help us to achieve responsible government and we will share power with you and help to remove those features of the proposed Union that you find obnoxious: '*You want our help as much as we do yours.*'[9] With unerring instinct Hincks had tapped the source of the Union's future sustenance.

5 NAC, LaFontaine Papers, Hincks to LaFontaine, 30 Apr. 1839
6 Ibid., Hincks to LaFontaine, 11 Dec. 1839 (italics added)
7 Ibid., Hincks to LaFontaine, 2 May 1840
8 Ibid., Hincks to LaFontaine, 9 January 1840
9 Ibid., Hincks to LaFontaine, 17 June 1840 (italics added)

For LaFontaine, the implications were startling. If Hincks was to be believed, here was the spokesman of an important and perhaps dominant body of Upper Canadian opinion, the reformers, cheerfully offering to subvert Durham's – and Sydenham's – whole purpose. But still, though tantalizingly close, no deal was struck. LaFontaine was suspicious of Baldwin's participation in Sydenham's ministry, and just when Hincks had managed to reassure him 'that Mr. R.W. Baldwin is incorruptible'[10] and he seemed on the brink of coming to terms, the incorruptible one himself, with his rigid cast of mind, would begin to raise difficulties. Only once did Hincks seem to despair: he had got LaFontaine so far as to discuss the names of possible participants in a future coalition ministry, only to have negotiations stall over a couple of harmless time-servers. 'I should like to know from you,' he wrote with a touch of exasperation, 'whether you would consent to any compromise, that is would you act with any of your old enemies provided they agree to carry out our policy.'[11] In the end, it took Baldwin's resignation from the ministry to cement a formal alliance, but by then all of the groundwork had been laid. In essence, when they could no longer afford to procrastinate, the two leaders agreed to the power-sharing arrangement that had been worked out by Hincks: they would join forces within the framework of the Union with a view to achieving responsible government and in a future coalition ministry would divide the major offices on an equitable basis. Thus, when Baldwin crossed into opposition, he was not (as Sydenham believed) entering the political wilderness: he was allying himself and his supporters with the most cohesive and arguably the largest single bloc of members in the new parliament – the French Canadian moderates.

There was, however, nothing inevitable about such an alliance, and indeed the odds were strongly against it. Neither Baldwin nor LaFontaine had ever shown much skill or inclination for the making of political bargains; both, in fact, had well-deserved reputations for unbending adherence to principle. What it took to bring them together was the initiative and imaginative intervention of Francis Hincks. It helped that LaFontaine and Baldwin were kindred spirits between whom a lasting personal friendship eventually blossomed, but their initial political alliance was not based on friendship. It was a deal, skilfully brokered, based on clear-headed perceptions of mutual inter-

10 Ibid., Hincks to LaFontaine, 22 Feb. 1840
11 Ibid., Hincks to LaFontaine, 14 Feb. 1841

est, and like all good deals it worked to the advantage of both parties. Had it been a business transaction, Hincks would have earned his commission.

Viewed in retrospect, what he achieved seems obvious. Anyone should have been able to see that the Union of the Canadas could only be governed – if it could be governed at all – by an English-French coalition. Of course, hardly anyone did see it, and among them was Governor General Sydenham. Ironically, at the very time when the latter was sending self-congratulatory despatches to the Colonial Secretary detailing his political 'triumphs' the real political process had already begun to stir.

III

The immediate impact of the alliance was dramatic. In a highly symbolic gesture, it was arranged for LaFontaine to enter the Assembly as the member for the Fourth Riding of York, a safe reform seat, in a by-election held in September 1841. (He was able to do so because under the existing electoral system 'double returns' were permitted, which meant that a candidate could run in more than one riding and, if successful, could then choose which to represent. Hence Robert Baldwin had run in both York and Hastings. The latter was a doubtful riding for reformers, but he had managed to win it nevertheless, thus conveniently opening up his other seat for LaFontaine.)[12] It was a favour LaFontaine was soon to repay.

The first session of the legislature was played out in an atmosphere filled with confusion, acrimony, and suspicions of betrayal. Sydenham had taken to summoning its members in groups to lecture them, schoolmaster fashion.[13] But free lectures, it soon transpired, were not exactly what many of them had in mind when they looked to the governor general to show some tangible appreciation of their support. Consequently, 'before the end of the session ten members of parliament held major offices, and nearly twenty others held minor offices under the Crown.'[14] Baldwin, for his part, was bitterly disappointed that so

12 Longley credits Hincks with this idea (*Hincks*, 75). Baldwin had originally intended to give his spare seat to his father, but the latter willingly stood aside and gave LaFontaine his enthusiastic support (Wilson, *Baldwin*, 131–2).

13 'What between lecturing members every morning and schooling my Cabinet every day my hands are therefore pretty full.' Paul Knaplund, ed., *Letters of Lord Sydenham to Lord John Russell* (London 1931), 146–7, Sydenham to Russell, 11 July 1841

14 Longley, *Hincks*, 81

few of those elected as reformers had seen fit to join him in opposition, for, apart from Hincks, only four others had done so. This, however, was hardly surprising. Given that the reform members were for the most part progressive, business-minded 'men of the Districts' and that their closest affinities were with like-minded local patrons upon whom they depended for electoral support (and who were itching to get their hands on Sydenham's promised expenditures on local improvements), they were most unlikely to sacrifice constituency interests – to say nothing of their patronage posts – to Baldwin's principles. Nevertheless, it did leave the latter with an embarrassingly small following to contribute to his alliance with LaFontaine. And faced with this reality, to make matters worse, he and Hincks began to part company over tactics: Hincks, with his eye on the next election, favouring a pragmatic course of supporting (and hence sharing the credit) for certain pieces of government legislation, such as currency reform, that were likely to prove beneficial; while Baldwin favoured a course of undeviating opposition to every government measure, even if it meant voting with the tories.[15] Meanwhile, on the irrelevant fringe of the circus, old tories like Tiger Dunlop, the redoubtable member for Huron, were having a field-day with the contradictions and hypocrisies of their opponents on both sides.

Sydenham's regime continued shakily for a few months, but it could not survive a second session of the legislature. By 1842 virtually the whole political landscape had changed: Sydenham was gone from the scene (removed by a fall from his horse that proved fatal), and the new governor general, Sir Charles Bagot,[16] was a professional diplomat who felt nothing but distaste for 'the unscrupulous personal interference' of his predecessor. But without Sydenham's lavish backing his ministerial appointees had nothing with which to keep the bulk of the Upper Canadian reformers behind them, and one by one – as Hincks had predicted – they began to drift back to Baldwin.

Throughout the summer Bagot and his ablest minister, William Henry Draper, manoeuvred ceaselessly to stave off the defeat that now loomed before them, but to no avail.[17] It had become obvious that the key to survival was the participation of the French Canadians in the ministry, and to this end some of their number were assiduously courted; yet none would accept the status of *vendu*: they would serve

15 See Ormsby, 'Hincks,' 154–5.
16 *DCB*, VII, 30–3
17 See George Metcalf, 'William Henry Draper,' in Careless, ed., *Pre-Confederation Premiers*, 44–6.

only under LaFontaine. To the dismay of his Upper Canadian colleagues, Francis Hincks did accept office, as did Henry Sherwood, an
ambitious tory, but neither carried any additional supporters with
them.[18] In September, after the opening of the House, Bagot had to face
the unwelcome fact that his ministry was on the brink of certain defeat.
He therefore belatedly entered into negotiations with LaFontaine. But
by delaying until the House was in session he was forced to bargain from
a position of weakness – thus practically ensuring that LaFontaine's
demands would be shockingly high: he would join a reconstructed
ministry, LaFontaine informed the governor general, but only with
Baldwin and only if three additional places were filled by their
supporters. Eventually, after further protracted wrangling – and the
forcing of the issue by Baldwin's introduction of a motion of non-
confidence – these demands were met.[19] In the reconstructed ministry
Baldwin took office as attorney-general West, LaFontaine as attorney-
general East; and when in the ministerial by-election necessitated by his
appointment Baldwin failed to hold Hastings, LaFontaine arranged to
have him elected for the riding of Rimouski.

Bagot had managed to salvage something, but not very much: an
outright defeat had been averted, and the ministry would still not be a
true party government since, in addition to Hincks (who was soon
reconciled with Baldwin and back at the centre of reform politics), it also
contained three survivors from the previous ministry. Baldwin and
LaFontaine, however, had gained almost everything: the ministry
would be a true English-French coalition; they had demonstrated the
power of their alliance, and, as Bagot was soon to admit, 'whether the
doctrine of responsible government is openly acknowledged or only
tacitly acquiesced in, virtually it exists.'[20]

18 Ibid. Hincks' motives in accepting office are obscure, and he offers no enlightenment
   in his *Reminiscences* other than to state that he supported the administration's
   policy (81). But he consistently believed that the object of the parliamentary game was
   to win office and that in virtually every circumstance there was more room to
   manoeuvre in office than in opposition. It is also probable that he had calculated
   correctly that in any future reconstruction of the ministry under Baldwin and
   LaFontaine, he would be included.
19 For accounts of these developments, from slightly different perspectives, see Wilson,
   Baldwin, 155–9; Metcalf, 'Draper,' 46–7, and Careless, 'Robert Baldwin,' in Careless, ed., *Pre-Confederation Premiers*, 123–4.
20 Bagot to Stanley, 28 Oct. 1842, as quoted in Wilson, *Baldwin*, 166

IV

In spite of enjoying an overwhelming majority in the Assembly, the coalition ministry was by no means beyond challenge – as events would shortly prove. But an important lesson was to be learned from the *method* through which it had obtained power (and equally, perhaps, by the conspicuous failure of the alternative methods of their opponents). Thereafter, it would become axiomatic that the government of the Union could only be conducted on the basis of dual, hyphenated English-French ministries. And those ministries could only be formed and held together through unremitting attention to the art of political brokerage. Practically from the start, therefore, successful brokerage was the prerequisite for the holding of power; and throughout the history of the Union its politics were dominated above all by brokers. The field of their activities, moreover, encompassed far more than English-French bargaining. Critical though that was, an equal or even greater challenge was often first to put together a coalition *within* Upper Canada, for only then could negotiations be opened with potential French Canadian allies. The latter tended to be more politically cohesive, if only because they feared that fragmentation would lead to cultural assimilation. But in Upper Canada there were no such concerns. There, fragmentation could bring rewards, with the result that brokerage became a pervasive, unavoidable fact of political life. The clientele system had already begun to evolve in that direction economically, but politically its development was greatly accelerated by union and, eventually, responsible government.

There was also every incentive to keep the old provincial boundaries intact. To that extent, the die-hard tories had not fought in vain. Upper and Lower Canada, though constitutionally united, for all practical purposes remained two separate and distinct political sub-systems, joined only at the top through a form of overarching accommodation between the members of their respective governing elites.[21] Even officially, there was clear recognition of their separateness in the organization of the machinery of government. The key posts were those of attorney-general West and attorney-general East, for, following Baldwin and LaFontaine, these were usually held by the leaders of the

21 This form of elite accommodation is a central feature of what has become known in political science as 'consociational democracy.' See, e.g., Kenneth McRae, ed., *Consociational Democracy: Political Accommodation in Segmented Societies* (Toronto 1974). The development of consociational practices in the government of the United Canadas is discussed more fully in chapter nine.

two parliamentary groupings who made up the governing coalition, one English and the other French, but other ministries too were administratively bifurcated, right down through the various levels of officialdom.[22] In strict constitutional usage, only one of the co-leaders would be asked by the governor general to form an administration, and hence would nominally become 'premier' (though formally and legally no such post was as yet recognized). But political reality dictated that they function in practice as co-premiers, each exercising independent authority over his own section of the ministry. The proportion of ministerial heads for Canada East who could be English remained a touchy issue, though one that could generally be resolved through negotiation and compromise. In time, however, it became a broadly accepted convention of the system that, as far as possible, the lines of administrative duality and cultural duality should fairly closely coincide. In practice, they did not always do so; but it was a sign of weakness in a ministry (and seen as such) if for any reason they did not.

There had to be co-operation across French-English segmental lines to make government possible at all – as Francis Hincks had so clearly foreseen, and as virtually every politician of any consequence had eventually come to recognize, but that co-operation did not have to extend very far down into the political sub-systems. In fact, it could be confined to an extremely narrow stratum of politicians from each sub-system and was no doubt thereby greatly facilitated, since it meant that large numbers of people had neither to be persuaded of its necessity nor brought into the negotiations that made it possible. But this also meant that just as no unified administration developed, neither did there develop a unified political process, for as long as accommodations could be reached at the top, the Union could be maintained without it. Elections, for example, were fought among different contending groups or coteries of politicians (in effect, embryonic political parties) in each segment, with no overlap between the two. The previous alliances and affinities of individual politicians and groups with their counterparts in the other segment were of course well known, and possibly had some small influence on their electoral fortunes, but basically they operated independently of one another. Aggregation took place only at the end, when all the results were in and politicians could take stock of the new balance that had been established within each segment. Hence there

22 J.E. Hodgetts, *Pioneer Public Service: An Administrative History of the United Canadas* (Toronto 1955), 56–7 passim

were no parties or movements or political organizations of any kind that appealed directly to the people across segmental lines. Instead, each segment retained its own internal political dynamic, which still strongly reflected its own history and political traditions. In Lower Canada *la survivance* and in Upper Canada *loyalism* continued to be potent and emotionally sustaining values of the political culture; a believable appeal to either could still have extraordinary electoral impact. Moreover, each segment had its own distinctive pattern of cleavages – economic, regional, ethnic and religious – which greatly affected its internal political balance and at times could even exert a compulsive hold over certain of its politicians or groups, as in the case of the Catholic-Protestant cleavage and the political influence of the Orange Lodge in Upper Canada.[23]

From the beginning, also, legislation was commonly passed that applied only to one or other of the segments; and in particularly important or sensitive matters, such as those dealing with education or municipal government, separate and very different legislation was invariably the rule. There was thus no attempt to legislate institutional uniformity. From the old regime to the new, in both sections, more remained the same than had changed, and this was on the whole accurately perceived by the public. Even the new names that were introduced in the Act of Union, Canada West and Canada East, failed to catch on in popular usage, and soon were not even used officially with any consistency. On the floor of the Assembly and in the press it was not only tories who continued to speak and write of Upper Canada and Lower Canada but practically everyone, including the most avidly pro-union reformers.

V

Since our concern here is with the emergence of brokerage as a dominant mode of elite behaviour, it is essential to return to the issue of responsible government, for it was that issue that more than any other defined the way in which brokerage politics would function in day-to-day practice. And it did so because it was inseparably bound up with the question of who, ultimately, was to control government patronage – the governor general, through the exercise of the Crown's prerogative powers, or the politicians in the Executive Council. In other words, did

23 See Hereward Senior, *Orangeism: The Canadian Phase* (Toronto 1972).

the spoils of office go to the victors? This was the acid test of responsible government. If they did not, then in no meaningful sense could responsible government be said to exist at all, for patronage was not something peripheral to nineteenth-century government but its very essence.

Whoever controlled patronage could exert enormous political power, as Sydenham had done with such deadly effect in the previous election. This was well understood by the politicians of the day and greatly influenced their choice of political strategies. For example, if patronage was understood to be a gubernatorial prerogative, there was strong incentive for politicians to develop a direct patron-client link with the governor general – and little scope for brokerage politics. Even after 1842, many conservatives continued to pin their hopes on the maintenance of that link, from which they had benefited so substantially in the past; indeed, it was precisely this arrangement which they defended as *constitutional* government (as opposed to subversive notions of *responsible* government).[24] But if it was understood that the Executive Council would in practice control patronage, then there was naturally a strong incentive to form combinations, alignments, and coalitions, for the rewards of success would then be not only the victory of a principle but the tangible spoils of office. Without the latter, responsible government was no more than a fine theory, sincerely believed in by proponents such as Robert Baldwin but lacking practical effect. The engine that drove it forward – and placed a premium on the art of political brokerage – was patronage.

In office, Baldwin and LaFontaine acted as though they were at the head of a responsible ministry, seemingly with Bagot's full concurrence. They did not claim the exclusive right to patronage, however, since they recognized that a certain share should legitimately rest with the representative of the Crown, but they did claim the right to control the great bulk of everyday patronage, which was essential to their operation

24 Essentially, in the 1840s, there were two versions of responsible government. The moderate conservatives fully accepted the *individual* responsibility of ministers, but not *collective* responsibility. In other words, they rejected the idea of party government. This was also the position of the governors, since in their view it was party government that threatened to extinguish the Crown's prerogatives. As Gordon T. Stewart points out, this was an important and legitimate constitutional question that had not even been fully settled in Britain at the time. For his insightful analysis of this issue, see *The Origin of Canadian Politics: A Comparative Approach* (Vancouver 1986), 44–58.

of the machinery of government.[25] Their problems with patronage did not stem from the governor general, who was old and weary and not inclined to make demands upon them, but rather from their own vast, clamouring army of supporters, who had waited long and hungrily for their reward and now expected patronage to rain upon them like manna from heaven. The new ministers, moreover, were none too adept in the unfamiliar business of distributing manna, with the result that their efforts were often counter-productive. 'While such men as William Rorke held the lucrative posts of Collector of Customs, Postmaster, Commissioner of Crown Lands, and lesser jobs, most of the party faithful were neglected.'[26] The result was not the satisfaction of their clientele but a flood of complaints.

The ministers had no system of distribution in place and, as it turned out, no time to create one. For, unbeknownst to them, Bagot's sensible and relaxed attitude towards their administration of patronage had never been sanctioned by the British government. The latter, it transpired, had merely *tolerated* it. And they had done even that with much uneasiness and out of an awareness that there was very little else they could do, short of humiliating the governor general (and perhaps forcing his resignation) by an outright repudiation of his views.[27] Hence the impression was created that the British had accepted responsible government as a *fait accompli* when in fact they had not.

But after Bagot left office in January 1843 the way was again clear for the assertion of British power; and the issue that brought the unresolved conflict over responsible government once more out into the open was, significantly, patronage. There were a number of reasons for this, but perhaps the chief among them was that British officials, no less than their Canadian counterparts, appreciated the central importance of patronage in the political process. In resisting responsible government, therefore, they were not merely resisting an *idea*; they were also resisting the implicit suggestion that they should hand over their claim to some tangible and valuable assets. Indeed, the more the small change

25 A memorandum by LaFontaine setting out the administration's attitude towards patronage is contained in Hincks' *Reminiscences*, 98–102.
26 M.E. Nish, 'Double Majority: Concept, Practice and Negotiations, 1840–1848,' MA thesis, McGill 1966, 88. LaFontaine, however, was a more efficient administrator of patronage in Lower Canada. See Jacques Monet, *The Last Cannon Shot* (Toronto 1969), 116–7.
27 Metcalf, 'Draper,' 47–8; see also J.M.S. Careless, *The Union of the Canadas* (Toronto 1972), 70–1.

of patronage was squeezed out of their own political system, the more tenacious they became in hanging on to whatever bits and pieces of it remained at their disposal in the colonies.[28] Indeed, they did not believe that they could rule effectively without them. It was thus in defence of those bits and pieces that Bagot's successor, Sir Charles Metcalfe, made his stand.

28 See J.M. Bourne, *Patronage and Society in Nineteenth-Century England* (London 1986).

8

The Juggling of Men and Money

They represent SIR CHARLES METCALFE *as an old Indian, disliking and incapable of understanding free institutions. They paint him mounted on an elephant, the despotic ruler of oriental slaves. They boldly assert that he is a foe to 'Responsible Government'; and then, forgetting their oath of secrecy as Executive Councillors, they tell in the Assembly a variety of stories about appointments to office ...*

– Edward Gibbon Wakefield, *Colonial Gazette*, 11 December 1843

Fancy such a state of things in India, with a Mahomedan Council and a Mahomedan Assembly, and you will have some notion of my position.

– Sir Charles Metcalfe, letter to Colonel Stokes (c January 1844)

I

The new governor general had spent most of his career in the administration of the British Raj, which left him with a well-developed sense of the Crown's prerogatives and a fine contempt for 'lesser breeds without the law' – among whom he was soon counting Baldwin and LaFontaine. The challenge he laid down to them was basic: he would not be bound by the conventions of responsible cabinet government, which in the colonial context he regarded as a dangerous constitutional heresy and a practical impossibility. Moreover, he had come armed with the clearest possible instructions from the Colonial Office to recapture the powers and prerogatives of the Crown that his predecessor had so regrettably allowed to slip from his grasp. He was to respect the very limited form of individual ministerial responsibility that had been practised under Lord Sydenham, but, he had been assured, 'you are yourself the head of your administration.'[1] Hence, as he was soon demonstrating through his actions, he was under no obligation to heed the advice of his Executive Council, nor, in seeking advice, would he be confined to its members. Instead, he flagrantly consulted their opponents in the Assembly, the leader of the Orange Lodge, the head of the Methodist Church, and indeed anyone he pleased. But what turned a smouldering issue into a flaming one was his determined grab for patronage. Without consulting his ministers, and at times without even informing them, he began to fill the offices of government with his own appointees, who were of course opponents of Baldwin and LaFontaine. From top to bottom, patronage was distributed to tories rather than reformers, from the speakership of the Legislative Council to the lowly post of district clerk of the peace – including some posts that ministers had already offered to their own friends and supporters.[2] There could have been no more public advertisement that the ministry no longer wielded effective power.

The ministry did not claim an exclusive right to patronage, but its leaders also knew that they could not long survive in office in the face of so direct a challenge. Hincks, displaying his usual cleverness, urged Baldwin to follow a pre-emptive policy in Upper Canada by recommending tories for appointment as district councillors and magistrates, which, he believed, would both pacify Metcalfe and weaken the conservative attack in the next election, but his advice was rejected as too cynical.[3] Meanwhile, within the Assembly itself the control of patronage was becoming ever more critical. The problem lay not with LaFontaine's side of the coalition but with Baldwin's, whose restless Upper Canadian reformers were becoming increasingly unreliable. They had deserted him before, and unless 'purchased to their duty' (to resurrect Governor Simcoe's apt phrase) they were likely to do so again. 'Really,' Hincks exclaimed in frustration, 'such men as Thorburn, Smith, Hopkins, Roblin, etc. are worse than enemies. We never know where to find them.'[4]

1 Colonial Secretary Lord Stanley to Metcalfe, 29 May 1843, quoted in J.M.S. Careless, *The Union of the Canadas* (Toronto 1972), 79. See also *Dictionary of Canadian Biography*, VII, 603–8.
2 George E. Wilson, *The Life of Robert Baldwin* (Toronto 1933), 174–83; and J.M.S. Careless, 'Robert Baldwin,' in J.M.S. Careless, ed., *The Pre-Confederation Premiers: Ontario Government Leaders, 1841–1867* (Toronto 1980) 126
3 R.S. Longley, *Sir Francis Hincks* (Toronto 1943), 129
4 Hincks to a friend, 5 Nov. 1843, quoted in M.E. Nish, 'Double Majority: Concept, Practice and Negotiations,' MA thesis, McGill 1966, 88

From Metcalfe's point of view, however, it was such men as Hincks, with their 'violence of party spirit,' who were precisely the sort of upstarts and rebels who needed to be put in their place. 'The council,' he wrote contemptuously, 'are now spoken of by themselves and others generally as the "ministers," the "administration," the "cabinet," the "government," and so forth. Their pretensions are according to this new nomenclature. They regard themselves as a responsible ministry, and expect that the policy and conduct of the governor shall be subservient to their views and party policy.'[5] It was his duty to disabuse them. And, he correctly perceived, the way to do it was through an attack upon their administration of patronage.

'I am required,' he claimed inaccurately, 'to give myself up entirely to the council; to submit absolutely to their dictation; to have no judgment of my own; to bestow the patronage of the government exclusively on their partisans; to proscribe their opponents; and to make some public and unequivocal declaration of my adhesion to these conditions.' He was therefore prepared for 'a rupture with the council' because 'I cannot consent to the be tool of a party.'[6] But for all his overweening arrogance, Metcalfe was no fool. He could see where the battle lines would be drawn and carefully prepared his ground.

Baldwin and LaFontaine were extremely vulnerable on the issue of patronage, for two reasons. First, their own hesitant and generally inexpert handling of it had caused widespread dissension among the Upper Canadian reformers, many of whom were puzzled by its meagreness or outraged that plums were still being given to those they regarded as less than deserving. 'Too much anxiety to do justice to all parties,' one dismayed reformer protested, 'will be the rock on which the present administration will split.'[7] Second, and even more serious, was the potential of the issue to unite their normally faction-ridden opponents. For if there was one thing upon which Upper Canadian conservatives of every stripe were agreed it was that *any* reform control of patronage was an affront to constitutional government and wholly illegitimate. And if that were not enough, many in Upper Canada (and the entire 'British' party in Lower Canada) regarded the very notion of LaFontaine and A.N. Morin systematically doling out patronage to French Canadians as positively sickening and treasonable. Metcalfe,

5 J.W. Kaye, *Life of Lord Metcalfe*, II (London 1854), 478, Metcalfe to Stanley, 12 May 1843
6 Ibid.
7 A.N. Buell to Baldwin, 4 Aug. 1843, quoted in Wilson, *Baldwin*, 183

moreover, was well aware of all this: from the moment he arrived his mailbag had overflowed with their shrieks of outrage.[8]

The anticipated rupture, when it finally came, was ostensibly provoked by a small and venal piece of patronage – the governor's appointment of a tory as clerk of the peace of the Dalhousie District.[9] This was exactly the sort of patronage the ministry could ill afford to surrender without a fight, even at the risk of appearing unduly partisan and small-minded, and having the larger issue of principle obscured. The result was a frosty confrontation with Metcalfe in which Baldwin and LaFontaine demanded that in future he should make 'no appointment, and no offer of an appointment, without previously taking the advice of the Council,' and that 'in deciding, after taking their advice, [he] should not make any appointments prejudicial to their influence.'[10] When Metcalfe confirmed his intention of continuing to dispense patronage without their advice, Baldwin, LaFontaine, and all but one of the other executive councillors thereupon resigned.

II

The one councillor who did not resign was Dominick Daly,[11] a survivor from an earlier era of imperial rule and, for the 1840s, something of a political curiosity – an avid place-man who studiously avoided politics, preferring instead to affect the manner of a permanent civil servant. And though he held a seat in the Assembly (he had been elected in Lower Canada under Sydenham's auspices), he appears to have regarded it as a handicap, for he rarely spoke or otherwise participated in the Assembly's proceedings. On the most charitable interpretation of his career, he was a useful administrator who 'knew the ropes' and loyally served whatever regime held power, and perhaps for that reason, and his impeccably uncontroversial demeanour, he had been kept on by Baldwin and LaFontaine. Less charitably, he may be seen as a political Vicar of Bray who would do anything to avoid being dropped from the official payroll, a sycophant who, in J.C. Dent's pithy summation,

8 He also received letters and addresses praising the ministry, which only served to confirm his belief that his true mission was to combat 'partyism.' See Stephen Leacock, *Baldwin, LaFontaine, Hincks* (Toronto 1907), 166–8.
9 Wilson, *Baldwin*, 184
10 Ibid., 185
11 *DCB*, IX, 189–93

'passed his life in coming to the rescue of the strongest.'[12] Whatever his true métier, it was definitely not government leadership. Yet suddenly, like a rabbit ferretted from its hole, he had been thrust forward out of the shadows into the unaccustomed heat and glare of the day. He was now himself the entire Executive Council – a solitary figure on the government front bench, upon whom rained the taunts and jeers of the Baldwin-LaFontaine majority. Since no new administration could be formed, it was in this state that the legislature was prorogued on 12 December 1843.

The governor general was in a relatively strong position. There was no principle of government at stake, he declared in words that were sure to resonate effectively among the Upper Canadian conservatives, but only a question of whether 'the patronage of the Crown should be surrendered to the Council for the purchase of Parliamentary support.'[13] In the meantime, of course, he had full control of that patronage, as well as the approval of the Colonial Office, and, if needed, the backing of British troops. He also had some influential voices raised on his behalf, including those of Egerton Ryerson, the Methodist leader, and Isaac Buchanan, a politically prominent business magnate.[14] Yet if Sydenham's bankrupt theory of gubernatorial prime ministership were to be tried once again, there had to be some semblance of an Executive Council, and it was here – surprisingly, in view of the rich inducements he had to offer – that Metcalfe ran into trouble: there were too few takers for the positions available. Such was the odium attached to the acceptance of office that again and again lucrative posts were offered only to have the chosen recipients back away. Even former Sydenhamites such as S.B. Harrison, who supported Metcalfe (or, what amounted to the same thing, opposed Baldwin and LaFontaine), could not be drawn in, with the result that nine months after the resignation of the reformers there was still no properly constituted Executive Council.

Instead, a provisional triumvirate had been formed, consisting of Daly (who remained the only one to hold an executive portfolio and draw a salary, but who was otherwise practically useless) and two other advisers, each of whom was more politically inclined but whose alliance was highly suspect and indeed astonishing. One was William Henry

---

12 *The Last Forty Years: The Union of 1841 to Confederation* (Toronto 1881; reissued 1972), 126
13 Governor's statement, *Kingston Chronicle*, 2 Dec. 1843, quoted in Wilson, *Baldwin*, 187
14 DCB, XI, 127

Draper, the enigmatic moderate conservative who had played such a key role as Sydenham's agent in steering the pro-union resolutions through the old Upper Canadian Assembly (thus earning for himself the undying enmity of the Compact tories), and who had so resourcefully tried to rescue Bagot. He had since taken refuge in the Legislative Council, but just as he had once put his undoubted talents at Sydenham's disposal, and then Bagot's, he now emerged again to put them at Metcalfe's.[15] In this he was at least being consistent, for he was above all a supporter of the British connection – which he interpreted as requiring his unswerving support for the representative of the Crown. Consequently, he favoured union but opposed responsible government.

His astonishing partner was a horse of an opposite colour – Denis-Benjamin Viger,[16] an elderly ex *patriote* and separatist who had previously been adamant in his opposition to union but who (for reasons of his own) had supported Robert Baldwin's concept of responsible government. Various explanations have been given of Viger's participation in the triumvirate, including the onset of senility, personal envy of LaFontaine, and fear that responsible government as practised by the latter and Baldwin had worked only too well, and if continued would mean the defeat of his nationalist aspirations. All perhaps contain a certain measure of truth, but it is also possible to offer a more sympathetic interpretation: J.M.S. Careless suggests that '*le Vénérable* had grown convinced that more could presently be gained for French Canadians through their working as a distinct national bloc under a governor who desperately needed their aid, than by holding to a mongrel French-English alliance in the Assembly.'[17] But such a stance, while plausible in retrospect, was hardly a sufficient justification at the time for what he had done – it was too much the rationale of a *vendu*.

It is revealingly indicative of the gap that divided the conservative elite of Upper Canada from Lower Canada that the normally astute Draper for a time actually believed that Viger could draw substantial popular support away from LaFontaine; but when month after month went by and still Viger remained unable even to fill the Lower Canadian seats in the Executive Council, the hopelessness of the situation gradually dawned upon him. In the end, he was left with no option but to patch together a largely English-dominated administration in which

15 George Metcalf, 'William Henry Draper,' in Careless, *Pre-Confederation Premiers*, 49–51
16 *DCB*, IX, 807–17
17 *The Union*, 85. For an examination of 'la crise Metcalfe' from a Quebec perspective, see Jacques Monet, *The Last Cannon Shot* (Toronto 1969), 137–92.

LaFontaine's old post of attorney-general East was finally filled (on the seventh try) by an obscure Montreal lawyer of no parliamentary experience, one James Smith.[18] It was obvious, however, that such a ministry faced the prospect of certain defeat on a vote of confidence if it dared to meet the Assembly. Acting on Draper's advice, Metcalfe accordingly dissolved the Assembly before it could meet and issued writs for a general election, to be held in November 1844.

III

Once again, as under Sydenham in 1841, there were effectively two separate elections. In Lower Canada, though Sydenham's gerrymander had been reversed, the English were still assured of disproportionately large representation; but, perhaps because troops were not used as extensively as before, the overall result was a victory for LaFontaine, who was returned at the head of a party of twenty-five.[19] Only two of Viger's supporters were returned, and Viger himself was defeated. LaFontaine, as it turned out, was the only clear winner in either province. In Upper Canada the campaign was even more violent than that of 1841 and very nearly as corrupt: Metcalfe, following in the footsteps of Bond Head and Sydenham, threw the full weight of the Crown's influence into the struggle, with telling effect. As usual, the careful selection of polling places and the appointment of partisan returning officers went a long way towards determining the outcome. In addition, the Orange Lodge played a crucial anti-reform role, as sanctioned through an 'understanding' reached between Metcalfe and the Orange leader, Ogle Gowan.[20] Metcalfe had ostentatiously consulted Gowan while in the process of divesting himself of his reform ministers and had used his vice-regal prerogative to reserve the Secret Societies Bill (a measure designed to curb the lodge's power to intimidate), which Baldwin had successfully piloted through the legislature.[21] In return, the Orangemen supplied the strong-arm squads necessary for the effective capture of many local polls, as well as a substantial bloc of

18 Metcalf, 'Draper,' 52, and DCB, IX, 728
19 Paul G. Cornell, *The Alignment of Political Groups in Canada, 1841–1867* (Toronto 1962), 92
20 DCB, X, 309–14
21 Metcalfe's reservation of this bill, without so much as an explanation to his ministers, was cited by Baldwin as a second reason for the ministry's resignation. See Wilson, *Baldwin*, 186.

votes. Moreover, the cry of 'loyalty' was still a potent one: a call for support of the Crown could still summon an automatic response on the part of a great many Upper Canadians. The cry of 'French domination' was also widely heard (and appeared to have some substance, since the reformers had voted to move the capital from Kingston to Montreal), while the dissension in reform ranks over patronage, personalities, and issues had only worsened as the election approached. ('I am sick of reformers,' Baldwin's own election agent later moaned; 'the infernal fools, they are so very independent.')[22] Overall, these factors, when added to purely local cleavages – the 'immemorial political feuds in the ridings'[23] – produced, if not a clearly conservative, then at least an anti-reform majority in the western section of the legislature.

Baldwin was returned at the head of the most coherent Upper Canadian grouping, a party of twelve ultra-reformers, but without Hincks, who had been defeated in Oxford. The remaining thirty seats were distributed among 'ministerialists' of various political shades and degrees of commitment to the government side.[24] Some were the same moderate reformers who had drifted out of Baldwin's camp in 1841, back into it in 1842, and now out of it again. They were evidently disinclined to move constitutionally quite as far or as fast as Baldwin, and still had their eyes fixed mainly on constituency benefits, but they had no other leader and in most respects were inclined to support him. Some were moderate conservatives, pro-unionists who had no great objection to responsible government as advocated by Baldwin, as long as control of it was kept out of the hands of the ultra-reformers. In their view power should be held by a more loyal and trustworthy group – namely, themselves. Some were die-hard Compact tories, who had again exhibited remarkable success in getting themselves elected. They were very nearly as hostile towards the moderate conservatives, whom they regarded as interlopers and sell-outs, as they were towards the ultra-reformers, but otherwise they could agree on little and devoted much of their energies to their own obscure internecine feuds. And finally, there were some who were thoroughgoing opportunists whose allegiance, essentially, would go to the highest bidder. Thus, when the

22 Heyden to Baldwin, 17 Feb. 1845, quoted in Careless, *The Union*, 93
23 Paul G. Cornell, 'The Genesis of Ontario Politics in the Province of Canada,' in *Ontario Historical Society, Profiles of a Province: Studies in the History of Ontario* (Toronto 1967), 63
24 Cornell, *Alignment of Political Groups*, 17, 92

new Assembly met on 28 November 1844, it was by no means certain that this volatile mixture would in fact support the government or, if it did, that it would continue to do so for very long.

IV

The choice of Sir Allan MacNab as speaker of the Assembly had the effect of temporarily sidetracking the most prominent and irascible of the tories whose inclusion in the ministry (to which he had a strong claim) would have alienated the moderate conservatives and sorely provoked the moderate reformers. It might even have driven some of them immediately into Baldwin's camp. But MacNab had only been chosen over the Baldwin-LaFontaine candidate, A.N. Morin, by a mere three votes, which revealed just how precarious the government's position really was.[25] In the fluid political circumstances of the time three votes could change sides between divisions of the House, or over dinner, depending on the issues and personalities – and inducements – involved. And to make matters all the more uncertain, the Draper ministry was woefully short of talent and experience. Draper himself had not even stood for election to the Assembly, opting instead to lead the government from his place in the Legislative Council – which quickly proved impossible. His ministerial colleagues who did hold seats in the Assembly almost immediately began to bicker openly among themselves, while the more aggressive of them could not resist jockeying for position: it was not long before even the obscure attorney-general East, James Smith, was grandiloquently styling himself 'head of the Administration.'[26]

By the time Draper could resign from the Legislative Council and have himself returned to the Assemby through a by-election, the damage was irreversible: so many of the fickle moderate reformers had drifted away that the government was unable to muster even a bare majority on any issue of consequence. That it survived at all was due entirely to Draper's superb skill in the game of parliamentary politics – and a macabre twist of fate that left him in possession of unprecedented and unrivalled powers of patronage.

Unlike Baldwin or LaFontaine, or even, to a certain extent, MacNab, Draper was a politician with no personal following; there was literally no

25 Donald R. Beer, *Sir Allan Napier MacNab* (Hamilton, Ont. 1984), 191–2
26 Metcalf, 'Draper,' 56

group or party on which he could invariably rely whatever the circumstances. Instead he was forced to deal for support wherever he could find it, often among individuals and factions whose first instincts were to oppose him, either because they were die-hard tories who had never forgiven him for abandoning the Family Compact and who were suspicious of his cool, pragmatic (or, in their eyes, cynical) approach to politics or because they were reformers whose views on most questions were more progressive than his and who were suspicious of his links with the tories and the Anglican Church. Yet somehow he usually managed to hold their support, or at least prevent them from combining against him, but the price to be paid was high: votes had to be purchased left and right, and still his government was able to do virtually nothing (thus inspiring the famous headline: 'The Great Government Measure of the Session, the Dog Bill, Carried – the Muskrat Bill Lost').[27] He was in fact the most artful of artful dodgers and a political broker of no small genius. To friends and enemies alike he was known as 'Sweet William' for his mellifluous voice and persuasive ways, or 'the Magician' for his ability to keep a government afloat with no visible means of support.

But above all he was a juggler of men and money. Through an extraordinary and bitter irony, Metcalfe, after fighting a fierce and apparently successful rearguard action in defence of the Crown's patronage prerogative and against the principle of responsible government, had no sooner won than he was forced to surrender both. From before the time of his appointment he had been afflicted with a painful and inexorably spreading cancer of the face, the ravages of which had by the end of 1844 left him almost totally incapacitated, horribly disfigured, and under the sedation of powerful narcotics. By default, therefore, all the Crown's patronage fell into Draper's hands, making him by far the single most powerful politician in the Canadas – the first true prime minister in every sense. Now, finally, exactly as Baldwin had all along insisted should be the case, patronage was dispensed by a politician who (however reluctantly) was responsible to the legislature.

Skilful juggling, however, while it could keep the administration alive from vote to vote, was not a satisfactory basis on which to govern. It was essentially a temporary expedient, a way of buying time, and the wonder is that it worked as long and as well as it did. But no one was more acutely conscious than Draper of the impossibility of governing effectively without French support; that had been the rock on which his

27 *Examiner*, 5 Mar. 1845

ill-fated combination with Viger had foundered, and it still loomed menacingly before him. Behind all his artful dodging, therefore, lay one consistent long-term strategy, and that was to win over at least some of LaFontaine's supporters. He pursued that strategy deviously and at times brilliantly, and on at least one occasion he appears to have been on the verge of success;[28] but in the end, in spite of the offer of 'handsome emoluments,'[29] the cohesion of the French proved unbreakable: they remained loyal to LaFonatine – and LaFontaine remained loyal to Baldwin.

When all else had failed, the Magician's final trick was a disappearing act: he arranged to have himself appointed to the Court of Queen's Bench of Upper Canada, leaving behind him a government dominated by die-hard tories to face the music in the general election of 1847.

28 See Metcalf, 'Draper,' 59–62.
29 R.-E. Caron to LaFontaine, 7 Sept. 1845, quoted in Leacock, *Baldwin, LaFontaine, Hincks*, 260

9

Brokerage and the Politics of Power-Sharing

You are, of course, aware how strongly LaFontaine holds to the principle of the two majorities ... I think this quite absurd, and I am inclined to think so do you. Nevertheless I would have no objection to see it tried. I am sure it would strengthen us materially as a party ... [and] it would drive the Tories here mad ...

– Francis Hincks to Robert Baldwin, 23 September 1844

I

The general election of 1847 brought LaFontaine and Baldwin triumphantly back to power, each with clear majority support in his own province.[1] The inauguration of their ministry marked the full and unambiguous acceptance by all concerned, including the British government, of the Baldwinian version of responsible government. In effect, the control of patronage that had been so completely exercised by Draper could no longer be withheld from the reformers. Theirs was seen as a party victory, and it was assumed that they would function in office as a party government; that is, it was assumed that they would have the right to allocate patronage as they saw fit. The new governor general, Lord Elgin,[2] who had replaced Metcalfe in 1846, would do nothing to

1 Paul G. Cornell, *The Alignment of Political Groups in Canada, 1841–1867* (Toronto 1962), 22–5, 100. LaFontaine was returned at the head of a party of thirty-three, including nine English members. Baldwin's supporters numbered twenty-three, to eighteen for the Conservatives. Hincks was later declared the winner of a disputed election in Oxford, increasing the Reform total to twenty-four and reducing the Conservative total to seventeen.

2 *Dictionary of Canadian Biography*, IX, 89–93

upset this assumption. Unlike his predecessor, he had no mandate, and no desire, to be a 'partisan governor.' Instead, he aimed to establish 'a moral influence,' which, he hoped, would 'go far to compensate for the loss of power consequent on the surrender of patronage.'[3] The age of 'governor generalities' had arrived. In fact, there was no sweeping introduction of an American-style spoils system, as the opponents of party government had feared. LaFontaine and Baldwin simply picked up where Draper had left off; that is to say, they dispensed the usual patronage in the usual way, but there was no wholesale turnover of public officials. Over the next few years, however, the public service was considerably expanded as the reform ministry pressed ahead with policies that expanded the role of government generally, and the newly created posts naturally went mainly to supporters of the winning side.[4]

Yet in the long run it was not the final establishment of responsible government that mainly distinguished the LaFontaine-Baldwin administration, nor even its record of progressive and reformist legislation in such areas as education and municipal government, but rather its entrenchment of a unique system of power-sharing. This was basically the system that the two leaders had successfully introduced in 1842–43, only now their positions were more secure, for not only had the British government decided not to intervene, but the whole course of the Draper administration had served to underline the essential practicality, even the necessity, of their approach. They were thus free to extend their system, refine it, and pragmatically adapt it to fit the political circumstances of the time. To satisfy Baldwin – who insisted that the conventions of Westminster-style responsible government could not be stretched to include a dual premiership – LaFontaine was nominally prime minister.[5] But in reality the ministry was a dual one in which they functioned as co-premiers, with each responsible for filling his allotted share of cabinet posts, the one in effect leading the government in matters pertaining to Lower Canada and the other in effect leading it in matters pertaining to Upper Canada.[6] Within the Assembly, their

3 Quoted in J.M.S. Careless, *The Union of the Canadas* (Toronto 1967), 116

4 J.E. Hodgetts, *Pioneer Public Service: An Administrative History of the United Canadas* (Toronto 1955), 56–7; and J.M.S. Careless, 'Robert Baldwin,' in J.M.S. Careless, ed., *The Pre-Confederation Premiers: Ontario Government Leaders, 1841–1867* (Toronto 1980), 133–4

5 George E. Wilson, *The Life of Robert Baldwin* (Toronto 1933), 243

6 Careless, 'Baldwin,' 132; and R.M. and J. Baldwin, *The Baldwins and the Great Experiment* (Toronto 1969), 215–18

respective parties retained their separate identities; that is to say, it was a genuine coalition and not a blending or amalgamation of the two.

Given the notoriously unstable nature of Upper Canadian party alignments, however, the question was bound to arise of whether, or to what extent, such a system of government required adherence to the principle of 'concurrent' or 'double' majorities. In other words, in addition to the ministry's maintaining the confidence of the Assembly as a whole – which was now totally accepted as the basic principle of responsible government – did each *section* of the ministry (the Lower Canadian under LaFontaine, the Upper Canadian under Baldwin) have to maintain majority support *within its own section of the Assembly*? There could be no doubt that the ministry would enjoy a considerable advantage if each of its sections could do so. But there could also be no doubt that it was not a constitutional requirement. The real question, therefore was whether it was an *operative* requirement. And if it was, what were its implications? Did it mean, for example, that 'sectional legislation should be the exclusive concern of the representatives from the affected section, and the majority from each section should govern only that section?'[7] Or did it mean only that the ministry should in general maintain the confidence of both sections of the House, but that on a day-to-day basis sectional exclusivity in the passage of legislation was not required? Also, considered more broadly, did it mean that, in future, whichever party won a majority in its own section would automatically be entitled to claim all of the ministerial seats for that section?

Both LaFontaine and Baldwin rejected the extreme sectionalist position, but otherwise their viewpoints diverged widely. LaFontaine supported the double majority principle in theory but recoiled from accepting its practical implications. In particular, as he had shown by his rebuffing of Draper's overtures in 1845, he was not prepared to participate in a coalition with the Upper Canadian conservatives. But it was only with great difficulty that he had been able to restrain some of his colleagues from doing so (for, following his own logic, they could see no reason why they should be deprived of lucrative ministerial positions for the sake of an alliance with the Upper Canadian reformers, who were plainly a minority in their own section.[8]) At the time, however,

7 M.E. Nish, 'Double Majority: Concept, Practice and Negotiations, 1840–1848,' MA thesis, McGill 1966, 146
8 See R.S. Longley, *Sir Francis Hincks* (Toronto 1943), 144–9.

responsible government had not been conceded; now that it had been, it was unlikely that LaFontaine would be able to prevent such a coalition from being formed should the situation arise again. Baldwin, by contrast, consistently denied the validity of the double majority principle in theory but, as it turned out, was prepared to accept its implications in practice. Hence, when in June 1851 he failed to secure majority support in his own section in a division on a strictly sectional issue – an opposition motion to abolish the Upper Canadian Court of Chancery – he promptly resigned.[9]

On the face of it there could hardly have been a more stunning demonstration of the practical force of the double majority principle: Baldwin still had the confidence of the House as a whole, since the motion had been defeated by a margin of thirty-four to thirty, yet had regarded a defeat in one section as sufficient to compel his resignation from the ministry. But beyond that obvious fact the matter remained shrouded in ambiguity. The other Upper Canadian ministers did not resign with him, nor did he ask them to, and in giving reasons for his resignation he cited almost everything *except* the double majority principle – including the rise of 'mere demagogue clamour,' which he blamed for the defection of his former supporters.[10] The principle remained, as Stephen Leacock put it, 'the will o' the wisp of the rival politicians.'[11] But it was a will o' the wisp that would haunt every ministry that followed.

As LaFontaine and Baldwin had shown, however, if a ministry possessed majority support in both sections of the Assembly, it could enjoy the luxury of appearing to comply with the double majority principle without having either to define it or declare undying adherence to it. Not surprisingly, this was Hincks' preferred approach. And since no realistic alternative was ever found, it remained a convenient evasion to the end of the Union era. The trouble arose, as it did for Baldwin, when a ministry lost its majority in one section or the other, for to do so was to advertise weakness, nearly always to invite trouble, and frequently to compel resignation.

Finally, the double majority principle itself was in many respects less important, and less influential in the long run, than the assumptions

9 To add insult to injury, the author of the motion was Baldwin's old enemy, William Lyon Mackenzie. See Wilson, *Baldwin*, 284–90.
10 Ibid., 289
11 *Baldwin, LaFontaine, Hincks* (Toronto 1907), 259

and understandings on which it rested. This was something the Upper Canadian tories understood perfectly, which explains their persistent inclination to view it purely in instrumental terms. For them it was a means of combating the centralizing tendencies of the Union and of maintaining the essential separateness of Upper Canada. In this attitude, ironically, they were closer to the Lower Canadian French than to any other group.[12] Hence, in spite of the apparent absence of consensus, the Union of the Canadas was not ungovernable. What was required to make it work was above all a tacit acknowledgment by each ministry of the validity of the old provincial boundaries, for once that acknowledgment was made, other political arrangements became more readily negotiable – such as the operation of government on a double majority basis as far as possible; the sharing of executive power on a mutually acceptable basis; and the distribution of patronage within each section by the members of the cabinet drawn from that section.

II

To maintain such a system required continuous attention to the art of brokerage politics, especially in the Upper Canadian section of the coalition. Baldwin's party, for example, was never as cohesive and disciplined as LaFontaine's. Many of its moderate reform members were in fact quasi-independents whose support generally had to be secured issue by issue – perhaps in this respect accurately reflecting the view of their constituents, who likewise tended to show little consistent attachment to reform principles. In consequence, in addition to dealing with their French colleagues, the Upper Canadian ministers had also constantly to deal with their own loose assemblage of supporters – a collection of local patrons, aspiring brokers, disappointed claimants for office, individualists, and political mavericks, among whom there were also potentially disruptive differences of region, religion, and business connections. As Donald Swainson observes: 'Backbenchers might be simple tools of powerful regional leaders; often, however, they were men of substance and local power who could and did challenge their party leaders, sometimes successfully.'[13]

Moreover, the reformers' appetite for patronage was insatiable. As James Morris (who would later be appointed postmaster-general) wrote

12 Nish, 'Double Majority,' 141–2
13 'Sir Henry Smith and the Politics of the Union,' *Ontario History* 66 (1974): 161

to Baldwin: 'Now that we have fully assumed the helm of state you will feel no surprise at the numberless missives which reach you asking for all sorts of favors, reasonable and unreasonable.'[14] Little wonder, therefore, that Baldwin attached such importance to brokerage skills in the filling of the Upper Canadian ministerial posts. Francis Hincks was of course indispensable, becoming in effect minister of finance (inspector-general), and in short order places were found for two more of the ablest brokers of their time, William Hamilton Merritt (who thus completed his passage across the political spectrum from tory to reform) and the young John Sandfield Macdonald,[15] the leading reform politician of Glengarry and the eastern counties – and the political heir of the old tory grand patron, Alexander Macdonnell, a line of succession that accurately reflected the evolution of the Upper Canadian clientele system as a whole in this period.

In its main features, the form of power-sharing that became entrenched in Union politics was of a type that has since become fairly common in culturally segmented societies and is now generally identified in the literature of political science as 'consociational democracy.' Its basic premise, as a theory, is that stable, electorally based political systems can function successfully in societies that are not culturally homogeneous as long as the following conditions are met: (1) at the top, power must be shared through some form of coalition, either formally or informally; (2) the political leaders of each cultural segment must be willing (and sufficiently trusted by their respective communities) to make the deals and compromises necessary to maintain the system (a process of brokerage usually labelled 'elite accommodation'); (3) proportionality must be observed in the legislature and in the distribution of government benefits, including patronage; and (4) in general the principle of 'mutual veto' must take precedence over the principle of rule by simple majority. The first three of these conditions obtained, if not perfectly, at least to a considerable extent in the political system of the United Canadas as it took shape during the LaFontaine-Baldwin era; and while more problematical, the fourth, in the form of the double majority principle, was at least honoured in the breach in that the political cost of contravening it was shown to be high. Though the LaFontaine-Baldwin coalition foundered in 1851, the system itself proved durable. Thereafter every administration more or less was

14 Quoted in Longley, *Hincks*, 276
15 DCB, X, 462–9

modelled on theirs, and, though over the years deadlocks grew more frequent and effective coalitions harder to achieve, no practical alternative emerged until the idea of forming a federation of all the British North American colonies found currency in the 1860s – but that federation, too, would retain certain strong consociational features.[16]

III

That the Union of the Canadas came to operate in a manner different from that intended by its imperial architects, reinforcing and entrenching cultural particularisms instead of obliterating them, is perhaps not in itself very remarkable; after all, the consequences of constitutional change were as unpredictable then as they are now. But that it operated in a manner so diametrically at odds with that intended, and yet on the whole so peacefully and constructively, is very remarkable indeed and requires further explanation.

Part of the answer undoubtedly lies in the economic context, for the period of the Union also happened to be a period of sustained and at times even exponential economic growth. The working out of a new set of political arrangements and understandings thus took place within a generally favourable economic environment. This was not something for which LaFontaine and Baldwin, or for that matter any administration, could claim responsibility. The immensely productive agriculture of Upper Canada and the forest resources of Lower Canada and the Ottawa Valley needed only the right combination of external factors to produce a booming economy, and with the rising cycle of world trade after 1850, fuelled by British and American industrial growth, new steam technology, and the Crimean War (which removed competing Russian grain and Baltic timber from British markets), that combination had arisen. For example, exports of wheat and flour via the St Lawrence grew from 3,645,000 bushels in 1849 to 4,547,000 in 1850 and to 6,597,000 in 1853. By 1856 it had reached 9,391,531 bushels. There was a similarly rapid increase in timber exports, both to the United States and Britain.[17] Ironically, in so far as government played a role, it was the public investment policies of the old Family Compact regime in Upper Canada, especially in improvements to the St Lawrence waterway, that had now

16 See S.J.R. Noel, 'Consociational Democracy and Canadian Federalism,' *Canadian Journal of Political Science* 4 (1971): 15–18.
17 Careless, *The Union*, 133–4

come to fruition – largely to the benefit of their reform opponents. But by the time the Hincks-Morin coalition lost power in 1854 it was abundantly clear that the Union of the Canadas, for all its peculiar anomalies, was a goose with a demonstrable capacity for laying golden eggs. Thereafter, for all but the most extreme sectionalists, it was the underlying premise of politics that whatever changes might be contemplated, nothing ought to be done that might risk killing that goose. And since it was also clear that the two Canadas were, and for the foreseeable future would probably remain, effectively separate entities, there was thus a strong incentive for the politicians of each to seek to maintain the Union through the processes of brokerage and accommodation, processes that success had endowed with an undeniable legitimacy.

A second factor that no doubt contributed to the distinctive *modus operandi* of the Union is more problematical but perhaps ultimately no less important: namely, the capacity of each subculture to produce political leaders who possessed a sure grasp of the mechanics of brokerage politics. This was most crucial in the early formative years, for the Union began as a constitutionally complex entity, unnecessarily burdened with hostilities and with an enormous potential for disaster. That it also began with two extremely able and creative political elites suggests that the old pre-1841 provinces of Upper and Lower Canada – of which those elites were the product – possessed more sophisticated political cultures than is generally realized.

Arend Lijphart has remarked on the extraordinary development of consociational devices in the United Canadas in spite of the fact that 'not even a trace of prior consociational traditions can be detected.' While this is obviously true, in the sense that neither Upper nor Lower Canada displayed the sense of cultural pluralism of the smaller European states that were once part of the Holy Roman Empire, and subsequently evolved consociational political systems, it is misleading to conclude (as Lijphart does) that there must therefore have occurred a 'spontaneous development of a series of key consociational devices arising from the necessity of ruling a plural society in the United Province,'[18] *for that development arose out of a significantly different historical experience*. In Upper Canada, as we have seen, brokerage politics evolved out of an indigenous clientele culture and directly reflected the transition of the society as a whole towards more complex, triadic forms of economic and social interaction. So far from being 'spontaneous,' then, the growth

18 *Democracy in Plural Societies* (New Haven 1977), 128–9

after 1841 of consociational arrangements was but a natural extension of brokerage politics. It was not by accident that a key role was played by Francis Hincks, the broker *par excellence.* And though brokerage norms might have been relatively weaker in French-Canadian political culture (though that has by no means been established – they might only have been less commercially oriented), the shrewd understanding of them on the part of LaFontaine, A.N. Morin, and their successors suggests that they were by no means alien or unfamiliar. Moreover, there clearly existed in that culture, even more strongly than in Upper Canada, another of the important prerequisites for the success of a consociational system: a bond of trust between the elite and the mass of the people such that the elite were free to make the deals and accommodations necessary to ensure the system's survival. It was that bond of trust that allowed LaFontaine, for example, to work so effectively with Baldwin, A.N. Morin with Hincks, and later, George-Etienne Cartier with John A. Macdonald.

None of these embraced consociationalism as a doctrine or practised it as a matter of rigid convention. Instead, in practising it they usually trod (and occasionally crossed) the fine line that separates the pragmatic from the cynical. And even those who attempted at times to enunciate and defend the 'double majority' principle, such as John Sandfield Macdonald, would not themselves be absolutely bound by it when circumstances dictated otherwise.[19] The result was a political system that was full of anomalies and inconsistencies. Some ministries, for example, were split down the middle along Upper Canadian–Lower Canadian lines, from top to bottom; others were partially split in a variety of ways; some maintained a semblance of administrative unity; others did not; and some actually were fairly well unified. Within the legislature, governing coalitions invariably formed across segmental lines, but their actual composition, in detail, was always subject to negotiation. Within each section of a ministry, moreover, the allocation of portfolios and the determination of who would be inside the cabinet and who outside it in practice involved a good deal of political horse-trading. Even the location of the capital was settled in a supremely realistic (and roughly consociational) way: Kingston was chosen first, but proved too much of a backwater to make a suitable capital; Montreal

19 The Macdonald-Sicotte ministry remained in office, to the derision of the opposition, after sustaining a defeat in the Upper Canadian section in 1863. See Bruce W. Hodgins, 'John Sandfield Macdonald,' in Careless, ed., *Pre-Confederation Premiers,* 274–7.

THE GOVERNMENT THIMBLE-RIG.

Choosing a capital – 'Sporting Bob from York' (Robert Baldwin) has his game
exposed by Mr Punch.

was next, but proved too volatile when an English mob rioted and set fire to the legislative chambers. Thereafter, from 1849 to 1865 the capital rotated between Toronto and Quebec City. This curious arrangement worked surprisingly well until, with Confederation in the air, Ottawa became the capital in 1866.

IV

That the Union of the Canadas was an economic success is undeniable, and indeed the visible signs of that success are still very much in evidence in such things as the splendid heritage of Union-era architecture and in the many contemporary institutions, both public and private, that arose originally out of its burgeoning growth. But what is less commonly acknowledged, perhaps because the evidence is less materially visible, is that the Union was also a political success. To view it merely as a prelude to the greater political act of Confederation, or as a 'problem' that Confederation solved, is grossly to undervalue its very real and very great achievements, not only legislatively in specific areas of public policy such as education, municipal government, social services, and communications, important though these were, but above all in its evolution of a unique political system that was in some respects in advance of any other in the world at that time.

It is useful to view the Union of the Canadas in comparative perspective. It was not without its defects, but no other form of government anywhere was conspicuously more successful in providing its people with a framework of peace and order, or in maintaining their rights and freedoms as individuals and as communities, or in generally supporting conditions favourable to the growth of economic, social, and religious institutions. It must be remembered that in the mid-nineteenth century the United States, for all its commitment to the idea of liberty, allowed nearly four million of its people to be held in slavery, a contradiction that would shortly tear the republic apart; in Europe for the most part the price of peace was still acceptance of autocratic rule, while in Britain it was deference to an aristocracy (except in Ireland, where submission was required). No student of European politics, especially, can fail to be struck by one startling feature of the political system of the United Canadas: virtually everything was open to negotiation. In contrast to the bi- or multi-ethnic European states and empires, where the forces of popular democracy were either suppressed or kept under tight rein and inter-elite bargaining restricted to a limited range of traditional rights and privileges, in the United Canadas the combination of responsible government and brokerage politics produced a system in which practically all the important areas of public policy (with the exception of external relations, which remained in the hands of the imperial government) were dealt with through the processes of bargaining, deal-making, and compromise; in other words, almost everything was legitimate grist to the political mill.

The result was a politics of byzantine complexity. At its worst it was flagrantly cynical, utterly scurrilous, and more than a little corrupt. But at its best it was innovative, practical, and wonderfully civilized. Such were its intricacies and so finely balanced were its mechanisms that almost invariably among the leading politicians, both French and English, those who were winners and held power had also at some point been losers and sat in opposition, and *vice versa*. And those who were on opposite sides of the House had always to keep in mind that in the next coalition they might well become allies; they were thus naturally disinclined to treat politics as a winner-take-all proposition, a zero-sum game. Moreover, the quality of decision-making does not appear to have suffered unduly: there were fewer stalemates than might reasonably have been expected, and the overall record of governmental accomplishment compares favourably with that of any other era, either before or since.

10

The Majoritarian Challenge

Population of Canada West: 952,000
Population of Canada East: 890,000

– *Census of the Canadas*, 1851–52

The representation of the people in Parliament should be based upon Population ...
without regard to any separating line between Upper and Lower Canada.

– George Brown, *Debate on the Representation Bill*, March 1853

I

Given the cultural duality of the two Canadas, any system of democratic political union between them was bound to be fragile. But it was nevertheless possible – if each section was governed by a political elite that recognized the perils of fragmentation and was willing to make the overarching accommodations and compromises that were essential to the preservation of such a union.[1] If, however, the political elite of either section were to split into those who supported and practised accommodation and those who did not (because of nationalist aspirations, for example – or because they were enamoured of some clear-cut doctrine, such as unqualified majority rule), the system would be placed at risk. And if electorally the non-accommodationists were to secure a majority of seats in their section, the system would become unsustainable.

---

1 This is one of the fundamental prerequisites of consociational democracy. See Arend Lijphart, *Democracy in Plural Societies* (New Haven 1977).

Of the Upper Canadian ministers in the reform coalition no one, not even Baldwin himself, understood this more perfectly or practised accommodative, consociational politics more constantly than Francis Hincks – whose career, ironically, has generally been interpreted, even by charitable biographers, as notable mainly for clever opportunism, and by the less than charitable, for constancy to nothing beyond the cynical advancement of his own private ambitions and interests.[2] Yet for all his undoubted cynicism, fondness for devious tactics, and seemingly ecumenical willingness to deal with anyone, from a consociational perspective there is also discernible in his actions (as well as in his writings) a consistent core of political belief and, following from that belief, a consistent sense of political purpose.

Above all, Hincks believed in the Union of the Canadas. He had supported it enthusiastically from the very beginning, both for its boundless economic potential and as an instrument for the achievement of responsible government. But earlier than practically any other Upper Canadian – possibly even as early as his correspondence with LaFontaine in 1839–40 – he had caught a dazzling glimpse of just how great and original an achievement it could ultimately become; and from that moment he had thrown himself wholeheartedly into the struggle to make it work. In the process, his political career had blossomed. The Union was the larger arena for his talents that he had always sought, and he delighted in the challenge of its dual, infinitely complex, multi-dimensional politics. As Baldwin's Upper Canadian lieutenant and the Union's inspector-general (minister of finance), he had carried an enormous workload and had thrived on it, becoming the administration's indispensable catalyst. 'During all important events, Hincks was almost ubiquitous: consulting here, arguing there, convincing, pleading and interfering.'[3]

---

2 R.S. Longley's *Sir Francis Hincks* (Toronto 1943) is distinctly ambivalent about many of the twists and turns in his career. William G. Ormsby's 'Francis Hincks,' in J.M.S. Careless, ed., *The Pre-Confederation Premiers: Ontario Government Leaders, 1841–1867* (Toronto 1980), is cautiously favourable, associating him with 'the politics of consensus and management' (193). The entry in the *Dictionary of Canadian Biography*, XI, 406–16 (also by Ormsby), is unsympathetic. For a hostile indictment of his career, focusing on his involvement in numerous railway and other private deals while minister of finance, see Gustavus Myers, *The History of Canadian Wealth* (Chicago 1914; reissued Toronto 1972), 170–83. Casual hostile references in general works abound: see, e.g., R.T. Naylor, *Canada in the European Age* (Vancouver 1987), 368–73.
3 M.E. Nish, 'Double Majority: Concept, Practice and Negotiations, 1840–1848,' MA thesis, McGill 1966, 304

Yet in spite of an unprecedented record of legislative achievement, and the putting into place of virtually a new system of government, by 1851 there were ominous signs that the Upper Canadian half of the coalition (which was itself a coalition of sorts) was rapidly falling apart, both in the Assembly and in the country. Hence, while Baldwin's resignation over his defeat on the Court of Chancery bill had come as a shock, the defeat itself had not come as a total surprise, nor could it be dismissed as an accidental outcome, caused perhaps by poor attendance in the House. For the issue in fact had been carefully picked and the dissension had been orchestrated.

The geographical locus of that dissension – in what by this time had become a familiar paradox of Upper Canadian politics – lay in the politically restless, economically prosperous agrarian communities of the western peninsula, which had spawned yet another radical movement. Its adherents were known, satirically at first, as 'Clear Grits,' in derision of their pretensions to political purity. But they had liked the connotation and had appropriated the name as their own.

II

The Clear Grits were in certain respects typical frontier populists, and as such shared many of the social and political outlooks of their counterparts in the American mid-west.[4] They believed in progress – and in their own ability to achieve it; they believed in individual equality – of opportunity but not of condition; they believed in private property – and implicitly in their own right to lots of it; they believed in minimal government and low taxes – which they equated with freedom; and they believed in democracy, in the form of universal adult male suffrage and the widest possible application of the elective principle to the institutions of government – which they assumed would ensure the rule of men like themselves. Some were no doubt influenced by the Chartists, the Cobdenites, and other contemporary movements of British radicalism whose ideas had crossed the Atlantic with new immigrants. Others

4 The background and ideological affinities of the Clear Grits are examined, from different perspectives, in F.H. Underhill, 'Some Aspects of Upper Canadian Radical Opinion in the Decade before Confederation,' in Craig Brown, ed., *Upper Canadian Politics in the 1850s* (Toronto 1967), 1–16; J.M.S. Careless, 'The Toronto Globe and Agrarian Radicalism, 1850–67,' ibid., 38–63; and Fred Landon, *Western Ontario and the American Frontier* (Toronto 1941; reissued 1967), 231–7.

were simply old followers of William Lyon Mackenzie who had kept the faith since 1837 and now had Mackenzie back among them, amnestied after an exile in the United States but as vituperative and irascible as ever. Their ideology was of the left in that it placed unqualified faith in the wisdom of the common man, but belonged more generally to the right in its atomistic view of society, its emphasis on individual rights, and its denial of the claims of community. While many of their orientations were plainly American, they were also in certain respects quintessentially Upper Canadian: as surely (and, to liberal-minded opponents, as maddeningly) as any die-hard tory, for example, they believed that Upper Canada was the absolute centre of the universe (and hence, of course, the target of endless take-over plots, particularly by the Pope and his French-speaking minions).[5] Whatever the sources of their radicalism, by 1851 they constituted a clearly identifiable, increasingly organized, and highly disruptive force in Upper Canadian politics, with their own newspapers, their own coterie of journalist-politicians, several aspiring leaders (including ex-minister Malcolm Cameron, a wealthy Sarnia lumber merchant and railway speculator, who had ostentatiously split with his former colleagues in the reform cabinet),[6] and already one member, Peter Perry, elected to the Assembly in a by-election.[7]

Their presence on the political scene posed an immediate threat to the unity of Baldwin's reform party, for though the reformers still ostensibly held a majority of the Upper Canadian seats in the Assembly, they remained basically the same precarious coalition they had always been, impossible to discipline and incorrigibly prone to split into factions. They had done so on numerous occasions in the past, and now, under pressure from the Clear Grits, they began to do so once again. Their sudden forcing of Baldwin's resignation had revealed just how far the process of disintegration had gone. Thereafter the Upper Canadian half of the reform coalition was under constant siege.

---

5 'Papal agression' was a favourite theme of the Clear Grit press in the 1850s, and presumably cost the Clear Grits whatever support their program might have garnered among the substantial body of Catholic voters in Upper Canada. See J.M.S. Careless, *The Union of the Canadas* (Toronto 1967), 177.

6 DCB, X, 124–9

7 DCB, VIII, 694–9. Perry, a declared annexationist, was elected for the Third Riding of York.

III

The Clear Grit cry, predictably, was that Upper Canada was subject to 'French domination.' And since in their eyes the French were a backward, unenterprising, priest-ridden lot – in contrast, of course, to their energetic, progressive, independent selves – such an aberration was plainly intolerable and could not be allowed to continue. Following their own logic, their remedy was to reform the constitution, specifically by ending the provision whereby the two segments of the Union were equally represented in the legislature. Instead they would substitute representation by population.

'Rep by Pop' had been a fairly unremarkable plank in early Clear Grit platforms, one item among a lengthly miscellany of demands for everything from the popular election of the governor general to lower fees for lawyers. But after the census of 1851–52 confirmed that Upper Canadians had become a majority, outnumbering the French and English of Lower Canada combined, the Clear Grit leaders were quick to recognize its propaganda value and soon elevated it into the major rallying point of the movement.[8] Its advantages were obvious: it was simple, easily understood, and it had about it a nice ring of moral virtue that appealed greatly to a certain Upper Canadian sensibility; one did not have to be a Clear Grit to be attracted by it. Political memories, it seems, are either very long or very short, depending on whose advantage is being served. Hence the tendency of many Upper Canadians to forget that only ten years previously, when they were in a minority, they had regarded full segmental equality as a necessary condition of union with Lower Canada – and had spurned as anathema the very same notion of representation by population that they now increasingly demanded.

Yet the public's fickleness on this question should not be exaggerated. In spite of its obvious appeal and growing acceptance, 'Rep by Pop' did not dominate completely, nor, electorally, did the Clear Grits. In fact, nothing more sharply differentiates their situation from that of similar agrarian populist movements in the United States than the stiff resistance they encountered to even their most attractive and seemingly modest and reasonable demand – a demand that to Americans threatened no real disruption of the existing political order and thus was too innocuous even to be an issue. In Upper Canada, however, it was too

8 Careless, *The Union*, 181–2

explosive not to be one. In other words, the Clear Grits had to function in a drastically different political environment from that of their American counterparts, and it was that environment that in the end largely determined their behaviour. For they had to contend not only with the dual reality of the constitution but also with some extremely stubborn features of the Upper Canadian political culture, features that just as surely prevented them from achieving a complete triumph.

First, the old traditions of loyalism and toryism were by no means dead, nor in many areas had the old clientele system lost its effectiveness as an instrument of political mobilization. This was especially true of the counties east of Toronto, where even moderate reformers had been unable to make much headway – unless they were eminent (and socially conservative) patron-brokers such as John Sandfield Macdonald.[9] There the radical message of the Clear Grits fell on stony, and predominantly tory, ground. But even in the counties west of Toronto, where the Clear Grits had their greatest strength, they did not enjoy a uniformly high level of support. The west was agrarian, but also more ideologically diverse than comparable areas south of the border. Perhaps the mythical 'tory touch' was, after all, too ingrained to permit an idealized Clear Grit version of Jacksonian democracy to pass unchallenged. Or perhaps there were simply too many moderate reformers, moderate conservatives, and proud old Baldwinites to permit the idea of a dual, responsibly governed Union of the Canadas to go undefended. In consequence the radicalism of the Clear Grits never assumed the status of a new orthodoxy; many rejected some or all of its main tenets; not a few vociferously attacked the movement, its leaders, and every subversive, republican tendency for which they believed it stood.[10]

Secondly, the institutions of parliamentary government and the processes of brokerage politics were more resilient than the Clear Grits had imagined, and perhaps also more broadly in keeping with the political assumptions and outlooks of Upper Canadians in general. The result was to leave the Clear Grits, after their initial surge forward, in what is always a confusing and awkward position for a radical movement: that is, with enough strength to shake the existing system but not enough to destroy it.

9 See Bruce W. Hodgins, *John Sandfield Macdonald* (Toronto 1971), and 'John Sandfield Macdonald,' in Careless, ed., *Pre-Confederation Premiers*, 246–314; and DCB, x, 462–9.
10 Even the *Globe* initially denounced the Clear Grits as 'a miserable clique of office-seeking, bunkum-talking cormorants' (10 Jan. 1850).

And finally, the Clear Grit leaders had a machiavellian nemesis lying in wait for them in the person of Francis Hincks.

In 1851 Baldwin had been ill, exhausted by the unremitting strain of office, and without the will to continue in the face of the rank treachery of those who had so recently purported to be his friends and supporters. LaFontaine too had been sickened by developments and announced that he would retire at the end of the session.[11] For the Clear Grits it seemed a stunning, indeed almost divinely ordained, manifestation of their power. There was, however, another consequence, unintended but none the less devastating to their prospects: they had unwittingly cleared the way for the rise of Francis Hincks as Baldwin's successor and new Upper Canadian co-premier (in partnership with A.N. Morin, LaFontaine's long-time lieutenant).

Hincks was neither ill nor wearied by the struggle, nor was he prepared to see the Union's promising beginning and hopeful ideals of tolerance and moderation washed away by a tide of anti-Union bigotry. He also suspected that among the Clear Grit leaders there were more than a few place-seekers jockeying for position. Baldwin's utter distaste for what the Clear Grits stood for, which neatly summarized virtually everything he despised in politics, had ruled out any possibility of a calculated attempt to split their ranks and so derail their popular momentum. But Hincks was under no such inhibition. And with Baldwin's restraining influence removed, he was at last free to deal with them by his own methods. With unerring instinct he began to engage in a little speculative bargaining with three of their most eminent and, as it turned out, most pliable leaders: William McDougall, the editor of the leading Grit newspaper, the *North American*; Malcolm Cameron, who held a seat in the legislature and who could therefore be immediately useful; and Dr John Rolph, who did not hold a seat but who was thought to possess a considerable following of old radicals.[12] They had all expressed vehement opposition to the existing system: yet were they

11 Stephen Leacock, *Baldwin, LaFontaine, Hincks* (Toronto 1907), 353–4. LaFontaine's announcement of his intention placed Hincks in an awkward position, since it effectively immobilized the ministry and had the opposition circling for the kill. It took his proffered resignation in the end to force LaFontaine to act so that he and A.N. Morin could get on with the task of reconstruction. See Longley, *Hincks*, 389–90.
12 Rolph's entire career is a study in ambiguity and double-dealing. He could be counted upon to undermine any movement with which he was associated, which is probably what Hincks saw in him. The real puzzle is why the Clear Grits thought so highly of him as to make him one of their most prominent leaders. See DCB, IX, 683–9.

not also politicians, actual or aspiring? And if so, would they not be attracted, as such men usually were, by the offer of influence and the prospect of high office, or by the honours, emoluments, and opportunities that only membership in the inner circle could bring? These were perhaps cynical suppositions, but they were not inaccurate. When, after months of bargaining, Hincks revealed the composition of his half of a reconstructed coalition ministry, it provoked a furore: among the new members were Cameron and Rolph. And when the *North American* next published, it was obvious that McDougall too had been included in the deal: the strident voice of Clear Grittism had overnight been turned into a tame ministerial organ![13]

For Hincks it was a masterful coup. He had taken the Clear Grits, who claimed that they had come to change the rules of the game, and turned them into players of it – but as players they were rank amateurs up against a polished professional. Hincks gave the impression of making substantial concessions to obtain their conversion, but in reality what he conceded amounted to little more than the shadow of power and the empty trappings of office. The new Grit ministers, while no doubt gratified to exercise administrative authority and to dispense the patronage that went with their offices, were unable to exert a determining influence upon any issue of consequence, since within the Upper Canadian section of the ministry they were outnumbered by pro-Union moderates. In terms of policy Hincks had surrendered nothing to them, beyond an easily made commitment to carry 'reasonable' and 'progressive' measures. In return, the Clear Grit leaders had surrendered the whole of their radical platform, their leading newspaper, and, it transpired, much of their movement's momentum as a new force in politics.

Radical opinion was divided. Some Clear Grits were satisfied to have so swiftly placed two of their number in high office; but for those who believed in 'Rep by Pop' as an article of faith, the deal with Hincks was no better than a deal with the devil. Some furiously attacked it, but to no avail: their leadership was in hopeless disarray. Eventually the dissidents would regroup under the leadership of George Brown and make another bid for power, but by then their early radicalism had turned sour and paranoid, its momentum irretrievably lost. In the meantime, Hincks had deftly rescued the Upper Canadian half of the reform coalition and given it a new lease on life.

13 Careless, *The Union*, 172; see also Ormsby, 'Hincks,' 162–3.

That, however, was only the immediate result; in retrospect his achievement looms even larger, though curiously its significance is today generally overlooked. Historians tend to view the great political watershed of the Union era as the party realignment that took place following the general election of 1854, when the reform coalition finally came to an end and was replaced by a new coalition of Upper Canadian conservatives and the Lower Canadian *bleus*, an event supposedly marking the transition from reform to conservative dominance.[14] But *in terms of the political system*, the shift from the Hincks-Morin ministry to the MacNab-Morin ministry that followed it was in no significant respect a break with the past; it represented continuity rather than change. A more critical turning point had occurred three years previously, when not just the regime but the system itself had been in danger of disintegrating. By opportunely co-opting the Clear Grit leaders, thus broadening the basis of the governing coalition – and more importantly, stopping the ominous shrinking of the middle ground of Upper Canadian politics – Hincks managed to preserve both, with profound consequences for the future of the Union.

IV

The presence of two Clear Grit ministers in a government dedicated to the maintenance of a dual union based on the principle of equal representation was an extraordinary – if somewhat tainted – demonstration of elite accommodation in practice. But it was a practice that, if the results of the 1851 and 1854 general elections are to be taken as indicative, was by no means rejected by the Upper Canadian public. In 1851 the reformers under Hincks were returned with eighteen seats, the same number of seats they had held at the time of dissolution.[15] In 1854 (in a legislature enlarged to sixty-five members from each section) they increased their number of seats to twenty-five, overcoming a strong challenge from the revived Clear Grits under George Brown, who managed to win only fourteen.[16] Hincks himself stood for election in Oxford South, in what was supposedly the heart of Clear Grit territory, and was returned with the largest majority he had ever won, in spite of

14 See Paul G. Cornell, *The Alignment of Political Groups in Canada, 1841–1867* (Toronto 1962), 36–43.
15 Ibid., 103
16 Ibid., 105

concerted efforts by Brown and William Lyon Mackenzie to unseat him.[17]

The Hincks-Morin ministry, however, was narrowly defeated by a combined vote of conservatives, Clear Grits, and Lower Canadian *rouges*. And in the jockeying that ensued, it was an aggregation of old tories and moderate conservatives who came out on top – with Hincks' connivance. Their nominal leader was Sir Allan MacNab, but their guiding spirit was the young John A. Macdonald, a moderate conservative with close ties to banking, insurance, and railway interests – and a political broker of genius, an apt pupil of William Henry Draper, cast in the same mould as Hincks himself. He was also, like Hincks, a fervent believer in the value of the Union.[18]

Macdonald is generally acknowledged to have been the broker of the deal that led to the formation of the MacNab-Morin administration (with himself in the key Upper Canadian portfolio of attorney-general West), but it is also noteworthy that Hincks played an important, if secondary, brokerage role. Again acting as the nemesis of the Clear Grits, the latter had thrown the full weight of his support behind the new administration.[19] This, as Macdonald well knew, was critical to its survival. In the Upper Canadian half of the Assembly the conservatives were in a minority, outnumbered thirty-nine to twenty-six by the other two parties combined. But the larger of the two groups, the reformers, were notoriously unstable: there was a strong possibility that in opposition a substantial number of them would be tempted to find common cause with the Clear Grits and so render the government's position untenable. To preclude such a result, Hincks himself provoked a split in the reform ranks by carrying eighteen of the party's members with him in support of Macdonald and a new coalition with their old ally and colleague, A.N. Morin, leaving only six in opposition. He would not participate in the new ministry: gathering clouds of scandal over his personal financial dealings had made him, he declared, a 'governmental impossibility.'[20]

17 Ormsby, 'Hincks,' 181
18 Macdonald was first elected in 1844. His substantial career in Union politics is examined in Donald Creighton, *Sir John A. Macdonald: The Young Politician* (Toronto 1952); and J.K. Johnson, 'John A. Macdonald,' in Careless, ed., *Pre-Confederation Premiers*, 197–245.
19 Longley, *Hincks*, 304–7
20 Ormsby, 'Hincks,' 183. See also Paul Romney, 'The Ten Thousand Pound Job: Political Corruption, Equitable Jurisdiction and the Public Interest in Upper Canada 1852–6,' in David H. Flaherty, ed., *Essays in the History of Canadian Law*, II (Toronto

But for his services he demanded, and was given, some major concessions – including the privilege of naming two members to the cabinet. His nominees were Robert Spence,[21] a wily pro-Union politician who had long been a thorn in the side of the Clear Grits, and John Ross,[22] Robert Baldwin's son-in-law and the president of the Grand Trunk Railway. Together they made a perfect Hincksian legacy to the new regime.

Obviously, the new conservative-*bleu* coalition was as much the product of brokerage politics as the old reform one had been: the deal that brought it into existence was essentially a matter of English-French elite accommodation, rather than an expression of the popular will; the tacit understanding that underlay it was still mutual acceptance of the Union's dual, consociational structure; and even the procedures and exigencies of coalition-building remained basically the same. They still required a two-stage system of brokerage, in that to form a government it was necessary to deal for support first within, and then across, segmental lines. The only transformation that took place was therefore in the personnel of the Upper Canadian half of the administration. But the new conservative ministers were, like Hincks, believers in the Union and avid promoters of economic development, and even suspect old tories like MacNab were closely tied to railway companies and commercial interests.[23] No less than their predecessors, they would be aware that their capacity to promote such enterprises depended in the last resort upon their political alliance with the French.

The combination supporting the MacNab-Morin ministry, however, was to prove more cohesive than previous combinations had been, and more tenacious in its grasp on power. Shortly before it was formed Macdonald had written to one of his associates: 'Our aim should be to enlarge the bounds of our party so as to embrace every person desirous of being counted as a *progressive Conservative.*'[24] Such a party had been difficult to mould in opposition, but in government, in full control of office and patronage, and under Macdonald's clever tutelage, something very close to it did in fact develop out of the moderate conservative

---

1983), 143–99. Ever resourceful, Hincks cushioned his fall by securing a choice plum of imperial patronage: in 1856 he was appointed governor of Barbados (DCB, XI, 414).

21 DCB, IX, 735–6
22 DCB, X, 631–3
23 See Donald R. Beer, *Sir Allan Napier MacNab* (Hamilton, Ont. 1984), 264–354.
24 Creighton, *Macdonald*, 199

and Hincksite reform elements in the coalition, becoming recognizably and by its own designation the *Liberal-Conservative party*. Within Upper Canada this was the party most in tune with the evolution of the clientele system towards a more complex, triadic form in which the brokerage role was paramount. It therefore functioned both horizontally, as an instrument of elite accommodation between the two segments of the Union, and vertically, as an instrument linking the clientele system in the the townships and districts, where the small change of patronage was important, to the cabinet and legislature, where large urban business interests, most notoriously the railways, were major elements in the political process.[25]

Over a period of nearly eight years (1854–62), through two general elections and five ministries (MacNab-Morin, MacNab-Taché, Taché-Macdonald, Macdonald-Cartier, Cartier-Macdonald), the Liberal-Conservative party's grip on office and power was unbroken (except in 1858 for a period of *two days* – the latter being the entire lifespan of the bizarre 'short administration' of George Brown and A.A. Dorion).[26] The Cartier-Macdonald ministry enjoyed a tenure of almost four years, making it the longest administration in the Union's history. And for all but two of the thirteen years before Confederation the Liberal-Conservatives were either the governing party or participants in an even larger governing coalition.

Its Upper Canadian section, however, was less secure than this record would seem to suggest, for although as a party it was electorally strong, it was by no means electorally dominant. Indeed, in the 1857–58 general election it failed by a narrow margin to hold its majority, being outnumbered in the new House by opposition reformers, thirty-three to twenty-eight; in the 1861 general election it again fell short of a majority, although this time it pulled even with the reformers, twenty-nine to twenty-nine, and secured the support of six 'coalition' reformers for a total of thirty-five; and in the final Union general election, in 1863, the positions were once more reversed, with the reformers coming out on top, thirty-eight to twenty-two.[27] Nevertheless, in spite of this fairly regular swing of the electoral pendulum (which was more or less a continuation of the pattern of pre-Union politics), there was no

25 For Macdonald's management of party and patronage in this period, see Johnson, 'Macdonald,' 209–19; and Gordon T. Stewart, 'John A. Macdonald's Greatest Triumph,' *Canadian Historical Review* 63 (1982): 3–33.
26 *DCB*, x, 97–8; see also Creighton, *Macdonald*, 261–70.
27 Cornell, *Alignment*, 45, 49, 55

corresponding alternation in office; instead, the Liberal-Conservatives normally managed to carry on even when in a minority. There were a number of reasons for this – including the presence in the legislature of some highly pliable 'independent' members – but above all Macdonald had the good fortune to face a profoundly divided reform opposition. His own supporters, on the other hand, if far from perfectly harmonious, could at least be pressed into line when it counted: 'Let there be no splits,' was Macdonald's incessant refrain.[28] On the whole, they were too pragmatically inclined towards brokerage politics, and perhaps too fond of the multifarious joys of office, to imitate the self-defeating factionalism of their rivals.

The reformers who remained in opposition following the party realignment of 1854 did not unite in the face of a common enemy but rather subdivided still further into two mutually antagonistic camps, following different leaders, advocating different policies, and broadly leaning towards different ideologies. Above all, their views of the nature and future of the Union were quite irreconcilable. For practical purposes they were not a single reform party but two separate minority parties, each claiming with some justification to be the true bearer of the reform banner.

One was in effect an agrarian populist party, consisting of a hard core of Clear Grits and their sympathizers, whose electoral base was largely confined to the western peninsula. They tended to favour the introduction of American-style direct democracy, demanded immediate and unqualified 'Rep by Pop,' were hostile to what they regarded as French and Catholic domination of the government, and if necessary to break that domination they were quite prepared to see the Union dissolved; at least incipiently, they were the party of western separatism. Their leader was George Brown, a wealthy Toronto businessman and newspaper proprietor – whose views, curiously enough, were the opposite of their own on a number of these basic questions.[29] Brown was neither a populist nor a separatist. In the columns of the *Globe* he had tirelessly attacked the excesses of American democracy (in terms reminiscent of those used by John Graves Simcoe) and extolled the virtues of British parliamentary institutions. Though for 'Rep by Pop' and against

28 Johnson, 'Macdonald,' 216
29 Careless, *The Union*, 169, passim, and 'The Toronto Globe and Agrarian Radicalism,' 45–6

'French-Catholic domination,' he also strongly supported the preservation of the Union (albeit in a new form that would recognize Upper Canada's numerical superiority). What brought Brown and the Clear Grits together was their shared loathing of Hincks, Macdonald, and the whole politics of accommodation, which they believed to be effete, opportunistic, immoral, and more concerned with French than English interests. They also shared a certain rough commonality of outlook, a tendency to view the world in demonic perspective: they were anti-Catholic, anti-French, calvinistically inclined to interpret political conflict as a conflict between good and evil (with themselves, of course, invariably on the side of good). In the long run this did not make them wholly immune to the blandishments, opportunities, and sheer necessities of Union politics, but for a time it did make them virtually impossible to accommodate in a normal coalition.

The other reform group was in effect a party of whiggish liberal-unionists, or 'Baldwinites.' They were dedicated to the maintenance of responsible parliamentary government, which their revered mentor had done so much to achieve, and the Union, which he and LaFontaine had done so much to establish on a basis of duality, accommodation, and co-operative French-English leadership. They were sceptical of direct democracy, utterly opposed to 'Rep by Pop,' and in general repelled equally by Grit radicalism and Brownite intransigence. In their eyes the dual union of the Canadas, though plagued by sectionalism and currently maladministered by the Liberal-Conservatives, was still a proud achievement – and still, in the circumstances, an appropriate and practical model of government.

Their leader and guiding spirit was John Sandfield Macdonald, the patron of Glengarry and member for Cornwall, a politician who bridged the gap between the old clientele system, where the roots of his power and influence still lay, and the new world of sophisticated financial and political brokerage. As a young man he had served as Baldwin's junior ministerial colleague and had been deeply influenced by him personally and by the general intellectual milieu of the great LaFontaine-Baldwin administration; thereafter, by his own preferred description, he was not just a reformer but a 'Baldwin-reformer.' And like Baldwin, throughout his career he not only practised but also defended the *idea* of a politics based upon accommodation, moderation, and tolerance, often against the strident attacks of sectarians on both the left and the right of the ideological spectrum. Where he went beyond Baldwin was in his conscious efforts to articulate a clear, theoretically defensible statement of the double majority principle.[30]

Coming from a self-professed reformer, these efforts particularly infuriated George Brown, for, however formulated, there could be no doubt that the double majority principle was the very antithesis of representation by population. Indeed, the *Globe* fulminated, it was not a 'principle' at all, but merely an invention of the 'priest party.'[31] Yet in Sandfield's view it was the only proven recipe for stable, humane government in a union in which, as even Brown had to admit, 'we have two countries, two languages, two religions, two habits of thought and action.'[32] Moreover, like the principle of responsible government before it, it was conventionally accepted in practice by politicians who denied its validity in theory: thus John A. Macdonald, for example, while dismissing Sandfield's case for it as a 'historical essay,'[33] nevertheless left no strategem untried in his efforts to obtain majority support for his own section of the ministry from the Upper Canadian section of the House.

There was, of course, an obvious danger in attempting to turn a flexible political prescription into a constitutional requirement: it could produce an impossibly disunited administration (as might very well be the result if the Clear Grits won a majority in the upper province and the *bleus* a majority in the lower). In other words, while it might guarantee a dual administration, it could not guarantee a mutual commitment to the process of accommodation. And the latter was essential to make a dual administration work. On the other hand, there was an obvious advantage in making the governing parties more clearly responsible to their respective electorates and in guaranteeing that majority status in either section would lead automatically to participation in the administration. The unspoken assumption of the double majority principle was that politicians from both sections, even Clear Grits and *bleus*, would prefer half a loaf to nothing at all, and consequently, when it came to the point, would be willing to share power – in other words, that the context within which the double majority principle would operate would be the familiar one of brokerage politics. In the event, it was never put to the test in quite so stark a fashion; but given the record of the Union's

30 Hodgins, 'J.S. Macdonald,' 259–60
31 Hodgins, *John Sandfield Macdonald*, 35
32 Hodgins, 'J.S. Macdonald,' 259–60
33 Hodgins, *John Sandfield Macdonald*, 35

politicians, and the distinct inclination towards brokerage at the elite level in both its political cultures, there is no reason to believe that Sandfield Macdonald and the other liberal-unionist proponents of the double majority principle were being naïve or unrealistic.

In terms of popular support, the liberal-unionists were strongest in the region east of Toronto where the Clear Grits were weakest, but even in the western peninsula they were not without their following. In London, in particular, they were powerfully backed by Josiah Blackburn and the *Free Press*. Blackburn was a 'Baldwinite' and his newspaper a counterweight to George Brown's *Globe* in that it was an able exponent of the double majority principle and a consistent admirer of Sandfield Macdonald.[34] The liberal-unionist appeal was thus to a fairly widespread body of moderate reform opinion, and though this was not easily translatable into seats, it did tend to make them a disproportionately influential group in the Assembly, where they occupied a key pivotal position between the Clear Grits on the one side and the Liberal-Conservatives on the other. Their leader, moreover, for obvious reasons, was highly regarded by the French-Canadian members and had close contacts among them; should the existing coalition break down, Sandfield Macdonald was likely to be the catalyst in the formation of the next one.

Small wonder, therefore, that John A. Macdonald tried to secure his addition to the administration; but in the event Sandfield's price proved too high.[35] Though closer in outlook to John A. than to George Brown, Sandfield and his followers also differed from the Liberal-Conservatives in certain specific respects that made an accommodation between them difficult to reach. As advocates of modest, inexpensive government, for example, they were appalled by what they regarded as the Cartier-Macdonald administration's grandiosity and wanton financial extravagance; and while privately not averse to a little profitable railway speculation, on the whole they lacked the Liberal-Conservatives' close ties with the major railway companies and big business generally (though the latter may have been due more to lack of opportunity than to lack of inclination).

Hence, when the Cartier-Macdonald coalition's long string finally ran

---

34 Ibid., 42–8; see also Orlo Miller, *A Century of Western Ontario* (Toronto 1949), 126–7.
35 He demanded seats in the cabinet for himself and three of his supporters. John A.'s final offer was one additional seat plus a compromise on one pro-government Hincksite. For their negotiations, and a fascinating glimpse into the process of Union cabinet-making, see Hodgins, *John Sandfield Macdonald*, 36–7.

out in 1862 – through loss of majority support in the Lower Canadian section, which caused it to be defeated on the floor of the House – it was Sandfield Macdonald who was the logical choice as the next Upper Canadian co-premier, in collaboration with L.V. Sicotte[36] (who had engineered the crucial split in *bleu* ranks). The new administration was unusually explicit in its declarations of commitment to the double majority principle, and indeed is mainly of interest for that reason. The procedures it intended to follow, and its major goals, are summarized by Bruce W. Hodgins: 'Recognizing "the Federal character" of the Union, the government pledged itself to see that the full cabinet dealt with most matters common to both sections; the portion from each section was primarily responsible for its sectional affairs. Each half of the administration, it was agreed, "should possess the confidence of a majority of its representatives," and local legislation should not be carried against the wishes of a sectional majority ... It would establish representation by population *within* a section, hold to Ottawa as the future capital ... and finally, secure financial and administrative reorganization, rigid retrenchment and a balanced budget.'[37]

The circumstances under which it took office, however, were not conducive to such plans: ironically, the new administration, the first to state plainly that it intended to live or die by the double majority, ended up trying to govern with no secure majority in *either* section. The reason for its predicament was that it had never won an election.

V

In the previous general election, in 1861, the Liberal-Conservatives under John A. Macdonald had actually improved their standing in Upper Canada, emerging with thirty-five supporters, making them the largest party and even sending George Brown down to defeat in his own riding. In Lower Canada, however, Cartier and the *bleus* had lost ground but still managed to come out with a bare majority.[38] What brought their administration down in 1862 was a single extraordinary issue, an issue moreover that was forced upon them by external pressures. At the time the American civil war was raging in full fury, to the Union's profit but also to its peril, for its neutrality was tied to that of Britain – and the latter

36 *DCB*, XI, 821–4
37 *John Sandfield Macdonald*, 57
38 Cornell, *Alignment*, 49

was on the brink of becoming a belligerent on the side of the Confederacy. If that happened the Canadas would inevitably be invaded by the North (whose rulers in any case were fond of claiming that they had a 'manifest destiny' to govern the entire continent). Thus threatened, and bombarded by British demands that they assume greater responsibility for defence costs, the administration introduced a bill calling for a massive increase in the size of the militia, with a correspondingly massive increase in a budget that was already in deficit. This alone would have stirred controversy, but the bill also rashly included a provision for the introduction of conscription – not necessarily, but if necessary – in localities where the militia quota could not be met by volunteers. For sixteen *bleus* the bill was totally unacceptable; on second reading, urged on by Sicotte, they voted with the opposition to defeat the government sixty-one to fifty-four.[39]

The long-maintained *bleu* solidarity was thus broken, but – as subsequent conscription crises also have shown – the issue on which it broke was one that virtually ensured the disruption of the normal processes of French-English elite accommodation.

When, contrary to expectations, Britain and the United States did not go to war, the whole issue of defence faded quickly into the background – and the *bleus* who had deserted Cartier just as quickly returned to their former allegiance. The result was to leave Sicotte short of a majority. Meanwhile, Sandfield Macdonald was facing precisely the same problem in his section of the legislature, for though he had initially secured Grit support through the Hincksian ploy of including three of their leading members in the ministry, that support too proved ephemeral. George Brown, livid at the hypocrisy of his former colleagues (whose ready acceptance of office in a government pledged to the double majority – after long years of advocating 'Rep by Pop' – he regarded as 'enough to sicken a horse'),[40] was soon back in the Assembly by means of a by-election, thundering against the perfidy of it all and with the non-ministerial Grits once more solidly behind him.

Surprisingly, in view of its plight, the ministry managed to survive for eleven months, mainly through its ability to keep the frustrated Brownites at bay; for when it came to the point the latter had no wish to bring about the return of 'Cartier and Corruption' – which, as Sandfield Macdonald astutely reminded them, was the only alternative.[41] Sicotte,

39 Creighton, *Macdonald*, 321–33; and Hodgins, 'J.S. Macdonald,' 265
40 Hodgins, 'J.S. Macdonald,' 268
41 Ibid., 276.

however, had no such card to play. On 8 May 1863 the ministry was finally brought down on John A. Macdonald's motion of non-confidence. It lost the Lower Canadian vote thirty-six to twenty-eight; but, with reluctant Grit support, won the Upper Canadian, thirty-one to twenty-eight.[42]

With a dissolution of Parliament assured and new elections in the offing, Sandfield, using his brother (who was also the member for Glengarry) as intermediary, entered into a long and complicated series of negotiations: with Brown and several other leading Grits, with Luther Holton (a Lower Canadian railway magnate, financier, and former Hincksite who now supported Brown), and with A.A. Dorion, the leader of the Lower Canadian *rouge* party. The outcome was a new administration headed by himself and Dorion as co-premiers, with Holton as minister of finance. Brown did not become a minister, but his influence was clearly paramount: the double majority principle was dropped and representation by population declared to be an 'open' question (in other words, the Baldwinites and Grits had agreed to disagree). The original Grit ministers to whom Brown had taken such exception were either purged or demoted, and two of Brown's nominees were added.[43] It was this uneasily balanced aggregation that faced the electorate in the general election of 1863.

When the results were in, the most conspicuous winner was Cartier, whose reunited *bleus* were restored to their accustomed position as the largest Lower Canadian bloc. In Upper Canada, however, the result was again problematical. Nominally the Grits and Baldwinites together had won a majority, thirty-eight to twenty-two, over the Liberal-Conservatives;[44] but in actual fact the differences between them had not been resolved, merely thinly papered over. Even had their solidarity been strongly maintained, it is doubtful whether the existing ministry could have survived for long, poised as it was on a knife-edge in an almost equally balanced House. But in the event, dissension was rife: Brown interfered in its business in overbearing fashion, while Sandfield Macdonald secretly bargained with the Liberal-Conservatives to dish the Grits and form a new coalition of the centre.[45] Before it could complete a single session the ministry collapsed, resigning without even

42 Hodgins, *John Sandfield Macdonald*, 67
43 Ibid., 67–8
44 Cornell, *Alignment*, 55
45 Hodgins, 'J.S. Macdonald,' 282–91

being defeated on a vote of confidence, and clearing a path for the return in March 1864 of Cartier and John A. Macdonald (in a coalition nominally headed by Etienne Taché). The weak point of that coalition, however, was John A.'s lack of adequate support in the Upper Canadian section of the Legislature. Consequently, the new ministry survived for barely three months before being defeated on a vote of censure – thus becoming the fourth government to fall in little more than two years. In spite of its impressive achievements, the Union, it seemed, was fast becoming ungovernable.

11

George Brown, the Great Reform Convention, and the Transition to Federalism

What a motley collection! Broken down Editors – political blacklegs, idiotic back-woodsmen, half starved reeves, ragged members of Parliament, hungry lawyers, simple-minded yeomen and cunning sharks ...

– Anon., *The Great Convention* (Toronto 1859)

I

Superficially, the deadlock of 1864 resembled that of 1854 in that in each case Lower Canada had produced a stable majority and Upper Canada had not, but in other respects the political landscape had changed greatly in the intervening decade, especially in Upper Canada. Above all, the Clear Grits of 1864 were not the same party as the Clear Grits of 1854; indeed, for the most part they were no longer *Clear* Grits at all, but simply 'Grits' or, more specifically, 'Brownites.' Gradually, through his undoubted ability, sheer force of personality (and a widely influential newspaper), Brown had not only made himself the Grit leader; he had recast the larger part of the reform movement in his own image. The turning-point was the Great Reform Convention of 1859, and to understand subsequent Union politics it is essential to look first at that extraordinary, and even somewhat bizarre, occasion.

It was the largest political convention ever held in the Canadas up to that time, a gathering of some 520 reform delegates supposedly drawn from all over Upper Canada but actually drawn predominantly (76 per cent) from the western peninsula and the Toronto region. Sandfield Macdonald and most other Baldwinites stayed away, thus accounting for the small proportion of delegates (11 per cent) from the eastern counties.[1] Those who attended were mainly former Clear Grit stalwarts. The purpose for which they had been called together was 'to consider the relations between Upper and Lower Canada, and the financial and political evils that had resulted therefrom, and to devise constitutional changes fitted to remedy the said abuses'[2] – a plain invitation to an organized outpouring of wrath against the alleged iniquities of the Union, the alleged immorality of the Cartier-Macdonald regime, the horrible prospect of life under 'the French yoke,' and every other real or imagined disadvantage of the *status quo*. Not surprisingly, it produced 'a political avalanche of outraged virtue.'[3]

It also produced an opportunity for George Brown to recoup his political losses, which in the preceding months had been considerable. A major electoral victory had again eluded him, while his ill-judged attempt to govern without one had ended farcically in the 'double shuffle,' the defeat of his and Dorion's two-day-old administration and the return of Cartier and Macdonald.[4] In consequence, 'Rep by Pop' seemed further away than ever. Faced with their own leader's evident failure, the persistent success of the Liberal-Conservatives, and the refusal of the Baldwinites to disappear, the Grit faithful had begun to grow restless and quarrelsome; if nothing were done, they would soon be seeking a new Moses to lead them out of the wilderness. Brown therefore badly needed an event, even a contrived one, that would place him once again at the centre of the political stage. At the same time, it had become unavoidable that the issue between himself and many of the leading radical reformers over the whole future of the Union should finally be resolved. For the fact of the matter was, they were separatists (or 'dissolutionists'), and he was not. What better way to settle the question than by an appeal to the rank and file at a Great Reform Convention?

Such affairs are rarely exercises in pure democracy, and this one was no exception. Brown and his allies had initiated it and were careful to

1 Percentages are calculated from regional totals contained in George W. Brown, 'The Grit Party and the Great Reform convention of 1859,' in Craig Brown, ed., *Upper Canadian Politics in the 1850s* (Toronto 1967), 24. Other sources give slightly different totals. See Elwood H. Jones, 'Ephemeral Compromise: The Great Reform Convention Revisited,' *Journal of Canadian Studies* 3 (1968): 28.
2 J.C. Dent, *The Last Forty Years: The Union of 1841 to Confederation* (Toronto 1881; reissued 1972), 274
3 Brown, 'Grit Party,' 17
4 See Dent, *Last Forty Years*, 265–73.

keep control over its procedures and organization in their own hands, thus enabling them, for example, to make it difficult for known opponents to obtain accreditation as delegates, and, more importantly, place their own supporters in charge of the committee set up to draft resolutions, whose role would be crucial. They could not rig the convention too blatantly without risking a fiasco – as would be the case, for instance, if it were to break up amid charges of fraud – but they could and did very skilfully 'manage' or 'engineer' it from beginning to end. It was meant to be a showcase for Brown, and it was; rising to the occasion, he dominated it with his ideas and his oratory, turning it into nothing less than a complete personal triumph.

Symbolically and substantively, the Great Reform Convention also turned out to be the last dying gasp of Clear Grit radicalism. The former party of American-style democracy and annexationist sympathies was won over by a leader who poured scorn upon all such notions. 'I have no fear,' declared Brown, 'that the people of Upper Canada would ever desire to become the fag-end of the neighbouring republic (Cheers).'[5] The former party of agrarian populism fell over themselves to prove that they were really more truly loyal than the tories, repeatedly declaring their unqualified devotion to the Crown and the British connection. The convention closed with a delegate named Wilkes (who had earlier made a reference that might have been construed as a defence of the rebels of 1837) begging leave 'in consideration of the false allegation against him that he had recommended rebellion in his speech ... to propose three cheers for the Queen.'[6] Finally, and most significantly of all, the former party of separatism, a majority of whom had come to the convention prepared to support the outright dissolution of the Union, instead were prevailed upon to endorse an ambiguous compromise resolution that, in effect, called for its preservation – albeit in a revised federal form. That, at any rate, was the construction that George Brown and the *Globe* would later place upon the outcome, even though the actual wording of the resolution called only for the creation of 'some joint authority charged with such matters as are necessarily common to both sections of the Province.'[7]

5 Brown, 'Grit Party,' 32
6 Ibid., 37
7 Ibid., 31. J.M.S. Careless interprets the amended resolution as being in favour of federalism. See *Brown of the Globe* (Toronto 1959), I, 322–5. Jones, on the other hand, argues that 'the dissolutionists pictured 'some joint authority' as delegated commissioners advising the two separate governments.' 'Ephemeral Compromise,' 24

A federal union, however, was Brown's prescient vision of where the political future lay – as well as being the obvious way out of the dilemma in which he had placed himself. He had always been inconsistent in demanding *both* representation by population and preservation of the Union, since the imposition of the former was almost certain to destroy the latter. But under a federal system perhaps the two could be successfully combined, with representation by population becoming the rule at one level and sectional equality the rule at another, as under the American constitution, with each section having its own government responsible for 'all matters of a local or sectional character.'[8] Such a system would also allow for future expansion should the other colonies of British North America wish to join, as its advocates enthusiastically pointed out to the convention.

It is a mark of Brown's development as a politician that earlier than most he had come to the realization that the 'Rep by Pop' horse had been ridden about as far as it could go – and it had run out of oats some distance short of effective political power. Quite apart from its failure to make headway in Lower Canada, the unpalatable truth was that in Upper Canada too, in spite of strong support, it had not by any means hopelessly outpaced its rivals. Upper Canadians, indeed, had shown little inclination to give their undivided allegiance to any party, perhaps because they were too heterogeneous in their interests, or too stubbornly local in their political perceptions and loyalties, to do so; or perhaps they were simply too disposed to view politics in traditional patronage terms, putting tangible benefits to themselves, their friends, and their district ahead of fine declarations of principle.[9] For whatever reasons, while many Upper Canadians were ardent Clear Grits or Brownites, the majority were not. Many supported the Liberal-Conservative alignment that John A. Macdonald had so patiently nursed into existence, which included under its broad umbrella a variety of elements ranging from progressive Hincksite brokers (who, apart from their strong attachment

8 Brown, 'Grit Party,' 31
9 This outlook was deeply entrenched in the political culture. Even conservatives (who were perhaps the main beneficiaries) sometimes thought it was carried too far, as in this complaint about a tory mayor who had the temerity to run against John A. Macdonald: 'Mr. Counter's politics are expressed in the simple word "Kingston"; that he knows nothing but "Kingston"; and that he will do anything and everything (if he can do anything) for "Kingston." If this has any meaning at all, it means that, be the government radical, whig, or tory ... Kingston will be placed at its disposal, under any and all circumstances, *for a consideration.*' Kingston *News*, 20 July 1854

to the Union, would have been equally at home among the Brownites) to dyed-in-the-wool tory patrons (who would have been equally at home in a pre-1841 legislature); others faithfully supported an old guard of Baldwinite reformers; while still others (for reasons rarely understood outside their own districts) supported an assortment of independents. 'Rep by Pop' was too important to be abandoned, but after 1859 Brown's main runner was federalism. 'Thereafter the *Globe* boomed it exultantly across the west as chosen party policy.'[10]

II

The full impact of Brown's triumph was far greater, though it was only gradually realized: essentially, he set in motion, or accelerated, four processes that together irrevocably altered the character of Upper Canadian politics.

First, perhaps even more devastatingly than Francis Hincks, though in a different way, he was responsible for the erosion of the spirit of radical democracy that earlier had been the most dynamic element in the reform movement and seemingly the inevitable source of its future ideology. Instead, under his aegis, the Grits turned towards the centre of the political spectrum and adopted the postures of mid-Victorian liberalism, becoming defenders rather than critics of parliamentary government, pro-British and anti-American, advocates of cheap, efficient administration, free markets and economic growth, fervently loyalist – and more than a little enamoured of the idea of empire; in short, they moved into the mainstream of the Upper Canadian political culture.

Second, by putting the Grits in the forefront of the movement favouring immediate westward expansion, Brown tapped the potent underlying imperialism of the Upper Canadian people. In the old loyalist tradition there had always been a streak of proprietary interest in the British Empire, which Upper Canadians, according to their own myth, had defended as no others. At the elite level, especially, they therefore tended to see themselves as an 'imperial' rather than as a 'colonial' people, which probably accounts for their leaders' peculiar (and quite unconscious) arrogance. John Beverley Robinson, for example, saw no anomaly in lecturing the British government when he felt it was neglecting its duty in Upper Canada, while Robert Baldwin always

10 *Dictionary of Canadian Biography*, x, 98

presumed that he understood the British constitution better than the British themselves. It was thus a small step for a confident, expanding, commercially ambitious Victorian community to extend its imperial proclivities to the point of demanding an empire of its own, in the vast territory west of Lake Superior, which the coming of the railway age had brought within its grasp. The *Globe* was eloquent in extolling the advantages, foreseeing the day when an expanded Canada would 'take its place among the empires of the earth' and leaving no doubt where its imperial centre would be: 'The wealth of 400,000 square miles of territory will flow through our waters and be gathered by our merchants, manufacturers and agriculturalists. Our sons will occupy the chief places of this vast territory, we will form its institutions, supply its rulers, teach its schools, fill its stores, run its mills, navigate its streams. Every article of European manufacture, every pound of tropical produce will pass through our stores. Our seminaries of learning will be filled by its people. Our cities will be the centres of its business and education, its health and refinement.'[11]

Third, by bringing the bulk of the Clear Grits under his leadership, Brown produced a politically formidable combination, a party tied on the one hand to the energetic commercial interests of Toronto, where his own business connections were located, and on the other to the prosperous agrarian communities of the western peninsula, where a large number of *Globe*-subscribing farmers provided the solid foundation of its political support. Their alliance was not really as odd as it might seem: Toronto businessmen tended to be free-traders rather than protectionists and to realize the extent to which the success of their enterprises depended upon the success of agriculture, whose role as the true economic foundation of society they never doubted. Moreover, culturally as well as economically there was a certain affinity between the two. The *Globe* idealized the 'intelligent yeomanry' of the countryside, and while this was obviously a flattering image for its readers, it was also the case that agriculture was held in genuinely high esteem by the upper classes. Like John Graves Simcoe, they saw it as the most desirable way of life.[12] Hence it was a mark of status for wealthy Toronto

11 22 Jan. 1863
12 In this respect, Upper Canadian attitudes had changed little: it was still the case that 'the gentry could not conceive of a society in political, economic or social terms that was not rooted in the land.' Robert Fraser, 'Like Eden in Her Summer Dress: Gentry, Economy and Society, Upper Canada, 1812–1840,' PHD thesis, University of Toronto 1979, 106

businessmen (including Brown himself) to be also 'gentleman farmers' with large estates, affecting keen interest in such matters as scientific livestock-breeding and the cultivation of new varieties of crops. At the same time there were wealthy farmers (including some Clear Grits) who invested their surplus capital in such essentially urban enterprises as banking, railways, and manufacturing.[13]

Fourth, by bringing into his immediate circle of advisers some extremely able young politicians, Brown substantially improved the calibre of the Grit political elite, thus compensating for his own lack of talent and appetite for the constant manoeuvring of Union politics. Foremost among the new men were Alexander Mackenzie, who would go on to become prime minister of Canada, and Oliver Mowat, who would go on to become premier of Ontario. The latter especially was invaluable. Unlike Brown, whose bellicose posturing frequently contrasted oddly with the moderation of his views, Mowat combined moderation with a shrewd grasp of the intricacies and uses of the broker's art. It was no mere coincidence that Brown's previously erratic political career advanced steadily while Mowat was his chief lieutenant.

III

Together these factors gave the Grits – now no longer quite so 'Clear' – a broader electoral base than they had hitherto enjoyed. They were still the party of Upper Canadian sectionalism, but by 1863 they had become also the party of loyalism, federalism, and western expansion. As the elections of that year and the ensuing parliamentary deadlock showed, the Union could no longer be governed without them; the question was, could it be governed with them? The problem was basically an internal one of Upper Canada, for there was no doubt that the *bleus* were the dominant party in the lower province. If the Grits would not co-operate with them, there was no prospect of any other Upper Canadian group being able to do so with any prospect of success. Thus, following the defeat of the short-lived Taché-Macdonald ministry on 14 June 1864,[14] yet another dissolution and new elections seemed inevitable, though there was no reason to believe that the outcome would be significantly different.

13 J.M.S. Careless, 'The Toronto *Globe* and Agrarian Radicalism, 1850–1867,' in Craig Brown, *Upper Canadian Politics*, 42
14 Creighton, *Macdonald*, 352–3

The Union of the Canadas had apparently reached an impasse, and its novel experiment in consociational politics seemed destined to end in failure. Yet it did not do so: instead of rejecting consociationalism, the Union's politicians, at a time of crisis, turned more than ever towards it. For in the last resort the Brownite Grits were federalists, not separatists; they wanted an expansion of the Union, not its dissolution; and in these circumstances, even they found the logic of elite accommodation irresistible. The result was the adoption of what is theoretically the ultimate consociational device – a grand coalition.[15]

As usual in Union politics, the brokers were active, and once again their intervention provided an essential step in the accommodative process. The fall of the government had not been unexpected and must have been preceded by a certain amount of negotiation, or at least the taking of 'soundings.' But as far as is known, it was not until the day following, 5 June 1864, that the outline of a potential deal between Brown and John A. Macdonald was first put forward, with two Liberal-Conservative brokers, Alexander Morris and John Henry Pope, acting as intermediaries.[16] It is extremely unlikely that Macdonald was unaware of their approach to Brown, and Brown could not have been unaware of the connection of Morris and Pope to Macdonald; basically, it would appear, what they were all doing was observing the conventional proprieties of brokerage politics. Face-to-face negotiations followed; a deal was struck in private and symbolically sealed on the floor of the Assembly, with handshakes all round.[17]

In the 'Great Coalition' that resulted, Cartier retained his nominal role as premier. In reality, however, the coalition was a tripartite affair made up of Liberal-Conservatives under Macdonald, *bleus* under Cartier, and Grits under Brown. The terms upon which it was formed were complex, embracing both personnel and policy and reflecting in both the new increased bargaining power of the Grits. It was agreed that they would have three cabinet seats, thus enabling Brown to bring two colleagues with him into the ministry – one of whom would be Oliver Mowat. Macdonald and Cartier, however, would remain in the traditional leadership portfolios of attorney-general West and attorney-general East respectively, while Brown would assume office as president of the council and Mowat as postmaster-general. As a condition of

15 See Arend Lijphart, *Democracy in Plural Societies* (New Haven 1977), 25–31.
16 For a detailed account of how to deal was made, see Dent, *Last Forty Years*, 283–4.
17 Creighton, *Macdonald*, 357

Grit support, the government would have to pledge itself to introduce in the next session whatever measures might be necessary and to negotiate with other interests beyond its control to secure assent to a new pact that would enable all the British North American provinces to unite 'under a general legislature based upon the federal principle.'[18] In other words, the government had to accept the main thrust of Grit policy since the Great Reform Convention of 1859. But by implication the Grits would have to drop their insistence on 'Rep by Pop' except in so far as it might form part of a future federal agreement. Macdonald, on the other hand, was required to do an even more complete *volte face*: only a few days previously he had been one of the leading opponents of federation; now he would have to become one of its leading supporters.[19] Unlike Brown, however, Macdonald adjusted easily to changing political circumstances; in the struggle for power, which the coalition could mask but not eliminate, he, rather than his Grit rival, would emerge the winner and go on to dominate the new era of federal politics that was fast approaching.

It is not part of our concern here to deal with the series of conferences at Charlottetown, Quebec City, and London that led to the British North America Act of 1867 and the birth of modern Canada, except to note that the *process* that characterized those deliberations was the familiar one of political brokerage. There was thus an almost exclusive focus upon the concrete and material aspects of the new system that was being formed, right down to the enumeration of specific 'classes of subjects' that would be the proper sphere of each level of government and a very considerable willingness to trade and bargain on all sides. Conversely, there was almost no inclination to indulge in rhetorical preambles or declarations of principle or other ideological flourishes that might stand in the way of an accommodation among the provinces. Certainly, for the Upper and Lower Canadian delegates, schooled as they were in the politics of the Union, such a functional, and pragmatic approach came naturally, for, more thoroughly perhaps than any other group of politicians in the world, they had learned to operate within a framework of shared power. Federalism, indeed, was in many respects a clearer, more straightforward system of power-sharing than the evenly balanced, infinitely negotiable, raffishly entrepreneurial, yet remarkably successful system they were leaving behind. It was not a step for which they were unprepared.

18 Dent, *Last Forty Years*, 285
19 Creighton, *Macdonald*, 350–5

IV

In 1867 Upper Canada formally resumed its status as a separate and distinct political entity, though in reality it had maintained that status, and its name, throughout the entire period of the Union. The British North America Act thus became the third major constitutional document under which its political institutions and processes were organized, in succession to the Constitutional Act of 1791 and the Act of Union of 1841, and was to prove far more durable than either. In the short run, however, it by no means transformed the fundamental bases of political life. Federalism required adaptation, particularly at the elite level, but the underlying web of political culture and the hard facts of political economy were not susceptible to sudden change. Therefore, in no meaningful sense can it be said that the province of Ontario began its political life in 1867. Confederation was but a milestone in its evolution, not a sharp break with the past.

At the grassroots, in the townships and villages where the mass of the people lived, politics continued to have a distinctly local flavour. In many places the old Upper Canadian habit of combining loyalism with clientelism remained very much its essence, while at the top the newest archetype of the clientele system, the broker, who had so powerfully dominated the politics of the Union, did not find his prospects dimmed by having two levels of govenment to work with.

Part Three
Ontario

12

The Patent Combination

What the hell has Strathroy done for me?

– John Sandfield Macdonald

The genesis of federalism lies in the recognition by two or more communities that sovereignty is divisible and that it would serve their mutual interests to divide it. Those interests need not be identical, or even similar; all that is required is that they should exist, or be thought to exist. Of the four original provinces of Canada in 1867 none had a greater reason to believe that Confederation would prove a mutually advantageous political deal – and that its own particular interests would be well served and protected – than Ontario. It had found a way of maintaining the best features of its union with Quebec, since the two would remain politically and economically integrated, but without the confining necessity of dual-majority rule; it had satisfied the insistent popular demand for representation by population, which was now fully accepted as the principle of representation in the new federal House of Commons; it had established a suitable political framework for the spread of its people and the expansion of its commercial interests westward across the continent; and, not least, it had preserved its old boundaries and its old political identity, since Upper Canada would live on as Ontario. Small wonder, therefore, that its political elite overwhelmingly saw the birth of the new Dominion as a cause for joyous celebration.

One of the few who did not was John Sandfield Macdonald. He had clung loyally to the idea of an exclusive, consociational union of Upper and Lower Canada, with the result that as the movement for a larger confederation gained momentum, he had found himself politically isolated, with no role to play in the great endeavour to build new constitutional machinery for British North America, and reduced at the end to arguing the case for a referendum on the issue against the combined opposition of George Brown and John A. Macdonald – neither of whom would countenance for a moment putting the hard-won achievement of the Quebec Resolutions at risk by an appeal (in Brown's words) to 'the ignorant unreasoning mass.'[1] Yet when the time came to set the new machinery in motion, the member of the political elite who emerged as the chief engineer for Ontario was not one of the builders of that machinery; it was none other than Sandfield, a failed saboteur, who was skilfully eased into the premiership by John A. Macdonald.

The latter had been called upon to form the first federal administration. He was aware that Conservative electoral fortunes were unlikely to be improved by constitutional change alone and so prudently opted to perpetuate at the federal level the old familiar pattern of the United Canadas: his government would be an English-French coalition, whose expected weakness in Ontario and the Maritimes would be balanced by Cartier's solid bloc of supporters in Quebec. The problem that demanded the greater exercise of his ingenuity was Ontario, where George Brown (who had resigned from the coalition ministry in December 1865) thundered ceaselessly against the return of the 'corruptionists,' and the election of a hostile Grit provincial administration seemed practically inevitable. To stave off such a result required a typically sharp piece of Macdonaldian chicanery. Having first secured the appointment of a pliant lieutenant-governor of the province (Major-General Henry Stisted, a military man of no political experience and in George Brown's opinion 'an old fool')[2] he opened negotiations with Sandfield with a view to duplicating the federal coalition at the provincial level. Sandfield was quick to appreciate the advantages of such an arrangement and on 10 July 1867 became Stisted's astounding choice to form the first Ontario administration. The resulting cabinet of Conservatives and Reformers was described by the premier as a 'Patent Combination'[3] – a label that stuck.

1 As quoted in Bruce W. Hodgins, *John Sandfield Macdonald* (Toronto 1971), 82
2 Ibid., 93; see also *Dictionary of Canadian Biography*, x, 667–8.
3 The derivation of the term is obscure. It certainly had no flattering connotation; but Sandfield was known for his plain-speaking, and his new ministry *was* patently a combination of conservatives and non-Brownite liberals.

There could have been no clearer signal to the people of the province that there would be no fundamental discontinuity between pre- and post-Confederation politics. John A. had been the single most dominant Upper Canadian politician for more than a decade, his career neatly epitomizing the transfer of power in the political system to a new generation of business-connected brokers. He had been raised in the old clientele culture, and his political outlook would always reflect its values – especially in his attachment to patronage as the essential cement of political relationships – but his experience of Union politics had also taught him the necessity of transcending its inherent localism. Better than any other Conservative he had understood the purpose and mastered the techniques of coalition-building, both across segmental lines, by power-sharing with the French Canadians, and within Upper Canada, by broadening the base of Conservative support. Both involved the use of patronage, and in the latter case, in particular, he had used it with telling effect in the Great Coalition formed in 1864. As Gordon T. Stewart points out, in the course of a superbly insightful analysis of his party leadership, Macdonald seized his opportunity to attach the Reform element in the coalition permanently to the Conservative side: 'He distributed government patronage liberally to these former Reform colleagues and to supporters in their constituencies. When loyal Conservatives complained of valuable plums being given to former Grit opponents, Macdonald sharply retorted that as long as these men supported the Conservative party, they would receive all encouragement to stay in the fold. To a group of Conservative supporters in Toronto who complained about patronage flowing to Reform members of the government, Macdonald replied characteristically: "As soon as Toronto returns Conservative members it will get Conservative appointments, but not before." '[4] The formation of the Patent Combination was thus a natural extension of the Macdonaldian system of coalition-building, a system whose effectiveness had been amply demonstrated.

Sandfield Macdonald was no John A. In general, his political orientation tended to be 'country' rather than 'court' for, although pro-Union and accommodative towards the French Canadians, he was inclined to share the Grit preference for small, economical government. Yet he too was in many respects an archetypal politician of the Union era, a familiar figure whose long career stretched back to the days of Robert Baldwin; in office or out he had been one of the grandees of

4 *The Origins of Canadian Politics: A Comparative Approach* (Vancouver 1986), 65

Upper Canadian politics for a generation. He was also a shrewd choice
as premier, as George Brown and the Grits discovered to their chagrin.
Sandfield's roots went deep into the old clientele system, of whose local
intricacies he was an acknowledged master; his personal power-base in
eastern Ontario remained a secure bastion, to some extent electorally
counterbalancing Brown's stronghold in the western region; throughout the province he still possessed sufficient credibility as a reformer, at
least among old Baldwinites, to deny the Grits exclusive title to that
label; in the very heart of Grit southwestern Ontario, for example, he
was again enthusiastically supported by the London *Free Press*;[5] and
finally, he appealed to the anti-confederate minority, for, though now
reconciled to Confederation, he alone of the leading politicians had
fought it to the very end, and his emergence as premier was for them a
reassuring legitimation of the new constitutional order.

Exactly how that order would work in practice, however, was still
something of a puzzle. The British North America Act offered little
specific guidance on even such potentially important questions as the
functions and status of the lieutenant-governor, and still less on the
interaction between the written federal provisions of the constitution
and the unwritten (but by now well-established) conventions of
responsible cabinet government. The latter were presumed to be
simultaneously applicable at both levels of government, but such an
arrangement had never before been tried in any political system, and
how it would work – indeed, whether it would work – was something
that only experience could determine. What, for example, would be the
role of political parties in the new system? Would they become a
mechanism for bridging the formal division of powers laid down in the
constitution, effectively nullifying federalism through control of the
political process at both levels of government? Or would they serve to
accentuate the federal division by making it political as well as
constitutional, with responsible ministers at each level being effectively
independent of one another through their command of separate (and
perhaps even conflicting) party organizations? Where in the new federal
structure would major economic interests such as railway companies
and banks choose to exert their influence? And in broadest terms, how
would the people respond to the requirement that they now support
two governments, maintain two capitals, and directly elect representa-

5 Hodgins, *John Sandfield Macdonald*, 92

tives to two legislatures? Would they focus their loyalty, and their complaints, predominantly upon one or the other?

The 1867 elections in Ontario provide no conclusive answers to questions such as these since neither the manner in which they were conducted nor their outcome established a pattern for the future. Nevertheless, they do reveal the remarkable ease with which Ontario adjusted to the inauguration of a federal system, and the same may be said for the four years of Sandfield Macdonald's administration that followed.

For the one and only time, both the federal and provincial elections were held on the same days, in constituencies with the same boundaries, using the same polling places, voters' lists, officials, rules, and procedures; for all practical purposes they were conducted as a single exercise – as in the United States, where federal and state elections are held together. In outline, the new electoral system was very simple. The most important change was the allocation to Ontario (under Schedule 1 of the British North America Act) of eighty-two seats in the federal House of Commons, a number corresponding exactly to the total number of seats in the provincial Legislative Assembly; otherwise, the conduct of the elections followed the familiar pre-Confederation pattern. Polling still took place constituency by constituency over a period of several weeks, with two days being allowed for polling in each constituency; polling was still 'open' (that is to say, there was no secret ballot); and the voting procedure was still the same, with this necessary variation, as explained by John A. Macdonald: 'When a man comes up to vote he will be asked, "Who do you vote for the Commons and who for the Assembly?" and the answers will be recorded in two separate books.'[6]

The tactical advantage, as usual, lay with the party in control of the government. Thus, through their respective offices, the two Macdonalds were able to determine the general timing of the elections, appoint their own supporters as returning officers, and fix the specific dates of polling in each constituency. The significance of the latter was that it enabled them to establish a favourable sequence of results – their safe seats would be polled first, then marginal seats, and opposition seats last – in the hopeful anticipation that early victories would produce a 'bandwagon' effect. Moreover, the fact that two days were set aside for

6 D.G.G. Kerr, 'The 1867 Elections in Ontario: The Rules of the Game,' *Canadian Historical Review* 51 (1970): 381–2

polling, with results being tallied at the end of the first, allowed the government to marshal its invariably superior resources of money, patronage, and sympathetic officials on the second day and also concentrate such resources in ridings where the contest was close. In the riding of South Ontario, for example, George Brown was leading at the end of the first day's poll but saw his lead disappear by the end of the second, in a contest of which Sir John Willison later wrote: 'If rumour was not unjust, there was an expenditure of money as lavish as ever fertilized a Canadian constituency.'[7]

The government was also better able than the opposition to exploit the practice of dual representation. There was no legal prohibition on candidates' standing for both legislatures at once, and in fact a number of the leading politicians on both sides attempted thus to insure their political futures, standing in one constituency for both houses or in one for the federal House and in another for the provincial. But the governing party could assist their own dual candidates by spacing their election dates at convenient intervals – while handicapping the opposition by ensuring that their dual candidates would have to face simultaneous contests. This also all but eliminated opposition 'constituency-hopping,' although one instance of it did occur when the government neglected to schedule simultaneous elections in the ridings of Kent and Bothwell. Archibald McKellar, a prominent Brownite, was defeated in the federal vote in Kent but managed to arrange the retirement of the Grit candidate for the provincial House in the neighbouring riding of Bothwell and substitute himself. Two weeks later 'the Rejected of Kent' (as he was inevitably dubbed) won a seventy-vote majority and went on to become leader of the opposition in the Assembly.[8] There were, however, few such lapses on the part of the Macdonalds. Both were seasoned election managers, and John A. in particular was a politician whose skill in such matters had already become legendary; sober, energetic, and endlessly calculating, in 1867 he was at the very peak of his form.

Since both first ministers led coalitions, it was vital to their success that their respective parties – Conservatives and coalition Reformers – should work closely with one another at the local level or, at the very least, not compete openly. This was no easy matter to arrange. In some cases there were rival claims to candidacies, rival organizations, and

7 *Reminiscences Personal and Political* (Toronto 1919), 25
8 Kerr, '1867 Elections,' 380

political animosities between local patrons that went back for years. The role of the leaders in settling such disputes is described by Bruce W. Hodgins: 'In one riding where a Conservative candidate seemed strong Sandfield would persuade a Coalition Reformer bent on a federal seat to settle for a provincial one. In another Sir John would attempt the same result with a Conservative. Then both leaders and their lieutenants would urge their followers to regard the resulting compromise as a binding ticket. Often a strong federal candidate pulled in a weak provincial one, frequently a man from the rival part of the coalition.'[9]

The continuity with the pre-Confederation political process is striking: as before, the shape of the government was essentially determined at the elite level, through a deal between brokers; but neither Sandfield nor John A. were the leaders of disciplined, monolithic parties: to make their alliance work they had first to make it acceptable to a broad constellation of more or less independent local interests, and that meant unremitting personal attention to the details of clientele politics.[10] Even the most sympathetic local patron rarely bestowed his favour without some form of reciprocity, which normally included a fulsome personal assurance of friendship from the party leader and a display of interest in his views, while those who were candidates had to be treated very solicitously indeed, and consulted in a detailed and meaningful way on such matters as the most suitable election dates in their riding, the choice of election officials, and local patronage appointments generally. Others who were less sympathetic might nevertheless be persuaded that the new administrations would operate to the benefit of their commercial enterprises; while still others who were frankly interested in some specific *quid pro quo*, such as railway or timber concessions, could be enticed by hints of future consideration – if their riding voted the right way. Local patrons were still the key to electoral success, and the two Macdonalds, both steeped in the clientele system, knew how to deal with them in the friendly, face-to-face manner that the social conventions of the system required.

Their task was made easier by the substantial growth of southern Ontario's railway network, for this enabled them to make their personal presence felt in practically every constituency. 'Hunting in pairs,' they criss-crossed the province in a manner unprecedented by party leaders

9 *John Sandfield Macdonald*, 89
10 See, e.g., D. Swainson, 'Business and Politics: The Career of John Willoughby Crawford,' *Ontario History* 61 (1969): 231–2.

in previous campaigns.[11] Also, of course, they enjoyed the inestimable advantage of being in office, with all the opportunities to exert influence that that implied. Sandfield lacked John A.'s finesse, but his knowledge of local issues and personalities and his blunt, plain-speaking style made him a formidable campaigner in his own right. His treatment of patronage, for example, was quite open: for him it was simply a matter of reciprocity – 'A government must support its supporters.'[12] Whenever he pointed out this truth to doubtful electors (as in Hamilton, where he told them they could expect 'some axes to grind'[13] if – and only if – they elected the coalition candidate), the *Globe* would respond with predictable outrage, but Sandfield's frank acceptance of the legitimacy of patronage was widely shared among the public. In a clientele political culture the mark of good government is not so much the absence of patronage as its efficient and scrupulous use. Hence Sandfield's reputation, so paradoxical to the modern eye, for honest, frugal administration.

The great issue of the elections (or non-issue, in view of the broad consensus that existed on the matter) was Confederation. All the parties were in favour of it: what divided them was the question of who should be entrusted with its administration. Once again, however, George Brown had painted the Grits into a corner; at yet another 'Great Reform Convention' in June 1867 he had orchestrated a fierce attack upon any continuation of coalition rule, which he held to be a diabolical conspiracy guaranteed to produce 'the lowering of public morality, lavish public expenditure and widespread corruption.'[14] Thus, by the time the elections were called in August, with coalition governments in place both federally and provincially, the Grits had trapped themselves into becoming the sole advocates of a switch to single-party government, which was not a popular position at the time and in any case was bound to make them appear factional and self-serving.

11 'It is positively disgraceful to see Sir John A. Macdonald hunting after victims through the country with Mr. Sandfield Macdonald. They resemble more closely Indians on the war-path than any other description of human being. Their movements are secret, they come upon their prey unawares, and they try to dispatch him in a hurry. How long is our system of government to be brought into contempt by these absurd and undignified attempts to construct a government in defiance of the well-understood wishes of the people?' *Globe*, 20 July 1867
12 W.S. Wallace, 'The Patent Combination: An Account of the First Administration of Ontario,' *Canadian Magazine* 38 (1912)
13 *Globe*, 7 Sept. 1867
14 Ibid., 28 June 1867

The result was a bizarre reversal of roles. Voters were treated to the spectacle of Brown, the former scourge of 'partyism' (and himself a rather reluctant and inept party leader) acting as the hard-line champion of party rule, while John A. and Sandfield, both consummate party managers when it suited them, portrayed themselves as modest and sweetly reasonable 'non-partisans,' the impartial guardians of Confederation. 'Party,' intoned John A. to the electors of Chatham, 'is merely a struggle for office; the madness of many for the gain of the few.'[15] Sandfield evidently was no less pious: his performance won an extravagant review from the Reverend Egerton Ryerson, chief superintendent of education for Ontario and an influential Methodist, who claimed that the leader of the Patent Combination had 'evinced more freedom from party bias and subserviency than any other leading public man in Upper Canada,' and for good measure attacked parties as 'un-British, factious, wasteful, irresponsible, immoral, and conducive to a decline in "religious feelings."'[16] For the Grits it was that kind of campaign; once again, George Brown had plucked defeat from the jaws of victory.

When the last votes were counted, John A. had secured a majority of Ontario's federal seats and Sandfield a correspondingly safe margin in the provincial Assembly. In the latter there were too many independents, ranging from genuine 'loose fish' to 'fair-play' ministerialists, to make possible a precise calculation of party strength, but overall the Patent Combination could count on the backing of around fifty of the eighty-two members. Sandfield had not been able to put together a particularly outstanding cabinet, in either administrative talent or political strength, but all of its members (two coalition reformers and two conservatives, in addition to the premier) had been safely returned.[17] The premier himself had also won election to the federal House – where, in the confused shuffling about that marked the opening session of that chamber, he ended up occupying the seat reserved for the leader of the opposition! When his own legislature opened, however, he was in his right seat and firmly in control of the government.

The administration of the Patent Combination is usually passed over

15 *Leader* (Toronto), 11 Aug. 1867
16 Hodgins, *John Sandfield Macdonald*, 92
17 Ibid., 93. The Conservatives were John Carling (agriculture and public works) and M.C. Cameron (treasurer). The Reformers were E.B. Wood (provincial secretary) and Stephen Richards (Crown lands). Sandfield Macdonald himself was attorney-general.

quickly in accounts of Ontario politics, largely no doubt because in form as in name it is without a modern equivalent; it appears therefore to have been little more than a curious anomaly that lasted for but a single term and then disappeared, making way for the long liberal ascendancy that followed. Nevertheless, the fact that it did hold power for four full years, the first formative years after Confederation, ought not to be lightly dismissed. During that time some of the most enduring features of the province's political life emerged, or, just as significantly, re-emerged. Perhaps foremost among these was the tradition of strong executive leadership.

The last decade of the Union of the Canadas had marked the high tide of parliamentary power and influence. Following full acceptance of the principle and practice of responsible government, the pendulum had swung all the way from the executive-dominated system of the Family Compact era to a system in which the executive was almost totally at the mercy of the legislature. Political parties had not yet acquired sufficient solidity to impose effective discipline within the chamber, while in the constituencies the old pattern of clientele-based politics, with its intensely local activities, still flourished. Members of Parliament were typically local magnates, or the nominees of local magnates, with their own independent bases of support and their own patron-client obligations to consider; they were not merely grist to some party mill. The result was that governments were made – and regularly unmade – at the top, essentially through a process of political brokerage at the parliamentary level. Sandfield Macdonald had been a product of that environment and had risen to eminence within it, but now, as premier, in one respect at least he chose to break with the recent past and revert to the old Upper Canadian tradition of executive dominance that had prevailed from Simcoe to Metcalfe. There could be no complete reversion to pre-responsible government methods or styles, of course, but for a number of reasons in 1867 the time was ripe for a more powerful premiership. 'Yes, I have taken two Tories into the government,' Sandfield told an audience in Whitby. 'But I am Premier – I have the power, and if these two Tories don't do just what I want them to, I'll put them out!'[18]

Sandfield's prominent role in the election campaign, his administration's large majority, the inexperience of so many of the new members (only thirteen had had previous parliamentary experience, and four of

18 *Globe*, 20 July 1867

those were in the cabinet),[19] the uncertainties that existed over the practical workings of federalism, and the general desire for a fresh start all contributed to push the pendulum back in the direction of greater executive authority and personal leadership. Equally influential, no doubt, was the fact that the Patent Combination was too fragile a creation, and too short of talent, to withstand the sort of parliamentary free-for-all that had demolished so many ministries during the last years of the Union. In essence it remained an aggregation of old rivals, political opportunists, and regional notables, thinly cemented together by the possession of office. But office alone was unlikely to hold it together for long, as Sandfield well knew. From the start, therefore, he was concerned to establish his control over the cabinet and the cabinet's control over the legislature.

He did not succeed entirely; the cabinet was at times openly disunited and the coalition majority in the Assembly was at times unreliable, in spite of its size. Indeed, it was not long before one coalition backbencher (Sir Henry Smith, the redoubtable tory patron of Frontenac) was accusing the premier of attempting to 'carry the whole policy of the administration in his breeches' pocket.'[20] The opposition, for its part, condemned the government for using its majority to vote large lump sums for departmental purposes without providing details, thus avoiding accountability and denying the Assembly its traditional right to oversee public expenditure – a protest that echoed from the past and would be heard many times in the future. Nevertheless, on the whole the Patent Combination represented a decisive shift in the balance of parliamentary power: thereafter the Ontario system would typically be characterized by strong leadership, a dominant executive, and a weak legislature.

The Patent Combination's record in office was also one that would be much emulated in years to come: it used patronage freely, but not to the point of financial extravagance; in social and economic affairs it was cautiously interventionist and moderately reforming; it was supportive of progressive agriculture; and in dealing with such matters as railways and natural resources it was generally on the side of development and developers. Moreover, the financial terms of Confederation proved highly favourable to Ontario, thus enabling the administration to show

19 Hodgins, *John Sandfield Macdonald*, 93
20 W.S. Wallace, 'Political History, 1867–1912,' in Adam Shortt and Arthur G. Doughty, eds., *Canada and Its Provinces*, vol. 17 (Toronto 1914), 112

a healthy annual surplus in the public accounts.[21] Its legislative achievements were by no means negligible and included a Free Grant and Homestead Act to counter the pull of free land in the United States by opening new northern townships for settlement; a new Election Act, which broadened the franchise and restricted polling to one day only, among other constructive reforms; significant additions to the province's social-welfare system, including new Institutes for the Deaf and Dumb and Blind; and a sweeping Education Act, inspired by Egerton Ryerson, which provided for free primary and secondary schools throughout the province, made attendance compulsory in the early years, established province-wide standards, and introduced science into the curriculum. Further enactments provided for the foundation of an Ontario School of Agriculture at Guelph and a Technical College at Toronto.[22]

Patronage considerations were not of the essence in such matters, but neither were they neglected. The new Deaf and Dumb Institute, for example, was located in Belleville, which had supported the Patent Combination candidate, and not in Hamilton (the site of the old institute), which had returned an opposition Reformer.[23] Like every expert user of patronage, however, Sandfield had learned to use it strictly as a reward for performance, and even then not too lavishly. (It was in response to a group of lobbyists from Grit Strathroy requesting that their town be made the site of a proposed provincial prison that he uttered his famous retort: 'What the hell has Strathroy done for me?')[24] In style as well as substance the Patent Combination was a curious mixture of political partisanship and careful guardianship of the public purse that, to be properly understood, must be seen in light of the operative norms of a clientele political culture. As Sandfield explained: 'I admit that I am niggardly. I deal with the public money as though I were dealing with my own personal funds.'[25]

The troubles that led to the early demise of the Patent Combination stemmed primarily from two sources. First, the confusion that attended the division of governmental powers into federal and provincial spheres (and which is to some extent endemic in a federal system) was particularly rampant in the early years of Confederation, when neither

21 Bruce W. Hodgins, 'John Sandfield Macdonald,' in J.M.S. Careless, ed., *The Pre-Confederation Premiers: Ontario Government Leaders, 1841–1867* (Toronto 1980), 299
22 Ibid., 296–8
23 Wallace, 'Political History,' 118
24 Ibid.
25 Wallace, 'Patent Combination,' 241

government nor opposition, nor the press or public opinion generally, made much distinction between the responsibilities of the different levels of government, a problem further compounded by the practice of dual representation. The result was that Sandfield's provincial administration suffered repeated political damage from issues that were constitutionally outside its jurisdiction. For example, it became entangled in the controversy that developed over the federal government's decision to grant more favourable financial terms to Nova Scotia, and (despite Ontario's own excellent financial position) ended up looking insufficiently protective of the provincial interest when it defended the federal position and weak or opportunistic when it subsequently yielded to opposition pressure and supported a resolution attacking it.[26] Even more damaging was the issue of Louis Riel's rebellion in the Red River territory and the execution by the rebels of Thomas Scott, an Ontario Orangeman. The latter incident unleashed a wave of anti-French, anti-Catholic sectarianism in the province, stirred by the inflammatory invective of the *Globe* and effectively exploited by the Grit opposition in the Assembly.[27] By adopting a moderate stance and by refusing to interfere in a matter over which it had no constitutional authority, the unfortunate Patent Combination brought down upon itself the wrath of militant Protestants, with a consequent erosion of its popular support.

These difficulties, moreover, were further aggravated by a gradual shift in the underlying Ontario attitude towards Confederation. For it was not long before the initial spirit of optimism and nation-building began to give way before older, ineradicable pressures of geography, culture, and politics – and once again older, exclusively Upper Canadian perceptions and interests began to assert themselves. Ironically, in view of the Patent Combination's opportunistic beginnings, it failed to adapt to its changing environment.

Sandfield's administration was never a puppet regime whose strings were pulled in Ottawa by John A. (though its Grit opponents naturally missed no opportunity to portray it as such), but it was also true that the two leaders did share a basically 'Macdonaldian' view of the constitution, a view that in practice, if not in theory, produced what amounted to a form of 'co-operative' or 'consultative' federalism. They had their differences from time to time, but on the whole the two leaders and their

26 Wallace, 'Political History,' 116
27 Joseph Schull, *Edward Blake: The Man of the Other Way* (Toronto 1975), 73

respective governments worked closely together. Bruce W. Hodgins summarized their relationship thus: 'The Ontario premier did not object to the prime minister's examination and private comment and criticism of Ontario legislation. The exchange of private and official correspondence between them is rather voluminous. The prime minister had the governor general disallow only two Ontario acts, but he often urged the premier to amend or repeal certain laws. Occasionally Sandfield was persuaded by the logic of the argument, often he fought back. Frequently he emerged victorious.'[28]

The give and take of brokerage politics was, of course, nothing new to either, except that it now took place within a federal context and was directed towards the maintenance of Confederation. Both, moreover, were convinced that the latter goal would require a constant 'harmonization' of the two levels of government, a view Sandfield had made plain from the very beginning, during the 1867 election campaign: 'We start with Conservatives and Reformers. As that is the foundation of the Central government at Ottawa, it would not do to have the local in opposition to it, begetting rancorous hostility as soon as measures sprang up.'[29] Through their long experience of Union-era politics, both leaders were acutely aware of the perils of political fragmentation, and likewise were inclined to try to overcome those perils by traditional means – through overarching collaboration at the elite level of the political system.

The trouble was, however, that for many Ontarians the perpetuation of the process had become increasingly unacceptable: in their eyes the granting of new financial terms to Nova Scotia represented a flagrant sell-out of Ontario's interests, and the Riel Rebellion a confirmation that 'French domination' had been tolerated in Manitoba; whereas they had supported Confederation precisely because they believed it would put an end to such accommodations and give-aways.

Above all, they feared that the west would be denied them as a legitimate sphere of influence. The basic Ontario outlook had crystallized in mid-century, and, unlike the prevailing sentiment of any other colony of the British Empire at the time, and for complex reasons, including the province's loyalist roots and its economic imperative of agricultural expansion, that outlook was more imperialist than colonial.[30]

28 'Disagreement at the Commencement: Divergent Ontario Views of Federalism, 1867–1871,' in Donald Swainson, ed., *Oliver Mowat's Ontario* (Toronto 1972), 61
29 *London Free Press*, 23 July 1867
30 See Douglas Owram, *Promise of Eden: The Canadian Expansionist Movement and the Idea of the West, 1856–1900* (Toronto 1980), 59–78.

Accordingly, Ontarians tended to see the west as *their* empire: they would not allow it to be swallowed by the Americans, but neither would they willingly share it with the French. It was to be a place where *their* children would be able to acquire land and achieve agricultural success, just as their parents and grandparents had done in earlier times on the Niagara Frontier and the Huron Tract. This was a concern almost entirely absent among the people of the Maritime provinces, for whom, moreover, Confederation meant *closer* political ties with Quebec and a net loss of independence compared to their prior status as separate colonies. In sharp contrast, for Ontario, emerging from the dual Union meant a *loosening* of such ties, and among the anticipated benefits of federalism were greater local independence and untrammelled westward expansion.

It is not surprising, therefore, that Sandfield Macdonald's modest visions of harmonious federal-provincial relations and cautious expansion northward into newly opened townships on the Laurentian Shield were soon challenged by more aggressive assertions of Ontario's provincial rights and more strident claims to its possession of the west. These positions came to be powerfully articulated by George Brown and the *Globe* (who had earlier espoused a contrary centralist view of Confederation) and were taken up with much success by the Grit opposition in the Assembly.

A second broad source of trouble for the Patent Combination stemmed from changes that were taking place in the clientele system, especially in areas where agriculture was overshadowed by the development of a political economy based on the extraction of natural resources, as in the Ottawa Valley. There a vast and lucrative timber trade had grown up under the control of 'timber barons' whose fortunes rested upon their ability to acquire government land grants, leases, and cutting rights, and who in turn became wealthy merchants, railway magnates, and large employers, with correspondingly great political influence. In the granting of new concessions the stakes were high, and the Patent Combination inevitably made enemies of those it disappointed. More unusually, and more seriously, it also made enemies of those it rewarded.

The main reason for this was its conservative approach to expansion; its policy was basically to extend the old agrarian pattern of Ontario society northward, which brought it into direct conflict with the timber barons.[31] For unlike earlier extensions of the frontier in the southwest,

---

31 See H.V. Nelles, *The Politics of Development: Forests, Mines and Hydro-electric Power in Ontario, 1849–1941* (Toronto 1974), 44–5.

under patrons such as Colonel Thomas Talbot, the timber trade did nothing to promote settlement and the growth of stable communities; its method was simply to extract as much wealth as possible in as short a time as possible before moving on to the next uncut lot. Permanent settlers were thus economically unnecessary; indeed, their government-encouraged encroachments were viewed by the timber barons as an intolerable intrusion upon their right to dispose of the forests as they pleased. The result was a focusing of their hostility upon the Patent Combination and 'a four-year battle ... that threatened Sandfield's hold on the Ottawa Valley and the ministry's control of the timber trade's legislative supporters.'[32]

Other developments also proved more than ordinarily troublesome. Members of the cabinet were openly in league with large railway interests, which produced an awkward lack of solidarity when those interests happened to be in competition with one another, producing at its worst a farcical 'Battle of the Gauges' between those allied with the Grand Trunk (who wanted standard-gauge railways only) and those allied with smaller companies (who wanted cheaper narrow-gauge lines).[33] Catholic patrons were threatening to withdraw their support because they felt they were receiving too small a share of government patronage and were additionally upset by the compulsory school attendance provision in the new Education Act; Methodists were alienated by the revelation that 'Methodist dollars' were being spent on a *ballroom* for Government House; and nearly everyone had designs upon the government's much-vaunted surplus.[34]

Yet none of these difficulties was necessarily fatal: Sandfield still had his network of loyal supporters, the Grits had troubles of their own, and the treasury's full coffers might still be turned to party advantage. What finally destroyed the Patent Combination was more than anything an unforeseeable and disastrous circumstance – the untimely collapse of its leader's health. It could hardly have come at a worse moment. Shortly after the House had been dissolved and new election writs issued, in the spring of 1871, Sandfield, who had never previously allowed his lack of a robust constitution to prevent him from pursuing his political career with great vigour, was suddenly felled by illness. Hence, instead of

32 J.D. Livermore, 'The Ontario Election of 1871: A Case Study of the Transfer of Political Power,' *Ontario History* 71 (1979): 40
33 Wallace, 'Political History,' 112
34 Ibid., 115; and Hodgins, *John Sandfield Macdonald*, 111

stumping the province as he had in 1867, appearing as the very model of a strong, effective leader, in 1871 he was conspicuously absent throughout the campaign, bed-ridden at his home in Cornwall. And to make matters worse, John A. could offer no assistance, as important treaty negotiations in Washington kept him out of the country.

The Grits, meanwhile, had come under the leadership of Edward Blake, an austere and imposing figure drawn from the old Upper Canadian reform elite (his father had been solicitor-general West under Robert Baldwin) and whose political ancestry thus connected him not with Grit radicalism but with the more conservative reform tradition that Sandfield also represented. In his hands the Grits completed their ideological journey to the right and towards loyalism. The long shadow cast by the Riel Rebellion dominated the 1871 campaign, reawakening old fears, reigniting old animosities, and, inevitably, stirring old ghosts, for ever since 1837 'rebellion' had been a word with profound symbolic associations in the Ontario political consciousness. The Grits in particular had long been tainted by the suspicion that they were 'soft' on rebellion and perhaps even somewhat half-hearted in their devotion to the Crown, in spite of their protestations to the contrary; but now, thanks to Riel, for the first time the banner of loyalism had fallen into their hands and they made the most of it, loudly demanding vengeance for 'the cold blooded murder for his outspoken loyalty to the Queen of Thomas Scott, lately a resident of this province,' whose rebel executioners, they charged, 'as yet go unwhipt of justice.'[35] It was as though a familiar drama were being played, but with one difference – the members of the cast had switched roles.

The Patent Combination were forced on to the defensive, lamely (if sensibly) arguing that the response to the rebellion was a federal affair. But the public for the most part was in no mood for such constitutional niceties: in an era when the British government would not hesitate to use gunboats and troops to maintain its far-flung empire and protect the lives and property of its subjects, imperial Ontario would accept no less of a response to rebellion and murder in a territory it regarded as part of its own domain.

Edward Blake, moreover, had begun to articulate a corresponding view of Canadian federalism that stressed provincial rights, in stark contrast to Sandfield's vision of harmony. His biographer, Joseph Schull, writes of him that he saw in the granting of better terms to Nova

35 Schull, *Blake*, 73

Scotia a conspiracy between two partners, the latter province and Quebec, 'united to bilk Ontario' – an approach to federal-provincial relations that would have a long history. In other respects too he was a prescient guide: 'In himself, as he foresaw in others, that prospect of mutual pocket-picking was reviving old jealousies. The old names – Upper Canada, Lower Canada – recurred in his arguments now. Common nationality, the achievement of Confederation, became a dwindling and fitful strain. As between the provinces, for Blake, "destiny" became "destinies."'[36]

Yet when the votes were counted, the outcome of the 1871 election was highly ambiguous. In spite of its ailing leader and its other handicaps, the Patent Combination had fared surprisingly well at the polls, electing more members than the Grits in every area of the province except the southwest, which reverted overwhelmingly to its former allegiance. Even there, however, it is noteworthy that the trend was not entirely uniform: Middlesex East, for example, switched from Grit to the government side (while Middlesex West did precisely the opposite), and in London John Carling, a Patent Combination conservative, increased his majority to 427 (up from 342 in 1867).[37] Elsewhere in the province the election produced a large number of changes, but these ran in both directions and only slightly favoured the Grits. Overall, the Patent Combination secured the election of all its cabinet members and at least twenty-seven backbenchers it could count upon as committed supporters, which left them only one short of the probable Grit total of thirty-three.[38] Therefore the decisive factor in determining whether the government would be able to survive or not would be the attitude of the remaining members of the House – seventeen 'loose fish' who might be persuaded to swim in either direction.

It was a situation reminiscent of pre-Confederation parliaments and as such, in normal circumstances, it would have presented no insurmountable obstacle to a political broker of Sandfield Macdonald's ability and experience. Initially, therefore, he was optimistic that by the time the new House met, the ministry would have a small working majority.[39] Most of the independents were members of a traditional kind, local patrons concerned mainly with their own business interests

36 Ibid., 60–1
37 Roderick Lewis, ed., *Centennial Edition of a History of the Electoral Districts, Legislatures and Ministries of the Province of Ontario, 1867–1968* (Toronto n.d.), 202, 211, 220
38 Livermore, 'Election of 1871,' 43
39 Hodgins, *John Sandfield Macdonald*, 113

and the distribution of benefits to their clients; there was good reason to believe that they could be attached to the government side by time-honoured means. As Sandfield wrote of one of the doubtful, William Robinson, member for Kingston: 'Perhaps we may make him, as we hope to make others of the same class, fall into line before the meeting of the House by talking a little Dutch to them.'[40]

What Sandfield did not count on, however, was that his health would fail to return and that one of his own pieces of reform legislation would come back to haunt him. During the spring and early summer, while he could do no more than test the curative properties of the mineral baths at St Catharines, the Grit leadership were furiously campaigning across the province in an attempt to forestall the drift of the independents towards the government. But ultimately their most effective tactic was to make use of the new Controverted Elections Act, which had been passed during the previous session, to unseat six members of the House, three Patent Combination supporters and three 'doubtfuls of Conservative inclination.'[41] The intention of the act was to remove contested elections from the legislature and place such cases before the courts, but 'it also provided, unwisely, that while the matter was before the courts, the member whose election was being investigated could not take his seat.'[42] The result was that when the Assembly met in December, with the cases still undecided, the Patent Combination was deprived of the crucial margin of support it needed.

Under constant harassment by the opposition, and with Sandfield's maladroit handling of tactics on the House floor showing only too plainly that he was no longer the politician he had once been,[43] the Combination's always-fragile unity began to crack. Two instances in particular assured its ultimate downfall. In an effort to cement the allegiance of R.W. Scott, an Ottawa Valley timber baron, promoter of the Canada Central Railway, and an independent Catholic conservative whose attachment to the government had always been rather tenuous, Sandfield had induced him to accept election as Speaker of the

40 Livermore, 'Election of 1871,' 43
41 Ibid., 45
42 DCB, x, 468
43 There would be much second-guessing of Sandfield's tactics. His failure to move for an adjournment immediately after the election of the Speaker, on the grounds that while so many election appeals were pending, the House was not complete, seemed particularly inexplicable to some observers. See 'A Bystander' (Goldwin Smith), 'The Recent Struggle in the Parliament of Ontario,' *Canadian Monthly and National Review* (Feb. 1872).

Assembly. But when the *quid pro quo* demanded by Scott – namely, 'that Sandfield shall do all Scott asks for his Canada Central'[44] (that is, provide it with land grants along its route from Ottawa to Carleton Place) – was not forthcoming, the government was left with a powerful and resourceful enemy in the Speaker's chair.

More devastating still was the defection of E.B. Wood,[45] the treasurer of Ontario and apart from Sandfield the most prominent Reformer in the coalition, of whom J.D. Livermore writes: 'A moderate, non-Brownite Liberal, first elected in 1863, he had gravitated towards the coalition largely because of his business and professional ties to the Buffalo and Lake Huron Railway and the Grand Trunk Railway controlled by C.J. Brydges and friends of the Conservative party. Since his economic interests were perceived to be dependent upon securing the co-operation of the government, Wood preferred power to either principle or party, and was not averse to "taking the shilling" when it was offered by Sandfield in 1867 ... in Wood's case, the co-operative concept of politics was rooted in considerations more concrete than a vague distrust of excessive partisanship.'[46]

On 15 December, in a House wearied by futile late-night sittings and filled with an atmosphere of intrigue, Wood dramatically resigned in the most damaging way possible, during debate on a non-confidence motion. Though he supported the government in the vote on that motion, two days later he joined the opposition.[47] His resignation spelled the certain doom of the Patent Combination, for its meaning was never in doubt: it was a clear signal to the independents and waverers in the House that the 'smart money' was deserting the government. Sandfield sought to disarm the non-confidence motion by means of a sub-amendment, but in a final ironic touch, his motion was summarily ruled out of order by the Speaker, R.W. Scott, who then called the crucial division. In it the government was defeated by a single vote, thirty-seven to thirty-six.[48]

From the vantage point of Ottawa, John A. Macdonald had little sympathy: the defeat, he believed, could have been staved off if Sandfield had purchased the support of some of the 'independents' by creating ministerial posts for them. 'I pressed him,' he complained to

44 Livermore, 'Election of 1871,' 48
35 DCB, XI, 934–5
46 Livermore, 'Election of 1871,' 46
47 Hodgins, *John Sandfield Macdonald*, 115
48 Ibid.

John Carling, 'to make a President of the Council and a minister of Education, which he half promised to do, yet he took no steps toward doing so. With those two offices, and that of Solicitor General and Speakership, he had the game in his own hands.'[49]

On 18 December Sandfield tendered his resignation to the lieutenant-governor, who then called upon Edward Blake to form a government. To no one's surprise, in the new cabinet the commissioner of Crown lands – the portfolio most coveted by the Ottawa Valley timber interests – was none other than R.W. Scott.[50] The former treasurer, E.B. Wood, did not receive office under Blake but was given the safe federal seat of West Durham, and when the Grits came to power in Ottawa they appointed him chief justice of Manitoba. For Sandfield defeat meant the end of his long career; he died less than six months later, on 1 June 1872.

The change of government was conclusive, since, with control of the spoils of office, the Grits were quickly able to consolidate their hold on power; in fact, prompted by Wood and Scott, the 'doubtfuls' shifted *en masse* to the government side, increasing Blake's slender majority of one to a comfortable twenty.[51]

Yet in the by-elections arising out of the controverted election cases no fewer than five of the six contested seats were won by supporters of the Patent Combination,[52] in the circumstances a truly remarkable electoral performance (and perhaps also a vindication of Sandfield's position that a vote of confidence should not have been taken while so many seats were vacant). Above all, these results demonstrated once again the stubborn strength of localism in Ontario politics and the importance of personal loyalties in the small communities where the elections were fought. The patron-client link is multifaceted, and clientele networks, though inevitably damaged by loss of office at the top, in the short run at least, are not destroyed by it. As premier, Sandfield had used official patronage openly, if perhaps somewhat niggardly by the standards of the day, much in the manner of an old-fashioned grand patron, but that alone cannot explain his persistent political strength. Even out of power, as the by-elections showed, the Patent combination had the capacity to rally substantial grass-roots support.

49 Sir Joseph Pope, *Memoirs of the Rt. Hon Sir John A. Macdonald* (Toronto 1921), 501–3
50 Hodgins, *John Sandfield Macdonald*, 116
51 Livermore, 'Election of 1871,' 49
52 Hodgins, *John Sandfield Macdonald*, 117

The change of government, therefore, hardly amounted to a ringing endorsement of Blake, and still less an endorsement of his attitude towards Confederation. Nevertheless, he took it as such and immediately set out to bury the concept of 'co-operative' federalism. Henceforth there would be no commitment to 'harmony' between the two levels of government: 'As citizens of the province of Ontario we are called upon to frame our own policy ... we deprecate, nay more, we protest most strongly against any interference on the part of any government with our perfect freedom of action.'[53] One of the first acts of the new government was to outlaw dual representation, a symbolic as well as a practical severing of ties between the provincial and federal legislatures. In actuality, Blake's notion of disentangling federal and provincial affairs turned out to be somewhat defective, at least in its application: also among the government's first acts was the posting of a five-thousand-dollar reward for the capture of Louis Riel.[54] The doctrine of provincial rights, evidently, was not meant to keep Ontario from interfering in federal affairs, nor in the affairs of other provinces.

Blake's premiership was otherwise unremarkable, except perhaps for its brevity. As a member of both legislatures he was himself among those affected by the law prohibiting dual representation (and in this matter, at least, was compelled to follow his own injunction). Faced with the choice of federal or provincial politics, he unhesitatingly chose the former and resigned in October 1872, after a mere ten months in office. Plagued by a political ambition considerably in excess of his political talent, and disillusioned by the sordid transactions it had taken to make him premier, he headed for what he hoped would be the grander and purer vistas of Ottawa – where his career came to nothing and his disillusionment was soon made complete.

His departure, however, left no vacuum at the top but instead resulted in a substantial strengthening of the government. For all his aspirations to high office, Blake had no feel for political life and indeed was generally discomfited by it: 'Take the leadership, I beg of you,' he once wrote to Alexander Mackenzie, '... for the work outside of the House I have long known myself to be utterly unfit and I know now that I shall never be more fit for it.'[55] But when the time came, Mackenzie too opted to make his career in Ottawa. For his other party colleagues Blake

53 Schull, *Blake*, 84–5
54 Ibid., 85
55 Ibid., 78

evidently felt scant regard, for in choosing his successor in Ontario he had gone outside the Assembly altogether to recruit a figure from the past, a once-prominent Grit who for eight years had sat in relative obscurity on the bench of the Court of Chancery. More importantly, however, Oliver Mowat was a politician to his fingertips, a man with all of the personal resilience and capacity for party leadership that Blake could not find in himself, and who more than made up for his lack of recent experience by his sharp instincts for the game of democratic politics. He was also no novice. Like Sandfield Macdonald, he had served a long apprenticeship in the politics of the United Canadas; he had been one of the Upper Canadian representatives at the Quebec Conference and hence one of the Fathers of Confederation; and his elevation to the bench by John A. Macdonald had worked as Macdonald had no doubt intended – it deprived George Brown and the Grits of their ablest tactician at a crucial political juncture.

The decision to make him the next premier was not Blake's alone, but neither was it taken by the party as a whole, for at the time there was no notion of intra-party democracy; instead, the decision was taken by a tiny cabal that included Blake and George Brown (who jointly called upon Mowat to offer him the leadership) and Alexander Mackenzie.[56] There was also no notion of a mandate to require a new premier to test the popularity of his government at an early general election. Consequently, when Mowat assumed office on 25 October 1872 he could look forward to three full years in power, provided that he could maintain majority support in the Assembly. Under his leadership Blake's uncertain mixture of Grits, deserters from the Patent Combination, and independent ministerialists solidified into a moderately reformist Liberal party.

There would, therefore, be no revival of the Patent Combination. In opposition it had fallen quickly into disarray, and after Sandfield's death it disintegrated completely. Among its more serious defects was its inability to find or produce a moderate-reform deputy to Sandfield to whom leadership might have passed, which left the field clear for Matthew Crooks Cameron, an extreme tory (whose toryism extended even to ardently defending the memory of the Family Compact) to become leader of the opposition. Under Cameron the surviving supporters of the Patent Combination were absorbed into the Conservative party.

56 See A. Margaret Evans, 'The Ontario Press on Oliver Mowat's First Six Weeks as Premier,' *Ontario History* 56 (1964): 125–7.

13

Oliver Mowat and the Politics of Husbandry

HUSBAND – an oeconomist; a man who knows and practises the methods of frugality and profit. Its sinification is always modified by some epithet implying bad or good.
To HUSBAND – to till; to cultivate the ground with proper management.
HUSBANDRY – Thrift; frugality; parsimony.

Dr Samuel Johnson, *Dictionary of the English Language*

I

The idea of managerial efficiency has always been one of the primary values of the Ontario political culture, shared alike by tories and reformers with only slight differences of emphasis. Even for John Graves Simcoe, in spite of his theoretical musings on the value of an hereditary aristocracy, a case can be made that 'in administration his fetish was efficiency' and his *operative* ideal to have 'neither a *sine cure* mind nor a *sine cure* body throughout the entire Province.'[1]

In Simcoe's time, and until approximately the 1830s, the dominant Upper Canadian model of efficiency, as of so much else, was basically drawn from the military; thus an efficient administration, for example, was understood to be one that in form and ethos resembled a well-run regiment; its officers were expected to be authoritarian yet at the same time paternalistic in their concern for the welfare of all ranks. But with the ebbing of military influence, and as a prosperous agrarian society emerged in mid-century, that model, though it did not disappear

1 See S.R. Mealing, 'The Enthusiasms of John Graves Simcoe,' in J.K. Johnson, ed., *Historical Essays on Upper Canada* (Toronto 1975), 312.

altogether, gradually gave way to another that more accurately reflected the new preoccupations of the age. In particular, efficiency now increasingly came to be thought of in agricultural terms, with an efficient administration being understood as one that resembled a well-run farm; it was expected to be economical but also progressive in outlook and concerned with the betterment of the whole estate.

The earlier notion of efficiency had been broadly in keeping with the patron-client basis of Upper Canadian politics since, initially, a patron's status commonly rested at least in part upon his capacity for military leadership. Moreover, the clientele system itself had proved an efficient means both of political control and, when required, as during the War of 1812 and again during the 1837 rebellion, of military mobilization. But later, in post-Confederation Ontario, the notion of efficient husbandry that was coming into vogue in agriculture had no such parallel with the existing political order; indeed, it could even be seen as an implicit criticism of it. Thus an administration such as Sandfield Macdonald's Patent Combination, despite its generally sound financial record, could also give the appearance of being managerially inept and, perhaps equally damaging, old-fashioned in style and approach. It was too obviously clientelistic, too entangled in parochial loyalties and feuds – and led by a premier who was much too frank about his use of government patronage. Progressive Victorians, it seems, were not amused by 'What the hell has Strathroy done for me?' In their view, good government, like good agriculture, required the application of more modern methods.

It was Oliver Mowat's peculiar political genius to be able to articulate this progressive outlook, translate it into concrete government programs, and, in time, make himself personally its symbol. When he first came to power in 1872, however, there was little to suggest such a result: he had acquired the premiership only through the machinations of a tiny cabal, having not even been a candidate in the 1871 elections, and after the previous premier, Edward Blake, had hastily decamped for Ottawa. It all must have looked very much like old-style 'politics as usual.' Nevertheless, in retrospect it is plain that Mowat's administration was in fact very different from its predecessors. Not only did it remain in power and under his leadership for an unbroken span of twenty-four years (something even Mowat himself could hardly have imagined possible, in a society long accustomed to short-lived ministries), but during that time it presided over and directed the transformation of Upper Canada into the province of Ontario. In the process it profoundly altered the old clientele system that it inherited, essentially bringing it into closer conformity with the new economic, social, and intellectual realities of the age. But for that to be understood, it is necessary to look briefly at the nature of those realities.

II

Ontario in the latter part of the nineteenth century was first of all an agrarian society whose agricultural foundations were undergoing a drastic restructuring. For generations the production of a single staple commodity, wheat, had provided the main impetus to the spread of settlement and the main engine of economic growth. In substantial fulfilment of Simcoe's original plan, Ontario had indeed become the home of 'a numerous and Agricultural people' – a people, moreover, who had achieved a remarkably high standard of living, with concomitantly high levels of capital accumulation and investment.[2] But by the 1870s the source of that affluence was being threatened by a combination of factors, including declining markets in the United States following the end of the Civil War and the abrogation of the Reciprocity Treaty in 1866, a deterioration in the quality of seed stocks, and, in some areas, soil exhaustion caused by a lack of crop rotation, but mainly by the competition provided by new western producers. As R.L. Jones explains: 'Fundamentally, the decline and passing of wheat as a staple in Ontario was made inevitable by the expansion of the railways which opened the prairies of the American West and later of the Canadian Northwest. These distant regions now had the cheap lands and the agricultural machinery requisite for successful extensive farming.'[3]

Ontario farmers had therefore to face a difficult challenge: after years of concentrating on wheat production, a familiar and relatively simple form of agriculture, they had now to turn to less familiar and generally more complex forms, such as dairying, livestock-raising, and mixed farming; or, to remain successful grain producers, they had to adopt

2 John McCallum, *Unequal Beginnings: Agriculture and Economic Development in Quebec and Ontario until 1870* (Toronto 1980), 45–53, passim; see also H.C. Pentland, 'The Role of Capital in Canadian Economic Development before 1875,' *Canadian Journal of Economics and Political Science* 16 (1950): 457–74.

3 *A History of Agriculture in Ontario, 1613–1880* (Toronto 1946), 248. The reasons given by Jones, however, have been disputed in some later studies. See Ian M. Drummond, *Progress without Planning: The Economic History of Ontario from Confederation to the Second World War* (Toronto 1987), 32–5.

new cereal varieties and more advanced methods of cultivation. Farming, in other words, was becoming increasingly diversified and intensive. And farmers were becoming increasingly aware that it was no longer enough to rely on the land's natural fecundity; many could now see that future success in agriculture would require also a knowledge of new crops and technologies and a more efficient use of available resources – in short, good husbandry.

Simultaneously with the restructuring of its agriculture, Ontario was also experiencing a rising trend towards industrialization and urbanization, with the result that although agriculture was undergoing a remarkable development in productivity, and though the number of farms continued to increase, the *relative* importance of agriculture was diminishing. Between the censuses of 1871 and 1901 the proportion of the working population engaged in agriculture fell sharply, with a corresponding rise in the proportion engaged in manufacturing. Over the same period the urban segment of the population increased from 21.9 to 42.9 per cent. Urbanization was in fact widespread, in that it was based on the growth of small-scale manufacturing in numerous towns dotted across the province; but a few larger centres also emerged, including Ottawa, Hamilton, and London, all of which more than doubled in size, and one metropolis, Toronto, whose population soared from 56,000 to 208,000, in these thirty years. The result was a marked decline in village-centred economic activity and in the rural non-farm population.[4]

Changes of this kind and magnitude are bound to produce some degree of social stress and economic dislocation. In Ontario, for the first time, there were now urban concentrations large enough to be seriously affected by problems of overcrowding, poverty, and a host of attendant social ills and pressures – and also large enough to produce a numerically significant working class. The latter responded to industrialization in much the same manner as workers elsewhere, by organizing to promote their common occupational and class interests: the number of trade unions sharply increased, the American-based Knights of Labor acquired a strong following, and the first efforts were made to co-ordinate labour activities, culminating in the founding of the Trades and Labour Congress in 1886, with 109 affiliated unions. By this time

4 Jacob Spelt, *Urban Development in South-Central Ontario* (Toronto 1972), 179–82. See also J.M.S. Careless, 'Some Aspects of Urbanization in Nineteenth-Century Ontario,' in F.H. Armstrong et al., *Aspects of Nineteenth-Century Ontario* (Toronto 1974), 65–79.

also the urban labour vote was becoming a factor to be reckoned with in electoral politics.[5]

Even more important, however, was the response in the countryside. Ontario was changing, but it did not change overnight and for many more years, indeed until well into the twentieth century, it remained significantly agrarian in economic character and overwhelmingly so in spirit. In the Upper Canadian mind the idea that agriculture was a morally superior way of life had been deeply ingrained, and its influence continued to be strongly felt. It was a myth that transcended all social divisions – even the new elites spawned by industrial and commercial success typically devoted a considerable portion of their time and fortunes to establishing their status as gentleman farmers and progressive agriculturalists. Nevertheless, for the first time the once-solid foundations of agrarian life were being threatened, and the threat was all the more insidious because it was not simply, perhaps not even mainly, economic; it was also social, cultural, and, in the broadest sense, moral. This was generally understood at the time. It was obvious, for example, that many of the young were not being forced off the land by its inability to support them; they were being positively drawn to the cities like iron filings to a magnet.

Not surprisingly, the commonest response of those who sought to combat this trend was to castigate the falsity and wickedness of city life, often by way of warning the young to beware its seductive (but of course hollow) attractions. Traditional rural life, on the other hand, was held up as an altogether more virtuous and rewarding model. Closely linked to this response, and in many respects a direct manifestation of it, was the rise of a new social movement whose purpose was to espouse the validity of the agrarian ideal. It was known as the Grange and its members as the Patrons of Husbandry.

It had been founded in the United States immediately after the Civil War and from there had rapidly spilled across the border into Canada. By 1875 the 'Dominion Grange' had expanded to several hundred chapters (or 'subordinate Granges'), the overwhelming majority of which were located in Ontario – 'presenting in fact the impression of an Ontario order with offshoots in other provinces.'[6] The reasons for its extraordinary appeal to Ontarians are not difficult to find. Ideologically

5 See Gregory S. Kealey, *Toronto Workers Respond to Industrial Capitalism, 1867–1892* (Toronto 1980). For an earlier but still useful study see Douglas R. Kennedy, *The Knights of Labor in Canada* (London, Ont. 1956).
6 H. Mitchell, 'The Grange in Canada,' *Queen's Quarterly* 22 (1914–15), 174

it was both progressive and conservative, and it arrived on the scene at a most timely moment with a most timely vision, a vision of agrarian life restored to pre-eminence through 'instruction in the art and science of husbandry.'[7]

The Grange was vaguely co-operatist, in that as it was opposed to what it considered 'a surplus of middlemen' in the agricultural economy and favoured as an alternative 'working together, buying together, selling together.' But it was also firmly attached to the values of individualism and the rhetoric of moral uplift, one of its objectives, for example, being 'to develop a better and higher manhood and woman-hood among ourselves.'[8] It believed in scientific progress towards a better future – even if the future it foresaw resembled nothing so much as some long-vanished Arcadia.

One reason for its appeal, as L.A. Wood has noted, was that it gave farmers 'an opportunity to join a widely extended social organization that would minister to their long-pent-up desires for self-expression.'[9] But it also did more than that. It gave agrarian Ontario a new formulation of an old – and flattering – image of itself, as the only 'true' creator of wealth. It also gave farmers a heightened consciousness of their own special interests in relation to those of other classes in society. Its ideals, moreover, were broadly acceptable. It was not radical, or even very egalitarian. In its ranks or 'degrees' (which for men ascended from 'Labourer' to 'Cultivator' to 'Harvester' to 'Husbandman' and for women from 'Maid' to 'Shepherdess' to 'Gleaner' to 'Matron')[10] it mirrored the divisions of society, albeit in a simpler and purer form. In the Grange's scheme of things there would still be a social hierarchy, but it would be a hierarchy of producers, in which an individual could rise through hard work and attention to the principles of good husbandry. In the long run such a vision could not be sustained, but it was understandably attractive in an agrarian society that was becoming inexorably more urban, industrial, and complex.

In politics such cross-currents and pressures typically produce sudden shifts of electoral fortune, a rapid turnover of leaders, the fragmentation of political support, and other similar manifestations of uncertainty or upheaval. Yet in Ontario they produced none of these

7 L.A. Wood, *A History of Farmers' Movements in Canada* (Toronto 1924), 45
8 Mitchell, 'The Grange,' 166–7
9 *Farmers' Movements*, 36
10 Mitchell, 'The Grange,' 165

things. Instead, the last quarter of the nineteenth century was dominated by a single administration.

Part of the explanation of this development undoubtedly lies in Ontario's favoured position within Confederation, for in spite of some periods of economic difficulty it was on the whole better placed than any other province to profit from the new transcontinental economy that Confederation had brought into existence. In effect, by retaining so large a share of the wealth generated by its earlier wheat-based economy, it had fuelled the beginnings of its own industrial development – which in turn left it well placed to dominate the new protected markets that were being created for Canadian manufactured goods. The pressures it faced from industrialization, therefore, while not to be underestimated, were the myriad pressures of successful growth, they had no concentrated focus and consequently produced no single issue of overriding importance. That alone, however, cannot explain the longevity of the Mowat administration. A further and more important part of the answer is to be found in the realm of politics: in governmental programs and policies that reflected the changing balance of economic and social interests; in an approach to administration that reflected a more modern notion of efficiency; in the consequent strengthening and centralization of executive power; and not least, in the creation of a disciplined, cohesive Liberal party machine.

III

It is important to realize that Ontario politics were actually much more competitive than Mowat's long unbroken tenure of office would seem to suggest, for although his government was victorious in six successive general elections at no time was its position ever invulnerable.[11] As Table 1 shows, the opposition Conservatives always managed to maintain a substantial presence in the legislature and a share of the popular vote that was only marginally less than that of the Liberals. Each election was therefore a genuine contest; the outcome was not a foregone conclusion, nor at the time was it generally thought to be.

11 According to Brian P.N. Beaven, 'the absolutely safe liberal seats were confined to 16 ridings, compared to 12–13 safe Tory havens, leaving approximately 60–62 in which the party balance was close.' 'The Last Hurrah: Studies in Liberal Party Development and Ideology in Ontario, 1878–1893,' PHD thesis, University of Toronto 1981, 56. On party competitiveness, see also Douglas Baldwin, 'Political and Social Behaviour in Ontario, 1879–1891: A Quantitative Approach,' PHD thesis, York University 1973.

TABLE 1 General Election Results by Party, 1875–94[12]
Seats (% vote)

	1875	1879	1883	1886	1890	1894
Liberal	51 (49)	57 (48)	50 (49)	56 (48)	55 (49)	51 (43)
Conservative	34 (46)	29 (48)	35 (47)	33 (47)	35 (46)	24 (31)
Other	3 (5)	2 (4)	3 (5)	1 (5)	1 (5)	19 (26)

The government's electoral base, moreover, while ostensibly secure, in reality was constantly in jeopardy, for it was located preponderantly in the old Clear Grit areas of southwestern Ontario, where the winds of agrarian discontent were blowing strongly. The Patrons of Husbandry were one striking manifestation of that discontent, and the sudden rise of that organization, though avowedly non-political, was none the less correctly perceived as a political signal by many of the politicians and aspiring politicians of the day. It was not long before they were assiduously aligning themselves with Grange values and attitudes, competing with one another for the privilege of addressing Grange gatherings (especially the annual Grange picnics, which often attracted huge crowds), and treating local Grange officers as clients worthy of special cultivation. Though the Liberals enjoyed the advantage of office, it was still by no means certain that they could hold the allegiance of a pressured and potentially volatile agrarian constituency, for they were

12 There is no standard method of reporting Ontario party standings in this period, since it is not possible to determine precisely the degree of party affinity of a small group of variously labelled 'independents.' The 'Independent-Conservative' John Thomas Grange, for example, is described by Charles Clarke, a former Speaker of the House, as 'one of the men whom any whip finds difficult to manage, voting with equal facility for "yea" or "nay," and who sees no use in party organization and regards responsible government as a will-o'-the-wisp, and ministerial consistency as an impalpable myth.' *Sixty Years in Upper Canada* (Toronto 1908), 165. Not surprisingly, therefore, different sources give slightly different totals. The totals in this table have been calculated from electoral data contained in Roderick Lewis, ed., *Centennial Edition of a History of the Electoral Districts, Legislatures and Ministries of the Province of Ontario, 1867–1968* (Toronto n.d.). But since the attribution of party affiliation in this work is in some cases inaccurate, the figures have been adjusted on the basis of contemporary press reports, various editions of the *Canadian Parliamentary Companion*, and divisions of the House during the first session of the legislature following a general election. They have also been adjusted to take into account the outcome of by-elections resulting from controverted elections and (in one case) from the resignation of a member before the opening of the first session.

also bound by the constraints of governing the entire province and they could not afford to become the singular voice of agrarianism.

It was also unlikely that the tories would want to adopt such a role, but there was an ever-present danger either that an organization such as the Patrons of Husbandry would turn openly to politics and field its own candidates or that some new parallel movement of agrarian militancy would be formed to do so. In either case the effect would be to create disaffection among local Liberal elites at the township and county levels and a potentially fatal splintering of the party's vote. The challenge Oliver Mowat faced as premier and party leader was therefore not an easy one; it was indeed essentially the classic challenge of democratic politics, which is so often the undoing of those in power: to accommodate change and the rise of new interests in society without at the same time alienating or cutting themselves off from those old interests and sources of support on which electorally they still depend. The pitfalls are always numerous in such circumstances, the chances of failure high. It is thus only in hindsight that Mowat's long-term success seems to have been assured; at the time it was very much in doubt.

There can be no doubt, however, about the quality of his response. It was partly traditional, partly original – and wholly effective.

On the one hand it was obviously governed by defensive considerations and was entirely characteristic of a politician steeped in the tradition of clientele politics. One of Mowat's first acts after assuming office as premier, for example, was to induce the sitting Liberal member for North Oxford to resign by offering him the lucrative sinecure of rain-gauger (an office worth two thousand dollars per year), thereby opening a seat for himself in the agricultural heartland of the province.[13] Since Mowat was personally about as unlikely a representative of agriculture as nineteenth-century Ontario was capable of producing (he lived in central Toronto, within walking distance of the legislature, and, unlike so many other leading Grits, made no pretence of being a gentleman farmer), his choice of seat was clearly a calculated gesture, a symbolic cementing of his leadership to the Liberal party's peninsular grassroots. In practical terms, it also ensured him of an ideal vantage-point from which to counter the periodic stirrings of agrarian unrest that threatened to upset that relationship, bringing directly to bear upon

13 'Nobody has yet been appointed Snow-gauger, a position that might suit another supporter of the Mowat administration,' commented the *Mail* (25 Nov. 1872). See A. Margaret Evans, 'The Ontario Press on Oliver Mowat's First Six Weeks as Premier,' *Ontario History* 56 (1964): 125–41.

them all the prestige and patronage that as premier he alone could command.

On the other hand, there was also an aspect of his response that was surprising, and perhaps even a little daring, especially coming from one who had supposedly been insulated from the milieu of active politics during his previous eight years on the bench. For he stepped into the premiership as though he had been long preparing for it, with a fully developed, up-to-date political program that he articulated from the start with unusual consistency. In it there was clearly reflected a conception of government as a benevolent instrument of social purpose; but that was an old and mainly tory notion in Ontario, going back to Simcoe. What was most striking about Mowat's approach was his confident promise of an active program of reform and modernization conducted with managerial expertise, efficiency, and financial know-how – and that he addressed it to the farming community in exactly the same terms as he addressed it to the most sophisticated of urban audiences. This is evident even in his first address to the electors of North Oxford: 'I hope soon to mature, with the aid of my colleagues, and to carry, at an early date, measures for the *satisfactory settlement* of the Municipal Loan Fund debts; for the *just appropriation* of the surplus revenues of the province; for obtaining an *augmented immigration*, principally of agricultural labourers and domestic servants; for the more *rapid development* of the agricultural and other resources of our country; for the *reform of the laws* in regard to various matters in which experience has brought to light defects and injurious anomalies; and for securing *increased efficiency* in the workings of our educational and municipal institutions, in the administration of justice, and in other departments of public service.'[14]

Mowat was of course always frankly supportive of agriculture (which, he declared, 'could not receive too much attention from the Government'),[15] but he never condescended to suggest that farmers were interested only in farming, nor did he pander to the agrarian defensive impulse or to the nostalgic yearning for an arcadian way of life that was so much a part of the rhetoric of the Grange. In sharp contrast, his rhetoric was always the rhetoric of the future, of progress, development, and increased efficiency in all things, including agriculture.

This was a bold line to take in rural communities whose economic

14 C.R.W. Biggar, *Sir Oliver Mowat: A Biographical Sketch* (Toronto 1905), I, 156
15 *Globe*, 30 Nov. 1872

underpinnings were being shaken, but it was also shrewd and in the long run politically rewarding. By addressing farmers in terms of equality, as though they were progressive businessmen who were every bit as interested as their urban counterparts in the advancement, modernization, and profitability of their industry, he struck a responsive chord in a growing sector of agrarian Ontario. Everywhere there were farmers and perhaps especially farmers' sons (to whom Mowat's government extended the franchise in 1877)[16] who were coming to realize that their future prosperity lay in diversification and more intensive and scientific methods of production. They tended to be more excited by higher yields per acre, new seed varieties and animal stocks, and the development of new products and new markets at home and abroad than by agrarian protest. And they were not slow to appreciate the translation of Mowat's ideas into concrete policies: they understood very well who the intended beneficiaries were of the creation of a department of agriculture (the first in Canada), of government-financed land-drainage projects, experimental farms, advanced research and education in agriculture and agricultural technology, and of government sponsorship of Farmers' Institutes and such special-interest organizations as the Ontario Dairymen's Association.[17]

Farmers, for all their similarities, were not a politically homogeneous group. Many were stubborn tories, and many more were radical Grits who were naturally attracted by agrarian populism; but in the middle there was also a solid, substantial core of Mowat liberals, and even some Mowat conservatives. They were the main reason his government was able to retain the support of the farm community for so long, in spite of strong political challenges and the besetting difficulties of governing during a time of economic adjustment. He had earned their support with agricultural policies that made those of his opponents appear primitive by comparison. But he also profoundly understood his audience. They were, for the most part, the sober, ambitious, forward-looking men of the townships who were pleased to think of themselves as 'progressive agriculturalists' – and what he promised them, basically, was nothing less than efficient husbandry in the management of the Ontario estate.

16 W.S. Wallace, 'Political History, 1867–1912,' in Adam Shortt and Arthur G. Doughty, eds, *Canada and Its Provinces*, vol. 17 (Toronto 1914), 145
17 See A. Margaret Evans, 'Oliver Mowat: Nineteenth-Century Ontario Liberal,' in Donald Swainson, ed., *Oliver Mowat's Ontario* (Toronto 1972), 142, and 'The Mowat Era, 1872–1896: Stability and Progress,' in Ontario Historical Society, *Profiles of a Province: Studies in the History of Ontario* (Toronto 1967), 100.

IV

Promises, however, are one thing, and successful execution another, for the latter depends at least in part upon good timing and the right choice of issues. But in these matters Mowat's political instincts were practically infallible, as his early mention of the Municipal Loan Fund so clearly illustrates. This dull and dusty issue now hardly seems the stuff of which brilliant reputations are made, but at the time it was a major source of contention between the provincial government and the critically important local level of Ontario politics. It was also unique in that it directly involved a full range of municipalities, from the smallest rural counties and even townships to the largest cities. Moreover, it was an issue that reflected unfavourably upon past administrations, which had either helped to create the problem in the first place or had conspicuously failed to solve it. A speedy and acceptable solution, therefore, would represent a considerable coup for Mowat's new administration, bringing it immediate credit with both agrarian and urban interests. There was no other issue of the day with so much political potential, as Mowat clearly recognized. 'Oliver is as busy as it is possible for a man to be,' Mrs Mowat wrote to a friend on 10 February 1873. 'The Municipal Loan Fund Act is like a millstone round his neck.'[18] But within six months of taking office he had personally engineered a legislative settlement that pleased virtually everyone – and in the process established once and for all his reputation as an administrator of peerless efficiency and financial acumen.

His Municipal Loan Fund Indebtedness Act (1873)[19] was a remarkably modern piece of legislation in that it was a prototypical piece of formula financing. The problem it addressed was basically a problem that had originated with the great railway boom of the 1850s, when municipality after municipality, caught up in the heady optimism of the day, had borrowed heavily and poured the money into railway ventures. In this they were aided and abetted by the provincial government, which in 1852 (during the Hincks-Morin ministry) had set up the Municipal Loan Fund to enable municipal councils to borrow at rates considerably lower than those offered by private lenders. The

18 Mrs Mowat's letter continues: 'Even his private secretary feels it is so; at least he told me the other day that he had had a frightful dream, part of which was that he was in a graveyard and had seen his own gravestone, on which were carved the letters M.L.F.' Biggar, *Mowat*, 205

19 For the full text of the act and its accompanying schedules, see *Journals of the Legislative Assembly of Ontario* (JLA), VI (1873): 206–11.

result was predictable. As W.S. Wallace writes: 'This fund ... proved a direct invitation to extravagance. Municipal corporations all over the province had borrowed sums far in excess of their actual needs, sums which in more than one case had been invested in unprofitable speculations. The town of Cobourg, for instance, with a population of less than five thousand, had borrowed half a million dollars from the fund and invested it in the Cobourg and Peterborough Railway, which, on the construction of a rival line from Port Hope, straightaway became a white elephant on the town's hands. A period of depression set in, and many municipalities found themselves involved in obligations which it was difficult, if not impossible, for them to discharge.'[20] Even Mowat, in his preamble to the act, felt compelled to speak of the 'mistaken representation' of the railway companies and the 'delusive expectation' of the municipalities that their loans would be repaid out of the profits of the railways.

The result was a tangled web of private enterprise and public finance. By 1872 some forty-four municipal debtors owed the province no less than twelve million dollars in unpaid principal and accumulated arrears of interest. That sum, however, was purely hypothetical. There was no way the province could collect it all, or even a substantial part of it, for the whole matter had inevitably become thoroughly embroiled in clientele politics. Local patrons and brokers (who in most cases were also the city fathers or township officials) had been the prime movers (and frequently the prime beneficiaries) of railway speculation and were now determined to prevent their financial chickens from coming home to roost. 'Some municipalities were so hopelessly involved that they did not trouble themselves; others were regarding the idea of Repudiation with too much complacency and practically were daring the central authority to collect. Still others insisted that the policy of subsidizing new railways with Provincial funds had been the cause of discrimination against the municipalities which had accepted all the burden of constructing the earliest railways.'[21]

And to add to the complexity, successive governments, up to and including Sandfield Macdonald's Patent Combination and Edward Blake's brief ministry, had been generally content to exploit the situation by doing nothing – for it suited them politically to keep the local patrons in a state of indebtedness: 'Sandfield Macdonald, it was suspected, was

20 'Political History,' 140
21 J.E. Middleton and F. Landon, *The Province of Ontario: A History, 1615–1927* (Toronto 1927–28), 437

not perhaps entirely averse to keeping the indebted municipalities at his mercy.'[22]

By Mowat's time, however, as he correctly perceived, there was more to be gained by settling the issue. Yet any move simply to forgive the debtors was unthinkable; it would have provoked a political storm that no government would willingly endure, for Ontario's municipalities, then as now, were jealous rivals, and those who owed nothing, or had faithfully kept up their repayments to the fund, were furiously opposed to any policy that amounted to rewarding the delinquent. What then was the answer?

Fortunately for Mowat, the raw material for an answer was close at hand in the form of the provincial government's accumulated surplus of some four million dollars – nearly all of which, ironically, had been set aside by the frugal administration of Sandfield Macdonald.

What Mowat proposed was in essence very simple: the government would allocate approximately two-thirds of the surplus ($2,705,047) to the municipalities, with each municipality, whether indebted or not, receiving credit for a sum calculated on the basis of $2.00 per capita. From this paper credit there would then be deducted the sum owed by the municipality to the Municipal Loan Fund, with the remainder, if any, being paid to the municipality as a cash grant. For those who owed nothing the result was a happy windfall: they were to receive the full amount. These grants were to be spent under provincial supervision, but the terms were hardly restrictive for, according to the act, expenditures could be made: 'in aid of railways [!], of drainage, of the building or improvement of the court-house or gaol, of the building or improvement of an hospital, of providing for the use of the municipality an industrial farm, a house of industry or of refuge, or in building or improving schools, public halls, bridges, harbours, piers or gravel roads, or ... other permanent improvements affecting the municipalities, or ... towards the reduction or payment of municipal obligations already contracted for permanent works.'[23] The amount of local political patronage thus created was of course substantial, and even as-yet-unincorporated rural districts were included in the bounty, only in their cases expenditures on 'permanent improvements' would be determined directly by the legislature – that is, by the members of Mowat's party.

The net effect was to place cash in the hands of all but the twenty-two

22 Wallace, 'Political History,' 140–1
23 JLA, VI (1873): 207

most heavily indebted municipalities, but these too were given ample reason to be satisfied since the act also included provisions for further reducing their debts to manageable limits. In essence, a ceiling was placed on each municipality's indebtedness by the application of a formula based on two principles or 'rules' – each would be issued new debentures at an interest rate of 5 per cent (the 'five-cent rule') equal to an amount on which the interest could be paid out of 2 per cent of its property assessment (the 'two-cent rule') after 'the ordinary and necessary expenses of the municipality (other than schools)' had been met.[24] In consequence, even such hopeless cases as Northumberland and Durham, Lanark and Renfrew, Port Hope and St Catharines were restored to solvency by having a large portion of their debts forgiven (though Mowat was careful never to put it in those terms). Since the new debentures were well within the municipalities' capacity to repay, they would be treated as negotiable and distributed among the creditor municipalities as part of the cash payments owing to them. The government could thus claim with some credibility that by distributing $2,705,047 of the provincial surplus, it had managed to collect $2,711,835 (the total of the new municipal debentures), or 25 per cent of a previously uncollectable debt.[25] The opposition press naturally grumbled that what the government had really undertaken was 'to strike $10 million off an asset of $12,500,000,'[26] but the municipalities, whatever their status, were generally too delighted with their new-found bounty to complain.

For Mowat the result was a triumph. It demonstrated his financial virtuosity and marked the beginning of a new-style rational-administrative government, more self-consciously managerial than the old and, in its almost mechanical application of rules and formulas, ostensibly less partisan. 'In this settlement,' Mowat proudly proclaimed, 'no party preferences were observed. We applied exactly the same rule to a Tory municipality as we did to a Reform municipality, and as we did to those which were neither Tory nor Reform – if any such there are.'[27] But at the same time it won for his government an incalculable amount of goodwill at the grass-roots level, even among the traditionally conservative local elites who dominated municipal politics.

24 Ibid.
25 Middleton and Landon, *Ontario*, 442
26 *Mail*, 26 Mar. 1873
27 Biggar, *Mowat*, 210

Mowat's reputation for expert husbandry – a hat too big for his opponents to fill

Ironically, the Patent Combination, which had once cultivated those same elites, had all the financial resources necessary to produce a settlement, and in fact its treasurer, Edmund Burke Wood, had even gone so far as to propose a settlement broadly similar to the one that Mowat eventually achieved, but nothing came of it.[28] For the Patent Combination, while not short of ideas or brokerage skills, lacked the sheer administrative expertise necessary to put it into practice – and administrative expertise was Mowat's strong suit. A further instructive comparison may be made with Edward Blake's ministry. Blake had promised in the 1871 election campaign to resolve the Municipal Loan Fund issue by a per capita distribution of the provincial surplus, but since this would not in fact have resolved the matter completely, he had also promised to forgive the debtor municipalities their debts[29] – a measure that would have made the government some friends but even more enemies, so once again nothing was done. The virtue of Mowat's scheme was that it was administratively sound *and* politically clever. It solved the problem through a masterly display of managerial know-how; but, so subtly as to pass almost unnoticed at the time, it also drew the municipalities more closely into a clientele relationship with the provincial government. And not least, in the unincorporated areas, it directly increased the amount of local patronage at the government's disposal.

Such outcomes were not incidental. Rather, they marked the beginning of a systematic effort on the part of the Mowat government to extend and strengthen its influence at the grass-roots level of politics. That indeed was in many respects the most difficult challenge it faced. For, as earlier reform governments had discovered, local reform organizations were often ineffectual, and the much-vaunted 'body of reform opinion' did not automatically translate into electoral support. To build a more efficient instrument for the delivery of votes was therefore essential if the Mowat government was to have any realistic hope of remaining in power.

28 Middleton and Landon, *Ontario*, 437. W.S. Wallace goes so far as to suggest that 'had Sandfield Macdonald possessed the foresight and energy to pass a measure similar to Mowat's, he would have escaped defeat in 1871.' 'Political History,' 141
29 *Mail*, 14 Mar. 1873

14

Northern Ontario: The Boundary Issue and the Bribery Plot

The traitor's hand is at thy throat,
   Ontario! Ontario!
Strike down that traitor with thy vote,
   Ontario! Ontario!

– Liberal campaign song (1883)

Leaving the court one day, I found myself walking beside the man Kirkland, and we fell into conversation. He seemed very much surprised at the fuss made over such a small matter as attempting to buy a few legislators ...

– Charles Clarke, *Sixty Years in Upper Canada* (1908)

I

It is against a background of intensely competitive party politics that the more familiar aspects of Mowat's premiership must be understood. This is especially so of his celebrated conflicts with the federal government over the interpretation of the British North America Act.[1] For, however dry and legalistic the subject matter, each judgment of the Judicial Committee of the Privy Council arose out of an otherwise irreconcilable

1 See J.C. Morrison, 'Oliver Mowat and the Development of Provincial Rights in Ontario: A Study in Dominion-Provincial Relations, 1867–1896,' in *Three History Theses* (Toronto: Ontario Department of Public Records and Archives 1961). For an astute assessment of Mowat's leadership and forensic tactics in these cases, see Paul Romney, *Mr Attorney: The Attorney General for Ontario in Court, Cabinet and Legislature, 1791–1899* (Toronto 1986), 240–81.

federal-provincial conflict; each was pressed forward to its conclusion by relentless political pressure; and each, symbolically and in substance, inexorably marked off the ground gained by one side and lost by the other in the tug-of-war within Canada between opposing governments, leaders and parties – pre-eminently between Toronto and Ottawa, Mowat and Macdonald, Ontario Liberals and federal Conservatives, and their respective clienteles.

Overshadowing all such issues, and intensifying the partisanship with which they were fought, was the long-standing dispute over the Ontario-Manitoba border. Though not strictly a constitutional issue at all – since its outcome did not hinge on an interpretation of the BNA Act nor did it have anything to do with the federal-provincial division of powers in Confederation – it was nevertheless inseparable from the other points of contention between Ontario and Ottawa, and politically of far greater importance. For what was in dispute was no subtle constitutional point concerning the lieutenant-governor's prerogatives or some esoteric legal technicality (such as which level of government had jurisdiction over 'escheats and forfeitures'),[2] but rather something familiar in everyday life and hence immediately understandable: namely, the ownership of a large and valuable piece of land. There could hardly have been an issue more guaranteed to rouse the possessive instincts of an inveterately land-conscious people.

Indeed, without an appreciation of the extraordinary significance of land in the Ontario political culture it is difficult to understand either the intractability of the boundary issue or the acrimony it aroused, since on the face of it there was ample room for a negotiated settlement. Ontario's western and northern boundaries had been left in an obviously undetermined state at the time of Confederation, and since there were no major geographical barriers to mark their 'natural' limits, it might be thought that they could with equal justification have been located almost anywhere within a very wide range. The trouble was, however, that Upper Canadians had become accustomed to viewing western expansion as their undoubted right, since their political leaders had long claimed extended authority in that direction and vehemently rejected the territorial claims of the Hudson's Bay Company.[3] Their

---

2 This issue involved the right to possession of property forfeited to the Crown. Its outcome had a significant bearing on the status of the lieutenant-governor. See C.R.W. Biggar, *Sir Oliver Mowat: A Biographical Sketch* (Toronto 1905), I, 242–6.
3 See J.M.S. Careless, *The Union of the Canadas* (Toronto 1967), 205–6.

post-Confederation expectations were therefore very high. Consequently, when the federal government acquired possession of the still-undetermined Hudson's Bay Company domain in 1870, it found itself confronted by a province whose territorial ambitions in the region were vast, whose government was unyielding, and whose people were in no mood to accept anything less than what they believed to be their full entitlement.

In the following year two boundary commissioners were duly appointed, one by Ontario and one by the Dominion, but so far from producing a solution their efforts ended unhelpfully and on a sour and farcical note: after much suspicious intergovernmental bickering each produced his own version of the boundary line – some 275 miles apart![4] Moreover, for reasons that remain unclear, the line proposed by the federal appointee was drawn *east* of Fort William, deep inside what had previously been undisputed Ontario territory. This might have been simply a bargaining ploy, or an attempt to shock Ontario out of its obstinacy, or even a genuine (if historically unsupported) counterclaim, but whatever the intent, the only effect was to confuse and embitter the issue still further. Not surprisingly, it appeared to Liberal Ontario that Ottawa's real aim in the northwest had been unmasked as nothing more nor less than a gigantic tory land-grab, thus prompting the breakdown of negotiations in May 1872. Thereafter Ontario was unwilling to yield so much as an inch – but neither could it gain one, as long as the Conservatives remained in power federally.

For Mowat, therefore, it was a stroke of fortune when the Conservatives were swept out of office in 1873 and replaced by a Liberal government headed by his old friend and fellow Grit, Alexander Mackenzie. Where once there had been discord, now there was only harmony, resulting in an agreement between the two governments to accept as final and binding the adjudication of the boundary dispute by a new three-member board of arbitration, which was subsequently appointed. In 1878 it handed down its decision 'unaccompanied by supporting reasoning or explanation' and wholly in Ontario's favour.[5] With the prospect of adding some 110,000 square miles to its territory, the province had reason to be jubilant. It meant a great increment in natural wealth, and with it, Mowat implied, a corresponding increment

4 Morris Zaslow, 'The Ontario Boundary Question,' in Ontario Historical Association, *Profiles of a Province: Studies in the History of Ontario* (Toronto 1967), 109
5 Ibid.

in Ontario's power and prestige. 'And so,' he had sanguinely informed the legislature, 'another of the problems which the government had to deal with was settled, and settled satisfactorily.'[6] But in fact it was not. Ironically, although both governments had agreed in advance to ratify and give legislative effect to whatever decision might result from the arbitration, the timing of the award was such that it came too late to obtain ratification before the 1878 federal general election – and this next spin of the electoral wheel put Mackenzie out and Macdonald back in. As Mowat was to discover, no doubt to his chagrin, what one election could give, another could take away: predictably, the Conservatives refused to act. Instead they claimed that there had been collusion and threatened to investigate the arbitrators. As the *Mail* put it: 'nothing seems more necessary than an inquiry into all the circumstances attending this arbitration. It was manipulated by two Reform governments accustomed to hunt in couples.'[7] So far from being over, the boundary conflict was becoming more tangled and more venomous than ever.

Macdonald's next move was to rush through Parliament a bill extending Manitoba's border eastward to the head of Lake Superior, in total disregard of the arbitration award.[8] Purely in geopolitical terms, this might have been a sensible and indeed far-sighted solution (there was surely much to be said for giving western Canada its own outlet to the Great Lakes, and perhaps also for enlarging and diversifying Manitoba's resource base), but under the circumstances there was no possibility that it would be considered as such. Manitoba was much too obviously being used as a pawn for Ontario to view its sudden injection into the fray as other than reckless and outrageous, virtually a *casus belli*. For no matter how tarnished with party bias the 1878 arbitration award might in fact have been, once it had been handed down, Ontario opinion would thereafter brook no interference with it, as Mowat well knew when he rose in the legislature to deliver this furious rebuttal:

'Why is it that our rights in that territory are persistently withheld from us? I would like to know some reason, some real reason ... Is it to make Ontario the smallest of the great Provinces? Does not the Dominion owe the greater part of its prestige to Ontario? [applause]. Is

6 *Globe*, 16 Dec. 1878
7 *Mail*, 21 Feb. 1880
8 J.C. Morrison concludes that the bill was a 'tactical manoeuvre ... designed to force Mowat to come to terms.' 'Mowat and the Development of Provincial Rights,' 137

not Ontario the great taxpayer – the Province that puts more money into the Treasury than she takes out of it? [applause]. Why the difficulty, the obstacle that stands in the way? I cannot account for it except that there is ... hostility somewhere and those who ought to stand up for Ontario are not doing so ... Well, it is for the people of Ontario to say whether they will yield or not ... If they have been asleep, I venture to say that they are aroused now – [applause] – and that they will be asleep no more, and that they will not rest until every mile of awarded territory is surrendered to us – [renewed cheering] – and our constitutional freedom and our Provincial rights are both respected and secured forever [long and continued cheering]'[9]

II

In the Ontario general election in February 1883 Ottawa's refusal to implement the arbitration award was inescapably a major issue, and for many Liberals the only one. It was not a normal contest between government and opposition, Mowat argued in his address to the electors, but rather between two governments: 'It is useless to deny it, Ontario is at one side, the Dominion government is at the other side. We contend not merely with the local Opposition, but with the whole power of the Dominion government.'[10]

The Liberal campaign was orchestrated accordingly: it was anti-Macdonald, anti-Conservative, and anti-Ottawa, and it spared no effort to impress upon Ontarians the immensity of the loss they would suffer if the northwest, which was rightfully theirs, should be denied them. In the *Globe's* view, 'the issues are great, sharply defined, and easily understood. Shall this province be cut in two?' And when one hapless Conservative candidate adopted the slogan 'Vote for the only speedy settlement of Ontario's rights,' it thundered in reply: 'The "only speedy settlement," according to the Tory program, is unconditional surrender to Federal aggression.'[11]

The Conservatives under W.R. Meredith were in fact trapped in a classic Canadian dilemma. At first, in deference to public opinion, they had supported the arbitration award, albeit somewhat grudgingly; but later, under pressure from Macdonald after his Manitoba gambit, they had done a complete turnabout and aligned themselves with their

9 *Globe*, 28 Jan. 1882
10 Ibid., 4 Jan. 1883
11 Ibid., 20 Feb. 1883

federal colleagues. This of course raised an awkward question: 'If the award was for two years valid, as Mr. Meredith said it was,' asked the *Globe* unerringly, 'why is it not so now?' The answer, it suggested, was obvious and the lesson clear: 'Mr. Meredith has been ordered to turn his back upon himself ... Ontario cannot afford to trust one whose willingness to surrender the citadel of our rights to the demand of the enemy is now a matter of public record.'[12]

But if the Conservatives were weak on the central issue of the day, they were by no means without compensating strengths in other areas, nor were the Liberals invulnerable. The latter, indeed, had put themselves at risk by concentrating so obsessively on waging holy war against the federal government that the effort caused them – for the one and only time during Mowat's long premiership – to neglect their normally much-vaunted reputation for managerial efficiency. The Conservatives were thus able to chip away at it: for example, by accusing the government of 'squandering ... Ontario's patrimony in the woods and forests' and of 'raising revenue in a prodigal fashion' through its timber-licensing policies; by suggesting to Ontario manufacturers (perhaps somewhat fancifully) that the high tariffs of which they were so fond were endangered by federal-provincial discord and that therefore 'the interests of the National Policy require Mr. Mowat's defeat';[13] and above all by hammering ceaselessly on their favourite theme, that Mowat's drive towards administrative centralization was a threat to 'local liberty' (that is, municipal autonomy) and hence to the traditional clientele system: 'There is no blinking the fact that unless the provincial electorate administer a sharp rebuke at the polls, the work of centralization will soon be consummated ... step by step the government in its eagerness to enlarge its patronage is usurping authority in all directions, and with another lease on power no institution will be safe.'[14]

By the mid-1880s the shortage of local patronage had in fact become a source of considerable discontent. Though the Conservatives had regained control of federal patronage, it still rankled with them that so much had been taken out of the hands of the municipalities (many of which they controlled) by the Mowat administration. Local tory patrons had felt the shortage with particular acuteness during the lean years of parallel Liberal rule in Toronto and Ottawa, and they were determined

12 Ibid., 4 Jan. 1883
13 *Mail*, 2–29 Jan. 1883
14 Ibid., 21 Dec. 1882

to get back their lost resources. Consequently Meredith was pledged to various specific measures of patronage decentralization, including, most importantly, the restoration of liquor licensing to local authorities.[15]

The Conservatives also managed to divert attention from the boundary issue by giving their campaign a novel, if somewhat bizarre, sectarian twist: after years of appealing to the Orange, ultra-Protestant vote, and denouncing Mowat for his 'unholy alliance' with the Catholic church, with no very notable success, in 1883 they abruptly switched to the *opposite* tack and appealed to the Catholic vote, this time denouncing Mowat for his alleged *hostility* to Catholic interests.

As usual in Ontario, however, it was patronage and not religion that lay at the heart of the matter. Mowat had always smugly maintained that 'by an equal distribution of patronage he had done justice to both Roman Catholics and Protestants';[16] but what the Conservatives now purported to demonstrate (in a broadsheet entitled 'Facts for Irish Electors') was that Catholics actually received a smaller share of patronage than they were entitled to on the basis of their share of the population and that the choicest plums were reserved for Protestants only.[17] The clear implication was that if Catholics helped the Conservatives to an electoral victory, they could expect a more generous portion of the spoils. Whether this had any direct effect on the outcome is difficult to determine. The Catholic hierarchy remained unmoved in their support of the government, and there is no evidence of a general shift of allegiance on the part of Catholic voters, but in a few constituencies where the outcome was decided by a handful of votes, it could conceivably have made the difference. Yet there can be no doubt about the effect of patronage of a more immediate and tangible kind, for it was soon evident that the *quid pro quo* of the provincial Conservatives' endorsement of Macdonald's position on the boundary question was a lavish infusion of money from Ottawa, both in the form of campaign funds and, even more tellingly, in the form of access to Macdonald's bottomless barrel of federal patronage. As one contemporary observer put it, 'the whole artillery of Ottawa was brought into play, and its fire told heavily on the result.'[18] The *Globe* concurred, though its summation

15 W.S. Wallace, 'Political History, 1867–1912,' in Adam Shortt and Arthur G. Doughty, eds., *Canada and Its Provinces*, vol. 17 (Toronto 1917), 1612
16 *Mail*, 27 May 1879
17 *Globe*, 17 Feb. 1883. See also Wallace, 'Political History,' 165–6; and J.E. Middleton and F. Landon, *The Province of Ontario: A History, 1615–1927*, vol. 1 (Toronto, 1927–8), 408–9.
18 *Bystander*, Apr. 1883

was predictably more caustic: 'The opponents of the Mowat government came into the contest flushed with their victory in the Dominion
elections, and resolved to capture Ontario even if the whole corruption
fund of the Tory party were exhausted in the attempt.'[19]

The outcome was nevertheless another Liberal victory, though by a
reduced majority. In the previous general election – when the Conservatives had run an anti-Catholic campaign that backfired disastrously – the
Liberals had won a total of fifty-seven seats, including a number that
were normally Conservative (Cardwell, for example, had elected a
Liberal for the one and only time in its forty-one-year existence as a
riding),[20] but in 1883 most of these reverted to their former allegiance. As
usual, the *Globe* and the *Mail* gave contradictory reports of the outcome,
the former claiming that forty-eight Liberals had been elected to
thirty-five for the Conservatives and the latter that forty-three had been
elected to thirty-nine for the Conservatives.[21] But in the end, after the
customary recounts, charges and counter-charges of electoral corruption, and delayed returns from the ridings of Algoma and Muskoka
(where voting did not take place until September), the Liberals emerged
with fifty seats and the Conservatives with thirty-five. In addition, two
independent-liberals and one independent-conservative were elected.[22]

III

In terms of the boundary dispute the result was critical. Had the
Conservatives won, the path would have been cleared for an accommodation between Toronto and Ottawa, a new arbitration by Conservative-
appointed arbitrators, and swift ratification by both governments. But
since they did not, the strategic advantage once again shifted to Mowat,
who, with a renewed mandate, was now in a position to outlast his
federal opponents. No one was more painfully aware of the consequences of this turn of events than Macdonald: 'It is the policy of Ontario
to play the waiting game,' he wrote, '& I consider the fate of the
conservative party depends on the speedy settlement of the question.'[23]

19 1 Mar. 1883
20 Roderick Lewis, ed., *Centennial Edition of the Electoral Districts, Legislatures and Ministries of the Province of Ontario, 1867–1968* (Toronto n.d.), 38
21 *Globe*, 1 Mar. 1883; *Mail*, 28 Feb. 1883
22 For the derivation of these figures see above, chap. 13, n. 2.
23 Macdonald to A. Campbell, 5 July 1883, as quoted in Morrison, 'Mowat and the
Development of Provincial Rights,' 154–5

Further weakening his hand, ironically, was the ineffectiveness of the Manitoba government in its role as a federal surrogate once the outcome of the Ontario election had been determined. For, from that point forward, it was plain to Manitobans that there would be no easy political resolution of the dispute, at least not along the lines favoured by Macdonald, and hence no easy gains for Manitoba. Instead, they now faced a different and infinitely less promising prospect: of a long-drawn-out, costly, and perhaps futile battle with Ontario – over a piece of territory that they did not actually consider of much value in any case, since it was unsuitable for wheat production and since, in creating Manitoba in 1870, the federal government had retained control over the province's natural resources. Moreover, in the domestic politics of Manitoba an increasingly large and influential element consisted of settlers from Ontario (and particularly from Grit southwestern Ontario) who had no desire to quarrel with their native province; rather they looked to it for moral and political support in their own quarrels with the Métis and the French. Not surprisingly, therefore, Manitoba became a weak and ambivalent carrier of the federal banner. It was no match for Ontario, whose tenacious government, backed by a drum-beating Liberal press, never doubted either the value of the territory or the rightness of its claim, which it pursued with single-minded zeal.

Accordingly, with the election safely behind him, Mowat began to strengthen his government's presence west of the lakehead, appointing new land commissioners, magistrates, and other officials and sending out a force of special constables to back up their authority and generally 'show the flag.' The ensuing clash with Manitoba has been described as 'a comic-opera war' – but it was clearly one with a nasty potential. As a contemporary observer reported from Rat Portage (later Kenora): 'Dominion Commissioner McCabe, with two policemen, Ontario Magistrate Burden, with twenty-five policemen, and stipendary magistrate Brereton, with fifteen policemen, acting on behalf of Manitoba, have been arresting each other all day, and the people have been siding, some with one party and some with another to the imminent danger of the peace and of loss of life.'[24]

It was the sort of confrontation, just short of what it would take to justify the armed intervention of the federal government, that Ontario relished – and for which Manitoba, as it turned out, had no appetite at all. Hence, when in December 1883 the Manitoba attorney-general, J.A.

24 Middleton and Landon, *Ontario*, 411

Miller, was invited by Mowat to come to Toronto to arrange a truce, and to discuss possible terms for a permanent settlement of the issue, he attended with alacrity and showed a most conciliatory attitude. The outcome of their negotiations was an agreement so one-sided that it is doubtful if even Mowat himself could have anticipated such a coup.

In essence, the agreement committed their respective provinces to a joint reference of the boundary question to the Judicial Committee of the Privy Council for final and binding adjudication, and provided, in the interim, for an administrative *modus vivendi* in the disputed territory. But it is clear from the memorandum of agreement that was signed,[25] and from correspondence related to it, that in every important respect the terms and conditions of both the Privy Council reference and the *modus vivendi* had been dictated by Mowat, down to and including the exact wording of the questions to be submitted to the court. Even more crucially, he had insisted that the decision of the council be binding not only upon the provinces but upon the federal government as well – obviously to permit Macdonald no loophole should the decision go in Ontario's favour. And, coming close to adding insult to injury, he had exacted a private undertaking from Miller that the Manitoba government would use its influence with Macdonald to that end. As Miller wrote to him in a confirmatory note: 'I quite understand that your government consents to the basis of the agreement arrived at to-day upon the condition that I am to procure the consent of the Dominion government as speedily as possible to pass such an order in council as would be necessary ... to submit the case as agreed to between us for the opinion of the Judicial Committee ... Also that the Dominion shall be bound by the opinion so to be given so far as the western boundary of Ontario is concerned, and would request the Colonial Minister if necessary to procure an Act of the Imperial Parliament to legalize that opinion so that the Act when passed would bind not only Manitoba & Ontario but also the Dominion.'[26] Politically, the effect was to separate Manitoba from its federal mentor: at a stroke its status had been changed from surrogate to go-between.

That Mowat would try to manoeuvre his adversaries into a reference to the Privy Council on terms of maximum advantage to Ontario is not surprising. That Macdonald would acquiesce in such a set-up most certainly is – yet after much stalling and equivocation he did so. There

25 Ontario, Sessional Papers, xvi, pt ii, 1884, no. 3, 3–8
26 Morrison, 'Mowat and the Development of Provincial Rights,' 154

can be no doubt that he needed the issue settled before the next federal general election; and it is at least possible that the Manitoba government was able to exert effective pressure upon him; but he also seems to have badly miscalculated his chances of winning. Perhaps once again his normally acute judgment was unbalanced by his personal loathing of Mowat (in his estimation, a 'mere jackal to Blake's lion').[27] Or perhaps he was simply the victim of poor legal advice. In any event, when the case reached the Privy Council in July 1884, it was still, astonishingly, in every essential detail the case that Mowat had constructed: the questions were his, Manitoba was his sole adversary, and the Dominion was to be bound by the verdict. Thus was the stage set. Drawing on his own vast experience of both Privy Council hearings and the background to the boundary dispute, Mowat himself led Ontario's counsel. Manitoba's counsel were assisted by federal legal advisers – who were evidently no great asset: when judgment was handed down, it was wholly in Ontario's favour.

The Judicial Committee ruled that although it found the original arbitration award of 1878 to be 'not binding' because it had never been ratified (a fairly obvious point), *'nevertheless, their Lordships find so much of the boundary lines laid down by that award as relate to the territory now in dispute ... to be substantially correct and in accordance with the conclusions which their Lordships have drawn from the evidence laid before them.'*[28] Thus, in the end, the highly political, undoubtedly partisan, and quite possibly rigged award of 1878 was judicially confirmed.

At first glance this might seem odd or even suspect, for why should that award have been so exclusively the focus of the court's ruling? The reason, of course, is that the court could address only the questions that were put to it – and these had been constructed by Mowat (as part of his deal with Manitoba) with a view to ensuring precisely such a focus, as is clear from the first two questions, which asked: '(1) Whether the Award is or is not under all the circumstances binding? (2) In case the Award is held not to settle the boundary in question, then what, on the evidence, is the true boundary between the said Provinces?'[29]

The effect, naturally, was to enhance the importance of the award and give it a priority and a *locus standi* it would otherwise have lacked, thus subtly shifting the burden of proof to the other side to show why it

---

27 Ibid., 145
28 Ontario, Sessional Papers, XVII, pt II, 1885, no. 8, 44 (italics added)
29 Ibid., 43

should not be upheld. In short, what in Canada had been a political ugly duckling became transformed in London into a legal swan. The wonder is that Mowat was able to get away with it. But it would appear that his opponents simply failed to grasp the significance of his earlier manoeuvring until it was too late: to the very end the Manitoba government remained unconcerned and Macdonald almost absurdly over-confident.

IV

The result was a bitter defeat for the federal Conservatives, while for the Ontario Liberals it was a triumph to be savoured. Mowat returned to a jubilant province and a hero's welcome, with mass public demonstrations of a kind not seen since those honouring the memory of the fallen Isaac Brock, heralding his progress from town to town. These were of course orchestrated by the Liberal party with its usual efficiency,[30] but there was no lack of genuine enthusiasm, even in tory Toronto, where the greatest demonstration of all took place. Like a conquering Napoleon, the 'little tyrant' was paraded through his capital in an open carriage accompanied by a huge procession. 'Altogether some twelve thousand men were in line and fifteen bands blared triumphantly until the procession halted in Queen's Park for an overflow of oratory'; and, as if to acknowledge the critical contribution to the outcome of the Liberal electoral victory in 1883, each Liberal constituency 'had in the march as many delegates as the majority of the sitting Member.' Along the route enormous crowds gathered: 'Possibly one hundred thousand people, in a city whose numbers were swollen by visitors to the annual exhibition as well as those who came in especially for this occasion, witnessed some part of the demonstration.'[31] A few days later in Woodstock, the county seat of his home riding of North Oxford, the town was filled to overflowing by a crowd of twenty thousand who had come from miles around to greet his return. There, a triumphal arch had been erected by the Liberal party; and emblazoned upon it like battle honours were the names of Mowat's previous Privy Council victories over the federal government: 'Escheats, Insurance, Licences, Rivers and Streams.'[32]

30 See Kenneth A. MacKirdy, 'National vs. Provincial Loyalty: The Ontario Western Boundary Dispute, 1883–1884,' Ontario History 51 (1959): 191–8.
31 Middleton and Landon, Ontario, 443
32 Biggar, Mowat, 449

Mowat serves lunch to William Meredith and John A. in the Provincial Rights Restaurant.

For Liberals, these were patriotic occasions: 'I rejoice to know that the one great cause, the principal cause of your enthusiasm is that you love Ontario as I love it,' Mowat told a cheering multitude at Niagara Falls. 'The display you have made this night shows that you are for Ontario, and that you are for those who maintain Ontario's cause.'[33] The *Globe* struck a similar note: 'The victory we celebrate,' it pronounced, 'is greater than victories which have cost thousands of human lives ... Ontario as now definitely bounded possesses within herself all the necessities and potentialities of a great nation.'[34] The Conservative press naturally took a dimmer view of the proceedings. But however regarded, there can be no doubt that the boundary decision had important consequences both immediately and in the long run.

First, for Mowat himself the result was a brilliant political and personal triumph. And the fact that he had not only won but had won so dramatically before 'the highest court of the Empire' (as proud Liberals invariably described it) made his victory all the more impressive, inspiring acclaim that raised his personal standing to near-Olympian heights. Thereafter, whatever other difficulties his government might encounter, his position as the champion of Ontario's interests was unassailable, his record transformed by his adoring followers into the stuff of political folklore: 'Mr. Mowat,' the *Globe* proclaimed as the next provincial election approached, 'has met and has beaten Sir John Macdonald at every point, has, in fact, figuratively swept with him the floor of the Privy Council.'[35] The result of that election, held in December 1886, was an easy victory for the Liberal party. Functioning in the constituencies with well-oiled smoothness, and aided by a Conservative opposition that had become demoralized and fractious, it increased its majority in the legislature to twenty-two seats.[36]

Secondly, for the Canadian federal system the consequences of Ontario's victory were paradoxical. On the one hand, there can be no doubt that it damaged the prestige and weakened the power of the central government; indeed, it may be said to have altered the balance of power in Confederation more fundamentally than any other issue of the

33 *Globe*, 16 Sept. 1884
34 Ibid., 1 Sept. 1884
35 18 Dec. 1886
36 The campaign was dominated by sectarianism and charges of corruption. 'The enemy has no case,' the *Mail* maintained. 'He relies upon ecclesiastical fulminations, upon the gerrymander, and upon his army of licence inspectors, road bosses, and bailiffs.' 27 Dec. 1886

nineteenth century, since it confirmed, with apparent finality, that although the provinces might be constitutionally equal, in reality one province and one province alone would be paramount in population, in economic power, in the richness and diversity of its territory. On the other hand, there can be no doubt that it also helped to cement that province's attachment to the federation and thus contributed in no small measure to the system's long-term preservation. For, once Ontario's territorial expectations were fulfilled, it also became unique in another respect: it became (as it remains) a province without a major grievance. This is not to say that there were no further quarrels between it and the federal government, for there were many, or that it did not vigorously promote its own sectional economic interests, for it did; but thereafter it was also the province that most consistently and powerfully supported the maintenance of the federal system, the one whose people most tended to identify the national interest as their own.

Mowat had once said, at the height of the boundary dispute, that 'he was as much attached to the Confederation, and felt as great an interest in its success, as anybody; but if ... they could only maintain Confederation by giving up half of their Province, the Confederation must go ... it was not worth maintaining.'[37] But in the end his victory was so complete that Ontario could not have gained more had he himself written the Privy Council's judgment, a fact that was soon absorbed into the province's political outlook. For entirely unconnected reasons, old tory eastern Ontario had always looked sympathetically on the idea of a larger nationality: now even the most hard-boiled Grit in western Ontario could unreservedly embrace the same idea. After all, in the young Dominion that was the embodiment of that idea, Ontario's pre-eminence seemed finally to be assured.

Finally, the boundary award marked a significant turning-point in the evolution of Ontario's political economy. Now, a century later, it is perhaps difficult to appreciate its true impact, for the vast new territory thus acquired still stands, as Morris Zaslow states, 'on the threshold of development,'[38] a resource hinterland that is home to a mere 5 per cent of the province's people. The '60,000,000 acres of fertile land'[39] that were once so optimistically claimed for it turned out to be little more than a fanciful dream. But in other respects its natural wealth was not

37 *Globe*, 27 Jan. 1882
38 Zaslow, 'Boundary Question,' 115
39 *Globe*, 20 May 1882

exaggerated. It was indeed rich in timber, minerals, and water power; and its rail link to the south and its accessibility to the expanding industrial centres of the United States via the Great Lakes gave it an obvious potential, which entrepreneurs were not slow to exploit. To old Ontario, whose wealth had arisen out of agricultural success and had been sustained and augmented by the growth of manufacturing industry, there was now added the burgeoning resource frontier of new Ontario – with a consequent opening up of new outlets for investment, new markets, and new sources of employment. The result was to impart a powerful northward thrust to the province's overall economic development.

It must be stressed, however, that Ontario's fierce determination to expand its territory had not sprung purely, and perhaps not even mainly, from economic motives; it had sprung also from an abiding and at times almost obsessive concern over status, as manifested, for example, in the fear so revealingly expressed by one of Mowat's ministers, T.B. Pardee, commissioner of Crown lands, that a truncated Ontario 'would be reduced from the proud position of the Premier province of the Dominion to the position, so to speak, of a third-rate power in the Confederation.'[40] Expansion was thus a matter of Upper Canadian pride (or, from other points of view, of Upper Canadian arrogance). Historically, it reflected the same peculiar assumption of entitlement that had been built into the Upper Canadian outlook from the very beginning; for, it must be remembered, land had been the original loyalist imperative, its grant from the Crown the symbolic confirmation of rightness and worth, of political vindication. With astounding fidelity that outlook had been passed on to late-Victorian Ontario, where, after the passage of a century, land remained a potent symbol and was still pursued with a visceral acquisitiveness.

V

It is clear in retrospect that Ontario's treatment of the new territory after it was acquired, and of the north generally, was also profoundly influenced by cultural factors. For in spite of the political excitement generated by the boundary issue, and the possessive instincts it aroused, the north was not actually very well understood by southern Ontarians – if for no other reason than that it was a kind of hard

40 Ibid., 21 Jan. 1882

"NOW THEN, ALL TOGETHER! ONTARIO! ONTARIO!!"

Laurentian land of which they, as an agrarian people, had had no direct experience.

Hence it is not surprising that they, and their government, at first tended to conceptualize it in essentially agricultural terms; indeed, for many years it was believed to contain large areas suitable for cultivation and numerous schemes were devised by government to promote agricultural colonization.[41] Nor is it surprising that Mowat and the Liberal party approached the development of the north's growing inventory of exploitable forest and mineral resources from a basically southern and agrarian perspective. That is to say, they viewed it not in terms of its potential value to the north but rather in terms of its value to the old, predominantly agricultural society of the south – in which their political power was based, whose interests they represented, and whose intellectual and cultural outlook they shared.

Accordingly, their development policies were framed within a familiar context and reflected familiar ideas. Their idea of efficiency considered as good husbandry, for example, was implicitly extended to it, their object being to maximize its benefit to the Ontario estate as a whole. It was as though a farmer had discovered that some distant acres (whose ownership he had vigorously contested but whose topography he scarcely knew) contained valuable mineral deposits and a seemingly endless supply of timber: he would not relocate his home there (mining or logging being in his view unsuitable occupations for a true Ontarian), but he welcomed the royalties paid by developers and used them to supplement his income and improve his farm.

Moreover, the means to pursue such an approach were readily at hand. As H.V. Nelles has so tellingly demonstrated, there was no need for any Ontario government to invent the concept of a positive, interventionist state since that concept had always been present in the province's operative political culture, a legacy of monarchical rule that from the time of Simcoe had been a powerful instrument in the hands of the executive. Specifically, the legal reality and political tradition of the proprietary rights of the Crown over natural resources – 'latent in the expression, crown lands' – meant that the rights to forest, mineral, and water resources remained legitimately in the public domain and were not automatically conveyed to individual landowners with the titles to their land. It was therefore both legitimate and politically acceptable that

41 See Morris Zaslow, *The Opening of the Canadian North, 1870–1914* (Toronto 1971), 160–1.

the allocation of wealth derived from those resources should be 'in accordance with the prevailing notions of the interests of the state'[42] – and, it might be added, the policies of its governing party.

There was thus no confusion over Ontario's objectives or over the instruments to be used. Confident of public support, the Mowat administration brought to bear upon the field of natural resources the same proclivity for centralized control from Toronto, and the same expertise in public finance, that it had earlier brought to other fields. For example, it maintained rigid control over timber rights on Crown land, yet leased such rights through a flexible system of competitive 'bonusing' – that is, it auctioned short-term licences to cut timber on specific tracts of land, the successful bidder being required to pay a 'bonus' to the government at the time of sale that was not contingent upon production; in addition, he was assessed ground rent and stumpage dues on timber actually cut.[43]

The advantages of such a system were twofold: first, it discouraged (though it did not totally eliminate) the non-productive holding of timber reserves for purposes of speculation, and second, it enabled the province to obtain an economic return from its forests that reflected the timber industry's own market valuation of their worth. Since timber was a commodity for which demand tended to be extremely volatile, that valuation tended to fluctuate widely. But as ministers and officials gained experience in the operation of the system, and in particular as their monitoring of the American timber market became more sophisticated, they were able to adjust the timing of auctions to avoid periods of glut and to sell whenever possible during periods of rising demand. By such means the government was able to exact a proportionate share of all but the most short-term and unpredictable of windfall gains that might (and sometimes did) occur in the industry. Though not infallible, the system was many years ahead of any other then in place in Canada or the United States – and in striking contrast to the still-prevalent pattern of Canadian resource development, in which provincial governments assume many of the major costs and risks of development in return for a trivial share of future benefits.

As a result, the Ontario treasury enjoyed an extraordinary financial bonanza throughout the last two decades of the nineteenth century,

---

42 H.V. Nelles, *The Politics of Development: Forests, Mines and Hydro-electric Power in Ontario, 1849–1941* (Toronto 1974), 1–19
43 Zaslow, *Opening of the Canadian North,* 161

with income from the Crown lands alone accounting for approximately 25 to 30 per cent of all provincial revenues, nearly all of it derived from the northern forests.[44] Moreover, this high level was sustained without a massive disposal of timber rights. Unlike the Blake ministry, which in a single year disposed of 5,031 square miles, the Mowat ministry *during the next twenty years* disposed of only 4,234 square miles. But whereas the former received an average price per square mile of $117.79, the latter received on average *more than ten times* that amount, and in especially good years, *as much as thirty times*. In 1887, for example, the leasing of a mere 459 square miles produced bonuses totalling $1,312,312 for an average price per square mile of $2,859. In the depressed market of 1890 the area leased was cut back to 376 square miles but increased to 633 under more favourable market conditions in 1892, when the average price rose to $3,657 and total bonus revenue to $2,315,000.[45] By contrast, in the province of Quebec, the nearest and most comparable jurisdiction, the government over the same period never managed to obtain more than an average of $283.00 per square mile or a total revenue of more than $687,743.[46] Little wonder, therefore, that the Ontario Liberals missed no opportunity to trumpet their leader's masterful husbandry of the public domain.

It must be remembered also that these were for the most part economically difficult years for Canada as a whole. Yet because of its resource revenue the Ontario government – alone in the Dominion – was able to maintain its public finances in a healthy and even flourishing condition, accumulating surplus after surplus while at the same time substantially increasing the level of public expenditure.

The principal beneficiary of this good fortune was, of course, southern Ontario, for it was there that the bulk of the resource revenue was expended, in the form of investment in public works and the improvement of social services; in effect, wealth was systematically transferred from north to south, with government acting as a conduit. The result was to shower upon the latter region all the advantages of increased expenditure on roads, schools, universities, vocational education, hospitals, and other amenities without any commensurate increase in the rate of taxation or in the public debt. There was scarcely a

44 Nelles calculates that 'between 1867 and 1899 bonuses, dues and ground rent from the lumber industry produced in excess of $29 million, or approximately 28 percent of the total provincial revenue.' *Politics of Development*, 18
45 Ibid., 18–19
46 Zaslow, *Opening of the Canadian North*, 168–9

southern community or industry that did not enjoy some benefit, either directly or indirectly, but none benefited more than agriculture, which in the 1880s (when resource revenue had grown to new heights) received a vital and timely infusion of new public capital as well as other forms of direct and tangible assistance. For Mowat and his ministers were no believers in the doctrine of *laissez-faire*: to an extent remarkable for their time they actively intervened to support agricultural modernization and diversification, creating a separate department of agriculture, establishing a bureau of industries to monitor production and provide accurate and comprehensive economic statistics, financing scientific research and training in advanced agricultural technology, and promoting specific developments that they deemed to be economically desirable, such as the bringing of the province's southern wetlands into production by subsidizing (through local authorities) an extensive program of tile- drainage.[47] In sum, the contribution of northern Ontario to southern Ontario was large and important, and its timing vital.

VI

Politically, the chief beneficiary was undoubtedly Mowat's Liberal party. Farmers were naturally avid for public works and other benefits and aids to agriculture, but (being 'land rich and cash poor') they were also naturally loath to part with hard-earned cash in payment of direct taxes. For them, the Liberal policy of financing such benefits very largely out of resource revenue was nothing short of brilliant – as Liberal politicians never failed to remind them – and again and again they showed their appreciation at the polls.

Moreover, northern resource development significantly increased the flow of patronage through the Ontario political system by increasing the number of appointments, contracts, concessions, and other rewards that the government had in its power to bestow, thus crucially replenishing the reserves of the Liberal party at a time when the countervailing weight of federal patronage was commonly thrown against it in provincial elections. Hence, just as Ontario's relatively high degree of control over its own revenues enabled Mowat to challenge Macdonald on constitutional questions with virtual impunity, so too did the Liberal party's control over its own large reservoir of patronage

47 See A. Margaret Evans, 'Oliver Mowat: Nineteenth-Century Ontario Liberal,' in Donald Swainson, ed., *Oliver Mowat's Ontario* (Toronto 1972), 43.

enable it to compete with the federal Conservative party on roughly equal terms – and even more impressive, to do so while simultaneously fending off (or buying off) sporadic movements of agrarian populism.

But there were also certain dangers involved. Though these were largely obscured as long as Mowat himself remained personally in charge, later, in the hands of less able leaders, they would do the Liberal party irreparable harm.

Above all, there developed in the north a type of clientele system that deviated significantly from the Upper Canadian model, not only because of the time-lag of nearly a century in its development but also because of the fundamental difference that existed in the region's economic base, which in turn affected the way that Ontarians viewed it. For in their outlook, which the Mowat government implicitly shared, resource extraction, while plainly lucrative, was also plainly transitory and therefore not a suitable foundation on which to build a permanent community: that would come in time, but only with the development of agriculture, just as it had in the south. (Ontarians, it would seem, had a need to believe in the north's mythical 'millions of fertile acres' since otherwise they would have had to believe that their coveted new acquisition, once stripped of its surface assets, would become worthless, a mere wasteland.) Hence, though the Mowat government's management of forest resources was both efficient and, for its time, progressive – as shown by its promotion of research, its creation of a forest ranger service, and its efforts to prevent forest fires[48] – modern notions of conservation and reforestation played no part in its thinking. As H.V. Nelles points out: 'the nineteenth-century image of the forest was that of an enormous non-renewable resource, not unlike a giant mineral deposit, which was permanent simply by virtue of its size and could be exploited only once *and then passed on to the farmers.*'[49]

The importance of this last step cannot be too strongly emphasized. Clearly, in the Ontario scheme of things, there was no permanent or even long-term place for the lumberman; though the land might be opened up by his enterprise, and though he might grow rich in the process, in the final analysis he was perceived as a transient who would move on as the edge of the forest receded, taking his capital and his expertise with him. In consequence, he could never become a patron in the old Upper Canadian sense, for the patron's role was one that

48 Zaslow, *Opening of the Canadian North*, 162–3
49 *Politics of Development*, 184 (italics added)

entailed the existence (or at least the expectation) of long-lasting economic, political, and social relationships. The patron, moreover, was bound into the clientele system both from above and from below – from above by his ties to the government and the social hierarchy, by virtue of his land grants and his various military and political preferments; from below by his ties to the local community, by virtue of his need to promote the success and maintain the loyalty of his clients. The northern lumberman, by contrast, was but marginally attached to either – he too needed the government, and the government needed him, but their exchange was essentially short term and impersonal. Likewise, while his relationship with those who worked on his timber concessions and in his sawmills retained certain clientelistic elements (in that personal and political obligations were typically involved in addition to economic ones), he had no real interest in promoting their settlement on the land once it was cut over, and hence no attachment to any local community more permanent than a lumber camp.

Not surprisingly, therefore, party allegiances in the north also tended to be geared to the short run and to be cemented by little more than cynical calculations of *quid pro quo*. But since agriculture never developed as expected, the Liberal party was never able to acquire the solid, reliable clientele that sustained it in the south; instead it was forced to contend with its captive and increasingly restless clientele in the timber industry, and to resort to more and more desperate means to maintain its hold. By the turn of the century those means had come to include flagrant electoral corruption,[50] but even under Mowat there had been signs of trouble, though of a different kind.

It was perhaps inevitable that his administration's timber-licensing policies would provoke antagonism, particularly over the curtailment of speculation. Moreover, many of those affected were American lumbermen accustomed in such neighbouring states as Michigan and Wisconsin to having outright ownership of timber lands, to do with as they pleased without government interference. Indeed, it was not uncommon for local legislators to be their clients. They were not accustomed to the idea of public property rights inherent in the concept of Crown lands – and still less to dealing with an administration like Mowat's, with its peculiar notion of husbandry, its assurance of power, and (incomprehensible outside the Ontario political context) its infuriating habit of assuming the patron's role and treating *them* as mere revenue-producing

50 Bryan D. Tennyson, 'The Cruise of the Minnie M,' *Ontario History* 59 (1967): 125–8

clients. Hence, as the costs of timber licences and other fees escalated, so too did their resentment, to the point of outright revolt. The last straw, from their point of view, was the return of the Liberal government following the extremely bitterly contested 1883 general election, which left them with no prospect of relief. Shortly thereafter, no doubt emboldened by the closeness of the outcome, some of their number set out to tip the balance the other way by means of a little discreet bribery.

Previously, the size of the government's majority had rendered it practically immune to overthrow by such means, but in the immediate aftermath of the election, with several seats unfilled because of delayed elections or court challenges, and its majority sharply reduced, it had become suddenly vulnerable: it could be brought down, after the election of a Speaker from among its own ranks, if only five Liberal members could be induced to switch sides – a risky proposition, perhaps, but far from impossible in the turbulent political atmosphere of the time. At a minimum, after the swearing in of a new ministry, there were bound to be some government backbenchers whose hopes of a cabinet seat had been disappointed and who harboured grievances. The question was: how far would they be willing to go?

The answer, as it turned out, was not far enough. Either through bad luck or bad judgment, two of the Liberals selected for bribing, Robert McKim (West Wellington) and W.D. Balfour (South Essex), proved unreliable; after pocketing large sums of cash ($1,000 and $800 respectively) and giving the impression that they had been well and truly bought, both turned around and secretly informed their party whip, who informed Mowat – their bulging and incriminating envelopes being temporarily deposited in the safekeeping of the Speaker.[51] Thus was the stage set for Mowat's deadly counter-attack. Without warning, on 17 March 1884, just before the planned motion of want of confidence in his ministry was to be introduced, he rose during a routine debate on supply to make an unusual request of the Speaker; namely, that he

51 The circumstances surrounding these revelations remain somewhat obscure. Mowat's chief party agent, W.T.R. Preston, writes in his memoirs that only one of the members (though he omits to say which one) originally came forward, but that was sufficient to raise a general alarm. 'Reliable information, indicative of a widespread plot, soon came to my ears; and eight or nine members of the new Legislature contributed further proof.' *My Generation of Politics and Politicians* (Toronto 1927), 149–51. See also the memoirs of Charles Clarke, the Speaker of the Legislature at the time: *Sixty Years in Upper Canada* (Toronto 1908), 277–91.

unseal the envelopes that he had been given by the members for West Wellington and South Essex and table their contents. The Speaker did so with electrifying effect, the sudden flash of money jolting the House out of its customary early-evening torpor. Mowat rose again, this time facing the opposition benches across a pile of banknotes. Amid a growing furore he proceeded to name the alleged corrupters. They were F.S. Kirkland, a Wisconsin lawyer and representative of various timber and mining companies; Frederick Stimson (*alias* 'Lynch'), also an American with timber interests; and three Canadians, all of whom were in some way connected with the Conservative party (though none was a member of the legislature), the most notable being C.W. Bunting, the managing director of the *Mail*, the chief Conservative organ in Toronto. The others were John A. Wilkinson, a well-known Conservative agent and party broker, and Edward Meek, a Toronto lawyer. Taken by surprise, Kirkland was arrested in the lobby of the legislature; Stimson was never apprehended and was presumed to have fled to the United States.[52]

A judicial commission was appointed to inquire into the matter and eventually reported in January 1884.[53] Among its more important findings was that the five named had attempted to bribe not only McKim and Balfour but also three other Liberal members: R.A. Lyon (Algoma), John Cascaden (West Elgin), and J.F. Dowling (South Renfrew); that the monies paid, though in themselves substantial, were intended only as first instalments, with matching amounts to follow upon delivery of the votes in question and the fall of the government; and that in addition to cash various other inducements had been offered, including lucrative appointments in Edmonton and Regina (to local posts which at that time were in the gift of the federal government). Criminal charges of 'conspiring to corrupt' were subsequently laid against those of the alleged bribers who could be found, but the law in this area proved problematical, and in the end, after prolonged wrangling over legal technicalities, the result was a verdict of acquittal, 'the judge, Sir Adam Wilson, charging strongly in that direction.'[54]

By then, however, the impact of the 'bribery plot' had reverberated to

52 Biggar, *Mowat*, 364–9; Middleton and Landon, *Ontario*, 409; and Wallace, 'Political History,' 166–7

53 Ontario, *Sessional Papers*, XVII, p III, 1885, no. 9

54 Clarke, *Sixty Years*, 291

the furthest reaches of the political system, and Mowat had left no doubt
as to its meaning. With a single well-aimed stroke he had exposed and
publicly humiliated its perpetrators, cast a cloud of suspicion over the
Conservative opposition, and, most important, taught the timbermen
and mining promoters of the north a chastening and salutary lesson:
thereafter they tamely bid on concessionary licences as instructed and
paid due homage to the Liberal party.

15

The Mowat Machine

A population may, so to speak, go to bed with an Organization and wake up with a Machine.

– M. Ostrogorski, *Democracy and the Organization of Political Parties* (1902)

I

One of the frequently noted marks of a 'developing' or 'modernizing' society is the increasing level of direct control imposed by the central government upon rural and geographically remote areas that were previously beyond its reach, or to which its reach extended only weakly or intermittently.[1] This trend is generally the product of a number of interrelated factors, including the growth of transportation and other technological infrastructures, the creation of national markets, urbanization, and increases in the size and functions of the state bureaucracy. But whatever the causes of centralization, and whatever the means through which it is effected, if electoral competition is also present – that is, if elections genuinely determine which party or group will control the government – it will almost inevitably be accompanied by a parallel development in the organization and structure of political parties.

This was the case in virtually every democratic political system in the nineteenth century, and the result in each was the development of some form of extra-parliamentary apparatus, most commonly through the

1 See, e.g., David Apter, *The Politics of Modernization* (Chicago 1966); and Samuel P. Huntington, *Political Order in Changing Societies* (New Haven 1968).

creation of hierarchically structured party organizations.[2] These were designed to link the party's leadership formally and institutionally to its component units at the constituency level, and also to co-ordinate the electoral and other activities of those units, often through regional committees or other similar levels of intermediate organization. Within this broad pattern, however, the specific *type* of party structure that emerged varied greatly from one system to another, and even within systems, depending upon the pace of change, the constitutional framework, past experience of party rule, and, in general, the operative norms and expectations of the political culture.

Post-Confederation Ontario is a particularly fascinating seed-bed of party structures, for out of it, more or less simultaneously, there arose two distinct variants of machine-type party organization,[3] one federally oriented and conservative, the other provincially oriented and liberal. Both were natural outgrowths of the old Upper Canadian clientele culture in that both were based on the pyramiding of patron-client alliances to form networks of exchange in which patronage and other material benefits flowed downward and electoral support flowed upward; and in both brokerage was a vital function.[4] But there were also

2 The classic study is M. Ostrogorski's *Democracy and the Organization of Political Parties*, 2 vols. (London 1902).
3 The literature on this type of party organization is large and confusing, since the terms 'machine,' 'political machine,' and 'party machine' are used in a variety of senses, often with unsavoury or sinister connotations. In most modern political science and anthropological studies, however, these terms are used analytically and neutrally to denote specific *types* of organization, though there is no agreement on an exact definition. V.O. Key, Jr, for example, defines a party machine as the 'inner core' of the party, a 'more or less cohesive group held together by the ambition to gain power' (*Politics, Parties and Pressure Groups* [New York 1953], 337); while James C. Scott seems to use the term more broadly to include the entire apparatus of party ('Corruption, Machine Politics, and Political Change,' *American Political Science Review* 63 [1969]: 1142–58). My usage is a broad one and follows that of Michael Johnston, who defines a machine as 'a party organization within which power is highly centralized, and whose members are motivated and rewarded by divisible material incentives rather than by considerations of ideology or long-term goals of public policy. These incentives – money or gifts, jobs, contracts, favors – are used to build an organization which obtains votes (legally or otherwise) in sufficient number to win and maintain control over public authority. Authority in turn is a source of more incentives.' 'Patrons and Clients, Jobs and Machines: A Case Study of the Uses of Patronage,' *American Political Science Review* 73 (1979): 385
4 In spite of their generally acknowledged prevalence and importance, party machines have received little attention in Canadian political studies, beyond Escott Reid's famous essay, 'The Saskatchewan Liberal Machine before 1929,' *Canadian Journal of*

striking differences between them, to some extent in their detailed organizational configuration, but more importantly in their societal bases and their modes of operation. To understand these differences it is useful to view them in terms of the distinction drawn by René Lemarchand between two sub-types of party machine, which he identifies as 'neo-traditional' and 'orthodox.'[5]

The *neo-traditional* machine develops mainly by incorporating into its organization pre-existing clientele clusters and networks; or, as Lemarchand puts it: 'exchange processes between the center and the periphery are mediated by, and contingent upon, the operation of traditional forms of clientelism at the local level.' In such cases, 'traditional micro-level solidarities provide the essential linkages between the party and the masses; the machine is superimposed upon, and in some ways tributary to, the clientelistic subsystem.' By contrast, the *orthodox machine* develops mainly by creating its own network of patron-client exchange, in which purely political patronage is 'the essential source of cohesion' and 'vertical solidarities are maintained through material inducements.' There are also significant differences in their intermediate levels of organization. In the latter 'the party structure defines the organization of the machine, and is co-extensive with its field of operation. The neo-traditional machine, on the other hand, seeks to enlist the support of micro-level clientelistic structures through bargaining with traditional patrons who act as brokers between the party elites and the masses.'[6] The result will likely be two broadly

---

Economics and Political Science 2 (1936): 27–40. Most of the American work on machines, moreover, is based on studies of urban politics in terms of a 'boss-reformer' dialectic, which tends to overstate the similarities between machines while ignoring the very different local circumstances which produced them. See M. Craig Brown and Charles N. Halaby, 'Machine Politics in America, 1870–1945,' *Journal of Interdisciplinary History* 17 (1987): 587–612. Such work therefore offers few theoretical insights that are of use in the Canadian context. Of much greater theoretical value is the work of the Dutch anthropologist Mart Bax, who, in his study of Irish politics, puts forward what he terms a 'generic model' of the political machine which places a strong emphasis on the role of the leader. See his *Harpstrings and Confessions: Machine Style Politics in the Irish Republic* (Amsterdam 1976), 69–72. For further discussion of the differences in the development of American and Canadian machines, see S.J.R. Noel, 'Dividing the Spoils: The Old and New Rules of Patronage in Canadian Politics,' *Journal of Canadian Studies* 22 (1987): 74–6.

5 'Political Clientelism and Ethnicity in Tropical Africa,' in Steffen W. Schmidt et al., eds., *Friends, Followers and Factions: A Reader in Political Clientelism* (Berkeley 1977), 114–5

6 Ibid., 114

different patterns of party activity and, equally likely, two broadly different styles of party leadership.

In Ontario these differences were reflected in the Conservative and Liberal parties, and in the leadership styles of John A. Macdonald and Oliver Mowat. There can be no doubt, however, that of the two parties and leaders it was the Conservatives and Macdonald who controlled incomparably the greater share of patronage resources, since at Confederation seemingly all the richest spoils of office had fallen into the federal maw. Macdonald was thus amply supplied with the means he needed to strengthen and expand the Conservative party organization – in effect, to complete the task to which he had devoted so much time and effort during the Union era. For he had been the most assiduous, and on the whole the most effective party organizer of that era. Better than any of his contemporaries he had learned to use patronage as a means of knitting together the always potent (but endemically anarchic) conservatism of the districts with the precarious coalition of tories and moderates who constituted the Conservative party in Parliament. But his efforts, while extraordinary for their time and in many respects the key to his political success, were also almost entirely idiosyncratic and personal: in so far as there was a Conservative 'organization,' he was it.[7] Not surprisingly, therefore, his approach to party-building in the post-Confederation era followed essentially the same pattern. In other words, the Ontario Conservative party machine was built by formalizing – and enriching with new federal patronage – the bonds that already existed between the party leadership and the local elites, whether tory or 'progressive' conservative, whom Macdonald had always cultivated. Yet while they were unquestionably the party's vital core, they were rarely the party's creatures. Their power and prestige, in fact, typically pre-dated their involvement in the party, and often their positions in commerce and local government enabled them to sustain substantial clienteles of their own. They were thus quasi-independent patron-brokers, and they expected leaders to bargain with them for their support. Dealing with them could be a trial: it required brokerage skills of a high order, a personal touch – and usually a great deal of Macdonald's famous 'soft sawder' – to keep them in line; yet no

---

7 For Macdonald's role as a party-builder, see J.K. Johnson, 'John A. Macdonald,' in J.M.S. Careless, ed., *The Pre-Confederation Premiers: Ontario Government Leaders, 1841–1867* (Toronto 1980), 214–20; and Gordon T. Stewart, *The Origins of Canadian Politics: A Comparative Approach* (Vancouver 1986), 67–90.

Conservative leader could contemplate fighting an electoral battle without them.

When opportunities arose (as they did, for example, in new federal constituencies in western Canada), Macdonald was not averse to creating new party structures and using party intermediaries of a more orthodox kind, but in Ontario he was largely stuck with the old system. To create parallel structures was practically unthinkable, for it would only have encouraged the local faction fights or 'splits' that he was forever mending, and if unmended were always so electorally damaging. As a result the Conservative party in Ontario tended to remain essentially 'neo-traditionalist' in structure and outlook. This contributed to its weaknesses: its stress on bargaining was cumbersome and time-consuming; it required constant 'hands-on' leadership; and its infusions of patronage were as readily converted to bolstering a local patron-broker's personal standing as to building a poll-by-poll party organization in his riding. But to understand its role in Ontario politics in the nineteenth century it is essential to realize that this type of party also had some enduring strengths: its structure corresponded to the social structure of local communities; its supports were diffused over a range of relationships rather than narrowly concentrated upon exchanging votes for favours; and while its thirst for patronage was enormous, like the camel it could survive long periods without drinking at all (as it had to do, for example, when the federal well dried up between 1873 and 1878). In provincial politics it could also survive repeated election defeats, wild swings of party policy, and the churning over of party leaders – and each time come back fighting. There was no election in the nineteenth century in which it was not a force to be reckoned with.

When Oliver Mowat became premier and Ontario Liberal leader in 1872, however, he was confronted by an altogether different, and from a party point of view, infinitely less promising prospect. First of all, the 'party' that sat behind him in the legislature was composed of the same motley collection of reformers, Grits, 'ministerialists,' and hyphenated 'independents' who had doomed every Liberal attempt to govern for a quarter of a century: when subjected to pressure, or inducements, such aggregations had in the past always fallen apart, and there was no reason to believe that this one would not do so as well. Second, the 'party' outside the legislature was not so much a party as a semi-organized 'tendency,' in that it was composed of a large but amorphous body of 'reform opinion,' a number of supporting newspapers, and a miscellany of constituency electoral committees or associations that varied widely in their levels of activity and effectiveness; its local leadership tended to be difficult to co-ordinate for electoral purposes and often drawn towards temperance, anti-Catholic, or other single-issue diversions. And third, there was the unresolved question of whether the province's seemingly narrow range of powers under the BNA Act gave it either sufficient reason or sufficient resources to sustain the existence of political parties of any kind; or, if they continued to exist, whether they would develop fully or eventually be confined to a minor or subterranean role, as in municipal politics.

Yet in spite of these apparent disadvantages, over the course of Mowat's first four years in the premiership there was put in place in Ontario a working prototype of a new Liberal party machine that was in many respects organizationally superior to its Conservative counterpart.[8] It was more straightforwardly orthodox in its hierarchy, more 'professional' in its ethos, and tended to rely more exclusively on political patronage to maintain (in Lemarchand's terminology) its 'core vertical solidarities.' While not averse to incorporating existing clientele clusters into its structure (particularly in places where local elites were traditionally 'Baldwinite' or otherwise not firmly attached to the Conservative party), for the most part it was forced to create its own cadre of intermediaries. While these were recruited for the most part from among the ranks of the respectable, progressive, upwardly mobile members of the community, who generally had solid roots in their own ridings, they also tended to owe their positions less to any independent social status or commercial importance than to their party connections. The result was a party apparatus that was more amenable to direction from the top, and a party in the legislature that was dependent upon it for electoral support and thus more easily whipped into line. Over the following decade it would be developed into an instrument that was without peer in the efficient use of patronage. Thereafter Mowat could not be dislodged: he remained premier for an unequalled span of twenty-four years, until 1896, and the Liberal machine did not finally go down to electoral defeat until 1905. But by then it had fallen under inept leadership and become rotted with corruption.

8 One measure of its performance, for example, is its success in getting out the vote. Gail N. Campbell has calculated that fluctuations in turnout accounted for only 15 per cent of the variation in the Liberal vote, in contrast to 23–30 per cent of the variation in the Conservative. 'Voters and Nonvoters: The Problem of Turnout in the Nineteenth Century: Southwestern Ontario as a Case Study,' *Social Science History* 11 (1987): 187–210

Originally, the rise of the Mowat machine was generally facilitated – and the significance of its organizational development generally obscured – by the coincidence (after 1873) of a Liberal government in Ottawa. But after the return to power of Macdonald and the Conservatives in 1878, it soon became evident that the Mowat machine was by no means dependent upon access to federal sources of patronage for its continued existence, and that, on the contrary, as it showed in the 1879 provincial general election, it was perfectly capable of operating effectively without it. For Mowat had always taken care, even during the interval of complete federal-provincial liberal hegemony, to base the party's operation primarily on the downward flow of *provincial* patronage, which under his aegis was systematically increased in volume and variety. The process through which this was accomplished, however, should be viewed in the context of the times.

II

Today, ironically, Mowat is best known (and frequently vilified by writers of a centralist bias) as a *de*centralizer, a wily exponent of 'provincial rights' whose victories before the courts undermined the original intent of Confederation.[9] Yet to concentrate too narrowly upon such struggles is to miss the other essential thrust of his approach to governing, which was towards the greater centralization of power *within* Ontario. There is, moreover, an essential connection between the two. Ultimately, it was only the Liberal party's hold on the Ontario electorate that enabled Mowat to challenge the federal government from a position of strength; and the vital machinery of that party had been created primarily through the consolidation of power and patronage within the Ontario government's own undisputed constitutional sphere, particularly vis-à-vis the municipalities. On the face of it, the latter was a politically dangerous course to pursue, for it seemed to run directly counter to the spirit of localism that had for so long been a pronounced feature of the Upper Canadian political culture. But in Mowat's view efficient husbandry and centralization went hand in hand, and his method of settling the Municipal Loan Fund issue clearly pointed the way to their future combination. In effect, by coating the pill of centralization with the sugar of financial benefits, it showed that

9 See, e.g., the harsh judgment of Donald Creighton, *Canada's First Century* (Toronto 1970), 46–9.

centralization could be made palatable to the municipalities. Thus, while the idea of local autonomy was still too entrenched to be attacked directly, in practice it could be overridden by appealing to another long-established value of the political culture – the idea, dating back to the original loyalists, of government as a benefactor of local communities. This was Mowat's approach. And following on the success of the Municipal Loan Fund Act there poured forth from his ministry a stream of centralizing acts and regulations, in such diverse areas as health, education, liquor licensing, and agriculture, which cumulatively amounted to a new definition of the role of the province – a definition that even after the passage of more than a century remains recognizable in the basic contours of Ontario government.

For Mowat, centralization was always justified on grounds of greater administrative efficiency. But it also meant projecting the presence of the Ontario government *directly and formally* into the local constituencies on a scale previously unknown. Provincially appointed commissioners, inspectors, agents, and trustees multiplied in number, many replacing municipal officials in fields taken over by the province. And since all owed their positions directly to patronage, they naturally tended to be partisan supporters of the Liberal party, thus giving it a more solid and extensive extra-parliamentary structure than any of the old Upper Canadian political groupings, reform or conservative, that preceded it. That structure, moreover, remained for a very long time unshaken by even a temporary interruption of its hold on office. As a result, Sir John Willison observes: 'For over a generation no Conservative was appointed to the public service in Ontario. Although fitness in appointments was seldom disregarded, the Civil Service was an essential portion of the organized political machinery of the Mowat Administration.'[10]

In fact, the first statement is not strictly true. It is a mark of the new sophistication that Mowat brought to the administration of patronage that – much like a modern-day premier, for example, and in sharp contrast to the approach of his predecessors – he always sought to give at least a modicum of credibility to Liberal claims of non-partisanship by appointing a certain number from the other party. Of some two hundred and thirty liquor commissioners appointed to 1883, for example, at least twenty-three were known Conservatives.[11] But there

10 *Reminiscences Personal and Political* (Toronto 1919), 95–6
11 This figure was accepted by the Conservatives themselves in their 1883 election pamphlet 'Facts for the People.' D.B. Weldon Library, University of Western Ontario, *Ontario Political Pamphlets, 1878–1900*, vol. 4

can be no doubt that Willison's conclusion is essentially correct. Indeed, nowhere is the process of centralization more clearly demonstrated, and nowhere is the connection between centralization and the growth of the Liberal party's 'political machinery' more immediately obvious, than in the area of liquor licensing.

In 1876 legislation was enacted that effectively stripped the municipalities of their long-standing power to license and regulate the sale of alcoholic beverages, and transferred jurisdiction to the province.[12] As in the case of the Municipal Loan Fund Act, Mowat's basic technique of administration was to apply a set formula. Under the new act (known as the 'Crooks Act' – not in judgment of its ethics but after the provincial treasurer, Adam Crooks) the government was to appoint three liquor commissioners for every city, town, and electoral division in Ontario, who would assume responsibility for the distribution of local tavern, bar, hotel, and other such licences. Further, the *number* of such licences that could be granted in each locality would be restricted by means of a formula based on population – one licence for each 250 of the first 1,000 of population and one additional licence for each 400 of population above 1,000. It thus went some way towards mollifying the temperance movement. But more important by far was its effect on the Liberal party: at a stroke a cadre of loyal Liberal office-holders was created, distributed across the province in careful parallel to the electoral system, who would fill the crucial intermediate positions as the machine expanded to its full pyramidal shape; and liquor licences were turned into valuable assets that the machine controlled. The holders of such assets were thus necessarily placed in a clientele relationship with the Liberal district bosses who filled the commissionerships, with predictable consequences: 'The liquor regulations were tempered to the behaviour of licence-holders. An adequate display of zeal for the Government was a fair guarantee of security when licences were renewed. Inactivity was tolerated. Open rebellion was often punished.'[13] Their ties to the machine, moreover, were further reinforced and placed on a continuous face-to-face basis by a new corps of provincially appointed liquor inspectors (lower-level Liberal party operatives), who replaced the local officials who had previously been responsible for the enforcement of liquor regulations.[14]

12 *Journals of the Legislative Assembly of Ontario* IX (1875–76): 209–10
13 Willison, *Reminiscences*, 93
14 Sir John A. Macdonald, then out of office, was well aware of the danger thus posed to Conservative electoral fortunes and promised to restore liquor licensing to the

OFF WITH HIS HEAD!

Mowat and Crooks dispose of Conservative liquor-licence holders.

The Conservatives had not been slow to perceive the political implications of the Crooks Act and had tried desperately to rally popular support against it. In what would become a constant Conservative refrain over the next twenty years, they denounced the whole trend towards greater centralization as 'fraught with danger for the liberty of the people' and staunchly defended the maintenance of local autonomy. In their view the act's partisan purpose was clear: 'In plain words, it proposes to put the trade under the surveillance of the politicians; for, as politics go now, the commissioners and inspectors appointed to regulate the traffic will, without doubt, be political partisans of local might and celebrity, and skilled in the low arts of electioneering and ward chicanery ... No sensible man, whatever his opinions may be as to the use and abuse of intoxicating liquor, will approve of this sweeping and despotic proposition. We know too well what desperate things petty government officers will do to please their patrons at election times.'[15]

The Conservatives' efforts, however, met with scant success. Many local governments were not in fact unhappy to be relieved of a jurisdiction that they found increasingly difficult to administer and full of political pitfalls, especially in communities where the temperance movement exerted strong pressure. And once again the pill of centralization was sugar-coated by guarantees to the municipalities of generous financial compensation for their loss of power, to be paid out of surplus licence revenues.[16]

The basic blueprint of the Mowat machine is thus plain: it was designed specifically to facilitate central control. And the ultimate controller was Mowat himself, whose position as premier was thereby immeasurably strengthened. Unlike earlier premiers (including those under the old regime of the United Canadas) he had no need to bargain in the lobbies of the legislature with capricious independents and local patrons who would never lend more than their conditional or nominal support to any leader. Instead, for the first time, 'the most influential

---

municipalities through federal legislation if returned to power. Accordingly, after his return, Parliament in 1883 passed a Liquor Licence Act (the McCarthy Act)
designed for this purpose, but on appeal to the Privy Council it was ruled *ultra vires*. See W.S. Wallace, 'Political History, 1867–1912,' in Adam Shortt and Arthur G. Doughty, eds., *Canada and Its Provinces*, vol. 17 (Toronto 1917), 161.
15 *Mail*, 26 Jan. 1876
16 *Globe*, 26 Jan. 1876; see also C.R.W. Biggar, *Sir Oliver Mowat: A Biographical Sketch* (Toronto 1905), I, 275–6

Liberals in the Province and the humblest were subject alike to the will of the Premier.'[17] The suppression of factionalism was also dramatic, for his pre-eminence in cabinet as in party was beyond challenge: 'He said that the Cabinet was a band of brothers; so it was, but he was the Elder Brother, the undisputed head of the household. The scholarly Crooks, the ebullient Fraser, the stormy Hardy, the clever Ross, all sat in the family carriage, but Mowat drove.'[18]

Yet for all the importance of patronage in securing his place in the driver's seat, it would be wrong to conclude that his use of it was either excessive or corrupt. In spite of the frequently asserted claim of the conservative press that 'Sir Oliver ... is more responsible than any other man in Canada for the introduction of the methods of Tammany and the spoils system,'[19] Mowat was no Boss Tweed, nor was his Liberal machine modelled after Tammany Hall. In Ontario there was an ethical line drawn between patronage and corruption that was generally understood and accepted, even if its precise location was unmarked and often hotly disputed in particular cases. Thus it was considered a perfectly normal part of politics by tories and liberals alike for the victorious party to reward its own supporters with public appointments. Where the controversy arose was usually over whether this or that individual who had been given a post was an honest and deserving recipient or a mere 'boodler.' On such questions, needless to say, opinion tended to divide along party lines.

But if there was room for disagreement on *cases* it was at least agreed *in principle* that rewards ought not to be given to corrupt or incompetent party hacks solely on the basis of services rendered – or still less, services claimed or services promised. On this Mowat was adamant, and there were no exceptions. The typical grass-roots operation of the machine may be seen in Elgin county: 'James Coyne, after his defeat by Andy Ingram (a Tory) in 1886 became the manager of patronage in the riding until he pulled out a plum for himself: county registrar. Coyne followed very definite criteria in sifting applicants: *capability, proven party service, proven support from party colleagues*. As well he was careful to make a fair distribution across all areas of the riding.'[20] These were not just the Elgin

17 J.E. Middleton and F. Landon, *The Province of Ontario: A History 1615–1927*, vol. 1 (Toronto 1927), 447
18 Ibid.
19 *Empire*, 24 Nov. 1893
20 Barbara A. McKenna, 'Farmers and Railwaymen, Patronage and Corruption: A Volatile Political Mix in Turn of the Century Elgin County,' *Ontario History* 74 (1982): 225 (italics added)

criteria: they applied everywhere across the province. And Coyne's own plum was likewise not his for the picking: it had to be vetted by those above him in the hierarchy.

At the higher levels of the system, however, additional considerations came into play. Liberal backbenchers (or local patronage agents such as Coyne in ridings held by the opposition) were allowed a fair degree of personal discretion in dealing with the minutiae of patronage, such as the employment of labourers on public works, for such discretion was important to their standing in the community. But in the case of even minor public-service appointments they could only transmit their recommendations upward to a more senior level of the party hierarchy, usually to a member of the cabinet. There the competing claims of the various ridings (and sometimes, within ridings, of the various townships) would be balanced and, if no more was involved than the filling of an existing post, a decision might be made at that level: cabinet ministers too had their prestige to maintain. It was understood by all, however, that the overriding authority belonged to the premier. He dealt directly with all appointments of a highly lucrative, honorific, or politically sensitive nature, as well as with a great many others that were less important but which, out of caution on the part of underlings, or on his own intitiative, were deemed to require his attention.

Finally, he alone regulated the *amount* of patronage in the system: hence, any requests or recommendations that went beyond the filling of existing posts to the creation of new ones were automatically referred to him. A request for the appointment of additional magistrates in Southwold Township, for example, received this characteristically Mowatian reply: 'Your letter of the 25th June to Mr. Hardy [provincial secretary] about new Magistrates has been transferred to me. I find there are already 49 Magistrates in the commission for Southwold, or one for every 106 of the population, while the ordinary rule is that of Magistrates acting and not acting one for every 250 is sufficient.'[21] Once again there was the familiar invocation of a formula and the implicit judgment that province-wide standards ought to prevail over local particularisms. Such formulas were not absolutely rigid, but neither were they easily bent, since the integrity of the system depended upon their general application. Certainly, personal appeals for variance were not encouraged. Mowat's letter continued: 'When I had the pleasure of

21 D.B. Weldon Library, University of Western Ontario, Coyne Papers, Mowat to J.H. Coyne, 29 Sept. 1888

seeing you here recently, we had some conversation about additional Magistrates. I took no note of what passed, and the effect of it has escaped my memory.'[22]

Obviously, not every Liberal appointee was blessed with outstanding competence and sterling character, nor was every Liberal patronage agent impeccably honest and judicious in his dealings. Yet there were standards that had to be observed. From the top down there was an undeviating insistence that public duties be faithfully and honestly performed, that contractors give value for money, that the party not be embarrassed. This is not to say that there were no infractions – but when they came to light, punishment was swift and severe, and the same standard applied at every level. Even so senior a Liberal as Archibald McKellar, a quintessential machine politician who had risen through the ranks to become Mowat's commissioner of agriculture and public works, and who was a favourite of the party for his skill in the rough and tumble of electoral warfare, was summarily banished to a minor post when his habit of buying votes and various other rather flagrant peccadillos exposed the administration to charges of 'McKellarism' – a clever opposition coining that threatened to stick in the public mind.[23]

Then as now, the use of patronage – like the use of alcohol – was constrained not only or even mainly by the law but also by the values of the community. A party machine that offended those values through abuse or excess was liable to do itself serious and perhaps irreparable damage. One of Mowat's greatest political assets was his sensitivity to those values and his willingness to work always within the limits set by them; he seemed to know instinctively where the boundaries of patronage lay. No party boss has ever been more effective in ensuring that patronage was used efficiently and productively. In nearly a quarter of a century in the premiership 'the little Christian Statesman' – as his more shameless acolytes were fond of referring to him – was never seriously tainted by the whiff of corruption.

It was not for want of trying. Ontario politics in the late nineteenth century was a rough and frequently vicious game in which no quarter was asked or given. The stakes, moreover, were extremely high, and repeated narrow losses had produced a Conservative party in opposition that had grown frustrated and desperate, obsessed with finding

22 Ibid.
23 *Mail*, 16 Jan. 1875. McKellar was given the shrievalty of Wentworth, a post worth $7,000 a year.

The Liberal machine at work – directed by Mowat, Public Works Minister C.F. Fraser imposes a new registrar upon Carleton County.

ROOT HOG OR (POSSIBLY) DIE.

MISS ONTARIO: 'Sir Oliver, that dreadful creature is destroying my garden, devouring my youthful plants and trampling down everything I deem precious. I want you to put this ring in his ugly snout *at once!*'

SIR OLIVER: 'Don't be unreasonable, madam. Such a proceeding would be putting the Hog to great inconvenience. Besides, what's the use of putting a ring on his nose, when before very long, perhaps, I may possibly be authorized to kill him outright?'

some damning piece of evidence that would bring down 'the Dictator.' In this they were supported by a host of Conservative partisans hungering for the spoils of office, a vociferous and at times scurrilous Conservative press, and a conservative intelligentsia whose most notable voice was that of Goldwin Smith. For the latter, Mowat's reputation for piety was especially galling – and an irresistible target for sarcasm: 'The Ethiopian does not change his skin, even when he becomes a Christian Statesman,' Smith sourly observed. 'What the chiefs would shrink from doing, underlings do: and the underlings, if called to account, are defended by the chiefs ... A Machine, by the law of its being, grows more corrupt and jobbing [sic] the longer it reigns.'[24] Yet for all the smoke that the Liberal machine inevitably emitted, there was remarkably little fire. And none that could be traced directly to Mowat himself.

For, in sharp contrast to Sir John A. Macdonald, whose 'neo-traditional' Conservative machine required his constant attention to the minutiae of party management – and whose personal involvement in party fund-raising had led to the 'Pacific Scandal' and his abrupt downfall in 1874 – Mowat had crafted an 'orthodox' machine whose disciplined hierarchy effectively insulated him from such activities. At every level, specific 'underlings' had well-defined responsibilities, and though the chain of command led ultimately to the leader himself, at certain critical junctures it functioned exclusively through dyadic, face-to-face linkages, which required no formal record of either promised rewards or reciprocal services. In this respect the *modus operandi* of the machine clearly reflected its roots in the Upper Canadian clientele tradition. But it was also characteristically Mowatian in its incorporation of such linkages into the structure of a large-scale organization and in its prudent use of intermediaries. Significantly, after the McKellar affair (which had driven home the risk of having cabinet members too directly involved in the handling of election funds), Mowat had placed primary responsibility for the day-to-day running of the machine in the hands of a party professional who did not hold a seat in the legislature and who was therefore less vulnerable to opposition attack. For this purpose he had systematically strengthened the role of the party's general secretary, effectively making its incumbent his confidential agent – nominally a servant of the party but in reality his personal client, with well-understood but unspecified powers as the machine's chief manager,

24 *Bystander*, Apr. 1883

fund-raiser and election organizer. It was typical of Mowat's preference for long-term organizational stability that the post was made full-time in 1883 and for the next decade was occupied by a single individual: the ubiquitous W.T.R. (later known as 'Hug the Machine') Preston.[25]

Preston's job was to ensure that the premier could maintain a statesmanlike detachment from the seamier aspects of party patronage and the excesses of party zealotry. He was the machine's whisperer of promises, its collector of debts, its fixer, its gatekeeper, its trouble-shooter, and in every Ontario election during his long stewardship, federal as well as provincial, its key co-ordinator and tactician. Those campaigns were not genteel affairs, and on both sides there were masters of electioneering chicanery – but none more expert (or less troubled by scruple) than Preston. It was his practice, for example, to use private detectives to keep his Conservative rivals under surveillance with a view to uncovering some personal weakness that might be exploited to advantage. In his autobiography he claims to have found out by such means that Roderick Pringle, the top tory bagman of the day, and some of his cronies were in the habit of gambling for high stakes, and to have infiltrated their circle with one of his detectives posing as a wealthy Detroit timber broker (presumably with an ample supply of Liberal money): 'A strong bond sprang up between him and Pringle's band of electioneers. His virtues as a poker-player appealed to them. He was invited to Tory headquarters for further meetings over the green baize.' This continued for three or four years, Preston gleefully recounts, the detective 'losing and winning with the same happy smile, keeping me informed of every important manoeuvre of our adversaries, bringing us the information which time and again made the difference between winning and losing an election.'[26]

In 1893, however, facing a difficult three-cornered fight in the next election – a fight in which a more sophisticated approach and skills of a different order would be needed – Mowat, with his usual canny sense of

25 Preston's own account of his career is contained in his predictably self-serving (and in certain respects misleading) memoir, *My Generation of Politics and Politicians* (Toronto 1927). He acquired the nickname 'Hug the Machine' in 1899 when a telegram he had sent to the party organizer who had run a successful campaign in the West Elgin by-election of that year, instructing him to 'hug the machine for me,' fell into the hands of the Conservative press. See P.D. Ross, *Retrospects of a Newspaper Person* (Toronto 1931), 126–7.

26 *My Generation*, 120–2. Preston also claims that his detective retired from the card game undiscovered and '$15,000 to the good.'

timing, eased Preston into the post of provincial librarian to make way for his successor, the young Alex Smith. Not yet thirty years of age, university-educated, and already (according to the *Globe*) possessing an 'extensive acquaintance with the personalities of political life,'[27] Smith had risen swiftly through the ranks of the machine on the strength of his superior abilities as an organizer and party publicist. An essentially modern figure who would not be out of place among the pollsters and campaign managers of the 1980s, he was a strategist rather than a riding-level tactician, less enamoured of subterfuge than Preston, and more attuned to the nuances of public opinion. His appointment marked an important step in the renewal of the machine and in devising a strategy to meet the unprecedented challenge that was about to be mounted against it.

27 11 Nov. 1893

16

The Anti-Party Reaction

I do not say a government can be carried on without compromise and without being influenced by expediency. I know it cannot. I know, too, that some of its members are likely in any case to be men of no real love for political and public virtue.

– Oliver Mowat to Alexander Campbell, 1 February 1858

I

The rise of a new political entity as electorally formidable and seemingly as omnipresent as Mowat's Liberal party was bound to arouse hostility, and not only among those who envied its success. For it must be remembered that in the nineteenth century, in Ontario as elsewhere, political parties were generally held in low regard. There were many who believed that they had no legitimate place in provincial politics – or indeed, in politics at any level – and their allegedly sinister and corrupting influence was commonly deplored by press, public, and politicians alike. Goldwin Smith, for example, in the columns of the *Bystander*, railed incessantly against the 'puerile apparatus of party government' and the 'noxious farce' of the 'lilliputian' provincial legislature. All that was needed to govern Ontario, he maintained, was 'a good practical council of reeves.'[1] Appeals to 'place government

---

1 *Bystander*, Jan. 1880. Three years later he was still hammering away on the same theme: 'We have all of the evils of party government, the sacrifice of conviction to discipline ... representation also suffers: it is taken out of the hands of the people by the Machines, and good local men, who might serve the province well, are excluded because they are not slaves.' Ibid., Jan. 1883

above party' or for 'government by the best men irrespective of party' were in consequence more likely to be heard sympathetically than they are today. And a patronage-fuelled party machine was, of course, a particularly provocative departure from the ideal of a pure, non-party politics.

While by no means unique in his devotion to party, Mowat was exceptional among the politicians of his time both for his frank defence of the *idea* of party politics and his insistence that it was as valid at the provincial as at the federal level. His thinking on these questions was undoubtedly influenced by his experience as a Reform member of Parliament in the United Canadas, where an unmanageable contingent of 'loose fish' – and the chronic inability of the Upper Canadian reformers to unite in a single party – had produced one unstable ministry after another. And, even more seriously perhaps from the point of view of a young reformer, this had contributed to the long Conservative ascendancy after 1854. But these perceptions were not new. Robert Baldwin had seen the necessity of party, though he was incapable of organizing one; while Francis Hincks, who was capable, had run up against the anti-partyism of the Clear Grits, the intransigence of George Brown, and, more importantly, the rising presence of John A. Macdonald.

Certainly by 1858 Mowat had come to the conclusion (as he wrote to Alexander Mackenzie) that 'the only principle on which free government appears to be capable of being worked' is 'the distinction of parties.'[2] By the time he assumed power his views were fully developed and were articulated in the very first throne speech debate in which he participated as premier, in January 1873: 'I confess that I do attach a great deal of importance to party, but I do not place party before country ... I am for party because I believe – because I know – that the interests of the country are best advanced by means of a well-organized party, founded on well-recognized principles ... *Our whole system of government involves party as a necessity.*'[3] His attitude towards party organization was thus rooted in an essentially modern conception of party as a constitutionally legitimate instrument, the only effective vehicle of political power, the mainspring of responsible parliamentary government.

These were themes to which he returned again and again, for the conflict over party government (or 'partyism' as it was termed by its

2 C.R.W. Biggar, *Sir Oliver Mowat: A Biographical Sketch* (Toronto 1905), I, 76–7
3 Ibid., 176–7

detractors) continued to smoulder throughout the entire period of his premiership, with important ramifications for other, seemingly unconnected issues. The two major sources of anti-party opposition, however, were in all other respects far removed from one another, both organizationally and ideologically – for they consisted on the one hand (rather curiously) of federally oriented Macdonaldite tories and on the other of agrarian populists. Their attacks were consequently very different in character, stemmed from different beliefs and values, and reflected different – and largely incompatible – political aims.

II

The tory attack on partyism may be easily dismissed as either a piece of rank hypocrisy (since the federal Conservatives were not notably less blatant in their attachment to party than the Ontario Liberals) or mere 'sour grapes,' since at the provincial level they were generally less successful in its practice. Nevertheless, buried amid much partisan rhetoric there is also a neglected tory critique that deserves to be treated seriously, for it correctly foresaw, and profoundly understood, the danger that Mowat's development of party posed – both to the old spirit of Ontario localism, in which toryism had long thrived, and to Macdonald's vision of a centralized Canadian state. They saw no contradiction in their position because, for them, both localism and centralization were wedded to the premise that party politics was a legitimate form of conflict *only at the national level* and ought therefore to be rejected by the provinces. The debate went on sporadically for decades but is perhaps best crystallized in the exchange between Senator D.L. Macpherson and Mowat.

Macpherson fired the first shot in 1879 in a pamphlet praising Sir John A. Macdonald, who, he argued, at the time of Confederation had 'preserved the coalition principles' in the government of Ontario and done all in his power 'to bury the dead differences of the past, and to unite and inspire with a feeling of brotherhood – in short, to Canadianise – the people of the different provinces.' This he contrasted with what he claimed to be Mowat's approach: 'The Ministers of Ontario, instead of serving the whole people, appear to devote their main energies to the cultivation of party spirit. Under their administration the public departments and the whole public service, it is alleged, have become great schools for its inculcation, for the ignoble purpose of securing to a narrow-minded and selfish clique the loaves and fishes.' Apart from such traditional slanging, however, the theoretical heart of Macpherson's argument lies in a narrow conception of provincial government: 'Most of the evils which afflict this province, including the extravagance of the government, are directly traceable to prejudiced and pestilent partyism. I ask, why should it be tolerated in the management of the business of Ontario? The people object to its embittering presence in their municipal offices, and the public business of Ontario is neither more nor less than the business of a group of municipalities. Ontario is not charged with any subject of legislation other than of a strictly municipal character, or with any question into which party politics should be admitted. Ministers should be chosen for their ability and aptitude as administrators, for beyond supervising legislation, their duties are simply administrative.'[4]

Mowat replied in a speech, which was later printed as a pamphlet, ridiculing Macpherson as 'a certain High Tory Senator, who, when it suits his purpose, claims to be a no-party man' and offering an unapologetic justification of provincial party politics: 'There was a goodly number of men sent to our [Ontario] Assembly in 1867 who had no confidence in the government that had been formed, and who, therefore, in accordance with the opinion and wishes of their constituents, did not hold it to be desirable that the old party lines should be destroyed – who believed that, in our system of government, opposition was a necessary and valuable feature.' As for the claim that Sir John A. had promoted non-partyism: 'Mr. Macpherson, though a no-party man, eulogizes the Conservative party leader, Sir John; and what for? Because Sir John did all he could to prevent a division of the people into parties after Confederation. And why? That all parties might support him. I do not know what party leader would not willingly dispense with parties on the same terms.'[5] For Mowat, then, the real question of politics was never *whether* there would be parties but *which* party would prevail, in the provincial no less than in the federal arena.

Underlying his view of party, moreover, was a concept of federalism that was deeply at odds with the Macdonaldite version and that provoked a series of legal confrontations between Ontario and the federal government over the extent and nature of the province's

---

4 D.L. Macpherson, 'Letter on the Increasing Public Expenditure of Ontario,' D.B. Weldon Library, University of Western Ontario, *Ontario Political Pamphlets, 1878–1900*, vol. 4. Biggar claims that it was 'generally understood' that the pamphlet was actually written by John Hague, a tory publicist. *Mowat*, 315
5 'Speech of Hon. Oliver Mowat,' *Ontario Political Pamphlets*, vol. 4

powers. Constitutionally, his position was derived from the classical theory of federalism as a system in which the constituent provinces or states and the central government each have their own defined spheres of authority and exercise their respective powers without one being subordinate to the other. Politically, however, and perhaps more importantly, it was rooted in Ontario's old Upper Canadian sense of itself as a community with its own historical identity and interests (and, it should not be forgotten, a formidable record of defending both). His response to the tory attack on partyism was therefore the same as his response to the tory notion of federalism: both were portrayed as a denial of Ontario's rights and status in Confederation – while his Liberal government alone acted as their champion, 'steadfast defenders of provincial rights and provincial liberties.'[6]

III

The second major attack on partyism came from a different part of the ideological spectrum and was in many respects more difficult to answer than the conservative one. More to the point, perhaps, it also posed a greater danger to the Liberal ascendancy, for its proponents were agrarian populists who appealed to the same Clear Grit radical tradition, and the same regional electoral base, as the Liberal party itself.

Implicit in the populist position was a generalized anti-political bias, a feeling that the activity of politics itself, to the extent that it involved the brokering and aggregating of interests, was morally suspect if not actually iniquitous. The rejection of party was but one form in which it was concretely expressed, echoing very obviously the populist rejection in economic affairs of the role of merchants, agents, and other intermediaries, which also had moralistic connotations. The trouble with such a view was that it was more easily preached than practised. Hence, just as rural merchants continued to thrive even in the southwestern peninsula in spite of the costly efforts of the Patrons of Husbandry to displace them with co-operatives, so too did political parties, and for basically the same reasons. The merchants were part of the fabric of their communities and were, on the whole, efficient and dependable providers of essential services to their farmer-clients. And the latter, it would seem, whatever their sympathies for populist principles, when it came to the point were reluctant to take chances in

6 *Globe*, 15 Feb. 1883

their personal business; that is to say, they preferred the known advantages of clientelism to the uncertain prospects of co-operative endeavour.

The Patrons of Husbandry never presented a direct challenge to the political parties, but in its footsteps followed a more militant agrarian movement known as the Patrons of Industry,[7] which did. Like its predecessor it swept across the American border from Michigan and spread rapidly, especially in southwestern Ontario, claiming two thousand branches for the province as a whole and a membership variously estimated at between fifty thousand and one hundred thousand by 1893. Its leaders were virulently anti-party, their rhetoric florid and extreme: party politicians, they proclaimed, were an 'aggregation of plunderers' and party politics nothing less than 'the anvil on which our chains are being forged.'[8] Its constitution specifically excluded from membership 'all persons of proved immoral character, and Lawyers, Doctors, Merchants, Liquor Dealers, Manufacturers, *Party Politicians*, and those whose interests conflict with those of Farmers and Labourers.'[9] On the face of it, this was not an organization much inclined to compromise. Though many of its concerns were federal, involving such matters as high tariffs and assisted immigration (it was against both), it made its bid for power in the provincial arena, fielding a slate of candidates in the Ontario general election of 1894, obviously with the intention of undercutting the Liberal party's agrarian support. But, like a country merchant faced with competition from a new co-op store, Oliver Mowat was not without resources when it came to holding on to his customers, as the Patrons soon discovered.

Mowat's response provides the classic, definitive illustration of brokerage-style political leadership. At no time did he attempt to answer the Patrons' anti-party diatribes in kind, adopting instead a restrained and accommodating approach that amounted to ignoring the broad innuendoes of corruption in his ministry and discounting the ideological gulf that separated him from those who propounded the theory of single-interest representation. His strategy was first of all to appeal directly to the Patrons' rank-and-file, and potential rank-and-file, rather

7 See S.E.D. Shortt, 'Social Change and Political Crisis in Rural Ontario: The Patrons of Industry, 1889–1896,' in Donald Swainson, ed., *Oliver Mowat's Ontario* (Toronto 1972), 211–35.

8 *Farmers' Sun*, 6 June 1893

9 *Constitution and Rules of the Patrons of Industry*, Strathroy 1892, 3–4, quoted in Shortt, 'Social Change,' 217 (italics added)

than to seek an accord with 'Grand President' Caleb Mallory and other officers of the movement, whom he judged unlikely to be receptive. And in any case they had yet to demonstrate that they could effectively deliver the votes of their membership. As Alex Smith, the Liberal machine's new chief organizer, shrewdly observed: 'They are well qualified to conduct an agitation by sensation and emotional methods but for further action they do not appear to have the capacity.'[10] The task of attacking the Patrons' leaders could therefore safely be left to the Liberal press,[11] while Mowat concentrated on mending his party's fences.

As early as December 1893, in the North Bruce by-election, Mowat had begun to counter the Patrons' argument that their organization alone represented the interests of agriculture. There was nothing in their platform, he stated, that gave evidence of 'any special interest of the Patrons being neglected by the Reform Government': 'I claim that the Reform party has always been specially a farmers' party, while faithful to every other class as well: and that the Reform party is the true farmers' party: that the candidate of the Reform party is a farmer, and I claim for him ... the support of the electors of North Bruce.'[12] Later he would also call attention to the Patrons' incongruous preoccupation with matters that fell under federal jurisdiction, pointing out that of the few articles in their platform 'affecting provincial matters, one only is not in accordance with the policy and practice hitherto pursued by the Ontario ... Government, *and that one is respecting patronage.*[13]

The latter was, of course, the crux of the matter, for the article in question demanded the election of all municipal officials and the decentralization to the county level of all local patronage appointments apart from judicial ones; in other words, a complete reversal of the program of centralization that had so materially contributed to the building of a strong provincial government and a strong Liberal party

10 National Archives of Canada, Laurier Papers, Smith to Laurier, 7 Dec. 1893
11 The *Globe*, for example, described them as 'mountebanks and adventurers' (26 June 1894). The Patrons had their own newspaper, the *Farmers' Sun*, but otherwise could count on little press support. Of the forty-two Ontario dailies in 1892, seventeen were liberal and nineteen conservative. In addition, there were 117 liberal and 119 conservative weeklies. See Brian P.N. Beaven, 'Partisanship, Patronage, and the Press in Ontario, 1880–1914: Myths and Realities,' *Canadian Historical Review* 64 (1983): 322–3.
12 *Globe*, 24 Nov. 1893
13 Biggar, *Mowat*, II, 500–1 (italics added)

THE PATRONS AND THE PATRON-AGE.

SIR OLIVER: 'Oh, oh! Gracious, goodness, dear Patron Giant! Take anything, everything you want, but spare, oh, spare this, my pet and favorite che-ild.'

machine. This was an issue Mowat could hardly avoid, and one that was potentially very damaging, but in typical fashion he managed to deflect it onto more favourable ground: '[Their] method prevails ... in the neighbouring Republic; but I hope that however kind may be our feelings toward that country, none of us have such a love for its institutions that the mere existence there of the proposed system is sufficient to make us determined to have it here. Let us have in Ontario the best methods and the best laws, whether they correspond with those of our neighbours or not. Several of our institutions and many of our laws are far in advance of theirs; and as regards these we should be retrograding, not advancing, were we to adopt their policy in place of our own.'[14] It was less a rebuttal of the Patrons' position than an evocation of the old Upper Canadian sense of pride in their own political institutions, but cleverly updated by the suggestion that the latter were now not only more patriotically British than the American but also (thanks to the reforms of the Liberal government) more progressive as well, which was very much in keeping with Ontario's evolving self-image.

A second critically important Liberal strategy was to blur the distinction between Liberals and Patrons not only in terms of policies but also in terms of candidates in a substantial number of constituencies. The objective, plainly, was to minimize the damage to the overall Liberal position by reducing the number of three-cornered contests. Thus, in eight predominantly rural constituencies no Liberal candidate was nominated or the non-Patron Liberal withdrew in favour of a Liberal who was also a Patron. Most strikingly, in a transaction that illustrates the extraordinary discipline of the Mowat machine, which made such a strategy possible, in Prince Edward the *sitting Liberal member* withdrew, in a seat that had been Liberal since 1875. In five other such constituencies 'Liberal-Patron' candidates were endorsed as the sole opponents of the Conservatives; in two (Lincoln and Dundas East) the field was left clear for other challengers; and in one urban constituency (Toronto East), which the Liberals had come within 125 votes of capturing in the previous election, it was left clear for a 'Labour-Patron' candidate.[15]

14 Ibid., 504
15 The Liberal effort to blur the line between Liberal and Patron candidates was so successful as to make it difficult to determine exactly how many Patron candidates there were. Different sources give different numbers. Shortt puts the number at 56 ('Social Change,' 222); Janet B Kerr puts it at 34 ('Sir Oliver Mowat and the Campaign of 1894,' *Ontario History* 55 [1963]: 7); and J.D. Smart puts it at 52 ('The

To complicate matters further, a militant anti-Catholic (and anti-party) organization called the Protestant Protective Association (PPA) also intervened strongly in the election, fielding its own candidates in some ridings, taking over Conservative nominations in others, usually with the connivance of leading Conservatives, and infiltrating the Patrons at the grass-roots level, even though 'the leaders of the Patrons movement fought tooth and nail against the influence of the PPA within their association.'[16] The result, inevitably, was a confusion of party positions and candidates. In at least two ridings local Patrons endorsed PPA candidates, while in a number of others Patrons ran with PPA endorsement; among Conservatives, some received the nomination of both organizations and ran openly as 'Conservative-PPA' candidates, while others avoided an open linkage but pledged themselves to support legislation abolishing separate schools and various other anti-Catholic measures if elected in return for covert PPA backing.[17]

The party least affected was the Liberal: it suffered only one serious defection (the sitting Liberal member for North Bruce switched to the PPA), and in only two other ridings was there a serious breakdown of party cohesion caused by sectarianism (in Middlesex East a 'Liberal-Patron' ran with PPA endorsement); all three, however, were opposed by official Liberals.[18] As the most centralized and disciplined party, the Liberals were thus able to turn the PPA intervention to their electoral advantage, for it assured them of solid Catholic support without costing them a proportionate loss of support among Protestants, many of whom were repelled by the PPA's fanaticism. By contrast, PPA infiltration divided the Patrons of Industry and caused them to lose momentum at a critical juncture; increasingly as the election date approached they were forced to centre their campaign around denying that they were religious sectarians instead of advancing their claim (as economic sectarians) that they were the true representatives of the agrarian interest.

Patrons of Industry in Ontario,' MA thesis, Carleton University 1969, 67). The confusion arises from double nominations and the varying degrees of closeness between the Liberal machine and local Patron or 'Liberal-Patron' candidates. The figures given here are based on data contained in Roderick Lewis, ed., *Centennial Edition of the Electoral Districts, Legislatures and Ministries of the Province of Ontario, 1867–1968* (Toronto n.d.), adjusted in some cases in the light of contemporary press reports.

16 James T. Watt, 'Anti-Catholicism in Ontario Politics: The Role of the Protestant Protective Association in the 1894 Election,' *Ontario History* 59 (1967): 64
17 Ibid., 62–3
18 Lewis, *Centennial Edition*, 31–2, 211, 295

The Conservatives clearly hoped to be the main beneficiaries of electoral fragmentation, as Mowat had been quick to warn: 'The hopes of their party now rest on the temporary diversion which they are anxious that the PPA and the Patrons of Industry may make. Neither of these recent organisations is in sympathy with the present Opposition, but the notion is that they may serve to withdraw votes enough to defeat some reform candidates, and thereby defeat the Reform government of the province.'[19] But hopes were not enough. In actual practice the Conservatives were unable to take advantage of the situation, partly because of the ineffectual leadership of W.R. Meredith, partly because of their ambiguous connection with the PPA, but above all because of their fatal aversion to central direction: they persisted in approaching the general election as an unconnected series of local contests, and paid dearly for it.

The outcome in 1894 was a conclusive victory for Mowat and the Liberal machine. Though their share of the popular vote declined, as was perhaps unavoidable in the circumstances, and their majority over the combined opposition was reduced, they remained indisputably the largest party in the legislature, with fifty-one seats. The Conservatives elected twenty-four (including six 'Conservative-PPA candidates). Seventeen Patrons were elected, nine as 'Liberal-Patrons.' The PPA elected only two.[20]

A breakdown of the results shows clearly the degree to which the Liberal strategy succeeded. Though they ended up losing four seats to the Patrons, they had adroitly shifted the main burden of the Patrons' intervention onto the Conservatives, who ended up losing six seats to Patrons or 'Liberal-Patrons,' all but one uncontested by Liberals; in addition, two previously Conservative seats elected 'Conservative-Patrons.' The net result was a devastating blow to Conservative prospects, for they had not been able to make compensating gains elsewhere, nor had they benefited appreciably from the sectarian issue.

19 *Globe*, 16 Jan. 1894
20 Different sources give different totals, depending on the method used to calculate party standings. For the derivation of these figures see above, chap. 13, n 12. Watts sets the PPA total at three and estimates that a further eleven members of the association were elected under the auspices of other parties, though their affiliation was evidently not always known at the time of the election. In the case of John McNeill, for example, who had been elected as a 'Liberal-Patron' for Perth South, it did not emerge until some months later (during his trial for corrupt practices) that he was a member of the PPA. Watt, 'Anti-Catholicism,' 65

Indeed, the intervention of the PPA on balance probably damaged the Conservatives more than the Liberals,[21] though the effects are difficult to determine with precision because of the variety of Conservative-PPA arrangements that existed. From riding to riding, local tory elites behaved differently, here collaborating with the PPA openly, there covertly, here leading it, there fighting it, seemingly at random though no doubt influenced by particular local circumstances, such as the relative size of the Catholic vote or rivalries among the different Protestant denominations in the community. There is some evidence that collaboration worked, particularly where it took the form of joint sponsorship of a single 'Conservative-PPA' candidate. But where local tories decided to fight the PPA, the result as often as not was simply to deliver the seat into the hands of the Liberals, as in North Grey, where the order of finish was as follows:

Cleland, James (Liberal)	1,646
Medcalfe, Charles (PPA)	1,433
Read, Nicholas (Conservative)	1,242[22]

At the other extreme, where they decided to withdraw from the field altogether in favour of a PPA candidate, the result, almost invariably, was not a victory for 'Protestant solidarity' but a humiliating rejection by a largely Protestant electorate. In other words, Conservative withdrawals in favour of the PPA had the opposite effect of Liberal withdrawals in favour of the Patrons of Industry. In straight two-party fights against the Liberals, the PPA lost seven out of the eight seats contested; and, ironically, even their one victory (in Middlesex East) was without practical value since the seat had previously been held by a Conservative.[23]

For Oliver Mowat the 1894 election was his most difficult as party leader and personally the most troubling. 'I have had more personal abuse in this campaign,' he complained, 'than I have had in any campaign since I entered political life in 1857, thirty-seven years ago.'[24] But the overall result must have been gratifying, demonstrating beyond

21 In the view of the Conservative leader, W.R. Meredith, 'the PPA's managed their campaign badly ... and the result is that instead of being a help to us they really weakened us.' Meredith to J.P. Whitney, 30 June 1894, ibid., 66
22 Lewis, *Centennial Edition*, 108
23 Ibid., 211
24 *Globe*, 23 June 1894

any shadow of doubt the value of the party organization he had built and vindicating both his electoral strategy and his stand on the great issues of the day. By taking a soft line against the Patrons and a hard line against the PPA he had correctly judged the temper of the Ontario electorate. And though the margin of victory it gave him was reduced, it was more than adequate – and even capable of being enlarged, as became obvious soon after the legislature reopened in February 1895.

For it turned out that the Patrons who had been elected were an innocent group of rustics: 'I still have a picture of them,' Hector Charlesworth (a member of the press gallery of the day) recalled in his memoirs, 'sitting in the House in warm spring weather with weather-beaten fur caps on their heads.'[25] Moreover, since none of the leaders of the movement had obtained seats, those who had were left unshepherded and in obvious danger. As Goldwin Smith so cruelly put it, 'the Patrons, with their political inexperience, and their simple-minded openness to intrigue, were between the two regular parties as a flock of sheep between two packs of wolves.'[26] In consequence they were swiftly devoured, nearly all of them by the larger pack of Liberals. The Conservatives tried to forestall such an unequal division, even proposing an amendment to the speech from the throne that they had lifted straight from the Patrons' platform, but to no avail: it was defeated sixty-two to twenty-five, the hapless Patrons voting with the Liberals against their own policies.[27] Most were in any case sympathetically inclined towards the government, and even those who were not could be won over by the perks, privileges, and patronage that support for the government was guaranteed to bring their way. (Mowat, a colleague once observed, 'occasionally found it necessary to study his fellow man with a view to their weaknesses.')[28] The fate of the Patrons was thus sealed early in the session, and by the end of it few traces remained of their short-lived independence. 'We got through the session very smoothly,' Mowat wrote to Edward Blake with evident satisfaction; 'our smallest majority on any vote was seven ... our average majority was twenty-six.'[29] With efficient management, of party as of everything else, the right outcome could be reasonably guaranteed.

25 *Candid Chronicles* (Toronto 1925), 173
26 *Reminiscences* (New York 1911), 448
27 Kerr, 'Mowat and the Campaign of 1894,' 9
28 Charles Clarke, *Sixty Years in Upper Canada* (Toronto 1908), 237
29 29 Apr., 1895, quoted in Kerr, 'Mowat and the Campaign of 1894,' 13

Postscript

By the end of 1895 Mowat's long premiership was drawing to a close. He was seventy-five years of age, and though the previous year's election campaign had probably been his finest, in terms of the sheer quality of his electoral generalship, it had also been a personally taxing affair that had taken its toll on his health and energies. At the same time, however, his prestige and power in national politics had never been greater, and it was this, rather than any provincial concern, that finally determined the manner and timing of his departure. For as premier of Ontario with his mandate freshly renewed, as the Liberal party's 'elder statesman' – and not least, as the head of the most disciplined and battle-tested party machine in the country – his position in the struggle that was then shaping up for national power was absolutely pivotal.

No one understood this better than Wilfrid Laurier. Though he faced a Conservative government in Ottawa that was approaching the end of its term in a state of disarray, with its leadership in flux and its ranks divided, his own party's problems were very nearly as great. First, the immediate cause of the government's condition was the Manitoba schools crisis, which the province had provoked by passing legislation abolishing French and Roman Catholic separate schools. But that buzzing hornet's nest of communal and sectarian animosities was something that neither party could touch without getting stung. And when the courts, in their wisdom, tossed it into Parliament's lap – by ruling that minority educational rights in Manitoba were subject to federal protection – not surprisingly, it sent Liberals as well as Conservatives scurrying in all directions.[30] Second, on any realistic view, the federal Liberals were not exactly a formidable electoral force even when they were united – which they seldom were. Their record spoke for itself, as Laurier knew only too well. In striking contrast to their Ontario cousins, who under Mowat had marched from victory to victory and had dined on the fruits of office for more than two decades, they had gone from defeat to defeat and had tasted nothing but the dry dust of opposition for sixteen long years. As a result, as often happens in the case of such parties, they had become riddled with conflicting interests and ambitions. Their Ontario wing was particularly a source of

30 For an excellent brief account of this issue, see M.S. Donnelly, *The Government of Manitoba* (Toronto 1963), 34–40; for a more extended treatment see Paul Crunican, *Priests and Politicians: Manitoba Schools and the Election of 1896* (Toronto 1974).

trouble: it was torn over the Manitoba issue; Sir Richard Cartwright (an irascible former finance minister whose nostrum for every ill was unrestricted reciprocity with the United States, and who showed scant respect for Laurier's leadership) still had a following; and as well there were a number of lesser lights with leadership pretensions of their own or who simply detested the idea of being led by a French Canadian. All made the mistake of underestimating Laurier. But it was part of Laurier's genius as a politician that he rarely mistook the shadow for the substance of power; and in Ontario the substance belonged to Mowat.

Accordingly, it was not the federal pretenders but the old provincial chieftain whom he courted, deferring to him as to a grand patron, flattering him with the thought that he might cap his career with one last triumphant march on Ottawa. As for the leadership of the federal party, 'I would most gladly make way for Sir Oliver,' he wrote to J.S. Ewart, a senior party broker (and Mowat's nephew) who served as their intermediary.[31] Of course, he had no real intention of surrendering the leadership; he also knew full well that Mowat would not accept it; but in the subtle ritual of patron-client relations a client must always make such an offer before a patron can agree to serve in a lesser position, which must always appear to be of his own choosing. By such means the way was cleared for the deal that was eventually struck: Mowat would commit himself and his machine wholly to the federal campaign; if the Liberals were victorious he would resign the premiership and join Laurier's cabinet with a seat in the Senate, at least until a settlement could be reached in the Manitoba schools crisis; and finally, in due course, he would retire to Queen's Park as lieutenant-governor.[32]

When the election finally came, on 23 June 1896, it produced the desired result. In Ontario the Liberals won forty-three seats and pulled even with the Conservatives, their best federal showing in the province since 1874.[33] As in the previous provincial election, there was strong intervention in certain areas by third and fourth parties, and Mowat's overall strategy in combating them remained basically the same; though his health was too weak to allow him to campaign extensively outside

31 See Carman Miller, 'Mowat, Laurier and the Federal Liberal Party,' in Donald Swainson, ed., *Oliver Mowat's Ontario* (Toronto 1972), 88.
32 Ibid., 89. See also W.T.R. Preston, *My Generation of Politics and Politicians* (Toronto 1927), 208–10.
33 J.M. Beck, *Pendulum of Power: Canada's Federal Elections* (Scarborough, Ont. 1968). In the previous election, in 1891, the Liberals had won forty-four seats to forty-eight for the Conservatives.

Toronto, he continued to stress his government's record of progressive legislation, especially in the area of agriculture, in order to weaken the appeal of the agrarian populists; he attacked the religious sectarians; and, above all, he relied on his trusty machine to deliver the vote. By such means rural Ontario was once again kept out of the hands not only of the Conservatives but also of the Patrons of Industry, the Protestant Protective Association, and other splinter groups who had hoped to profit from the Manitoba issue. No less remarkably, Liberal party cohesion was maintained behind an untried national leader who was a Catholic and a French Canadian. With a clear victory in Quebec, where the Liberals won forty-nine seats to sixteen for the Conservatives, Laurier was thus assured of an overall national majority.

Mowat accordingly turned the premiership over to Arthur S. Hardy, was named a senator, and on 11 July 1896 joined Laurier's cabinet as minister of justice – where one of his first acts (which the old master of patronage must surely have performed with a certain glee) was to withdraw a list of 173 tory lawyers that the outgoing government had recommended for appointment as Queen's Counsel.[34] His tenure of office, however, was brief. As was expected of him, he devoted his attention primarily to the Manitoba schools question and was instrumental in arranging a compromise agreement with the Manitoba government that quickly settled the issue without federal legislative intervention – which, as a defender of provincial rights, he had always insisted should be the case. But once that agreement was reached, his role was effectively over; there was nothing of comparable importance to occupy him politically, and understandably, he found the drudgery of routine departmental administration 'exhausting and burdensome.'[35] On 18 November 1897 he resigned to become lieutenant-governor of Ontario, in which post he remained, keeping a watchful eye on the province where all his affections lay and which he had done so much to shape, until his death on 19 April 1903.

34 Paul Romney, *Mr Attorney: The Attorney General for Ontario in Court, Cabinet and Legislature, 1791–1899* (Toronto 1986), 281
35 Mowat to Edward Blake, 1 July 1897, as quoted in Miller, 'Mowat, Laurier,' 92

Conclusion:
Clientelism in Practice and Theory

In this book I have attempted to demonstrate that the political culture of Ontario, from its origins in eighteenth-century Upper Canada to the post-Confederation era of Oliver Mowat, can be usefully illuminated if approached from the perspective of a developmental model of clientelism. Accordingly, the main focus throughout has been upon the operative realities of the political process, and particularly upon the critical linkages in that process – the 'core vertical solidarities' – which evolved gradually from simple patron-client dyads into progressively more complex forms of brokerage and machine politics.

My approach, however, departs in two important respects from the approach followed in most studies of these subjects. First, it treats the political process historically. That is to say, it seeks to account for long-term patterns of behaviour, whereas most political science studies, by contrast, tend to be narrowly situated in time and mainly interested in accounting for specific functional interactions or outcomes. Second, it treats clientelism more broadly than most anthropological studies. In particular, it goes beyond the micro-level of analysis, where the emphasis is primarily on the internal dynamics of patron-client and brokerage-based exchange, and attempts to relate local clientele structures to the workings of the political system as a whole. In doing so it may help to fill a generally acknowledged gap in clientelist theory, for, as Luigi Graziano has observed, 'much is known about clientelistic forms of association, but relatively little about the systematic implications of patron-client ties.'[1]

---

1 'Center-Periphery Relations and the Italian Crisis: The Problem of Clientelism,' in Sidney Tarrow et al., *Territorial Politics in Industrial Nations* (New York 1978), 293

In this conclusion I shall not try to summarize the presentation of the main argument, which should be clear from the preceding chapters. Instead I should like to end by addressing a number of issues that seem to me to be implicit in the analysis or to arise from it, about both the nature of Ontario politics and the theory of clientelism. These may be conveniently categorized as follows.

The Ontario Political Culture

Between 1791 and 1896 Ontario experienced a profound transformation of virtually every dimension of its life as a political society. To generalize about its 'political culture' is hence necessarily a risky proposition. There are bound to be exceptions, and much will depend on the particular sub-period that one has in mind. Nevertheless, a century is a fairly long time in the life of any society, and in Ontario's case it represents fully one half of its history: patterns that persisted, even if unevenly, and even if evolving in their exact configuration, are unlikely to have been merely accidental.

To focus on the political process – and specifically on the relationships of exchange and brokerage that were central to its operation – is not to deny the presence of ideational factors in the political culture, I should perhaps reiterate, but it is certainly to question the significance that has traditionally been attached to them. And more importantly, it is to bring into sharp relief certain distinctive features of the province's collective identity that have not been sufficiently noticed or understood. The chief reason for the latter, I wish to suggest, is the wide – and fundamentally misleading – gap that existed in Ontario between political rhetoric and political behaviour.

The Upper Canadian period provides a striking illustration. Its politicians, its press, its religious leaders, in fact just about everyone involved in political conflict, were inordinately fond of clothing their arguments (regardless of what they happened to be about) in a dire Manichean rhetoric: *loyalty/disloyalty*, *trust/betrayal*, *honour/dishonour*, *gratitude/ingratitude* were words they intoned over and over, as though by rote. This may, of course, be revealingly indicative of the state of the Upper Canadian psyche. Or it may be taken to represent an 'underlying' ideological dialectic that shaped the course of 'surface' events. But however interpreted, the image projected of Upper Canada is of an unformed, fractious society – a society whose members were locked in elemental combat with one another, a society poised on the brink of ruin, politically immobilized.

Yet such an image is so far removed from the actual political and economic *performance* of Upper Canada, and so at odds with the everyday *behaviour* of Upper Canadians, as to constitute a paradox that fairly demands explanation.

The Upper Canadian political system was not without its disintegrative tendencies, including some so extreme as to produce an attempt at armed rebellion. There can be no doubt, from a democratic point of view, that it was substantially flawed. But it must also be acknowledged, on the record of half a century, that it contained as well some substantial strengths. It was especially strong at the local level. There, for the most part, power and authority effectively rested in the hands of leaders who typically combined governmental office (for example, as justices of the peace, in which capacity they were responsible for a wide range of administrative as well as adjudicatory functions) with important social and commercial roles in the community. They were not mere petty officials sent out by the central administration to impose its writ. Rather, they were local 'men of standing' whose offices contributed to their status but who at the same time lent their own considerable personal weight to those offices. They belonged, in other words, to that vital low-level elite whose members I have termed the 'local patrons.' And if their leadership was often idiosyncratic, overly zealous in the pursuit of perquisites, and stubbornly resistant to central direction, it was rarely weak.

There is no convincing evidence, then, that the necessary functions of civil society – which are always, in the end, 'local' matters – were performed any less well in Upper Canada than elsewhere. Nor, on the whole, do Upper Canadian communities appear to have been to any measurable degree unusually fragmented.

Similarly, there is nothing in the economic performance of Upper Canada to suggest that its overall level of social cohesion was low, and much to suggest that it was relatively high. The type of agriculture practised almost from the very beginning was of a type that *presupposed* an accompanying framework of economic relationships – in effect, a system of collaborative endeavour. For it made no sense to pursue a life of marginal self-sufficiency on agricultural land that was so productive it could be made to yield huge surpluses. But to capitalize on the land's productivity a farmer had to have, in all but exceptional circumstances, the support of a dependable patron. The latter, of course, was often a supplier of land, on terms of indebtment or tenantry;[2] and always he was an essential source of credit and supplies, of milling, transportation, and marketing. Even transactions of barter between neighbours commonly passed through his books for valuation of the goods traded.[3]

The relationship of patron and client, however, is always complex and personal. It is not *in essence* a matter of legal contract (though some aspects of it might be) but rather of mutual trust, of good faith on both sides. In a certain percentage of cases, however, the outcome will be failure – and when that happens, the recriminations are inevitably loud and bitter.[4] There is thus a dark side to the psychology of clientelism: the fear that trust will turn out to have been misplaced, that good faith will be repaid by treachery; that a patron, for example, will renege on his promise of a piece of land, or a client surreptitiously sell his crop to a third party. In Upper Canada, moreover, such fears were probably heightened by the closeness of the American border: feckless clients commonly abandoned their debts (and sometimes their families as well) to skip south, and occasionally a failing merchant-patron would take the same route.

Little wonder, therefore, that in Upper Canada – as in every known society where patron-client ties are pervasive – the rhetoric of conflict obsessively revolved around the dichotomies of *loyalty/disloyalty*, *trust/betrayal* and all the other familiar terms of that canon. Cries of 'Traitor,' 'Ingrate,' 'Judas,' 'Serpent,' and so on punctuated virtually every quarrel, including, perhaps especially, political ones. To enter the world of the local patrons is thus to encounter an archetypically clientelist mode of political discourse: the conflicts seem personal because they very likely *were* personal; as in family quarrels, the 'real' issue was often

2 The extent to which tenantry played a part in Upper Canadian clientelism is a subject that requires further research. It was undoubtedly of some importance from the beginning and seems to have persisted strongly, particularly in long-settled areas of high agricultural productivity. William L. Marr reports that in 1871, in such areas as Niagara, York, and Durham, between 25 and 30 per cent of Ontario farms were tenant-occupied. 'The Distribution of Tenant Agriculture: Ontario, Canada, 1871,' *Social Science History* 2 (1987): 169–86

3 Douglas McCalla, 'Rural Credit and Rural Development in Upper Canada, 1790 to 1850,' in Roger Hall et al., *Patterns of the Past: Interpreting Ontario's History* (Toronto and Oxford 1988), 43–4

4 For an extreme example of patron-client breakdown see the darkly comedic proceedings between the much aggrieved Archibald McNab (a failed patron in the Ottawa area) and his equally aggrieved ex-clients, *Dictionary of Canadian Biography*, VIII, 584–9.

hidden; and the verbal flourishes oscillated absurdly between civility and venom.

But what does all of this tell us about the political culture, other than that its rhetoric was conventionally clientelistic? It should not distract our attention from the practice of politics, which, I have argued, was overwhelmingly rooted in the material conditions of life and conceived as a process of exchange. A saw mill, too, emits an impressive amount of noise and friction, but all it means is that the wheels are turning, that the logs are being sawn – that it is 'business as usual.'

In the Union era 'business as usual' came to mean the artful making of political deals. The Manichean rhetoric did not disappear; indeed, a few new screeds were added to it, 'French domination,' 'the Pope and his minions,' 'the Cartier corruptionists' being among the more vivid. But what none of this could conceal was that the political process in practice functioned through the subtle balancing of interests, the blurring and undermining of ideological tendencies, and the pragmatic building of coalitions. It is difficult, perhaps impossible, to separate out those aspects of brokerage politics that arose out of the internal dynamics of Upper Canadian society, particularly in the spheres of finance and commerce, and those that arose out of the day-to-day necessity of governing through an overarching accommodation with the political elite of Quebec. The effect, in either case, was to place a premium on negotiating skill and mastery of the techniques of political management.

The Union of the Canadas, I have insisted in this book, must be viewed ultimately *as a political system in its own right*. To treat it merely as a 'prelude' to Confederation or as a 'problem' that federalism later solved is to fail to understand how it actually worked; it is also to undervalue its demonstrable and very great political success. There is much yet to be learned about the Union – and from it – for the whole period is in need of fundamental reappraisal, especially perhaps from a comparative perspective. But there can be no doubt that for Upper Canada it was a powerfully formative political experience.

The post-Confederation political culture of Ontario, in its core outlooks and orientations, naturally remained essentially Upper Canadian in character. But it did not remain static. Over time, under Mowat's long tutelage, it acquired some distinctive nuances of its own, and an even clearer definition of Ontario's long-term interests.

The nuances, while partly a matter of style, also reflected a significant consensus on the nature of politics. That consensus had two related components. The first, which flowed from a growing concern for agricultural modernization, amounted to a predisposition to view government as above all a matter of 'good husbandry' in the management of the Ontario estate. And as a corollary, there was general approval of political leaders who could demonstrate their managerial expertise – for example, by keeping taxes low while balancing the budget, by improving the efficiency of public administration, or by sorting out the tangled financial affairs of the municipalities. The second component, which flowed in part from long experience and in part from close acquaintance with Mowat's Liberal party machine, consisted of a general understanding that patronage was a normal aspect of political husbandry. It could be used well or badly, efficiently or inefficiently, honestly or corruptly, depending on the expertise and integrity of the user.

The definition of Ontario's long-term interests that emerged was by no means new or even very different. From Simcoe on, every government had conceived those interests in material terms, and primarily in terms of the acquisition and development of land: to see arise 'a numerous and Agricultural people,' to establish the security of the community on a foundation of economic success. But under Mowat they were defined more specifically, and pursued more aggressively, than ever before.

Under his aegis, Ontario rejected the status of a mere convenient 'jurisdiction' or 'level of government' within Confederation, as some had hoped or pretended it might accept, and instead decisively reasserted its long-standing interests. What Ontario demanded, basically, was a huge addition to its territory (in the shape of what is now northern Ontario), and a huge increase in its legislative powers. Both of those demands – for land, for local autonomy – resonated from the very core of the Upper Canadian political consciousness. And in the end both proved irresistible. Knowing exactly what it wanted, and led by a premier of surpassing ability, Ontario achieved a stunning, overwhelming victory. Not surprisingly, in view of the outcome, Ontarians thereafter preferred to see their provincial and national interests as basically compatible; to this day, perhaps more than the people of any other province, they remain disinclined to see fundamental conflict between them.

The Uses and Limits of Clientelist Explanation

The chief value of employing clientelism as an organizing and explanatory model is that it brings into sharp focus a type of social and political interaction whose presence is generally familiar but whose systematic importance might otherwise remain obscure. Used in a historical context, it also provides a clear framework for the analysis of changes in prevailing patterns of behaviour, and in the structure of political power, that might otherwise be overlooked or appear to be merely random.

It must be stressed, however, that a model of this kind – technically a mid-level empirical model of transactional exchange – is conceptually valuable precisely because it does *not* purport to explain everything. Rather, it purports to explain only a specifically defined sub-set of transactions that, however important or characteristic they may be, are but part of the total fabric of society. Such a model is therefore most appropriately used, I would argue, when the behaviours it identifies are treated not in isolation but in relation to their surrounding context (including, for example, in the case of Upper Canada, the economic and constitutional context), and at as low a level of abstraction as possible. Clientelism, then, should not be seen as a 'grand' or all-encompassing social theory: it belongs rather among what Francis Bacon called the 'middle axioms' – 'the true and solid and living axioms on which depend the affairs and fortunes of men.'[5]

Unlike Marxian theory, for example, the clientelist model offers no explanation of the origins and causes of social inequality. Instead, it treats inequality simply as a *prerequisite* for the development of patron-client relationships – a 'given' whose presence cannot be accounted for within the logic of the model itself. Hence, in this study the pronounced inequalities of wealth and status that were built into Upper Canadian society at the start are attributable mainly to external causes, including imperial policy in the wake of the American Revolution, the ideology of the British governing elite, and the influence of the military. But *from that point* the clientelist model powerfully directs our attention towards and offers a coherent framework of explanation for, the linkages between unequals that became so dominant a feature of the province's political and economic life. It also provides a basis on which to construct a developmental model of the political process as it evolved through successively more complex stages over the course of a century. Implicit in the clientelist approach, therefore, as Christopher Clapham has noted, is the perception that 'patron-client bonds by their nature ally members of different classes, and foment factional divisions between members of the same class. They are legitimized through a language of mutual obligation which discounts ... the idea of class conflict and the

5 *Novum Organum*, I, aphorism CIV

possiblity of class solidarity.'[6] It is perhaps for that reason that Marxist scholars have generally been uneasy about clientelist analysis and have hesitated to incorporate its insights into their work.[7]

In general, moreover, the clientelist model is of very limited usefulness in explaining the behaviour of political organizations that are built around feelings of common identity, whether of class or nationality or religion, and in which the rewards of membership are essentially psychological or emotional rather than material. Of course, such organizations may *also* provide certain material rewards (just as patron-client exchange may *also* involve certain intangible satisfactions), but on the whole their workings are best studied from other perspectives. The Patrons of Industry and the Protestant Protective Association, for example, should be seen not as arising out of but as a challenge to the clientelist norms of nineteenth-century Ontario. The clientelist model, therefore, cannot adequately explain either their rise or their internal dynamics – though it does offer, I would suggest, a good explanation for their swift and ignominious demise.

The Stages of Clientelism

Central to the thematic structure of this book is the proposition that clientelism developed through three distinct, historically identifiable stages: from the simple dyadic clientelism of early Upper Canada to brokerage at mid-century and subsequently to machine politics. Further, each of these stages is defined as the product of a specific set of conditions in the surrounding economic, social, and constitutional environment. In adopting this overall conception, however, I do not wish to imply that the inauguration of the second and third stages necessarily entailed the sudden or widespread disappearance of the stage before it. Rather, the stages should be viewed as analogous to geological strata, each changing the surface configuration but also metamorphosing with the one below. And the bedrock underlying it all, so to speak, was the old land-based clientelism of Upper Canada. The dating of the periods of transition must therefore be treated with caution, and this is especially so in the case of the transition to

6 'Clientelism and the State,' in Clapham, ed., *Private Patronage and Public Power* (New York 1982), 31

7 For a notable exception, see Peter Flynn, 'Class, Clientelism and Coercion: Some Mechanisms of Internal Dependency and Control,' *Journal of Commonwealth and Comparative Politics* 12 (1974).

brokerage. In Part Two, I place the transition mainly in the Union era and interpret it as a response to new economic conditions, new transportation and communications infrastructures, and new pressures generated by constitutional change. But while 1841 precisely dates the transition to the Union, it is admittedly a fairly arbitrary point to choose in dating the transition to a brokerage-based political process. As the remarkable career of William Hamilton Merritt so clearly shows, the broker was already active on the scene by the 1820s. My argument, therefore, is that brokerage could not become fully operative *until political power had shifted decisively to the democratically elected Assembly*.

The effects of the transition, moreover, were by no means immediately apparent at the grass-roots level, where traditional local clientelism largely retained both its commercial vigour and its political efficacy. In some respects, indeed, it was seemingly strengthened by the infusion of brokerage activity, since the latter tended to foster the growth of horizontal links among local patrons, thus remedying one of the old system's most conspicuous weaknesses. Also, in the political system generally, after the introduction of responsible government, the increasingly high stakes being played for at the top tended to heighten the competition for electoral support at the bottom – support that the local patrons were still well positioned to deliver. As a result, those in power were given added incentive to court their favour; which they did by showering them with fulsome praise, bestowing upon them honorific tokens of their civic worth, and – no doubt more to the point – supplying them with the patronage they demanded, both for themselves and for distribution to their clients.

For this reason, it may be postulated, *in the short run* the patrons' position in society was not seriously eroded by the declining relative importance of land as a factor in patron-client exchange: in effect, as land became less available they were able to substitute patronage of a specifically political kind. The two, however, were not perfect substitutes. Bonds based on political patronage were rarely as enduring as those based on land; they tended to need constant reinforcement; and ultimately, by making the patron dependent upon the downward flow of ephemeral benefits, they tended to narrow the base of his power and reduce his independence. Hence, *in the long run*, the result was the growth of a more integrated political system in which the broker increasingly acted as the key allocator of scarce resources.

This finding, it should be noted, confirms the analysis of the shift to brokerage contained in numerous other studies of political clientelism, both contemporary and historical. The following summation of René

Lemarchand and Keith Legg, for example, strikingly fits the Upper Canadian case: 'What was previously a rather fragmented, locally centred nexus, limited to traditional exchanges ... becomes a far more encompassing network of relationships, directly dependent upon the volume and allocation of resources from the centre, and more clearly susceptible to the techniques of political bargaining.'[8] When Sharon Kettering, writing of the rise of the early modern state in seventeenth-century France, paints a compelling picture of brokers who 'played the functionally equivalent role of patrons in distributing royal patronage from which they took a commission for brokering, sometimes diverting the flow of royal patronage for their own use,'[9] she could as easily be describing Francis Hincks.

The transition to the third stage is more precisely marked than the transition to brokerage in that it is identified with a specific institutional change: namely, the emergence of the formally organized, hierarchical party machine. That transition, too, I have interpreted as a response to changes in the society at large, including population growth and urbanization (which increased the size of local electorates, thereby rendering old methods of exchange and mobilization less reliable). Also, new political exigencies were created by Confederation. But nothing in this analysis is meant to suggest that the development of machine politics superseded brokerage or in some way reduced its functional importance in the political system. On the contrary, my point is that it was precisely *within* the Mowat machine that brokerage attained its fullest, most systematic expression. The machine, in other words, dramatically improved the efficiency of brokerage. It not only mediated the flow of benefits from centre to periphery and the counter-flow of electoral support; it also monitored and regulated the exchange. It made the administration of patronage more accountable, by introducing uniform criteria for rewards, and more economical, by cutting down on its unproductive or extravagant use. And in the process it successfully adapted the norms of clientelism to the modern age.

In contrasting the Liberal and Conservative party machines in this period I have suggested (following Lemarchand's distinction between 'orthodox' and 'neo-traditional' types of machine organization) that the differences between them were both structural and broadly socio-economic, stemming largely from their very different situations after Confederation. In essence, the Liberals were compelled to build from

8 'Political Clientelism and Development: A Preliminary Analysis,' *Comparative Politics* 4 (1972): 159
9 *Patrons, Brokers and Clients in Seventeenth-Century France* (New York 1986), 5

the ground up, by promoting the advancement of new local elites whose prospects were closely tied to those of the party. The Conservatives, however, having been long in office and now additionally enriched with federal patronage, naturally preferred to build on their existing foundations. And that meant continuing their old alliance with the quasi-independent local patrons who had always been the conservative mainstay but who also demanded personal negotiation with the party leader. They were not easily incorporated into a disciplined hierarchy.

It should be added, however, that both these patterns of development have implications that go beyond the immediate concerns of this study. In particular, both seem to lend additional support to Martin Shefter's 'critical experience' theory of party-building. Shefter puts forward the proposition that 'the way a party initially acquires a popular base is a character-forming or "critical" experience' that profoundly affects its subsequent behaviour.[10] Hence, parties that first acquire their popular base 'by distributing particularistic benefits through local notables and politicians' (as in Ontario) – unlike parties that first mobilize support through trade unions, churches, or other such organizations – will be more likely to develop long-term 'constituencies for patronage,' to which they respond and whose continued existence they foster.

Finally, it may be asked, what happened to Ontario clientelism after Mowat? Did it advance to a new stage, or (as my colleague George Emery put it) did it 'just peter out, like old man Mowat himself?' There is, unfortunately, no simple answer. The Liberal machine chugged on into the twentieth century, but increasingly its internal workings were impaired. It was no longer renewing itself at the local level, while in the cities, where it had never been strong, it was reduced to a shadow; the thorny issue of prohibition was seemingly unamenable to its techniques of brokerage; and it was growing undisguisably corrupt. Any study of the Liberal party in the period 1896 to 1905 would therefore almost inevitably have to be titled 'the decay of clientelism.' Yet, equally significantly, any study of the Conservative party would probably suggest just the opposite: that the period in question was a time of renewal and fresh beginnings; that out of it grew a new web of alliances that would more accurately reflect the political economy of twentieth-century Ontario – and that might aptly be termed a new stage of 'corporate clientelism.' But that is another story. This one, it seems to me, ends with the Mowat era in 1896.

10 'Party and Patronage: Germany, England and Italy,' *Politics and Society* 7 (1977): 403–51

Index